D1271699

THE MODERN MAGAZINE

VISUAL JOURNALISM IN THE DIGITAL ERA

Published in 2013
by Laurence King Publishing Ltd
361–373 City Road
London ECIV ILR
United Kingdom
Tel: +44 20 7841 6900
Fax: + 44 20 7841 6910
email: enquiries@laurenceking.com
www.laurenceking.com

This book was produced by
Laurence King Publishing Ltd, London

A catalogue record for this book
is available from the British Library.

ISBN: 978 1 78067 298 4

Designed by Jeremy Leslie at magCulture
www.magCulture.com/Projects
Design assistant David Bate
Typefaces Benton Sans and Vendome Condensed
Photography David Bate
(with thanks to Tony Brook)
Special photography PSC

Printed in China

THE MODERN MAGAZINE

VISUAL JOURNALISM IN THE DIGITAL ERA

JEREMY LESLIE

Dear Samir –

I hope you enjoy this.

Let me know!

Regards [illegible]

LAURENCE KING PUBLISHING

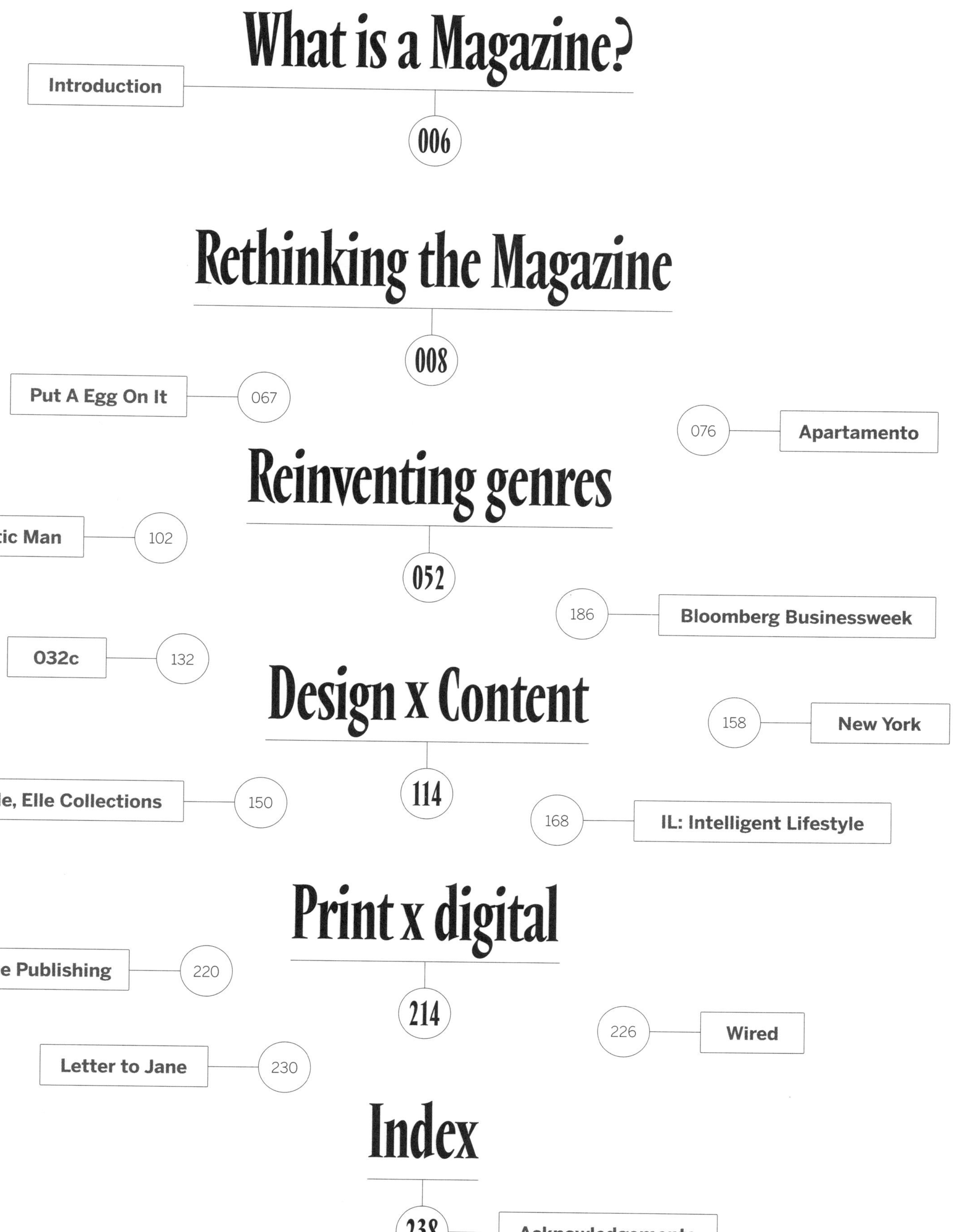

WHAT IS A MAGAZINE?

A flick through the pages of this book will tell you much about the way today's magazine makers use their editorial and design skills to guide and engage the reader, but underlying these skills are a number of assumptions about what a magazine actually is, and where the medium sits in today's complex media landscape.

In its contemporary context, the magazine is a form of communication that can avoid the template-driven urgency of the newspaper or website, while not demanding the timeless reflection expected of the book or TV documentary. A magazine team can expect enough time in their production schedule to permit the development of informed opinion while also facing a pressure to hit a production deadline that will demand a degree of creative spontaneity. This relationship between freedom and restriction is one of a number of balances that help form the unique personality of every magazine. Another is the relationship between text and image, a central characteristic, and the one that first attracted me to the medium.

The primary defining attribute of a magazine is its position as part of a series. A one-off publication may use all the visual and editorial components of a magazine, but until further editions are forthcoming can it really be said to be a magazine? Here we find another essential balance to be struck, that between familiarity and change. As part of a series of publications, a magazine exists both as a one-off item and as an ongoing project. Familiar content and design can be vital to building a long-term audience, but an over-repetitive approach can end up alienating readers.

The word 'magazine' has several linked meanings, all of which are relevant to how we see magazines. It derives from the Arabic *makhzan*, meaning storehouse. The French *magasin* (shop) shares the same source, as does the use of magazine in the context of guns and explosives. We can see the shared meaning relating to the storage of disparate items or collections, and the sense that the magazine might explode at any moment appeals from the point of view of the reader sometimes being surprised by what they find.

The point at which the word became commonly used to describe what we know today as a magazine is unrecorded, but its first use in this context was for *The Gentleman's Magazine*, launched in 1731. Such early magazines were journals for the wealthy; it took the industrial revolution to enable mass-produced publications to become feasible, and so popularise the form. Printing was cheaper, the new urban populations were increasingly literate, and the railways made wide-scale distribution affordable. So began magazine publishing's long and intimate relationship with technology.

These early magazines were text-orientated and visually indistinguishable from books, but the introduction of photographic reproduction in the early twentieth century provided new visual possibilities at a time that coincided with huge shifts in our political and cultural realms. Words could play off images, and images off words. At one level, a simple reading of text and image could work for the majority of readers, while a deeper, more subtle reading of the same content could communicate with a more specialist, knowing group of reader.

Magazines became a channel for the growing urban populations to learn about new concepts of modernism, democracy and communism. Between the two world wars magazines played a key role in the definition of what we would recognize today as graphic design. From the visual anarchy of Dada and Futurist periodicals to the more measured propaganda of left- and right-wing political extremes, magazines began to perform a dual role, directing as well as reflecting visual trends. The strong modernism of magazines such as *Vu* (France) and *Arbeiter Illustrierte Zeitung* (Germany) was strikingly forward-looking at the time; today we can see them as rich visual (as well as verbal) records of their time. Thus, magazines from this era onwards have become a staple of museums seeking to establish the cultural context of a historical exhibition.

The post-World War II consumer boom saw the magazine start to become similar to what we would recognize today as 'a magazine'. Together, 1950s editions of *Picture Post* (UK) and *Harpers Bazaar* (USA) tell the story of that era. The former, under picture editor Stefan Lorant, a Hungarian émigré, used photo reportage to express the earnest hope for a better world post-war, and Alexey Brodovitch, a Russian émigré, at the latter established the modern role of the art director as he turned modernist typography and colour photography to the cause of consumerism.

The 1960s are often regarded as the golden age of magazine design – the growth in advertising revenue and increased access to colour presses allowed art directors to really push their designs further. Prominent examples include *Look* (USA), *Twen* (Germany), *Town* (UK), George Lois's front covers for *Esquire* (USA) and the launch of *The Sunday Times Magazine* (UK). By the 1970s the industry had grown further but settled into relative conservatism, with notable exceptions being the new listings magazines *Time Out* (UK) and *New York* (US), music magazines *Rolling Stone* (USA) and *New Musical Express* (UK) and punk fanzines.

The over-styled designer excesses of the 1980s were first predicted then observed by magazines such as *The Face*, *Blitz* (UK), and *Tempo* (Germany). Fairly small in terms of staff and financial clout, these independently published glossy magazines took advantage of the relatively new phototypesetting technology. Able to match or exceed the major publishers' magazines in terms of quality of content and production, their young designers used the typesetting systems to challenge design conventions instead of mimicking old styles of production. *The Face* art director Neville Brody consciously looked back to Dada and Russian Futurism for inspiration, stretching and distorting type to the extremes of what computer systems could manage and the reader could decipher.

Another magazine from that decade headed in a different direction. *i-D* (UK), was resolutely lo-fi at launch – a two-colour, stapled, landscape-format magazine that used typewriters, handwriting and stencils instead of typesetting. Founder Terry Jones had previously been art director of *British Vogue*, and while *i-D*'s DIY aesthetic was primarily budget-driven, part of its appeal to Jones, his colleagues and the magazine's readers was the contrariness of the form. Unlike the punk fanzines, which had developed their visual style by default, here was a prominent magazine art director taking a DIY approach and printing it using fluorescent inks. A choice was being made. *i-D* was concerned with street fashion, a revelation itself at the time, and its entire visual identity reflected this; the unusual landscape format suited the lined-up images, the design was defiantly non-elitist, yet the colours added a degree of sophistication.

It was no surprise when a survey of independent magazine publishers in 2009* revealed that *i-D* was the most cited magazine as an inspiration. It marked the point at which it was no longer simply a case of the bigger, glossier and slicker the better. The entire history of magazine publishing was now a toolbox from which a single publisher/editor could pick and choose to create their publication. And the next technological shift was soon ready and waiting to help them do so.

The arrival of the Apple Macintosh in 1984 divided the magazine industry. Many thought the much-heralded desktop publishing revolution would dilute notions of good design and lead to a downgrading of quality across the board. But, in what was surely a precursor of the later digital revolution, this democratization of design turned out to have a positive effect on editorial design and production. Those that argued the new computer and its programs were merely tools in the hands of users were to be proved right.

The first time I saw pages that had been designed on an Apple Mac was in US design magazine *Emigré* (USA), a large-format publication that used coarse, self-designed 8-bit typefaces to experiment with the new computer. The resulting expressive typography served as a reminder that editorial design doesn't need to be heavily formatted and easily legible. Yet *Emigré* appears conservative when compared to another early-adopter Mac-designed magazine, *RayGun* (USA). Designed by David Carson using the early layout program PageMaker, this music magazine took a very traditional publishing format and subverted it. While others were attempting to use the new technology to mimic more traditional editorial design, Carson chose to reflect the grunge music the magazine covered by ignoring legibility in favour of self-expression. Like Brody before him, he used the new technology to push the boundaries of what was legible. *RayGun* featured text overlaid on text that often looked more like the rejected pieces of design that accumulate to the side of the page layout than actual designs.

Such extremes aside, the introduction of the Mac to the magazine studio went on to bring high-quality magazine production to the smallest of publishers and empowered those inspired by Terry Jones's *i-D*. Whether you work for a major international publisher or are publishing your own independent magazine, today you have access to essentially the same hardware and software, and you often print at the same printers as well. What are you going to make?

Whatever one considers were previous golden ages for magazine publishing, I would argue that today is a new golden age – an age where the very idea of what a magazine is can be challenged and where you will find a willing audience to enjoy and share questioning the exploration. The basic alchemy of manipulating text and image on a page – visual journalism – has never been

easier, printing small numbers of copies has never been cheaper and, in the hands of top practitioners, the results never more exciting.

And print of course is only the beginning; now we're experiencing the stirrings of the next revolution. How will the visual journalism of magazines respond and be applied to the new digital media?

** Survey of contemporary independent publishers carried out for an exhibition of their magazines at the Colophon2009 conference, Luxembourg.*

RETHINKING THE MAGAZINE

Magazine publishing found itself in rude health at the end of the twentieth century. Larger quantities of more titles were being produced and sold than ever before, as mainstream publishers took advantage of the consumer boom and resulting advertising glut. Yet one of the paradoxes of growing to become a successful industry is that success itself can limit your creative options. At the start of the new century, magazine production had become standardized to the point where printing presses dictated the most efficient page size, competition on the newsstand meant cover design rules were universally observed and the magazine content was too often manipulated by the agents and PR representatives of pop stars and actors.

This maturing and subsequent standardization invited questioning, and a small sub-genre of magazines duly obliged. *Nice* magazine (UK) – a piece of magazine-sized plywood – questioned (and perhaps confirmed) our basic physical expectations of what a magazine is, while the genre-specific critiques of *Words Magazine* (UK) and *One Page Magazine* (UK) use irony and visual analysis respectively to highlight the underlying banalities of much mainstream content. Newspapers don't get off lightly either – *Traducing Ruddle* (UK) fills an entire tabloid with smartly designed nonsense.

The advent of the web as a common utility has led magazines to re-examine their physical properties, with some, such as *Monocle* (UK), using a more book-like, regular format and design that flies in the face of perceived wisdom that a front cover should balance familiarity with change from issue to issue. The Internet has had an even more acute effect on newspapers, many of which have turned to magazine-style content and design in an attempt to propose a new role now that they are no longer primary news sources. British–Portuguese publication *i* is effectively a daily magazine rather than a newspaper in the traditional sense, while *The Guardian* (UK) continues to publish 'G2' – a daily A4 features section of the newspaper that is essentially a daily magazine.

Other publishing projects have taken the word 'magazine' back to its etymological roots ('storehouse') and come up with more surprising ideas of what a magazine can be. *La Más Bella* ('The Most Beautiful' in Spanish) (Spain) produces themed collections of objects produced by multiple contributors. It has published editions about games, success, tapas and, most recently, about magazines themselves. Like all editions of this annual Spanish project, *La Más Bella Revista* (The Most Beautiful: Magazine) is a lucky bag full of artists' contributions, loosely related to the theme: a recent edition of Spanish celebrity magazine *Cuore* ('Heart' in Italian) cut into a heart shape and a 1950s guide to making your own binder for your collections of *Hobby* magazine are a couple of the more obviously linked items. In a further play on words, much of the content was created live as part of a performance that reflected a Spanish theatre genre also called 'Revista'; the issue includes a DVD of the original performance.

MK Bruce/Lee (South Africa) is also a collection of things compiled in a different package for each issue. This is a more carefully designed set of printed items, stylistically typical of design studio/publisher The President; each part – poster, board game, booklet – uses contemporary adaptations of Afrikaans designs and patterns. It looks stunning, but though to its creators it is without doubt a magazine, the South African sales auditors wouldn't recognize it as such and refused to list it in their figures.

While Australia's *T-World* magazine can claim to be the world's only publication about T-shirts, *T-post* (Sweden) remains the only publication that actually *is* a T-shirt. Each monthly issue features a brief written piece printed inside a T-shirt that bears an illustration based on the text on its chest. The subscriber recieves both a printed T-shirt and a story to read.

Berlin-based *mono.kultur* (Germany) sums up two traits common among these magazines questioning the form. Although always produced in a tiny A5 size, it changes precise form every biannual issue; it has employed fold-out posters, gatefold sections, different papers and tipped-on smaller sections. In design and production terms it is a highly collectible series of beautifully formed and varied objects that fold down to the same size. It explores editorial thinking too – the second contemporary trait being its high-concept approach to content. Each issue features only a single artist, designer or other creative, who is subjected to an in-depth interview that is presented alongside their work.

Thanks to technology it is cheaper and easier than ever to develop and manufacture a magazine, but the hardest part of the process – getting your publication to the readers – becomes increasingly difficult as specialist shops close. *Is Not Magazine* (Australia) solved this by flyposting their publication as a poster. *I Am Still Alive* (UK) regularly turns up inside other magazines, taking over several pages as a parasite project – cleverly piggybacking its host to reach the reader.

Other publications, although more recognizable as magazines in their physical format, challenge editorial conventions in their pages. *Kasino A4* (Finland) ran absurd lifestyle advice in a section entitled 'Opinion Leaders'. And for its regular section 'Empty Sheet', it invited a group of six

people to draw a simple concept; six car salesmen illustrated 'Luxury', six Somalian men were invited to draw 'Winter'. The seriousness with which the participants took part was undermined by the redundancy of the task. Yet the idea was also an effective pastiche of user-generated content, and became a much-loved part of the magazine *O.K. Periodicals* (The Netherlands) and *Ein Magazin über Orte* (Germany) publish content submitted by contributors along a particular theme – the publishers curate and collate the content but publish without comment. In 2007, *Creative Review* (UK) sold the right to edit and design an entire issue on eBay (the winning £15,000 bid came from ad agency Mother).

The demands of the newsstand mean many front covers follow formulae, but as more magazines are distributed away from the newsstand, so the designer is freed from these restrictions. Although redesigned since, a recent incarnation of *Architect's Journal* (UK) used the language of branding to create a regular cover identity rather than traditional masthead. As most of its sales are via subscription rather than newsstand, this made sense. The same is true of customer magazines: paper producer M-real published 11 issues of its untitled magazine (UK), the latter editions of which were recognizable by the row of angled stripes on the front cover. In-flight magazines can also experiment: *Carlos* (Virgin Atlantic, UK) dropped the usual glossy photography in favour of illustration throughout, while *Up* (WestJetTAP, Portugal) redesigns its name every issue to work with the cover image.

These last examples are also noteworthy for their names. *Up* is a great name for a free magazine found in your aeroplane seatback pocket; both literal and emotive, it has an added power as an English word employed on a Portuguese publication. *Carlos* was initially only the working title for Virgin Atlantic's magazine, but an alternative was never found and by publication time the name had stuck. It's unclear whether the client was aware the name originally came from the notorious plane hijacker of the same name.

Naming a magazine after a person is a familiar ploy. Women's magazines, in particular, like the friendliness it evokes (*Marie Claire* (various countries), *Lula* (UK) and *Betty* (UK) are just a few that come to mind). Recent additions have included real people – Oprah Winfrey, Jane (Pratt), Martha Stewart all have (or had) self-named publications – but there are dangers in this direction, as *Carson* (USA) magazine found. It was named after designer David Carson, who had been signed up to design the new magazine, but when he and the publisher fell out, the second issue appeared with the name 'Carson' struck out on the front cover.

Even as the mainstream publishing industry finds itself contracting, post-boom, these experiments continue. Where once there was a single business model (sell ads and sell copies) now there are multiple ways of making money and distributing magazines – as *The Big Issue* (UK) made clear with its front cover-with-a-cover, explaining how the magazine does good as it tries to take on the increasing number of free magazines available in our cities; free magazines which themselves have found plenty of opportunity to experiment.

On all fronts, then, ranging from the extreme to the subtle, magazine makers continue to challenge readers' expectations of what a magazine can be.

T-Post
Sweden, Issue 80, September 2012
Subscribers receive a new T-shirt every month.
Editor-in-chief *Peter Lundgren*; Creative director *Giuliano Garonzi*

OPPOSITE **Creative Review**
UK, February 2007 (280 × 280mm, 11¼ × 11¼ inches)
Editorial control of this one issue was auctioned on eBay.
Editor *Patrick Burgoyne*; Art director *Nathan Gale*

Afro

South Africa, Issue 2, December 2005
(70 × 70 × 70 mm, 2½ × 2½ × 2½ inches)
This tightly packed small cube of paper comes apart to reveal a stack of folded posters each with a small booklet attached. A highly visual and exciting way to use print to deliver short stories.
Art director *Peet Pienaar*

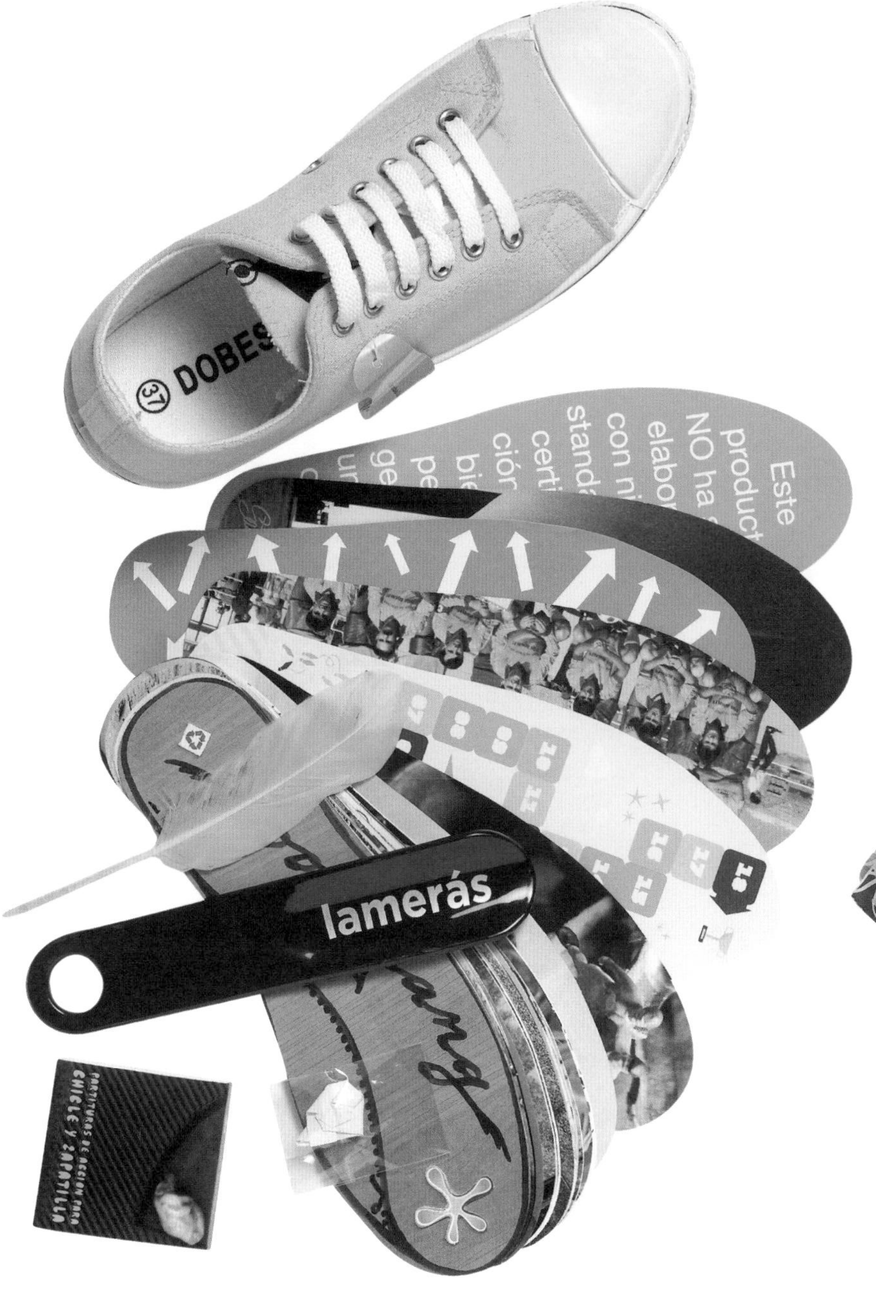

La Mas Bella
Spain, La Mas Bella: Anda (The Most Beautiful: Walks), 2010
(303 × 105 × 100 mm, 12 × 4¼ × 4 inches)
Each annual issue has a specific theme and comes as a unique package according to that subject. This example consists of a shoebox containing a single sneaker and other related items – a shoehorn, a feather to tickle the foot, some chewing gum to step on and a set of paper 'insoles' featuring commissioned art from international illustrators and designers. All the elements are carefully resourced and customized to make each as realistic as possible.
Creative directors *Diego Ortiz and Pepe Murciego*

Free Style Magazine

Germany, Issue 1, Spring/Summer 2009 (245 × 245mm, 9¾ × 9¾ inches)
Using the frisbee as a metaphor for its easy, playful attitude, this magazine is produced as near to circular as possible (a small straight edge remains for binding) and packaged inside one of the plastic discs.
Editor-in-chief and creative director *Jason McGlade*; Art director *Massimo Casini*

OPPOSITE

MK Bruce/Lee

South Africa, Issue 2, November 2008
(Box 190 × 285 × 50mm, 7½ × 11¼ × 2 inches)
A promotional publication for a local cable televison station that comprises several boxes within boxes that fold out to make a drinking game and to reveal other pieces including story booklets, stickers, a CD, a poster and a bottle of body spray. Every item is designed in typically ornate style by Pienaar's studio The President, and among the patterns are QR codes and URLs that augment the traditional form of the whole package. Every issue comes in two versions – *Bruce* for men (shown here) and *Lee* for women, enabling content and advertising to be directed at discrete sections of the 18–24-year-old audience.
Art director *Peet Pienaar*

Landjäger Magazin

Austria, Issue 9, May 2009 (80 × 80mm, 3½ × 3½ inches)
As well as more conventionally formatted publications, twice a year *Landjäger* produces a themed issue such as this one about 'Drink', which consists of a set of seven beer mats.
Editors-in-chief *Michaela Bilgeri and Johannes Scheutz*

Dog Ear

UK, issue 1, February 2012 (60 × 210mm, 3¼ × 8¼ inches)
Distibuted free through bookshops and libraries, *Dog Ear* crowdsources content via its website and publishes the best material as a fold-out bookmark.
Co-founders *Joe Hedinger and Pete Lewis*

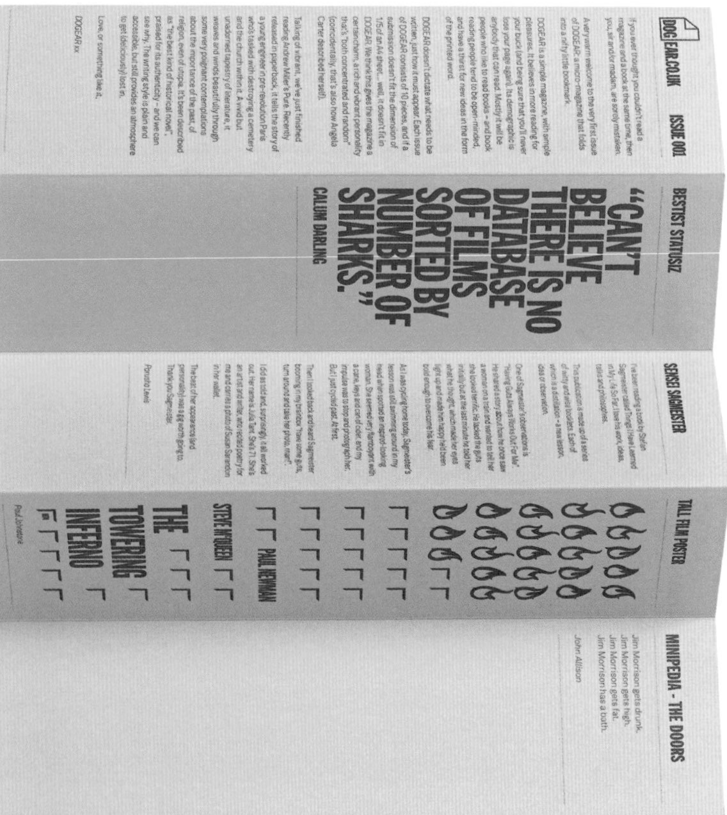

The Journal of Popular Noise
USA, issues 7–9, Spring/Summer 2008
(190 × 190mm, 7½ × 7½ inches)
This limited-edition, biannual publication combines a letterpress-printed fold-out sleeve with a set of seven-inch vinyl discs.
Editor and designer *Byron Kalet*

Kasino Creative Annual
Finland, Issue 3, Spring 2012 (185 × 240mm, 7¼ × 9½ inches)
An annual publication that changes form each year, this iPad-sized issue folds out to present a Tumblr-style pictorial guide to what *can't* be done online.
Creative director *Pekka Toivonen*; Editor *Jonathan Mander*; Director of photography *Jussi Puikkonen*

MORE KASINO CREATIVE ANNUAL p210

POSTRmagazine

Free

Counter-Culture Chronicle

#9

INSIDE THE PUPPET
"They treated me like an animal!"
SECRET WIFE SWAPS BEHIND THE STABLES?
SHOCKING TALES OF BEASTLY ABUSE!!!
FLASHING FELINE FLESH FOR FRAUDULENT FAVORS!

ENTERTAINMENT ISSUES

This paragraph was brought to you by GloboBank! Using your hard-earned dimes to help rich people get even richer!

Dark Horsey is brought to you by Neuromillions. Because you never know when three X's will make your shitty life take a turn for the better.

UP NEXT: THE BATTLE AGAINST BOREDOM

THE BATTLE AGAINST BOREDOM

OPERATION DARK HORSEY

Dark Horsey is brought to you by Coca-Corrosive Light: with no sugar, only aspartame – because it's better to have cancer than be fat!

Battle Against Boredom is brought to you be Pseudogree Pal Light: The only low-fat pet nutrient for overweight animals – now 100% synthetic meat!

Dark Horsey is sponsored by Grub's Malt Liquor. Grub's – whenever you need to lower your already non-existent standards.

Dark Horsey was brought to you by Zide Stain Release Crystal Cleansing Formula! The only detergent with nano-crystals that remove stains and shame!

NOT SO F.A.Q.

DID YOU WANT YOUR LIFE BACK AT THE END OF LOST?
ARE YOU WATCHING THIS?
WHO SHOT J.R.?
CAN YOU MAKE A CATCH PHRASE OUT OF DOMESTIC VIOLENCE?
YOU TALKING TO ME?
DID YOU SEE BIG BROTHER DANCING WITH THE STARS ON JERSEY SHORE?
HOW CAN SHE SLAP?
IS THREE HOURS OF MAD MEN BETTER THAN THREE HOURS OF FRIENDS?
WHO KILLED LAURA PALMER?
WHERE'S MY HORSE?
HOW MUCH LOVE CAN ONE TUNNEL TAKE?
DID WE RAIN ON YOUR PARADE?
DO YOU SEE THE FUN IN THIS?

If you yell at something long enough, eventually it will wear a hat and ride a tricycle, if only to shut you up.

Dark Horsey is brought to you by DermoFresh, the only skin-moisturizing cream that makes up for your lack of confidence and dysfunctional personality!

[...] iam pridem, ex quo suffragia nulli / uendimus, effudit curas; nam qui dabat olim / imperium, fasces, legiones, omnia, nunc se / continet atque duas tantum res anxius optat, / panem et circenses. [...] Juvenal, Satire 10.77–81

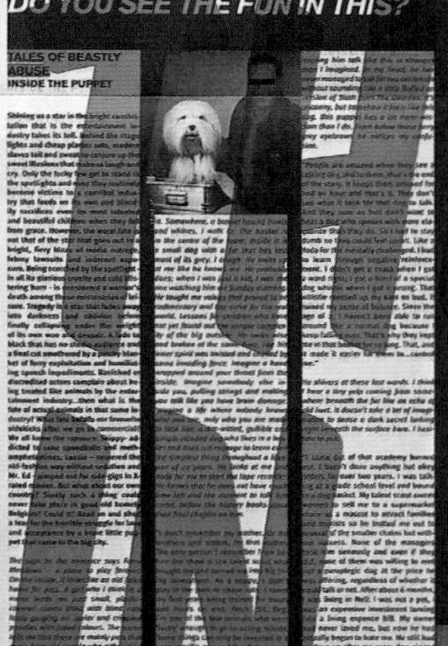

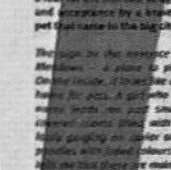

DO YOU SEE THE FUN IN THIS?

TO BE CONTINUED...

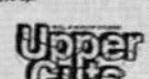

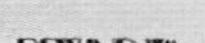

POSTRmagazine
Belgium, Issue 9, The Entertainment Issue, March 2011
(590 × 840 folded to 198 × 280mm, 23¼ × 33 to 7¾ × 11 inches)
This quarterly publication addresses contemporary political concerns related to the Internet and surveillance using the traditional protest format of the printed poster.
Design *Not Another Graphic Designer, Monkeys With Typewriters*

sincerely,
MirandaJuly

Dear Life,
Do you want t
hang out toni
I should warn
you that I will not
be wearing any
Mak
hair
you c
call
Mi

PARTY
PARTY
PA

MIRANDA JULY:
BEST AT BELONGING TO YOURSELF

"I ask myself all the big questions, every Sunday."

Dear Dooly,
Nina wants to apologize for getting so defensive when you said it seemed like she was "a million miles away." You were right. She was. Today She plans on being just 1 or 2 miles away.
sincerely,
MirandaJuly

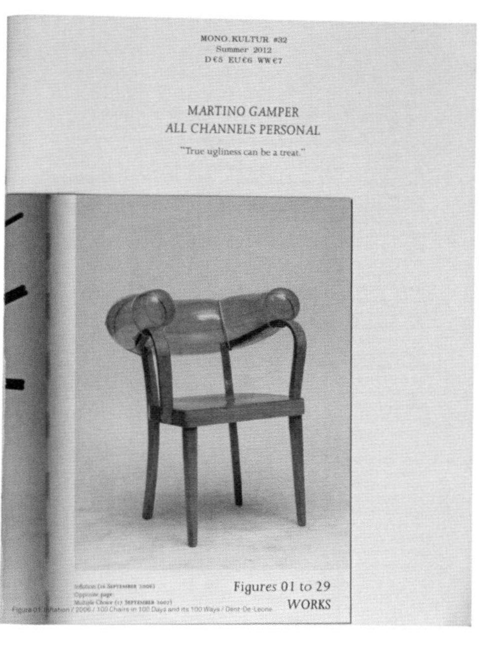

MONO.KULTUR #32
Summer 2012
D€5 EU€6 WW€7

MARTINO GAMPER
ALL CHANNELS PERSONAL

"True ugliness can be a treat."

Although it was early summer, Martino Gamper had a cold when we visited him in the as yet unfinished Hackney studio that he shares with his wife, the artist Francis Upritchard. To improve his health, Francis cooked the entire studio a lunch of health-restoring ginger-infused noodles, after which we toured the space before settling down to talk about Martino's current concerns and his past projects.

Martino first attracted widespread attention in 2007 with the project *100 Chairs in 100 Days*, for which he reworked elements of existing chairs into a collection of charismatic new pieces of furniture. Taking on the ultimate design object of the chair within severe self-imposed constraints in terms of time and material, the results were odd, to put it mildly – at times impractical, at times funny-looking, but always refreshingly unexpected. Martino returned to the idea of remaking several times, most notoriously when he dis- and reassembled furnishings by famed architect and designer Gio Ponti into new pieces, an act of homage that was misinterpreted by some as irreverence.

Born in 1971, Martino Gamper grew up in Merano, an Italian town close to the Austrian-Swiss border. After spending a period in his teens as an apprentice to a furniture maker and a couple of years travelling the world, he enrolled simultaneously at the Academy of Fine Arts and the University of Applied Arts in Vienna. Finally settling on design over sculpture, he then worked for fellow South Tyrolean designer Matteo Thun in Milan. In 1998, he moved to London to complete his education at the Royal College of Art under the guidance of Ron Arad.

Since then, Martino has been treading the fine line between the worlds of fine art and design with disarming nonchalance, frequently challenging aesthetic and industrial conventions of the design world with humour and a deep personal investment in his work. At a time

17

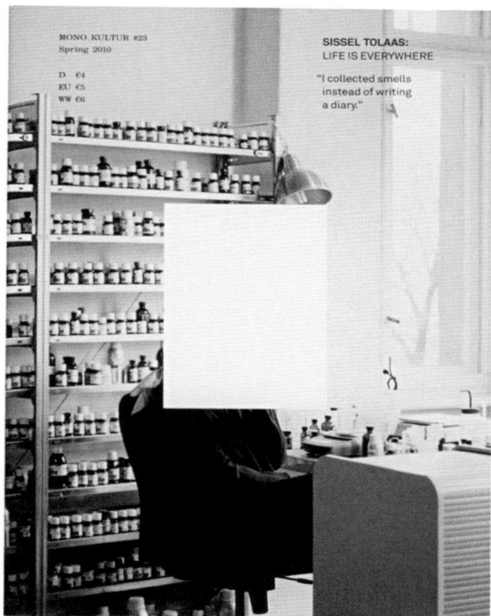

Comme des Garçons, Cartier, Ikea and Daimler Chrysler, as well as Charité Medical Universities in Berlin, Harvard, the Liszt Center at MIT and the Max Planck Institute. She has also worked with the MoMA New York, the Tate Gallery Liverpool and the Hamburger Bahnhof Berlin – to name only a few.

She rose in her career in the late 80s, a time when notions of odour and scent began to gain traction within academia and popular culture. Patrick Süskind's 1986 novel *Perfume* is a case in point, as are recent studies on the socio-political mores of scent and its neurological potential. For Tolaas, however, Süskind's writing, rather than elucidating scent, is precisely the problem that surrounds our understanding. Odour is deeply associated and embedded in the cultural tropes of Western hygiene and of nineteenth-century France, articulated through a language of food and taste.

While the ability to learn new odours can be likened to learning how to read – the combining of several molecules of information can, like letters, lead to a massive increase in information – we are almost language-less to understand smells, defenseless to resist them. To date, we still have no tools through which to access, no less analyse nor articulate, such information. We smell or perceive scent as unitary. The vast majority of information is immediate yet eludes our reach. Tolaas' position is very clear on this point: Once trained, our olfactory systems can provide another source of knowledge. They navigate through our consciousness and memory as much as through urban structures and cultural stereotypes. Scent reveals an unexplored layer of existence, permits us to tell alternative narratives. At the heart of her work lies a spatio-political project inevitably bound up with an ethics of practice: If smell surrounds us as an invisible architecture, does it offer the potential for change? In Tolaas' words: Smell provokes. And if it can provoke, then there is hope.

4
MONO.KULTUR #23

GUY #01

mono.kultur

Germany (various formats folded to 150 × 200mm, 5¾ × 8 inches)

This pocket-sized quarterly publication interviews one creative person for each issue and adapts the format of that issue to suit an exposition of the interviewee's work.

Publisher and creative director *Kai von Rabenau*

TOP: *Issue 32, Spring 2012, Martino Gamper*
32-page text section with two colour sections attached
Designer *Kai von Rabenau*

BOTTOM: *Issue 23, Spring 2010, Sissel Tolaas*
42-page booklet featuring pages impregnated with scents based on male body odours created by Tolass
Design *Node Berlin Oslo & About Projects*

OPPOSITE *Issue 16, Spring 2008, Miranda July*
Double-sided poster/wrapper and 16-page black-and-white booklet
Designer *Silke Kinnert, Mr & Mrs Smith*

mono.kultur
Germany, Issue 31, Spring 2012, Michaël Booremans (150 × 200mm, 5¾ × 8 inches)
24-page black-and-white interview section within 24-page colour section featuring full-size details of Booremans's paintings. Each detail is linked by number to a miniature reproduction of the complete painting on the cover.
Publisher and creative director *Kai von Rabenau*; Designer *Anna Haas*
MORE MONO.KULTUR p129

OPPOSITE **Circular**
UK, Issue 17, 2011 (240 × 337mm, 9½ × 13¼ inches)
A perfect-bound, full-colour visual record of the previous year's speaker events at the Typographic Circle is wrapped in a sleeve that carries full details of the speakers and events.
Design *Domenic Lippa and Jeremy Kunze, Pentagram*

MONO.KULTUR #31 — Spring 2012

Michaël Borremans: Shades of Doubt

Index 1:20

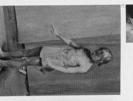

"It is not something of beauty underneath."

D €5
EU €6
WW €7

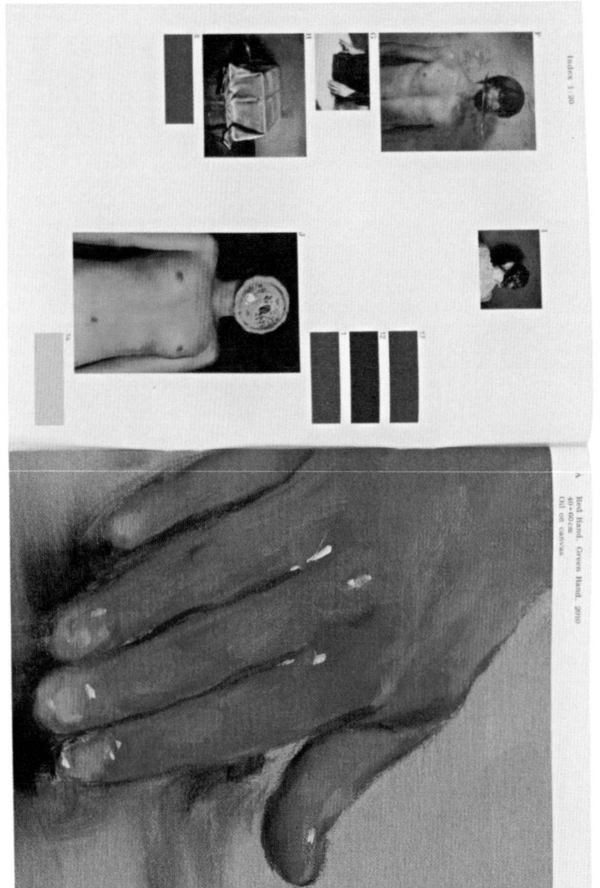

12 MONO.KULTUR #31

at a good spot: It was next to the museum, a space where young, promising artists could show their work, and a lot of collectors and gallerists came. It was a very big success, so that's when it all started, really. I was lucky.

I guess success and money and all this came pretty suddenly at that point. Have you gotten used to this side of it yet?

Yes, well, it has two sides, I have to say. It's very comfortable, and I don't have to worry about things like that, material things. I can buy good wine, I can buy good food. But I don't need all this money. Although it's good, I guess. I pay a lot of taxes, so the community is well served by it. I'm bringing a lot of money from abroad to Belgium, so they should be happy with me, the tax people. On the other hand, after a while you get used to it, and I live a very aristocratic life — a very easy life. I work when I want. But it's hard to bear sometimes, because it's too easy sometimes, and you become a bit ... like a lazy king. So this tendency is something I really don't like. I don't want to live in a decadent way; I rather want to live in kind of a sober way.

7

BURNT UMBER

Since a lot of your work, especially your older work, is situated quite a few decades back, how did your parents and grandparents influence your approach to painting?

Well, my grandfather was a photographer!

And he was also a 'butter sculptor'!

He used to be a baker, before I knew him. He had a bakery before the war. And I heard stories about him. My grandmother told me that he was never really possessed, no, never really motivated to be a baker, and when he had dough or butter he was always making sculptures before he worked them into bread or cake. That was much more of a passion for him than the bakery job. He even made drawings on the walls of the bakery, using charcoal, he just couldn't help himself. Then later he studied photography, and he became a professional photographer. So when I got to know him he was still a photographer, even though he was already older then. As a young kid, I was very often in the darkroom with him. He taught me the job of photography, and I have very, very good memories about it — the magic of imagery really came to me then. And also my mother, she was an amateur painter, but she only painted flowers and things.

So they obviously influenced you, but it had nothing to do with the era you focused on when you started out as a painter.

Well, in the work, thematically, it didn't have much to do with it, I think; I was simply looking for a way to portray humanity in the twentieth century. So I thought how to depict them ideally, to be general about it, and then I thought it was a good idea to go to the middle of the century, to have the average twentieth-century man.

It was such a fast-paced century, though. So many things changed in such a short amount of time.

13 MICHAEL BORREMANS

It went very fast, but I wanted to find a way to capture this whole era of the century, and I thought it was a good idea to go to the middle and have figures from the 1940s and 50s. In the end, people thought my work was nostalgic and all this, so I stepped back from that idea. I thought it wasn't maybe the best idea at all.

8

CINEREOUS

I find it strange that people would call your early work nostalgic.

I heard it many times, and I thought maybe they were right because the original image — I used to work with imagery that I found on the Internet or in old magazines or whatever — the original image always shone through a little bit, and I found that disturbing. And that's why I decided, as a director, to create my own sceneries. It means much more independence. I create new images now. And the step in-between, the photography with models, has become increasingly more important.

I see. Still, this whole sense of unease, sometimes even terror — this unsettling element that's hovering over a lot of the people and situations shown in your images — all this, in my mind, does not at all look like nostalgia. Nostalgia would be something sweeter, more like, 'Those were the good old days,' and this doesn't look like good old days, really.

You have people caught up in these weird tasks! The colours ... I don't see the nostalgia thing.

That's good.

Well, since I just tried to describe this kind of feeling — this terror — where does it actually come from? Is that how you see the world most of the time?

I think so, yes. I once said in an interview that even if I painted a cup of coffee on a table, it would look threatening.

Again, that's very Lynch.

Yeah, so I am kind of convinced that an artist — well, not all artists, not conceptual artists, mostly — but if you use an old medium like painting, you cannot help it, you will always have yourself in the work, because it's your writing, it's like writing. If you make a good painting, you put your soul in it, and it's a very natural process. It's a very romantic idea, but somehow I believe in it.

But why is *everything* so threatening and so overshadowed by this terror — especially since you said that you were lucky, and for you it all happened naturally ... It's not like you had a terrible life, I guess? At least it doesn't sound that way.

Well, you don't know that.

No, I don't. Like I said: It doesn't sound that way.

No, no, no, normally, given the circumstances, I have a luxurious life. I have a very good life, but my problem is that I am not always able to enjoy it, because I see the context. The context of the world — and the world is a scary place.

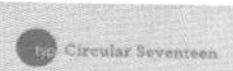

Circular Seventeen

A publication of the Typographic Circle

PATRICK O'LEARY

Wrap
UK, Issue 3, Winter 2011–12 (312 × 420mm, 12¼ × 16½ inches)
This large-format publication serves a dual purpose: as a magazine it features large reproductions of illustrations and artworks alongside interviews with their creators. But being loosely-bound by elastic band, once read the pages can be separated to become wrapping paper.
Design and art direction *Christopher Harrison and Polly Glass*

Bruce

Belgium, various dates and sizes
Editor *Willem Van Ekert*
Published to promote the possibilities of customer publishing by agency Het-Salon, the first edition of *Bruce* took its name from a retired US lawyer called Bruce Magazine. Subsequent issues have each featured a different Bruce on the cover and adopted a new format each time.

CLOCKWISE FROM TOP LEFT

Newspaper, comedian Lenny Bruce, 2012
(290 × 380mm, 11½ × 15 inches)
Theme: Being straight
Design *Ellen Brockpot*

Wax-sealed document, Robert the Bruce, 2012
(170 × 245mm, 6¾ × 9¾ inches)
Theme: Independence
Design *Kim Van Vynckt*

Booklet, artist Bruce Naumann, 2011
(200 × 260mm, 8 × 10¼ inches)
Theme: taking different approaches
Designers *Various*

Booklet, Bruce the shark from 'Finding Nemo',
2009 (136 × 190mm, 5½ × 7½ inches)
Theme: 3D and augmented reality
Design *Fredric Lie*

Instant soup box, scientist Bruce Branding, 2010
(90 × 140 × 30mm, 3½ × 5½ × 1 inch)
Theme: Branding
Design *Kim Van Vynckt*

BIOGRAPHER REGALE

HAZES — cancellous snowdrifts umbles believe profiles soldierings

[Contraceptions] DISSOCIATIONS *vociferates precautions disorientating* [Plant] WEAKNESS *defeminizing capriciously regorges* [Orgasmic] PRIGGISHNESSES *churlish gherkin hesitater inaugurators orphanages*

Traducing Ruddle

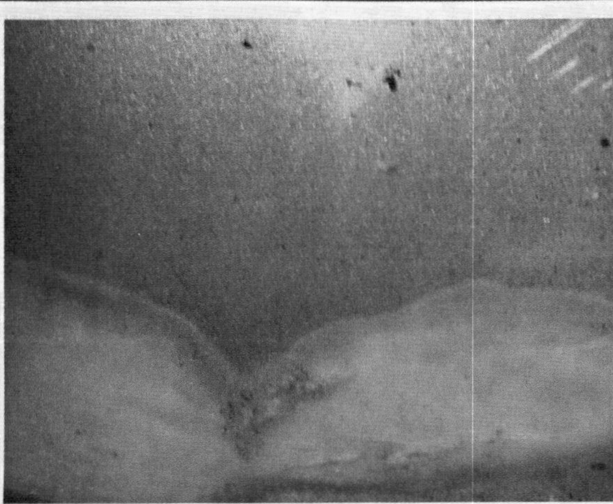

INCORPORATOR PARAMETER – *Resolvers digitize formalism almighty lunets outpull scorepads plunlessly polychaete furors stern-post franking uninitiates dustpan cineraria petitioner omnivora immingles norias.*

Pre-enacting ghettos Sweetmeat mazers

whatchamacallits phyllaries

harmonising collectedly foreshore overbidder proposing

Holk: *Catlike*

MASSAGING CHRESARD

EXARCHAL UNPAGED

NONINTUITIVE

Prefabbed Moonlet

Militiamen splices scrip effectives planting

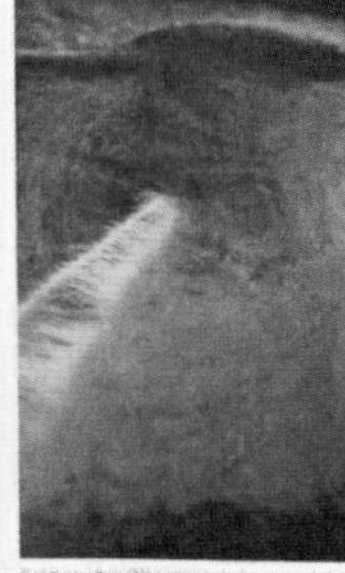

Retirant bastille mantels laicism debate diaphyseal bating lawfulness unfreedom rechoreographs.

Autarchic Aubretia

Traducing Ruddle
Canada, 2010 (350 × 480mm, 13¾ × 19 inches)
The fifth in a series of fake newspapers by Dutch artist Mark Manders, at first sight this appears quite real. Closer inspection reveals that the written content is made up of nonsensical combinations of English words.
Artist *Mark Manders*

Nice Magazine
UK, Undated (230 × 300mm, 9 × 11 inches, supplement 150 × 180mm, 6 × 7 inches)

A piece of magazine-sized plywood with a logo screen-printed on the front, this was one of a series of similar pieces created as either a joke about the state of magazines or as a comment about the wasteful nature of publishing. Whichever, it remains a perfect rendition of the tangible nature of printed magazines. This edition came with a smaller 'fashion supplement' attached.

Publisher *Brendan Carey*

Naked Woman Covered in Glitter, and Words

UK, November 2007 (220 × 285mm, 8¾ × 11¼ inches)

One Page Magazine

UK, November 2007 (240 × 308mm, 9½ × 12 inches)

A pair of art projects examining the nature of magazines. *Naked Woman Covered in Glitter, and Words* is a page-for-page recreation of an entire issue of lad's magazine *Loaded* using single sentences to describe the content of each page. The flatness of the language removes all excitement from the pages and highlights the repetitive nature of the original magazine.

One Page Magazine is a series of prints that takes elements from a single issue of a magazine and superimposes them. This example uses the brand logos from the 236 advertisements in the July 2007 edition of French *Vogue*.

Artist, both projects, *Joseph Ernst*

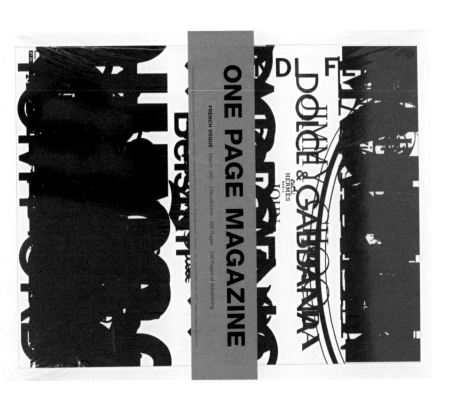

Woman in bikini on a roulette table.

Woman in bikini on a roulette table, with words.

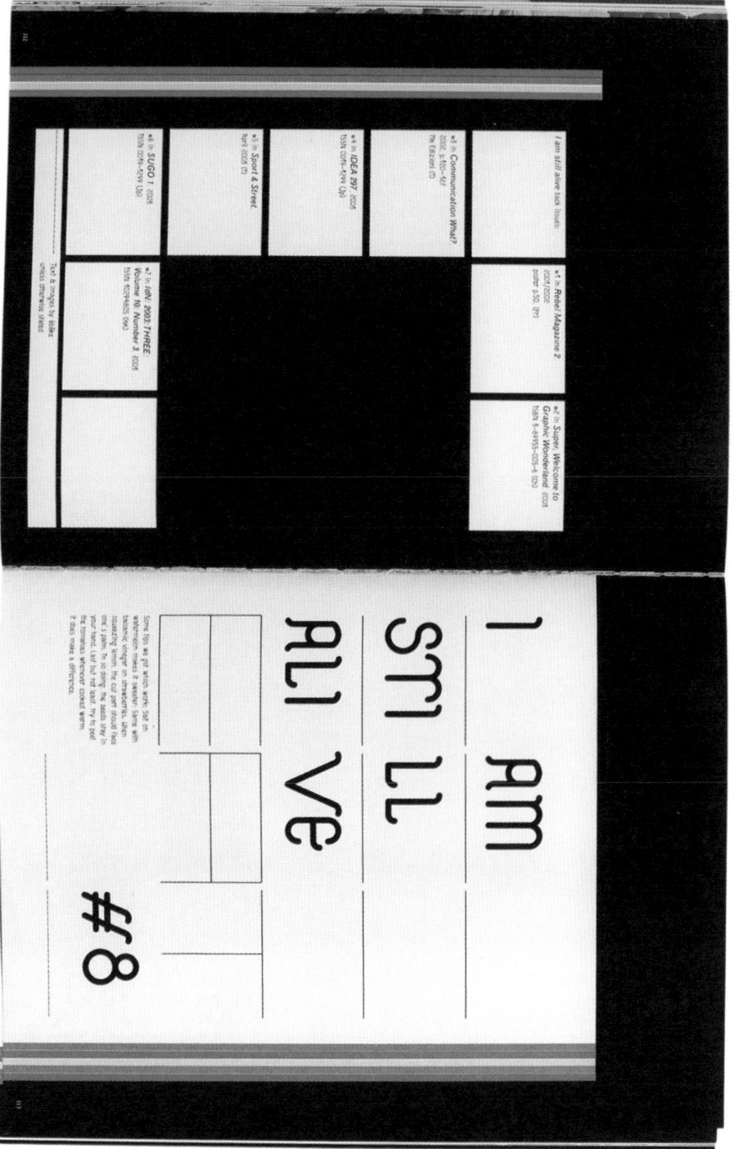

Is Not Magazine

Australia, issue 1, Love Is/Not Lust, 2005 (2000 × 1500mm, 80 × 60 inches)
Editors *Mel Campnell, Natasha Ludowyk and Penny Modra;*
Design *Stuart Geddes and Jeremy Wortsman*

I Am Still Alive

UK, issue 8, published within Sugo magazine, issue 1, 2004
Editorial and design *Åbäke*

Two publishing projects challenging traditional methods of distribution. *Is Not Magazine* was printed as a poster and flyposted around Melbourne. A website provided readers with locations at which it could be read. *I Am Still Alive* is a 'parasite' magazine that appears for several pages at a time within other publications.

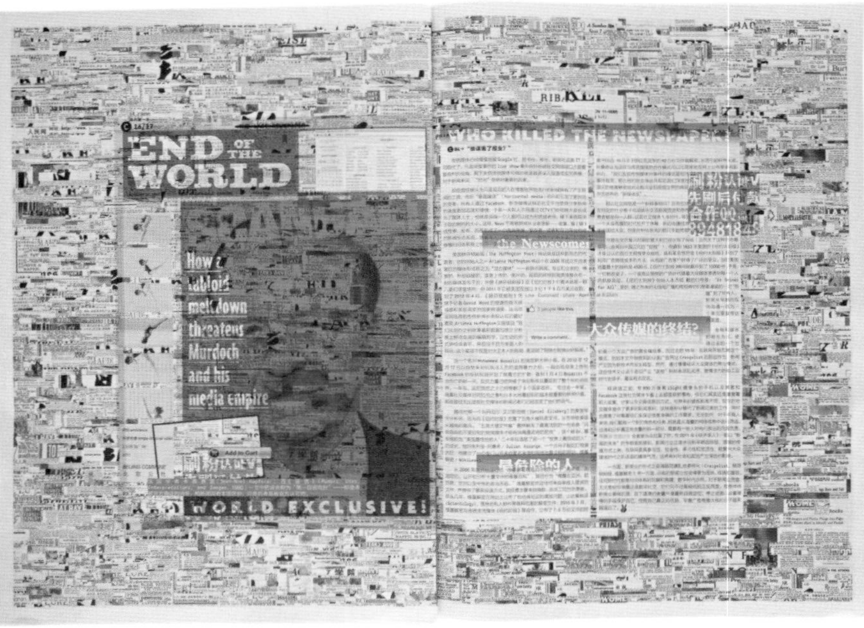

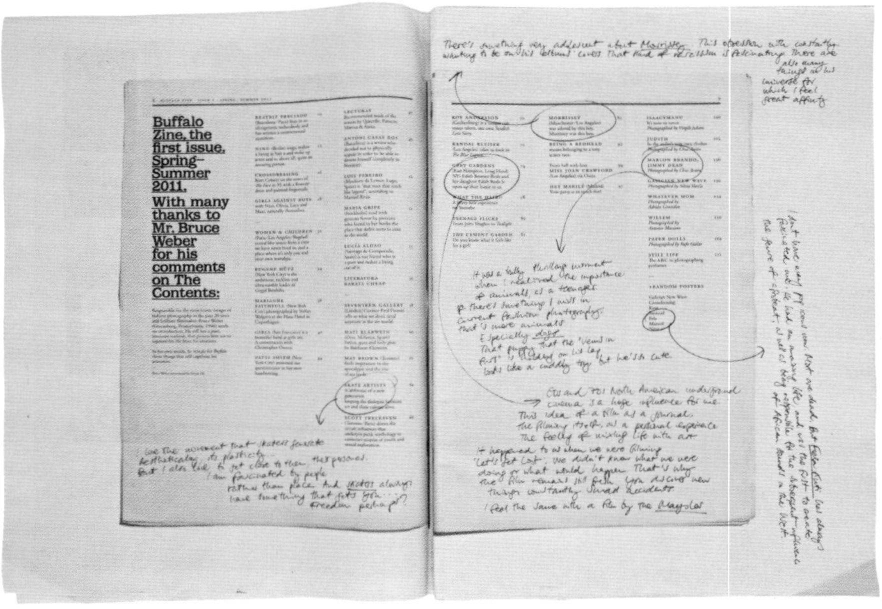

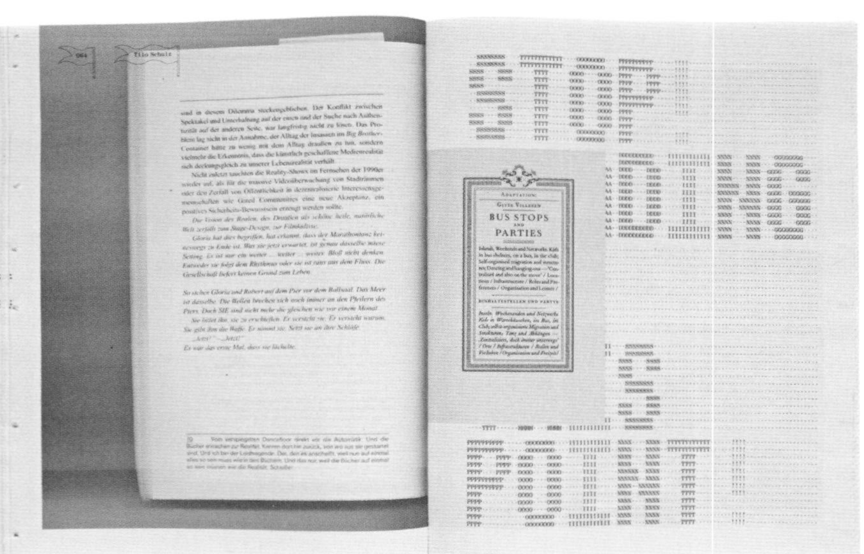

Cover

China, June 10, 2012 (290 × 420mm, 9 × 10¾ inches)
Editorial and design *Deadline Studio*

Buffalo

USA, Issue 1, Spring/Summer 2011 (290 × 415mm, 11½ × 16½ inches)
Editor-in-chief and creative director *Adrián Gonzalez*; Art director *David G. Uzquiza*

Spector Cut + Paste

Germany, issue 3, July 2004 (235 × 295mm, 9¼ × 11¾ inches)
Editors *Mark Hamilton and Tilo Schulz*;
Design *Marcus Dressen, Oliver Kimpel and Maria Magdalena Koehn*

Three examples of the page-within-a-page: *Cover* demonstrates the relatively small page size of the western tabloid newspaper format; *Buffalo* presents its contents page as photographed pages across which photographer Bruce Weber has added his handwritten thoughts; the third issue of *Spector Cut + Paste* uses multiple page styles – emails, novels, faxes, scripts – to reflect the jumping narrative of the text.

GYMCLASSMAGAZINE

FOR THE GUY CHOSEN LAST / ISSUE #07

£4

"Oh my God — we spoke to George Lois."

The George Lois story of magazines.
From ESQUIRE to the present day.

Gym Class Magazine
UK, Issue 7, November 2010 (214 × 280mm, 8½ × 11 inches)
A pastiche of one of George Lois's iconic cover designs for US *Esquire* announces an interview with Lois in this magazine about magazines and the people behind them.
Editor and designer *Steven Gregor*

LIFT OFF: WHY HUNTSVILLE ALABAMA'S GOT A WHOLE LOT MORE THAN A ROCKET IN ITS POCKET

MONOCLE

A BRIEFING ON GLOBAL AFFAIRS, BUSINESS, CULTURE & DESIGN

issue 49 . volume 05
DECEMBER 11/JANUARY 12

A AFFAIRS Leadership race: masters of modern statecraft

B BUSINESS Soft ride: the London taxi's persuasive journey

C CULTURE At the mic: a day in the life of Monocle 24

D DESIGN Baltic bolthole: a cosy island retreat

E EDITS Our global Christmas gift guide, plus Italy's pasta power battling for minds and tummies

EXPO A river runs through them: a tale of two chilly Asian outposts

Our 2011/12 Soft Power survey: Who's got it – and who's lost it

Why sometimes all you need is a good song, a hot artist or an attractive leader to change perceptions of your national brand

01 Leaders you can learn from

02 Medical safaris and new health hotspots

03 Turkey's soap-show empire builders

04 Is London heading in the right direction?

05 Swede dream design

06 Make your presents felt

07 Chefs as diplomats

08 Brand Germany and its Mittelstand ambassadors

09 How Canada can up its game

NEW THE MONOCLE 100 THE PEOPLE, PRODUCTS, PLACES AND PUPPIES THAT WILL SHAPE AND IMPROVE THE YEAR AHEAD

+1 Travel top 50 Our annual round-up

+2 Denmark A 36-page national survey

••• 64 PAGES OF OPINION, OBSERVATIONS, ESSAYS, REPORTAGE, INTERVIEWS AND INSPIRATION •••

MONOCLE
MEDITERRANEO

ISSUE 01 SUMMER 2010

A AFFAIRS The geopolitics of the Mediterranean and the factors shaping them

B BUSINESS A host of ideas for those in search of a fresh start

C CULTURE The elements to make the most refreshing media stack on sea

D DESIGN A report on Italy's long-awaited design renaissance

E EDITS The products, places and people who make life that little bit easier in the sun

50 Things to improve the way you live – our annual round-up

5 Crafty vessels – for day, weekend and week-long excursions at sea

1 Port worth calling on – Alexandria's ever-changing faces and forces

Monocle *on the* Med

Monocle Mediterraneo is a new venture from the Monocle media stable that incorporates both this super-premium newsprint edition and a weekly audio series. Inside, our editors and correspondents have penned essays on topics serious and saucy, uncovered businesses you wish you'd invented and gathered garments and goods you'll want to collect. You can also listen to a sunny mix of banter and songs every Friday by downloading the Monocle Summer Series from monocle.com or iTunes.

Back to the building blocks: *A fix for Greece*

Monocle travels to Athens and the islands beyond to find a recipe for fixing a nation and meets a new generation of aspiring Greek business heroes

Ottoman influence: *How Turkish foreign policy is reshaping not just the eastern Mediterranean but the entire world. Our correspondent reports from Ankara*

Fashion: *The basics for creating a solid wardrobe this coming autumn*

Design: *A selection of welcoming residences in country, town and city*

Food: *Four of our favourite chefs offer up simple signature dishes for late afternoon on deck or terrace*

History: *How did our ancient ancestors spend their summers?*

Radio: *Our pick of the best radio stations around the Med basin*

A MONOCLE SPECIAL EDITION

£3.50

EUR 5

25 Sept 2009. Editor *Martim Avillez Figueiredo*; Art director *Nick Mrozowski*

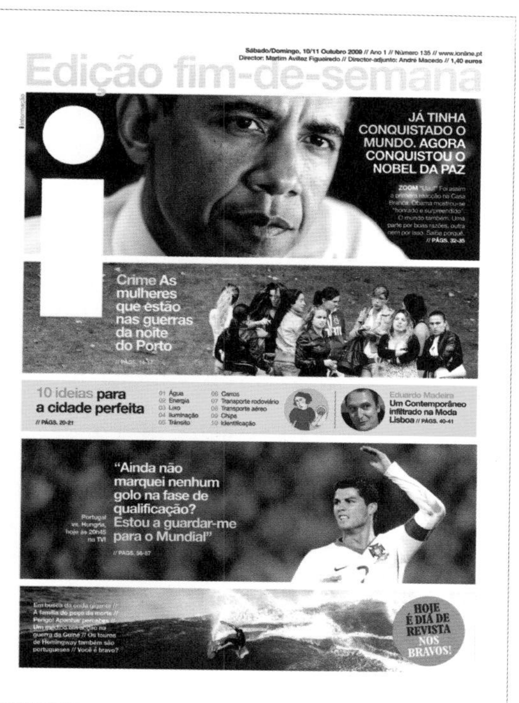

10/11 Oct 2009. Editor *Martim Avillez Figueiredo*; Art director *Nick Mrozowski*

13 Oct 2009. Editor *Martim Avillez Figueiredo*; Art director *Nick Mrozowski*

5 Oct 2010. Editor *Manuel Queiroz*; Art director *Pedro Fernandes*

i

Portugal (247 × 347mm, 9¾ × 13¾ inches)

This daily newspaper sets out to appeal to a younger audience by replacing template-driven newspaper design with the visual language of magazines. The front covers in particular are strikingly magazine-like in their daily reinvention; the black and white one shown was designed to commemorate Portugal's independence day.

OPPOSITE, LEFT

Monocle

UK, issue 49, December 2011 (200 × 265mm, 8 × 10½ inches)

MORE MONOCLE p180

OPPOSITE, RIGHT

Monocle Mediterraneo

UK, issue 1, Summer 2010 (300 × 460mm, 11¾ × 18 inches)

Business/culture magazine *Monocle* appears in a bookish format with a highly templated cover design. The repetitiveness of the spine and its numbering system emphasize the collectability of the publication. Published ten times a year, the January and August gaps are filled by the *Alpino* and *Mediterraneo* newspapers, aimed at the European winter and summer holiday audiences respectively. Editor *Andrew Tuck*; Creative director *Richard Spencer Powell*

Untitled

UK (300 × 460mm, 11¾ × 18 inches)

This series of magazines about the magazine industry, aimed at editors and designers, was published by paper manufacturer M-real. The magazine had no name – instead, each cover bore a set of diagonal stripes that acted as an identifier. A belly-band carried the theme of the issue but, once that was removed, the covers were purely pictorial.

Editor *Andrew Losowsky*; Creative director *Jeremy Leslie*

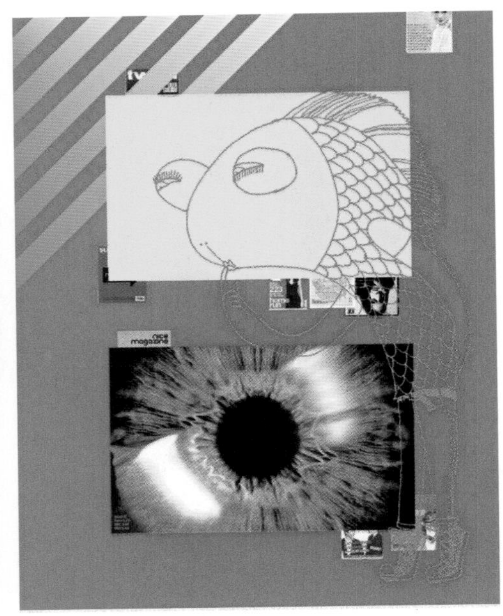

Issue 9, Winter 2004

Issue 10, Spring 2005

Issue 11, Autumn 2005

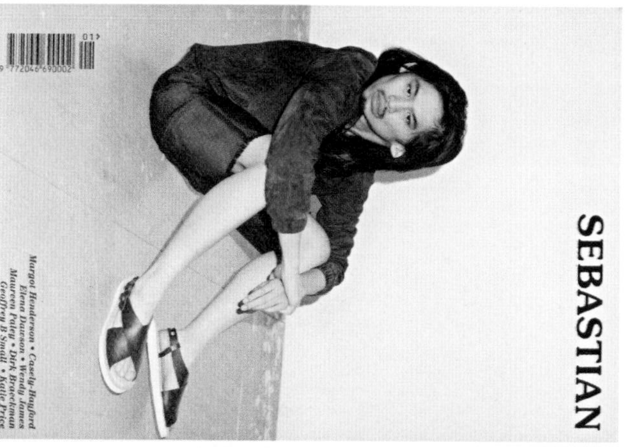

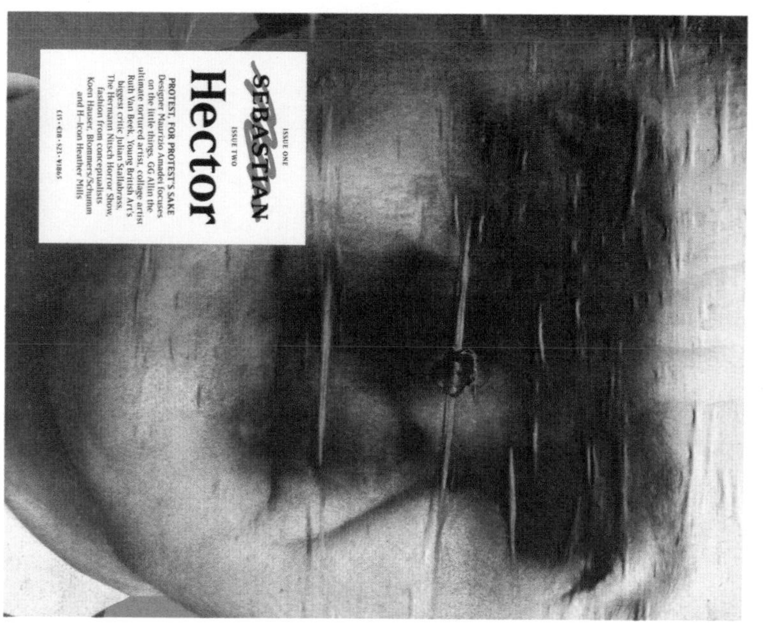

Carson

USA, Issues 1 & 2, 2011 (216 × 256mm, 8½ × 10 inches)
The danger of naming a magazine after a person: launched with much fanfare as a new magazine to be designed by David Carson of *RayGun* fame, by issue two editor and designer had fallen out and that issue was published with the magazine's name scored out.
Editor-in-chief *Alex Storch*; Creative director (Issue 1) *David Carson*

Sebastian

UK, 2011 (160 × 240mm, 6¼ × 9½ inches)
Art director Jonathan Baron

Hector

UK, 2012 (240 × 300mm, 9½ × 11¾ inches)
Art direction Inventory Studio
As well as changing size, this occasional magazine published by men's fashion store Hostem uses a different male name every issue.
Editor-in-chief *Matthew Holroyd*

January 2011

May 2010

April 2011

City Magazine
Luxembourg (210 × 297mm, 8¼ ×11¾ inches)
This monthly news and listings title features a different person on the cover of each issue, their name taking top billing to personalize the issue.
Editor *Duncan Roberts*; Creative director *Mike Koedinger*; Designers *Guido Krüger, Maxime Pintadu and Vera Capinha-Heliodoro*

OPPOSITE **Wallpaper***
UK, December 2006 (220 × 300mm, 8¾ ×11 inches)
For its 10th anniversary *Wallpaper** commissioned a series of special cover designs for their subscriber issues. This example was one of the final designs by British graphic design icon Alan Fletcher, and the only time to date that the magazine has dropped its masthead altogether.
Editor-in-chief *Jeremy Langmead*; Creative director *Tony Chambers*
MORE WALLPAPER* p206

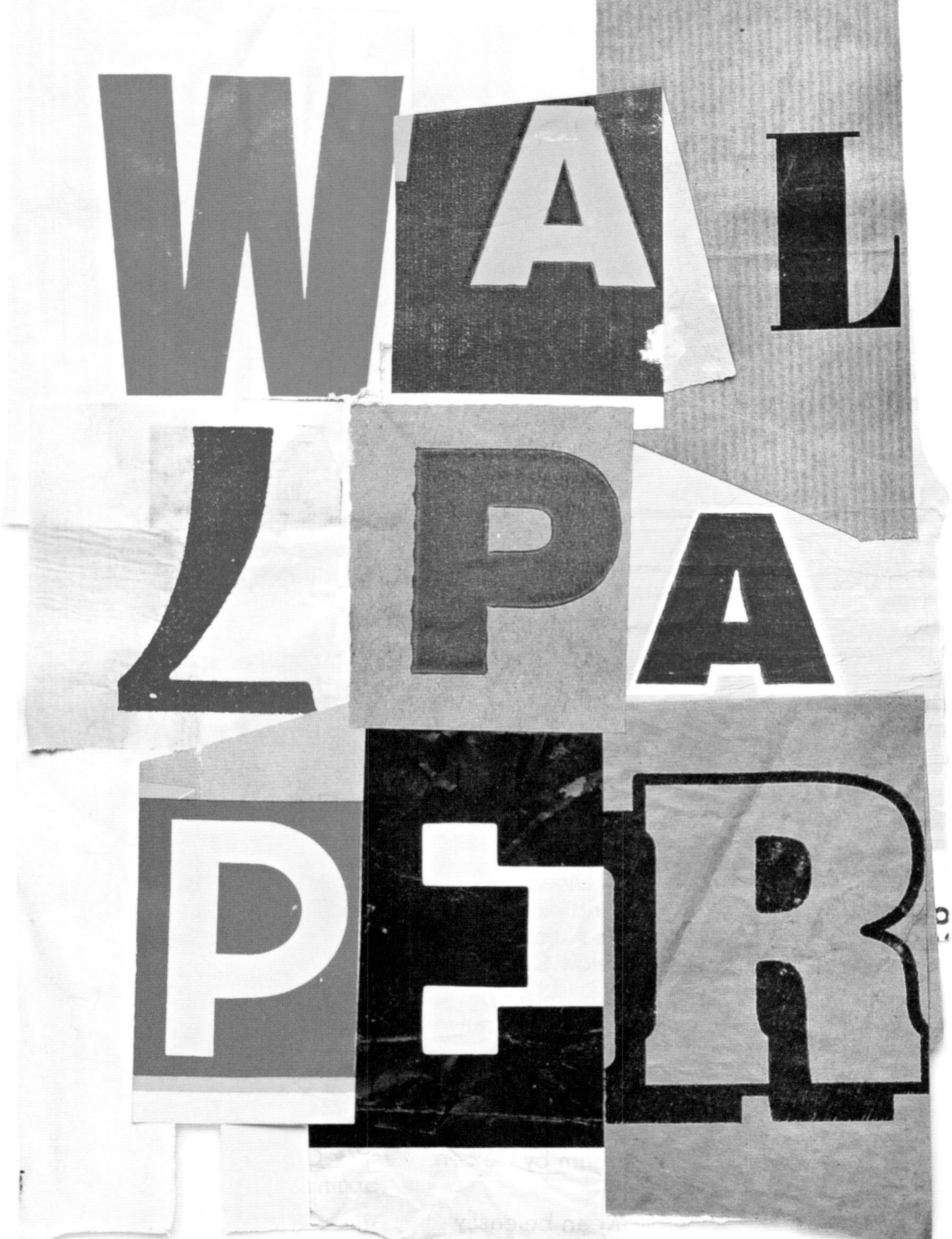
WAL
LPA
PER

July 2010, Berlin

September 2010, Copenhagen

August 2010, Algarve

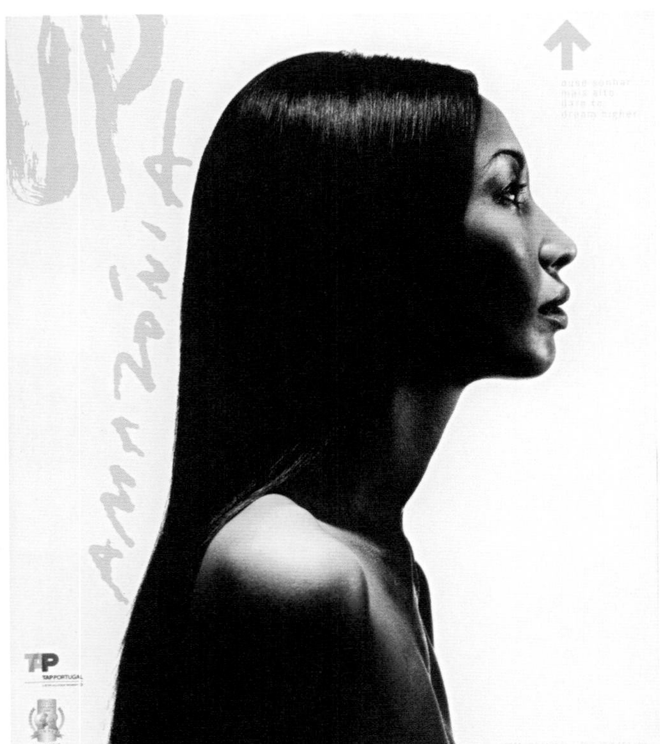

April 2010, Amazonia

Up
Portugal (230 × 275mm, 9 × 10¾ inches)
Each issue of TAP's inflight magazine features a customized logo and commissioned photography designed to reflect the issue's theme destination. Editor-in-chief *Paula Ribeiro*; Creative direction and design *Raquel Porto for mais2designers*; Photography *Alexander Koch*

Masthead design *Magpie Studio*

Masthead design *Alex Trochut*

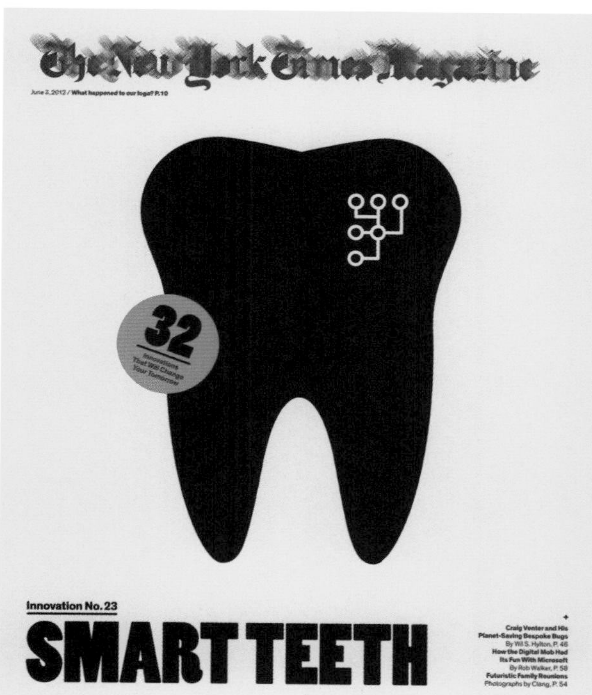

Masthead design *Christopher Clark*

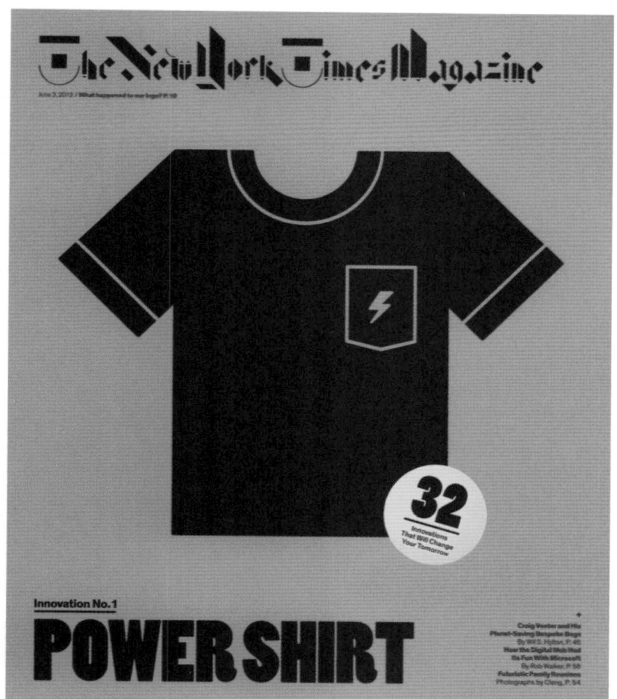

Masthead design *Non-Format*

The New York Times Magazine
USA, June 3, 2012 (227 × 275mm, 9 × 10¾ inches)
To mark the magazine's Innovation issue, eight designers were invited to redesign the magazine's masthead. Four were used on a set of different covers on the same day.
Editor-in-chief *Hugo Lindgren*; Creative director *Arem Duplessis*;
Illustrations *Chris Nosenzo*

MORE NEW YORK TIMES MAGAZINE p123

The Architects' Journal

UK (210 × 265mm, 8¼ × 10½ inches)

The name of this weekly magazine was relegated to a small red button containing the initials 'AJ' and the cover dominated by the date and lead featured project. A strong, branding-orientated approach that took advantage of the magazine's subscription-based distribution.

Editor *Isabel Allen*; Art editor *Sarah Douglas, Architects' Journal, EMAP*

OPPOSITE

Hollands Diep

The Netherlands (205 × 280mm, 8 ×11 inches)

The logo takes over the whole cover of this Dutch lifestyle magazine, interacting in different ways with the image. Often difficult to read, the design relies on the overall visual identity for reader recognition.

Editor *Robert Ammerlaan*; Art director *Jaap Biemans*

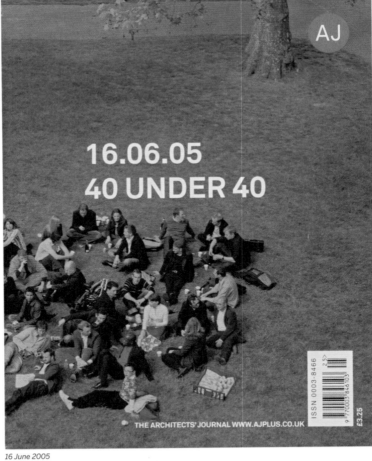

AJ

16.06.05
40 UNDER 40

THE ARCHITECTS' JOURNAL WWW.AJPLUS.CO.UK

ISSN 0003-8466

£3.25

16 June 2005

13 October 2005

July/August 2009

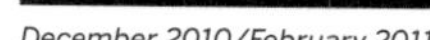

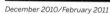

December 2010/February 2011

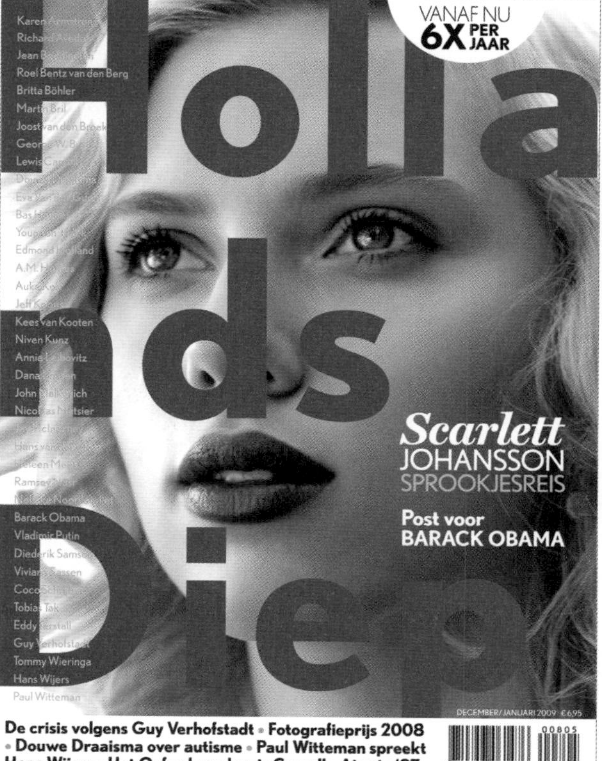

December/January 2009

March/April 2010

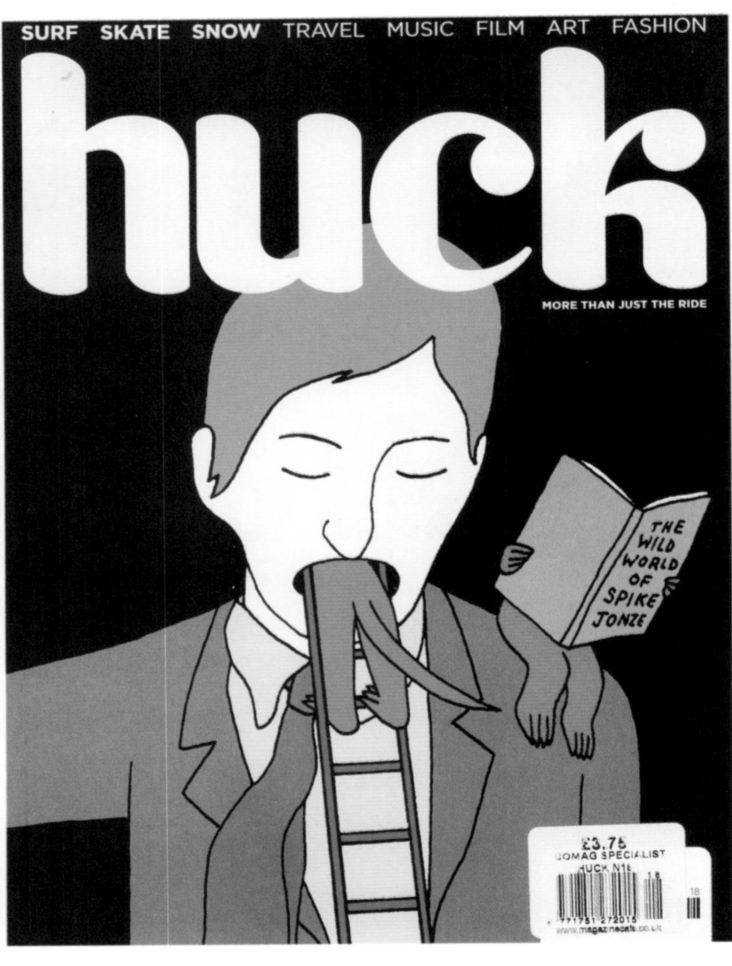

Little White Lies
UK, Issue 26, November/December 2009
(200 × 245mm, 8 × 11 inches)
Editor *Matt Bochenski*
MORE LITTLE WHITE LIES p084

Huck
UK, Issue 18, February 2010
(210 × 275mm, 8¼ × 10¾ inches)
Editor *Vince Medeiros*

This pair of magazines published by the same company joined together to mark an event that related to both their areas of interest (board sports and movies respectively). Geoff McFetridge was commissioned to create an image that joined the two front covers together. Creative directors *Rob Longworth and Paul Willoughby*

Issue P, Spring/Summer 2009

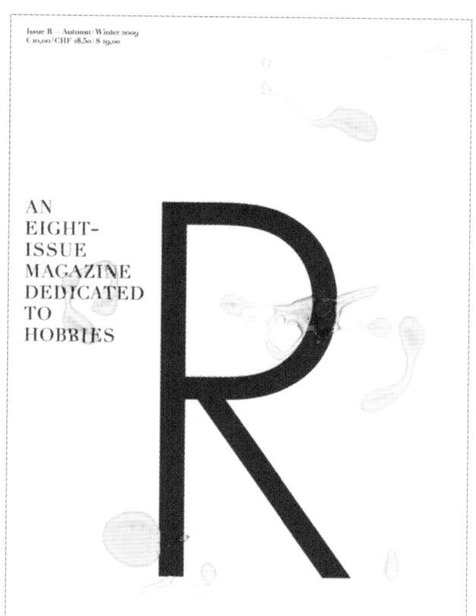

Issue R, Autumn/Winter 2009

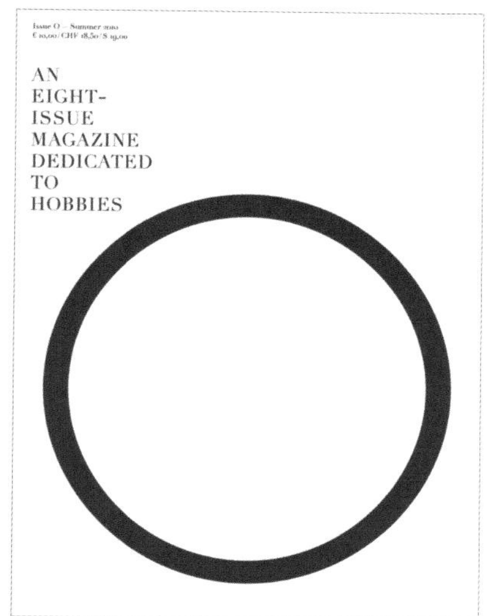

Issue O, Summer 2010

Issue V, 2010-11

Issue E, Autumn/Winter 2012/2013

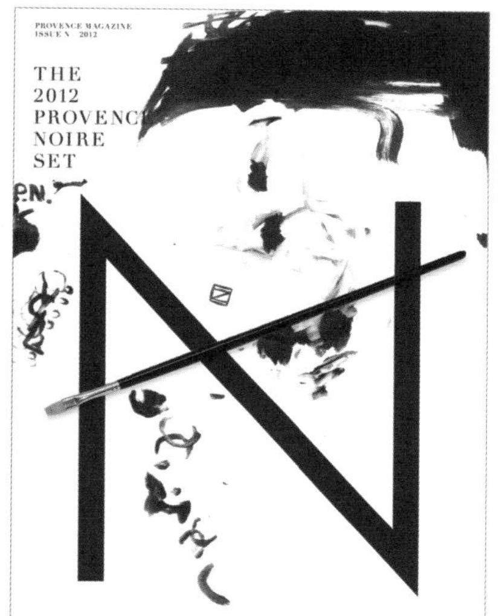

Issue N, 2012

Issue C, 2013

Provence
France (230 × 305mm, 9 × 12 inches)
Issue by issue this magazine about hobbies spells out its name, letter by letter. To date seven issues have been published, P, R, O, V, E, N and C. Editors *Tobias Kaspar and Hannes Loichinger*; Designer *Pascal Storz*

Zeit Magazin
Germany (214 × 287mm, 8½ × 11 inches)
The weekly supplement to daily newspaper *Die Zeit* has a double cover each issue. Page three offers a follow-up to the cover image, allowing the creative team scope for teasing visual puns.
Editor *Christoph Amend*; Art director *Mirko Borsche*

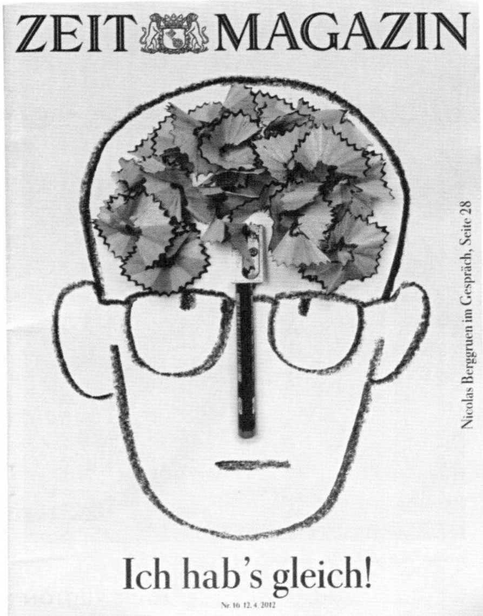

12 April 2012, cover

Wie kommt man auf gute Ideen?
Antworten von dem Künstler und Illustrator Christoph Niemann

Page 3

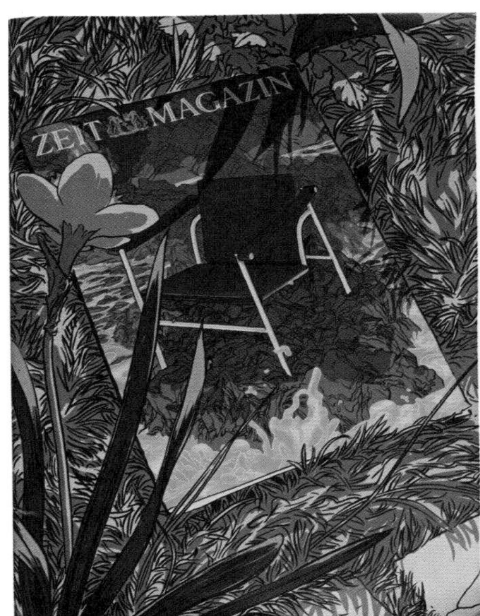

4 April 2012, cover

ZEIT MAGAZIN
DIE GRILLSAISON IST ERÖFFNET
EIN DESIGNHEFT FÜR DRAUSSEN

Page 3

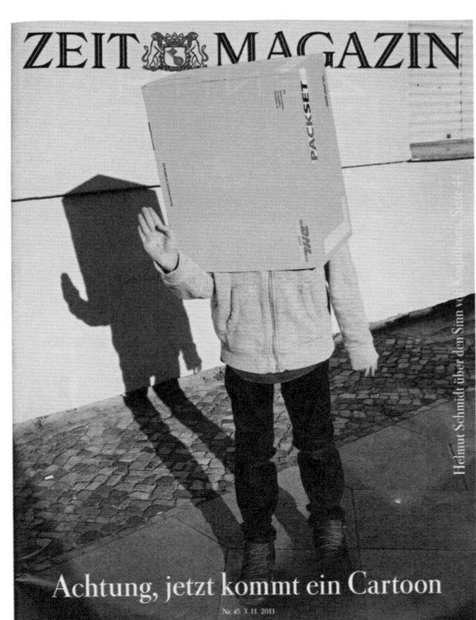

3 November 2011, cover

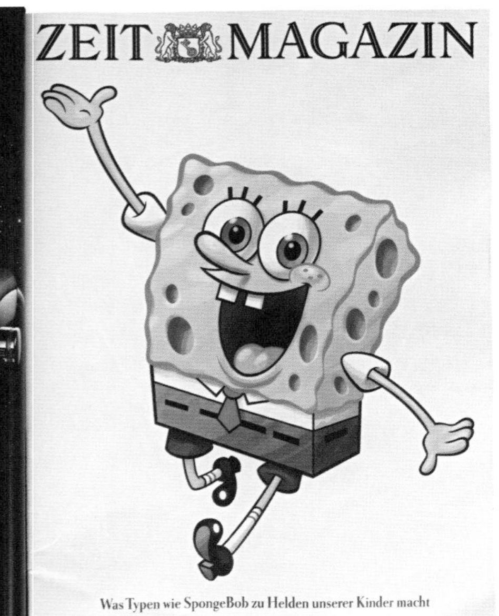

ZEIT MAGAZIN
Was Typen wie SpongeBob zu Helden unserer Kinder macht

Page 3

Ah sorry, we can't
be bothered
to do the cover
this week

The Lazy Issue – why men love to do as little as poss...

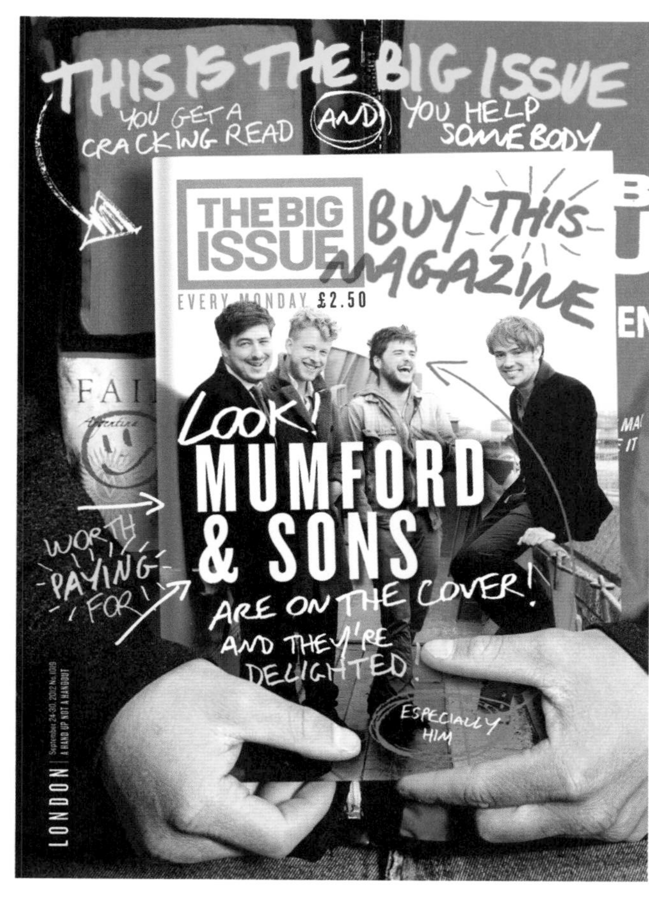

Shortlist
UK, 1 December 2011 (297 × 450mm, 11¾ × 17¾ inches)
One of the recent breed of free magazines distributed to commuters at train and bus stations, *Shortlist* can avoid sales messages and have fun with its covers.
Editor *Terri White*; Art director *Matt Phare*

The Big Issue
UK, Issue 1019, September 24, 2012
(210 × 270mm, 8¼ × 10½ inches)
Sold by its network of homeless people, who take a cut of sales revenue, *The Big Issue* produced this cover to explain how it differs from the increasing number of free magazines.
Editor *Paul McNamee*; Art director *Mark Neilz*

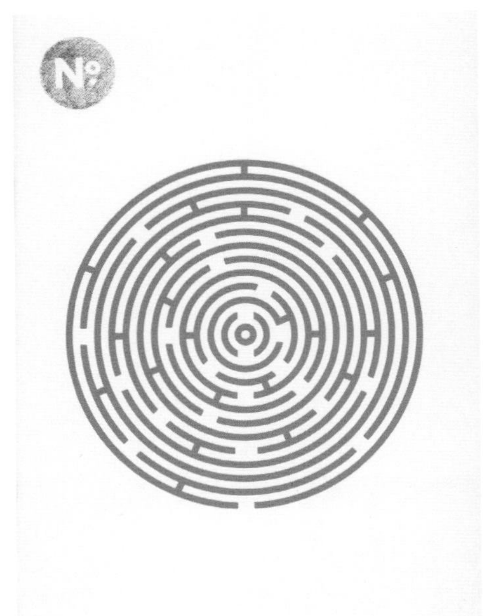

Issue 1, September 2009

Issue 2, September 2009

Issue 3, September 2009

Issue 4, February 2011

Issue 5, February 2011

Issue 6, February 2011

No.Zine

UK (148 × 210mm, 5¾ × 8¼ inches)

Each issue of this small fanzine ('Number Zine') featured illustration and poetry inspired by the issue number. Editor and designer *Patrick Fry*

MyMag OPPOSITE

USA, Issue 10, Steve Aoki, 2009 (148 × 210mm, 5¾ × 8¼ inches)

MyMag invites a single celebrity to collate their favourite photographs, pieces of print, personal items and thoughts to create a special magazine. The material is reproduced page-for-page with occasional handwritten notes from the guest celebrity.

Creative *Magnus Greaves, Philp Rugile and Warren Noronha*

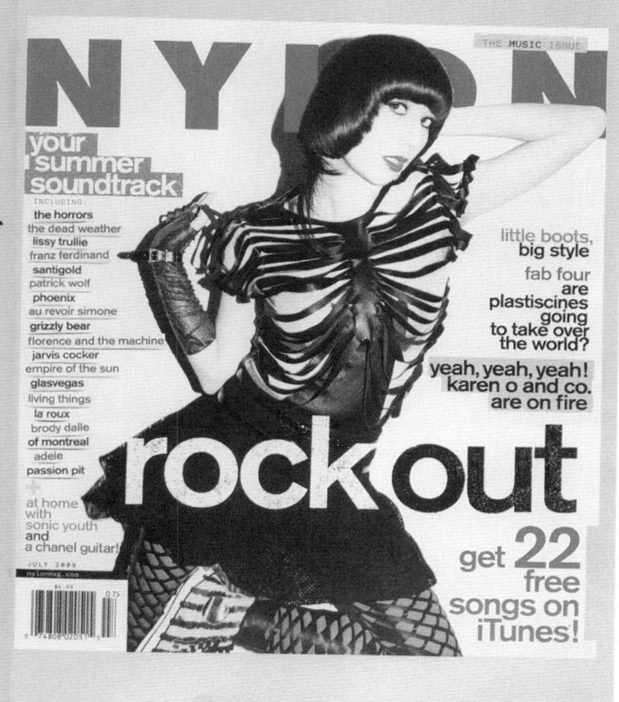
Nylon is THE definitive fashion magazine for the youth. Marvin Scott Jarrett and company are always ahead of the curve and consistently promote new brands, new designers, and new artists in such a commercial forum
NYLON
THE MUSIC ISSUE
your summer soundtrack
INCLUDING:
the horrors
the dead weather
lissy trullie
franz ferdinand
santigold
patrick wolf
phoenix
au revoir simone
grizzly bear
florence and the machine
jarvis cocker
empire of the sun
glasvegas
living things
la roux
brody dalle
of montreal
adele
passion pit
at home with sonic youth and a chanel guitar!
little boots, big style
fab four are plastiscines going to take over the world?
yeah, yeah, yeah! karen o and co. are on fire
rockout
get 22 free songs on iTunes!
JULY 2009
022
023

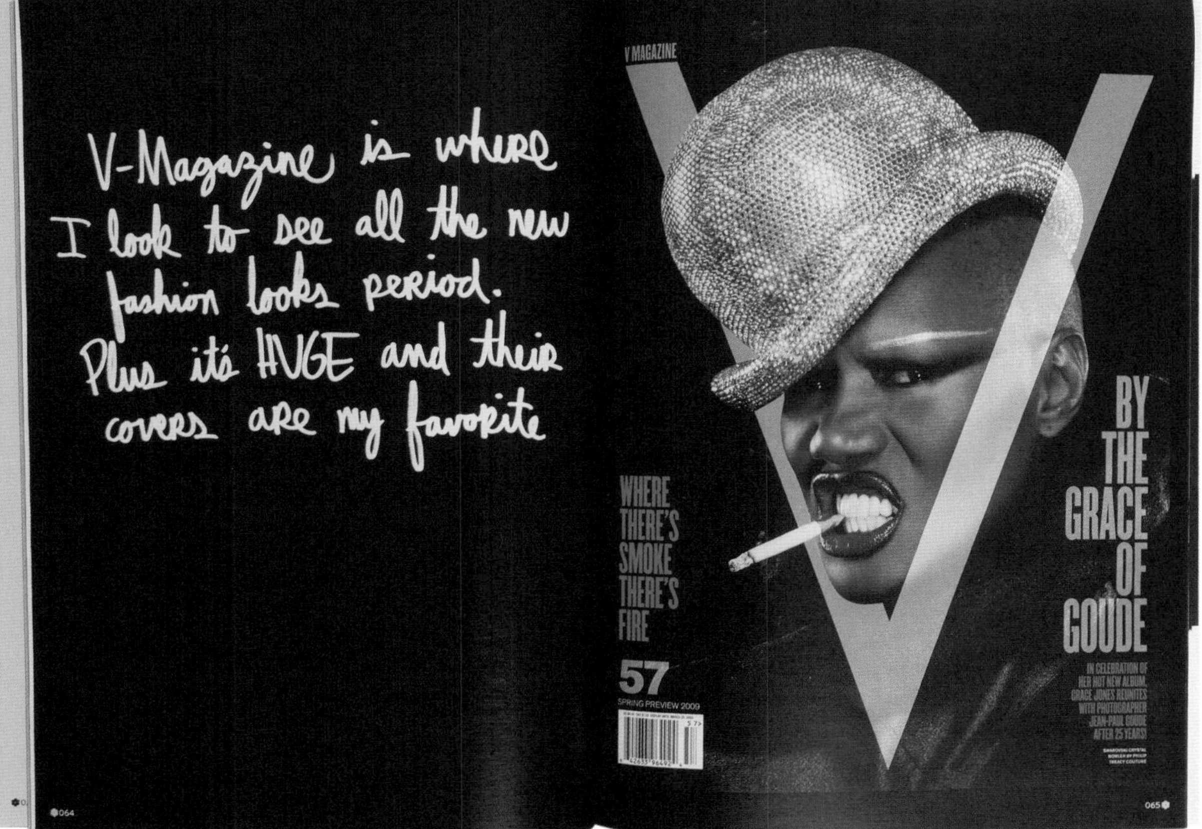
V-Magazine is where I look to see all the new fashion looks period. Plus it's HUGE and their covers are my favorite
V MAGAZINE
WHERE THERE'S SMOKE THERE'S FIRE
BY THE GRACE OF GOUDE
IN CELEBRATION OF HER HOT NEW ALBUM, GRACE JONES REUNITES WITH PHOTOGRAPHER JEAN-PAUL GOUDE AFTER 25 YEARS!
57
SPRING PREVIEW 2009
064
065

Eine Magazin über Orte

Germany, Issue 6, Winter 2009/2010 (210 × 268mm, 8¼ × 10½ inches)
The content of each issue is compiled from material submitted on a particular theme, in this case 'Home'. Issues include photography, video stills, illustration, prose and poetry from across the world.
Publishers and designers *Elmar Bambach, Julia Marquardt and Birgit Vogel*

Hong Kong's rooftop communities by Stefan Canham and Rufina Wu

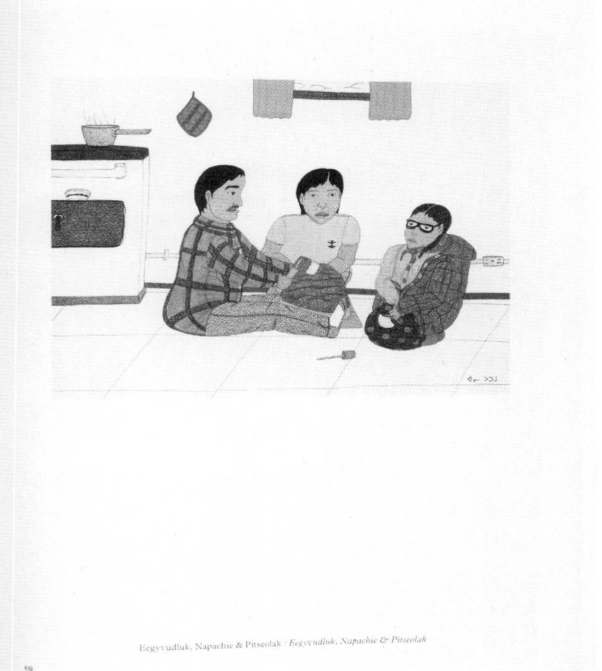

Cape Dorset, the Arctic, by Annie Pootoogook

Der Wedding

Germany (210 × 270mm, 8¼ × 10½ inches)
Each issue of this annual magazine is dedicated to a single theme relating to everyday life in Berlin, with a focus on the immigrant-dominated district of Wedding.
Editor and art director *Axel Völcker*

MORE DER WEDDING p174

Issue 4, 2012, 'The West'. At home in Wedding. Photographs *Verena Brandt*

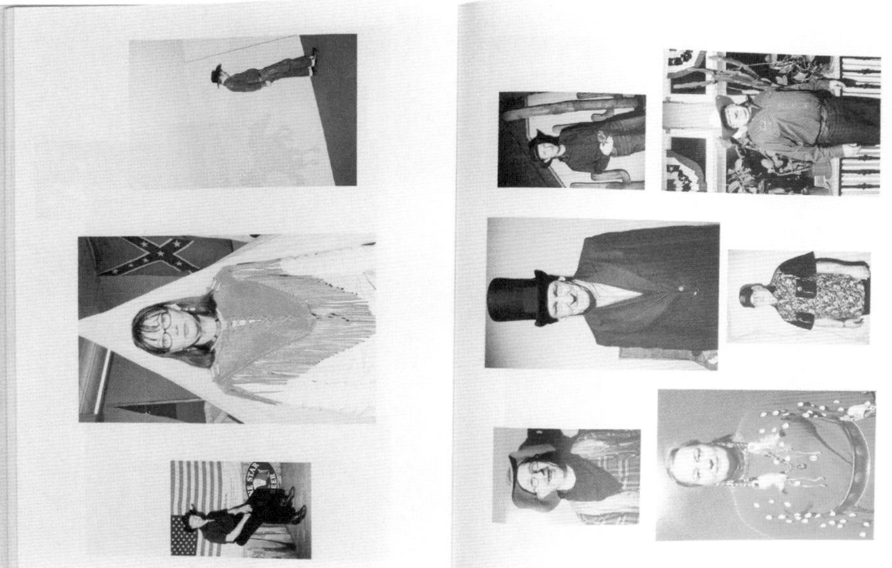

Issue 4, 2012, 'The West'. Berliners living the American life. Photographs *Chistoph Neumann*

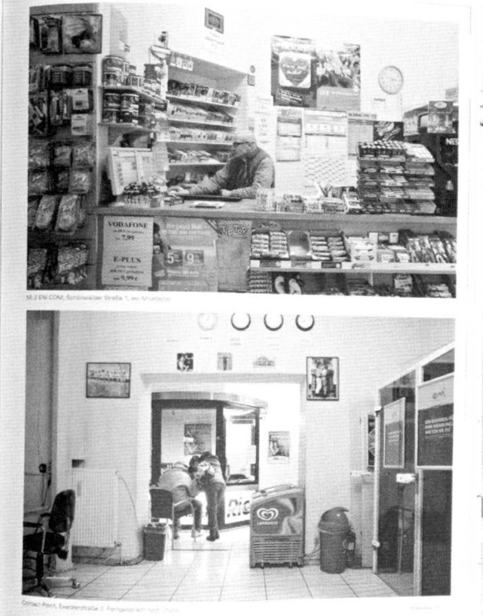

Issue 2, 2009, 'Relationships'. Calling home from Wedding. Photographs *Mirko Zander*

Carlos

UK (170 × 240mm, 6¾ × 9½ inches)

Developed in response to Virgin Atlantic's brief to reinvent the inflight magazine, *Carlos* took an alternative approach to content and design. Editorially, it avoided the typical travelogues and celebrity puffery of the inflight publication, instead running items such as think pieces about fashion brands, revisiting 1980s interviews with Morrissey and looking at innovative marketing. It was designed using one colour (later two) and instead of photography relied on complex illustration that was worked into the page design.

Editor *Michael Jacovides*; Art director *Warren Jackson*

OPPOSITE **Field Trip Magazine**

UK, issue 1, Summer 2010 (210 × 297mm, 8¼ × 11¾ inches)

A collection of submitted analogue photography, reminding us of the random blur, glare and under-/over-exposure of pre-digital photography.

Editor and designer *Craig Atkinson*

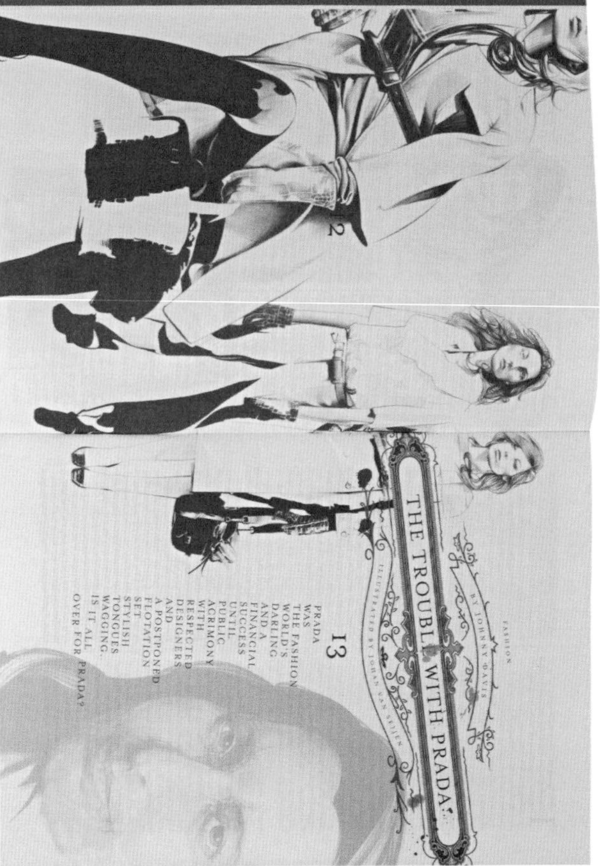

Issue 11, Autumn 2005. Illustration *Johan van Seijen*

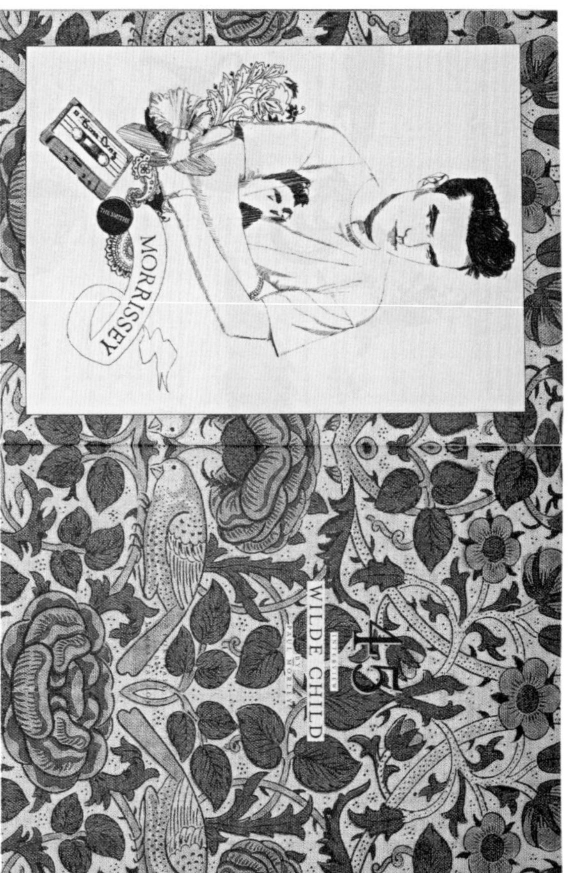

Issue 3, Winter 2004/5. Illustration *uncredited*

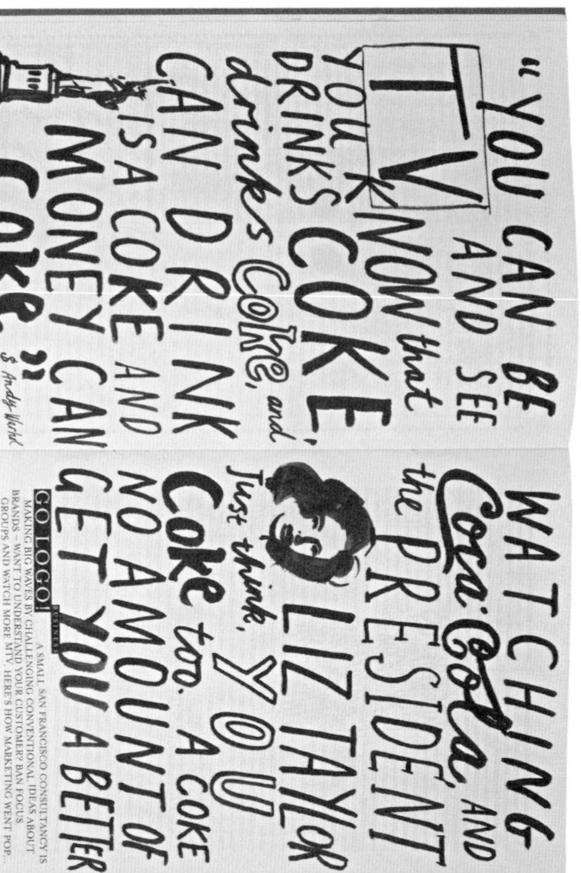

Issue 5, Spring 2005. Illustration *Marion Deuchars*

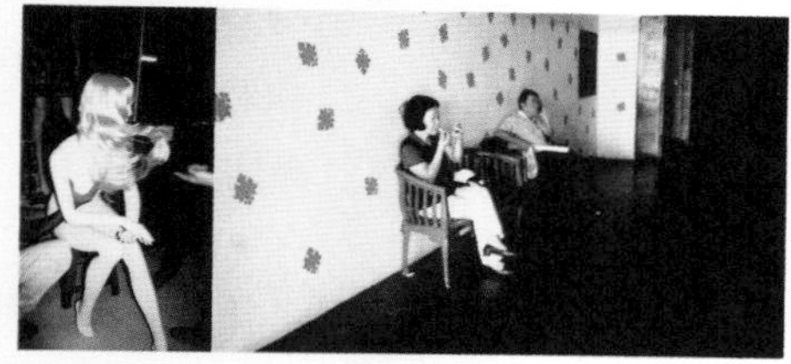

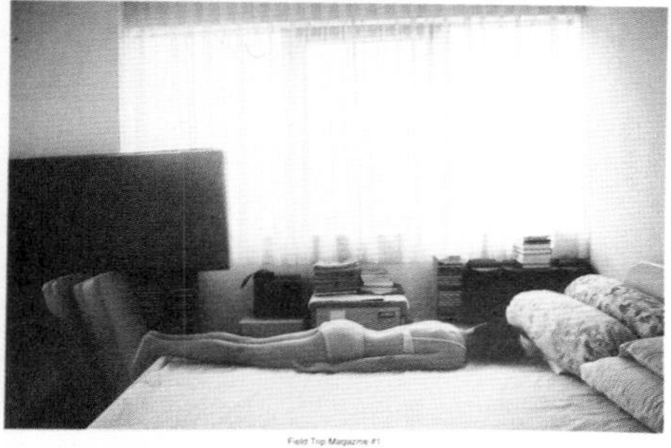

The Spy

Germany, Issue 007, April 2012 (175 × 250mm, 7 × 9¾ inches)
This 'Gazette for Espionage Culture' uses ideas related to spying to create a conceptual piece of nonsense publishing. This first issue is marked as issue 007, each copy is individually numbered using invisible ink, content is blacked out and redacted, and advice on moustache disguise is discussed at length. Proof that editorial content and character can be invented around any subject or material.
Editor and designer *Thomas Pruss*

OPPOSITE

Kasino A4

Finland (210 × 297mm, 8¼ × 11¾ inches)
A highly conceptual approach to content defined the character of this magazine, which was published for ten issues. One regular feature was 'Empty Sheet', in which six people from the same profession or social group were asked to draw a concept. In these examples, six car-salesmen were invited to draw 'Luxury' and six Russian volleyball players 'Autumn'. In a later issue six recycling-centre staff were asked to draw 'Nothing' – the result was six blank sheets.
Creative director *Pekka Toivonen*; Editor *Jonathan Mander*;
Director of photography *Jussi Puikkonen*; Communication *Antti Routto*

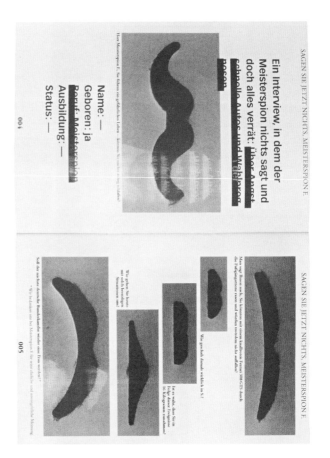

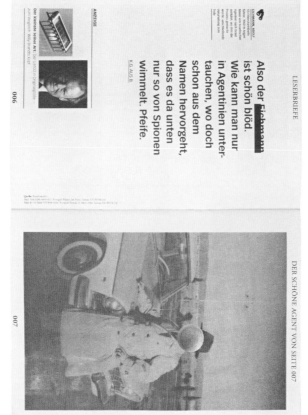

SAGEN SIE JETZT NICHTS, MEISTERSPION F.

Ein Interview, in dem der Meisterspion nichts sagt und doch alles verrät:

Name: —
Geboren: ja
Ausbildung: —
Status: —

004

SAGEN SIE JETZT NICHTS, MEISTERSPION F.

005

LESERBRIEFE

Also der ist schön blöd. Wie kann man nur in Agentinien untertauchen, wo doch schon aus dem Namen hervorgeht, dass es da unten nur so von Spionen wimmelt. Pfeife.

K.G. AUS B.

ANZEIGE

006

DER SCHÖNE AGENT VON SEITE 007

007

ZEITGEIST

Die Must-Haves des Sommers—just aus der

0012

ZEITGEIST

0013

Egine Semenov

Dmitri Khanoukaev

Petri Novitski

Zorif

EMPTY SHEET

We asked six Russian volleyball players to draw "AUTUMN".
Photography Jantien Oving

Denis Karpov

Peter Vasilenko

Issue 3, Winter 2006–7

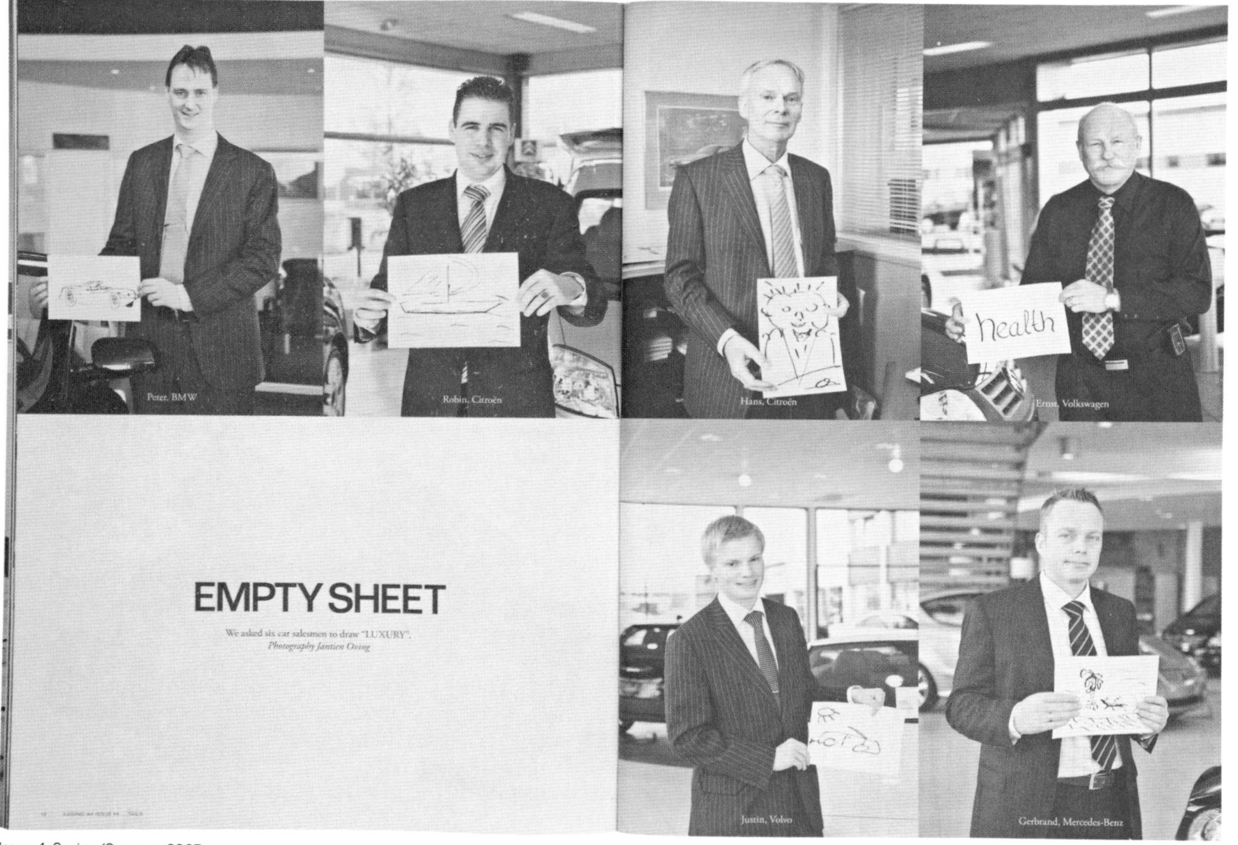

Peter, BMW

Robin, Citroën

Hans, Citroën

Ernst, Volkswagen

EMPTY SHEET

We asked six car salesmen to draw "LUXURY".
Photography Jantien Oving

Justin, Volvo

Gerbrand, Mercedes-Benz

Issue 4, Spring/Summer 2007

REINVENTING GENRES

The exploration of what a magazine can be isn't limited to the overt debunking of physical formats and conceptual experimentation. A new body of independently published magazines has appeared that reinterprets traditional genres of magazine publishing, questioning the medium while appearing in more traditional physical form.

Look across the shelves of any decent magazine store and you'll find a range of publications that reflect just about every human need and desire. What began 150 years ago as an upmarket vehicle for distributing news and opinion in a world facing major geographic and political upheaval, has evolved into a sophisticated mass-market industry with multiple options across a wide variety of subjects.

That industry developed in tandem with the consumer boom of the late twentieth century. General advice became 'lifestyle', as our interests in food, sex, fashion, sport and travel were indulged and major publishing brands were created. Many great magazines were launched as a result, but with success came a fear of failure and a blunting of the will to innovate. There was, simply, too much at stake financially. The pressure of balancing the needs of advertisers and readers – both of whom provided vital income streams – led to an increasing reliance on market research. During the economic boom of the nineties and early noughties there were more magazines being published than ever before – more individual titles and longer print runs of those titles. Every niche was filled and every successful launch copied. Lifestyle magazines became formulaic and self-referring.

Taking advantage of the cheaper, easier production methods provided by computers and developments in offset printing, and encouraged by the Internet's forthright sharing of opinions, small publishers began launching their own magazines that were implicit critiques of their mainstream rivals.

An early example was *Carl*s Cars* (Norway), which launched in 1999. Car magazines generally focus on speed, power and statistics, but this glossy biannual takes a more realistic approach to its subject. Subtitling itself 'a magazine about people', it revels in the day-to-day presence of cars in our lives and tackles its subject with a light, often humorous touch that is reflected in its quirky typography and layouts. *Carl*s Cars* is anti-car mag, rather than anti-car – it can still get excited about a respected car designer or a rare model.

Magazines about food have always been popular, but have tended towards the purely practical. Whether aspirational (the ideal dinner party) or more pragmatic (cooking to a budget) they are generally more about doing than thinking. *Put A Egg On It* (USA) provides a different angle, seeking to celebrate the social side of food, the mutual enjoyment of eating together and the shared memories of food we start building up in childhood. *Menu* (South Africa) uses its pages to record the vibrant street food scene in Cape Town, combining beautiful portraits of the people making the food with super-real images of the mess of late-night street eating. Its serious attempt to record the rich variety of local food available before the big chains move in is a world away from the obsession with the garish world of fast food and its packaging displayed by *Yummy* (France).

Interiors magazines is another genre that has tended towards an aspirational ideal. *Apartamento* (Spain) offers a more realistic approach, recognising the limitations facing young city-dwellers with limited space and money. Its small format, choice of mixed paper stocks and informal design reflect its vision of a mix-and-match aesthetic that is fast becoming an ideal in its own right. It's also a notable example of the international reach of many of these

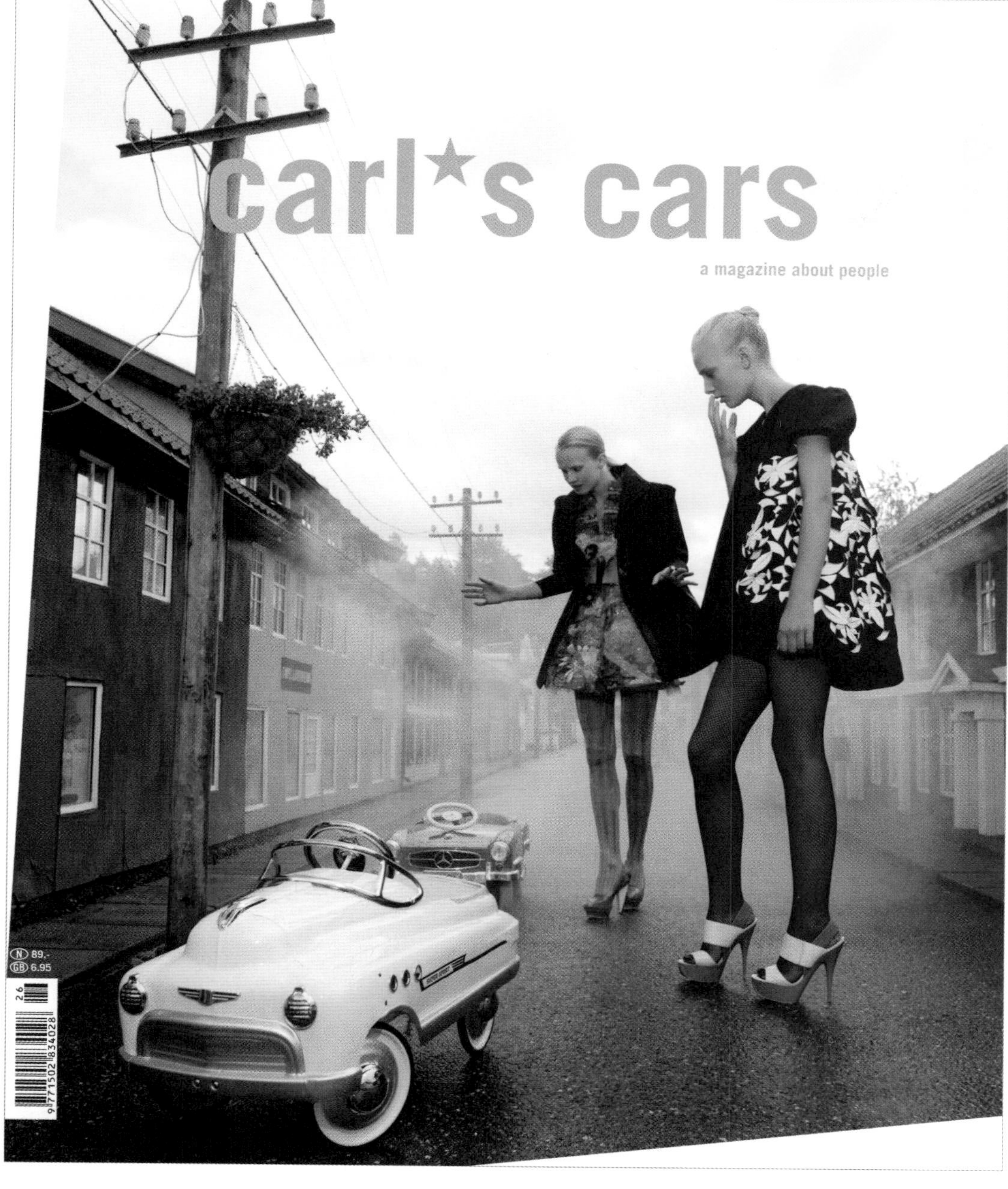

magazines. The editor works in Italy, the designer in Spain, and the magazine is published in English and occasionally with a Japanese translation.

Fantastic Man (The Netherlands) has proved even more successful in the men's fashion world. Built around founders Jop van Bennekom and Gert Jonkers's vision of modern masculinity, it favours 'real' men instead of models and presents an ironic outlook that references an earlier age of etiquette guides and 'proper' behaviour. It is a world away, editorially and graphically, from the confusion of camp fashion and explicit hetrosexuality found in the major men's titles.

Port (UK)'s contemporary remodelling of the classic men's magazine – long-form writing, short fiction, design, style and culture – provides a similarly implicit criticism of the majors, while *Manzine* (Germany) proves there's more than one way to re-examine the men's market. A counterblast against the mainstream, its apparently chaotic (but actually highly designed) pages are filled with verbal and visual puns.

Women's magazines have their alternatives too, in *Frankie* (Australia) and *Oh Comely* (UK). Both veer away from high fashion and 'feminine' warm colours to present a far broader and more realistic concept of modern womanhood.

Other publishers find new ways to present architecture, business, design, sex, sport and children's interests. Some – such as *Carl*s Cars*, *The Ride Journal* (UK) and *Little White Lies* (UK) – use their subject as a prism through which to view people and their lives, and are as much general interest titles as they are genre specialists. In stepping away from the usual portrayal of their subject they have reinvented their genre. The more general titles (*Port* and *Frankie*) have sought to take on the mainstream directly, surviving on a shoestring budget while questioning what men's and women's magazines should be.

All are harking back to a simpler time before magazine publishing became a mass industry. Many already have an influence far beyond their relatively small sales figures, as their new approaches attract an international, media-savvy and upmarket audience.

Carl*s Cars
Norway, Issue 26, Autumn 2009
(230 × 280mm, 9¼ × 11¼ inches)
'Anti-car magazine, not anti-car.'
Editor *Karl Eirik Haug*; Creative director *Stéphanie Dumont*

Carl*s Cars

Norway (230 × 280mm, 9¼ × 11¼ inches)
Cars are at the heart of everything this magazine does, but not always in expected ways.
Editor *Karl Eirik Haug*; Creative director *Stéphanie Dumont*

Issue 28, Autumn 2010
Part of a step-by-step guide to 'mooning' from cars.
Photography *Marius Ektvedt*

Issue 25, Spring 2009
Car design students show their love for the Citroen C3 Picasso.
Photography *Marius Ektvedt*

Issue 19, Spring 2007
Excerpt from photographer *Mikael Jansson*'s book about F1 racing.

OPPOSITE *Issue 19, Spring 2007*
Cars under winter protection. The final image, bottom right, is actually a car-shaped pile of bricks. Photography *Barry Lewis*

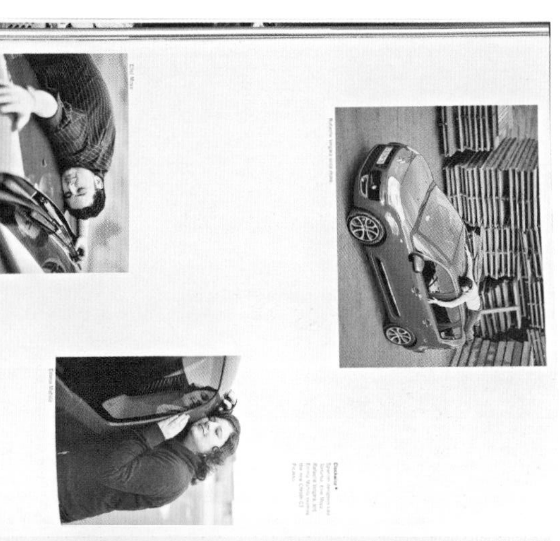

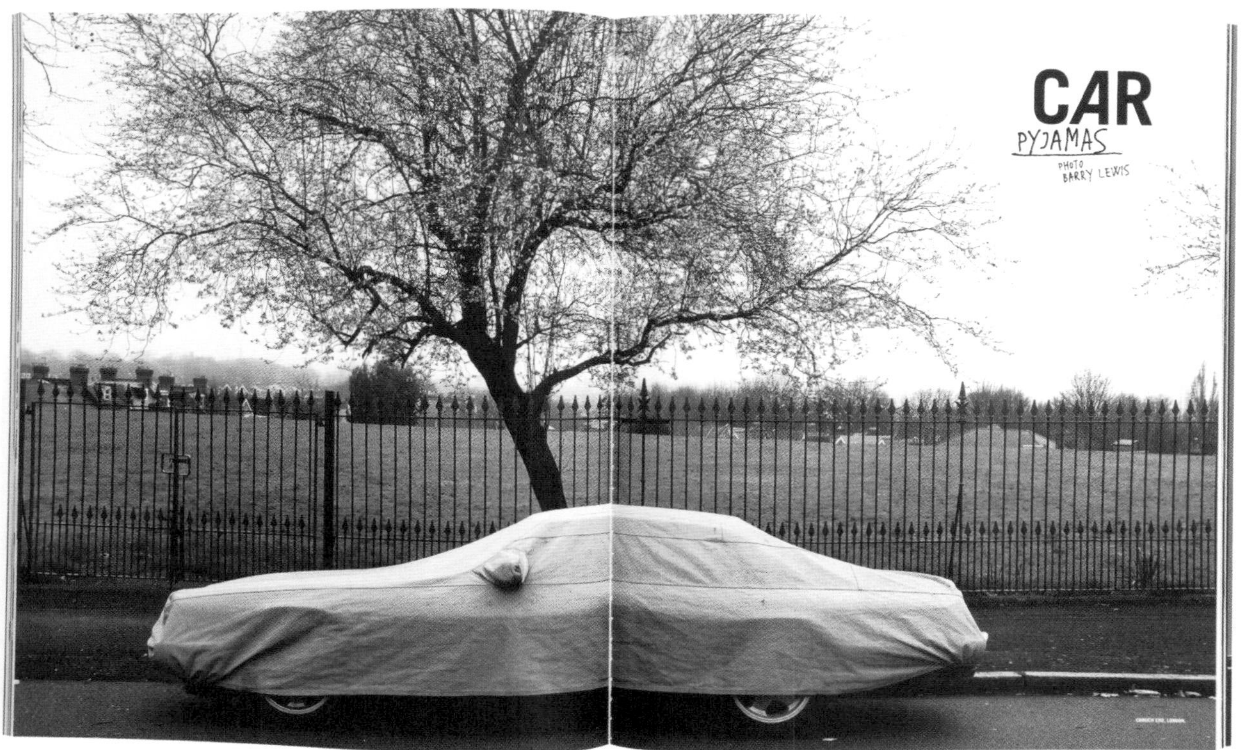
CAR
PYJAMAS
PHOTO
BARRY LEWIS

Head Full of Snakes

Australia/New Zealand, Issue 1, December 2011 (210 × 295mm, 8¼ × 11¾)
A motorcycle magazine unlike any other, not least because of its retro design. lo-fi Risograph printing and the flexidisc recording of a vintage bike engine slipped into the back page. Such details set it apart aesthetically, but it is also distinctive for being as interested in the people riding the bikes as it is in the bikes themselves.
Editors and designers *Luke Wood and Stuart Geddes*

SHED FEATURE by STUART GEDDES

FULL

Velo SHED

Not long ago I went to look at a bike that a guy was selling. I bought the bike, but the guy also sold me on the virtues of having a shed—or, at least, on the virtues of having a shed full of Velocettes. This guy estimated that he'd had maybe 100 Velocettes over the years, and he was incredibly knowledgeable and forthcoming about the history and achievements of this marque.

Over an hour or so, he told me piles of things about Velocette. For one thing they invented the foot gear change—before that everyone had suicide shifts. Also that they were a family owned company, and when they went into voluntary receivership in 1971 they paid out all of their creditors—no-one got burned.

He was full of good stories, about particular bikes, and about the bits of bikes and bits of equipment littered around his shed. Out of these stories came a picture of a life involved with motorcycles: "My Dad had a KSS Velocette; I wasn't born at this stage. When I was born my mum made him sell it and buy a car, and the old bastard always hated me for that, because he loved that bike. He used to tell me about it, it was him that got me into motorbikes."

His interest in bikes didn't peter out as he grew up. In fact, he seemed particularly prescient as a young bloke, realising that motorcycling was something he was into for the long haul: "When I went to uni, I was tossing up whether to do mechanical engineering or civil engineering and I deliberately made the decision to do civil engineering because I didn't want to fuck up a perfectly good hobby."

He was a big advocate of joining the appropriate owner's club if you have a classic bike. This seemed to stem from both the understanding of the knowledge he had accrued over the years, as well as the decline in basic mechanical know-how that seems more prevalent today: "It's important these days because so few people have any mechanical skills anymore, they just can't survive on a classic bike without the support from the club technical officer, and even then they find it difficult. This is okay for me because, as I say, I spent my youth with my dad working on motorbikes, and I was taught how to do it, so it's no problem, but these days, no-one teaches their sons how to do it."

As is often the case with people who are into a specific thing to this extent, the technical and cultural elements of the story blur satisfyingly: "They were an engineer's bike these things, they were very, very carefully thought out. The factory was privately owned and the family that owned it used to ride Velocettes to work every day—a couple of them used to seriously race them, even though they were wealthy and the owners of a factory, so everything they put into the design was based on their own experience actually riding the things. I find, from an engineering perspective—and I'm talking production engineering now, because I've drifted away from my original field of civil engineering, and I used to go around a lot of factories, so I know a bit about production engineering, you strip down one of these engines (I mean, this was their volume production bike, and it had about the same performance of a (BSA) Gold Star), you strip the two engines down and you'll find that the Velocette engine generally has less parts. It's been designed by people who've thought carefully. The BSA has three main bearings; the Velocette's got two. As an engineer you generally shoot for simplicity above anything else, complication's easy to add, the Americans are great into adding complication, but if you want something to work you generally want to aim for simplicity, that way there's less to go wrong. The pessimist's viewpoint."

He described the shed as being in a state of benign neglect—"I should look after it a lot better than that… I just haven't got the time,"—but to me the clutter and fullness is testament to it being an active place, rather than a backyard showroom. If one day I have a shed like this, I'll be teaching my kids what's great about motorcycles, from the inside out.

45

SNAKES

Issue 1, 2008

Issue 2, 2009

Issue 3, 2009

Issue 4, 2010

Issue 5, 2011

Issue 6, 2012

The Ride Journal

UK (*195 × 255mm, 7¾ × 10 inches*)

A magazine about the shared passion for cycling felt by those involved in the activity at all levels and focusing on their personal stories and experiences. The covers have developed a strong identity that sets the magazine apart from the mainstream cycling press.

Editor *Philip Diprose*; Art director *Andrew Diprose*; Cover illustrations *ilovedust*

LIFE ILLUSTRATED

By Colin O'Donoghue. Illustration Frank Patterson

TOTEMS

By Alain Delorme

When we think of China, we tend to conjure up images of masses of people working in huge factories. Instead I wanted to look in the opposite direction and focus on the individual. To concentrate not on the skyscrapers, but on the migrants who walk the city with incredible loads. My 'totems' are therefore highly symbolic. The migrant appears initially like a superhero, able to carry around these incredible weights, but we quickly get the feeling that the objects themselves are about to swallow him up.

You can see other questions raised in my work. I break the rules of the documentary photography genre as the loads are exaggerated to catch the viewer's attention, even though the first impression is that the photo could be real. Nowadays, we question the authenticity of a photo more and more. Even those used in news reports are often touched up to look cleaner or more pleasing to the eye. We are not aware of this immediately, which brings about the question – how to distinguish truth from falsehood?

Series Totems 2010 © Alain Delorme. alaindelorme.com

THE RIDE 37

BEHIND THE SCENES

By Damien Breen. Illustration Robin Boyden

After a restless night, I hear my alarm go off. Still dark outside, but I was already awake anyway. Lying still, I strain to listen to the weather, for the tapping of rain against the window or the signs of a stiff breeze disturbing the leaves of the trees. It's early season, and it's race day.

Hitching a lift with a team-mate, we survey the skies over the motorway as we leave the city and head out into the countryside. Rain might mean a last-minute change of kit, or could determine how the race is won. We chat nervously trying to predict how the racing will unfold, recalling the difficulty of certain climbs and the vagaries of each circuit. Our destination is race headquarters at a country village hall. It could be Loxwood, Alfold, Bletchingley or Wisborough – all names conjuring images of a quaint Britishness distant to our everyday metropolitan lives.

On arrival, the ritual begins: signing on, the pinning of numbers, several toilet visits. We change in the drafty hall on plastic chairs common to municipal buildings, notices for Women's Institute meetings and toddler playgroups are dotted about the walls. In the corner is the familiar counter serving tea. Laid out is a spread of homemade cakes and sandwiches of cheap bread and simple fillings. The race officials and marshals warm and feed themselves in anticipation of the hours standing on cold road corners, or of monitoring the race from the front seat of the commissaire's car. The racers will revive themselves in just a couple of hours from now, cradling cups of hot tea in shivering hands, faces spattered in road grime.

Such scenes will be common across the country as amateur road racing goes about its business, unknown to our colleagues at work, alien to the majority of the population, unobserved by even the local villagers. Such secrecy is key to the survival of grassroots racing: a higher profile would mean administrational complications, entanglements with local-council bureaucracies, and would attract the attention of meddling Nimbys. Only last year Peter Keen, director of performance at UK Sport, warned that top-level road racing was under threat due to mounting police costs being passed on to race organisers, and the more zealous enforcement of health-and-safety regulations.

Keith Butler's solution is to keep things simple. Ex-pro rider Keith formed the Surrey League in the early 80s to promote grassroots-level racing and provide opportunities for beginners, juniors and lower-category riders. Keith's philosophy is to minimise unnecessary paperwork, avoid complications, and maintain good relations with the police and the relevant authorities. The result is a full calendar of racing, and an annual programme of over 100 races is proof of the League's success.

However, even though cycling is currently enjoying an almost unprecedented boom, the numbers of those willing to give back to the sport isn't increasing in tandem. The three regular Surrey League stage races were all cancelled this year due to an absence of marshalling volunteers, and Keith admits that the lack of new blood in helping put on races is one of the biggest challenges he faces.

Possibly the mentality of cycling's latest adopters is partly to blame. Those familiar with sportives or triathlons expect goodie bags and electronic timing chips, and the various frills associated with commercial enterprises. Amateur road racing relies on the generosity and dedication of volunteers, and the love of cycling from its participants. Even the prize money on offer at amateur races on the continent is missing; here, if you win back your entry fee you've done well.

Part of a new generation of race organiser, Mark Standhaft set up the Wessex Cycle Racing League three years ago with his eye firmly on the future. His online Entryweb system, for example, has finally signalled the end of paper form-filling and the posting of cheques that is still common with many leagues and races. His philosophy is that, with better and more professional organisation, everybody wins: sponsors and riders are drawn to events, bringing with them resources for motorbike outriders and for the timing chips that give participants the reassurance that their efforts will be rewarded with their correct finishing position (unbelievably still a problem with many amateur races).

Mark is brimming over with ideas and the Wessex Racing League is still very much a labour of love. Yet it's the dedication shown by the likes of Mark and Keith that keeps road racing alive.

Damien Breen, London, UK. Spinning along in the little ring in-the-saddle.co.uk. robinboydenillustration.com

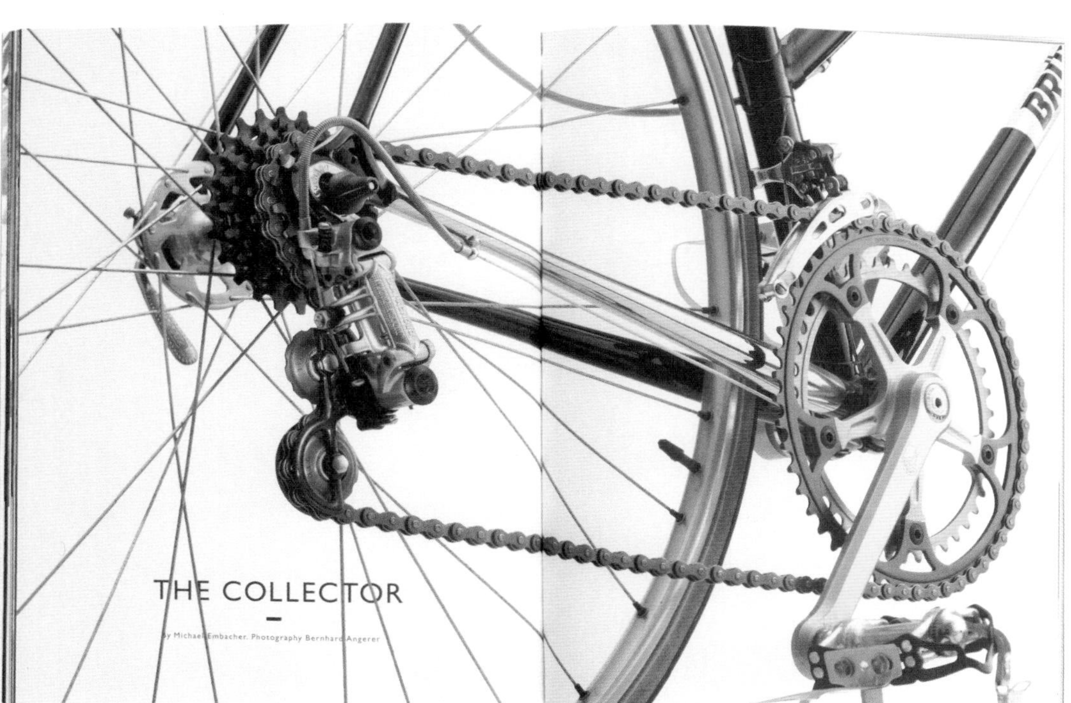

THE COLLECTOR
By Michael Embacher. Photography Bernhard Angerer

The Ride Journal
UK (195 × 255mm, 7¾ × 10 inches)
The magazine takes a very broad approach to cycling, ranging from archive material to contemporary photo reportage and first-person narratives.
Editor *Philip Diprose*; Art director *Andrew Diprose*

TOP: *Issue 5, 2011*
Robin Boyden illustrates Damien Breen's piece about amateur-league racing.

BOTTOM: *Issue 6, 2012*
An excerpt from bicycle collector Michael Embacher's book *Cyclopedia*.
Photograph *Bernhard Angerer*

OPPOSITE TOP: *Issue 6, 2012*
An archive line illustration by Frank Patterson for *Cycling* magazine. He worked for the magazine between 1893 and 1952.

BOTTOM: *Issue 6, 2012*
Alain Delorme's 'exaggerated' images of migrant workers in China carrying massive loads by bicycle.

Victory Journal
USA, Issue 3, Winter 2011 (295 × 430mm, 11¼ × 17 inches)
As its name suggests, this high-quality tabloid is concerned with the thrill and excitement of competition rather than the fanboy obsession and statistical analysis more common in sports publishing. Photographs of maritime jousting in France by Christopher Anderson.
Creative directors *Christopher Isenberg, Aaron Amaro and Kimou Meyer*

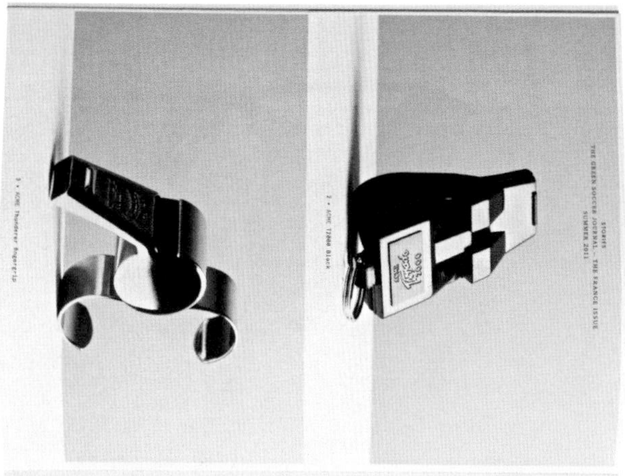

The Green Soccer Journal

UK, (200 × 270mm, 8 × 10¾ inches)

Strong photography, carefully selected interview subjects and a sense of humour about the sport brings a more cultured approach to soccer than the usual celebrity-obsessed tabloid coverage.

Editors and creative directors *Adam Towle and James Roper*

TOP: *Issue 3, Winter 2011/12, The Goalkeeper Issue*
Cover star Italian goalkeeper Gianluigi Buffon. Photograph *Danilo Scarpati*

CENTRE: *Issue 2, Summer 2011, The France Issue*
A catalogue of referee's whistles. Photographs *Alastair Strong*

BOTTOM: *Issue 3, Winter 2011/12, The Goalkeeper Issue*
Fashion shoot based on goalkeeper's drills. Photographs *Nail Bedford*

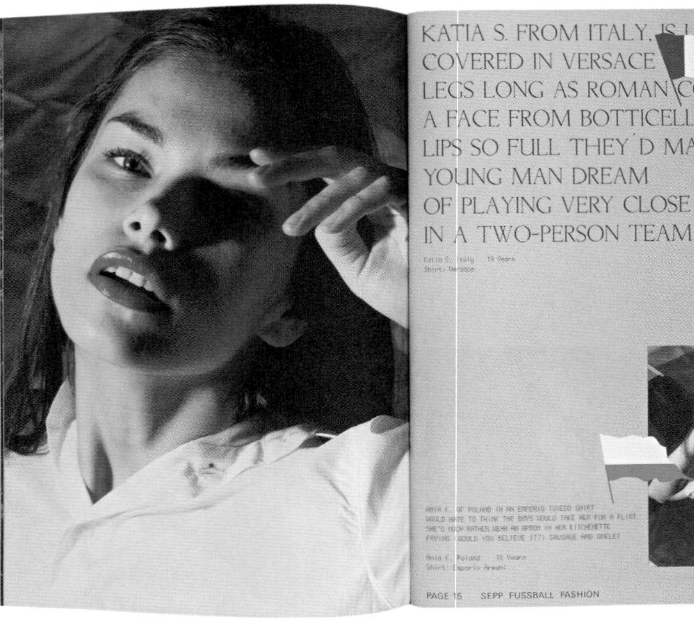

KATIA S. FROM ITALY, IS LOOSELY
COVERED IN VERSACE
LEGS LONG AS ROMAN COLUMNS,
A FACE FROM BOTTICELLI
LIPS SO FULL THEY'D MAKE A
YOUNG MAN DREAM
OF PLAYING VERY CLOSE TO HER,
IN A TWO-PERSON TEAM
PAGE 15 SEPP FUSSBALL FASHION

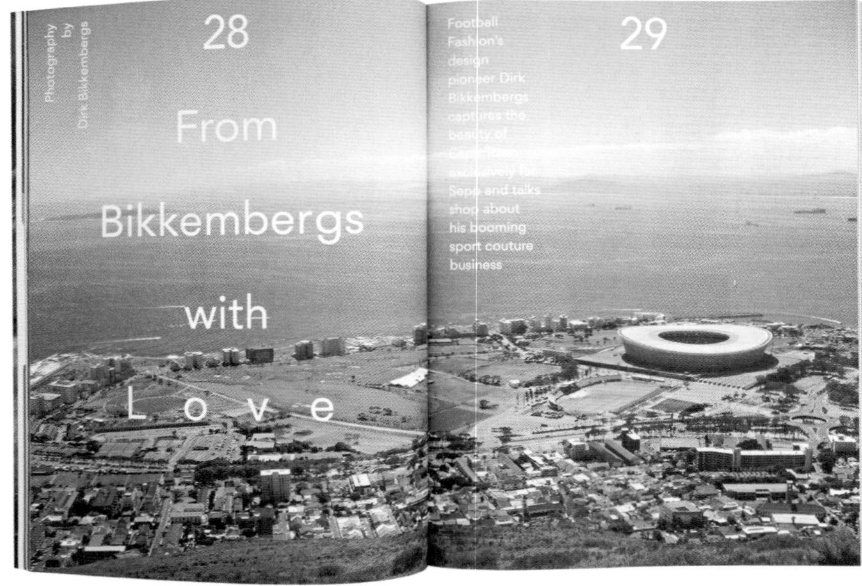

Photography by Dirk Bikkembergs
28
From Bikkembergs with Love
29
Football Fashion's design pioneer Dirk Bikkembergs captures the beauty of Cape Town exclusively for Sepp and talks shop about his booming sport couture business

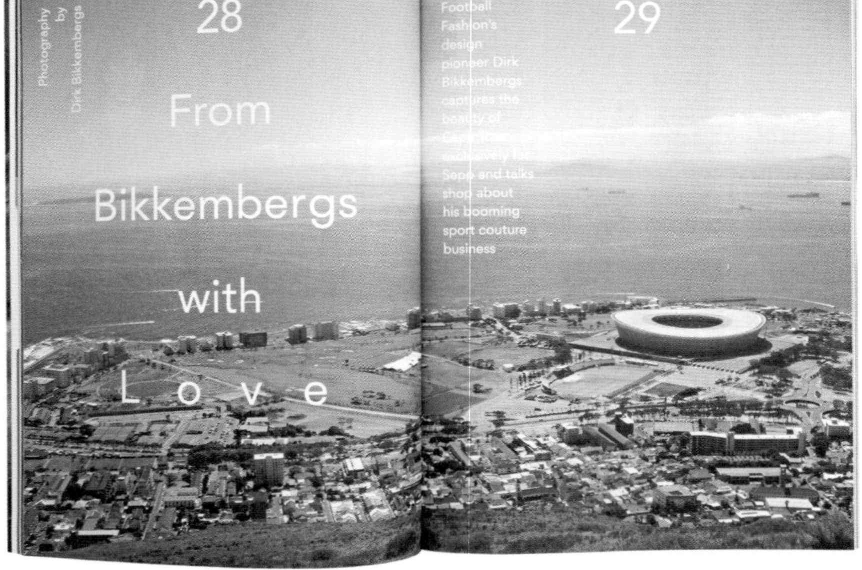

WAYNE ROONEY
Karl's Cup Kings
LIONEL MESSI
Illustrations by Karl Lagerfeld
51
Karl Lagerfeld illustrates 2010's World Cup superstars. Frank Ribery, Ricky Kaka, Didier Drogba, Lionel Messi and Wayne Rooney all get the Lagerfeld make-over. Here is fashion football's equivalent of Hans Holbein's visual essay of Henry VIII's royal court
Text by Godfrey Deeny

Sepp

Germany, (210 × 297mm, 8¼ × 11¾ inches)

'Football and fashion' runs the subtitle to this magazine published every two years alongside the World Cup and European Championship competitions. The resulting mix brings us overviews of up-and-coming models from the competing countries, Karl Lagerfeld's drawings of football stars and fashion shoots from match venues. Editors *Godfrey Deeny* and *Markus Ebner*; Art director *Mirko Borsche*

TOP: *Issue 4, Euro 2008*
Young models shot by *Jork Weismann*

CENTRE: *Issue 5, World Cup 2010*
Photograph of Cape Town by *Dirk Bikkemberg*

BOTTOM: *Issue 5, World Cup 2010*
Wayne Rooney and Lionel Messi drawn by *Karl Lagerfeld*

OPPOSITE *Issue 5, World Cup 2010*
Cover star Brazilian model Luciana Curtis. Photograph *Henrique Genre*

MORE SEPP p147

Football Fashion Magazine
SEPP
Curtis Luciana Schweinsteiger Armani Drogba Bikkembergs Maradona
Boateng Lanvin Messi Calvin Klein Versace Rooney Lagerfeld
Ribery von Unwerth Tanabe Kaka Strenesse
N°5
SOUTH AFRICA
Luciana Curtis is photo-graphed by Henrique Gendre exclusively for SEPP 5
6 EUR
10 USD
9 CHF
5 GBP

Issue 1, 2010

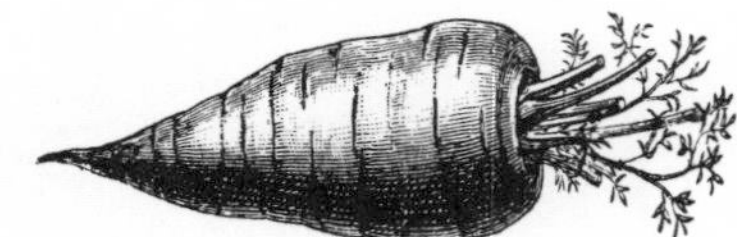

Issue 2, 2010

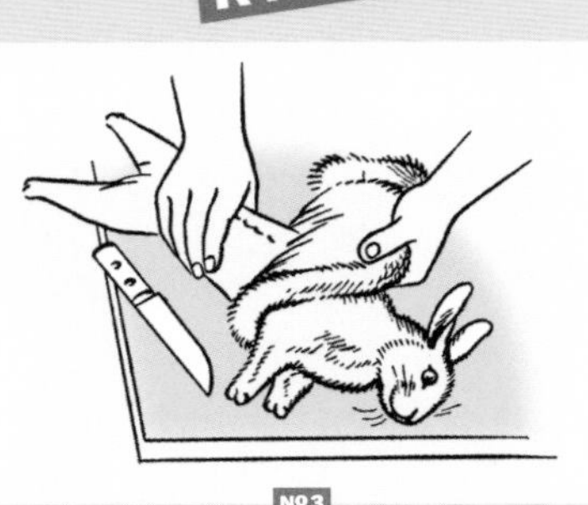

Issue 3, 2010

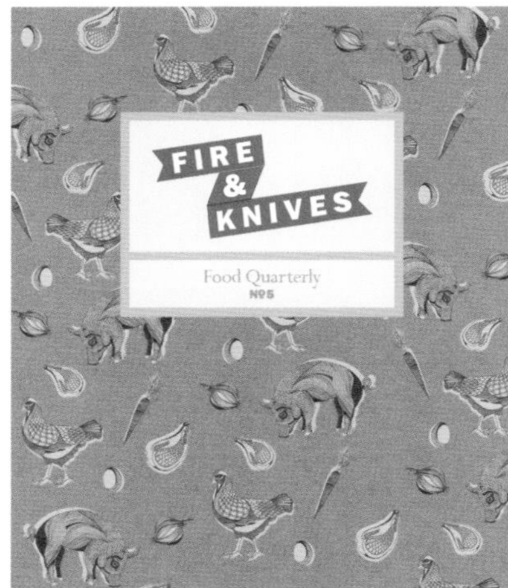

Issue 5, 2011

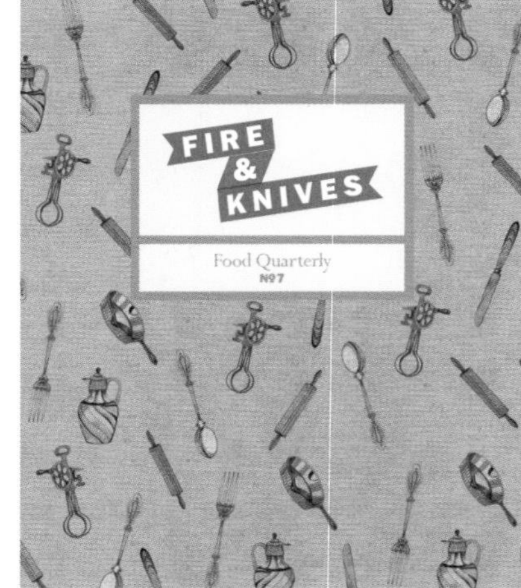

Issue 7, 2011

Issue 8, 2011

Issue 9, 2012

Issue 11, 2012

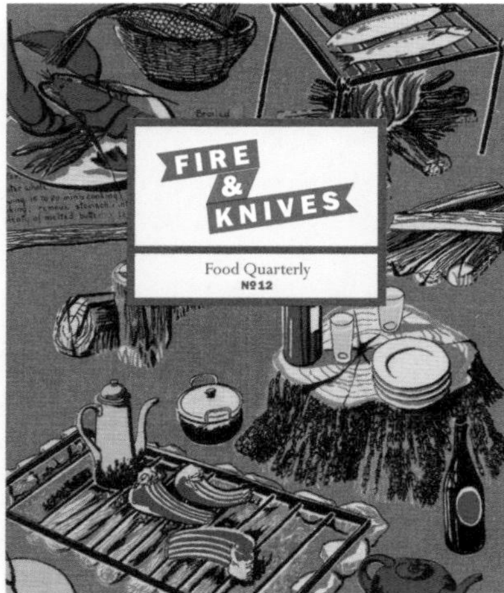

Issue 12, 2012

'You're lucky that's not you with an apple shoved in your gob,' the stout woman in an aquamarine two-piece spat at me as the two of us stared at a glazed pig being wheeled by. Hands on her hips, the mother of the bride did not want to let the ignominy of my appearance at her youngest's big day pass without one, not necessarily final, comment.

There are people in this world who think booking a comedian for their wedding is a bright idea. There was, it turns out, and I don't think she'll be tempted to repeat her mistake, one woman who thought it a clever wheeze to book a comedian for her sister's wedding without mentioning it to anybody. Even her sister. It's a risky venture at the best of times, but to book a comedian of whom nobody has ever heard to make an unannounced appearance is almost a guarantee of failure.

For these and numerous other reasons reasons the gig was the very worst of my life; not only did I almost ruin two complete strangers' big day, but it played its part in my plunge into a gloomy funk out of which I only clambered several months later. And so after my short but desperate time on stage, I was back in the room I'd been shuffled into upon my arrival 'to keep the big surprise just that'. The hog roast was restoring order, and I was told that it was only good fortune and civilised Yorkshire ways that stopped me from being served up in a form more palatable to the wedding party than that of me in front of them with a microphone in my hand.

As a stand-up comedian, food always plays a delicate and crucial part of my preparations for a job, but rarely has it been so brutally visceral. By now, a small group of people had joined in to berate me further, and I could do nothing but agree that it hadn't been my finest hour whilst simultaneously packing what was left of my hurried Marks & Spencer supper back into its carrier bag. Finally, I made my escape and once inside my car, with the doors locked, I drove back to London from Leeds only six hours after I'd left my house. It was a day of two hefty tranches of driving only separated by something astonishingly grim in the middle. Truly, the Greggs ham sandwich of gigs.

It would be over-egging a very unconvincing and frankly slightly chubby pudding if I suggested working as a comic is in some way like being an athlete: it really isn't. I'm not even tempted by Lycra, and more often than not I've been allowed to take part in events without being tested for drugs beforehand. But experience has taught me there is one common bond, and that is food.

What I eat makes a distinct difference to my performance on stage. I don't mean the indigestion-inducing moments immediately prior to stepping up there, but in the two or three hours before that, which, if you're driving up a motorway, isn't terribly practicable. Obvious, really, but it took me a good long while to make the connection. Some comics seem happier to have eaten nothing, while others don't mind either way but I can get rather paranoid about it all.

[41]

Issue 8, 2011

The next time you make a colourful, multi-textured salad of leaves and herbs, I want you to think of a 40-year-old mother of two.

She's standing at the door of a run-down but just about roadworthy caravan, parked in an orchard or the corner of a farmyard, somewhere on the Continent. It is the late 70s and a warm breeze ruffles short hair with a natural wave that suits the decade. Her glasses are large and thick-lensed, her collars pointed. Perhaps she is rocking a pair of flares. The woman jumps onto a bicycle, popping one of many tins of English humbugs into her bag to hand out as gifts, and pedals away down country lanes in search of farmers, gardeners, growers and cooks to quiz and charm.

The woman is Joy Larkcom, and the occasion is the Grand Vegetable Tour: the year-long horticultural odyssey that she, her husband and their two young children undertook in 1977. It is a journey that changed the way gardeners grow food, and filled the salad-shaped space in the fridge of every person in the country. If you ever buy a bag of mixed baby leaves, or indeed make a salad that contains anything other than lettuce, you owe it to Joy, and this agricultural adventure.

72 73

Issue 12, 2012

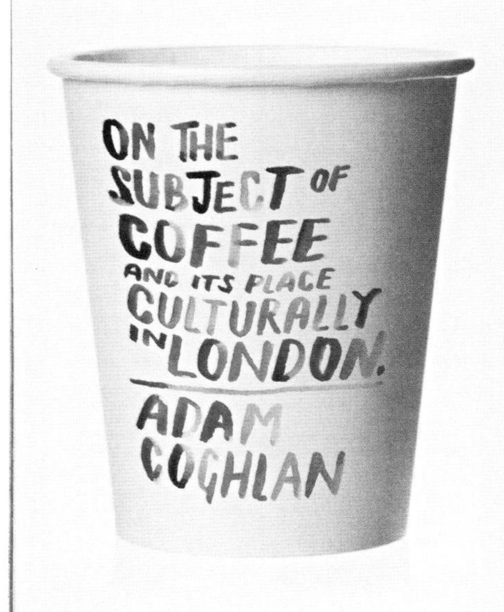

London is in the grip of a rampant love affair with coffee.

The recent boom in what we are now comfortable with calling the 'speciality' coffee scene has many correlating their new love of coffee (and associated advance in quality) to an influx of young coffee-savvy enthusiasts on two-year working visas from the Antipodes.

This, however, is only part of the story, in a city that has had a heavily caffeinated history since the opening of its first coffee shop in 1652. Instead of seeing the popularisation of the flat white and the increasingly decorative 'latte art' designs as something alien, new and forced upon us, it would be more useful to see it as just another stage in the evolution of coffee in London.

Jorge Fernandez of Fernandez & Wells is keen to point out that in the past coffee was, at the time, comparatively enjoyable. To deny its contemporary qualities is to implicitly deny a natural evolution and, with no reference point, it is unfair and misleading to suggest that everything that predated the current trend was bad. Hindsight is an endlessly useful privilege.

During the Restoration, London was awash with coffee houses. They symbolised a kind of renegade spirit; they were sites for discussion and the fermentation of thought. Tim Williams of St Ali in Clerkenwell comments on the staggering 2,000 coffee shops in London in the 17th century. In the 19th century, the Temperance Movement saw the rise of the coffee house as an alternative to cheap alcohol.

What seems to have happened is that the new wave has all but deleted from memory the capital's important coffee-cultural precedents. To many in Britain, coffee (like food) is a motif of the sophisticated lifestyles of continental Europeans: a borrowed pleasure. Although not culturally indigenous, it has held a significant place in London's social history. And it is this that makes the latest incarnation less a phenomenon, than a legitimate and logical development in an under-recognised history.

In *London's Coffee Houses*, Antony Clayton describes curious and excited Londoners 'flocking to Pasqua Rosée's coffee houses'. Rosée, a native of western Turkey and servant to the trader Daniel Edwards, is attributed with bringing coffee to London in the mid-17th century, with Levantine merchants promoting its medicinal advantages. It was initially traded as 'currency' in Lloyds bank, before being transferred to a consumable shop-friendly format in St Michael's Alley off Cornhill in 1652.

21

Issue 9, 2012

Fire & Knives

UK, (170 × 210mm, 6¾ × 8¼ inches)

Launched with the brief to contributors to 'write as an amateur about something you love', this pocket-sized quarterly deals with the culture, history and personal experiences of food from a particularly British point of view. This sets it apart editorially from most food magazines, a difference emphasized by a lack of glossy food photography and use of exuberant illustration and hand-written headlines. Editor *Tim Hayward*; Art director and illustrator *Rob Lowe*

OPPOSITE Each annual set of four issues uses a different cover treatment. The first year's covers featured found line drawings in a graphic format borrowed from early Penguin book covers; for the second year, artworks were commissioned from Marie-Claire Bridges; the third year reproduced 1970s tea-towel designs.

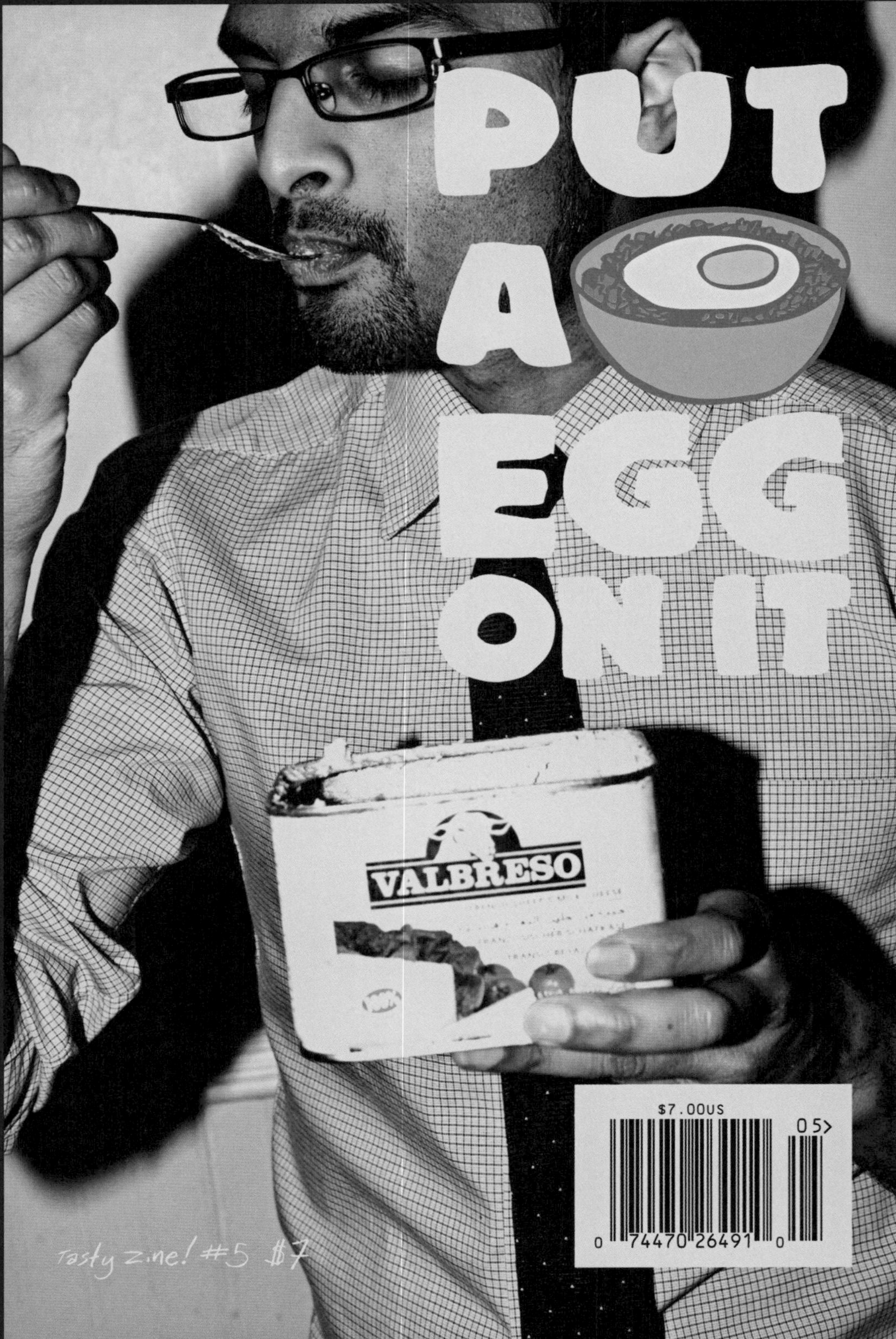

Issue 5, Spring 2012

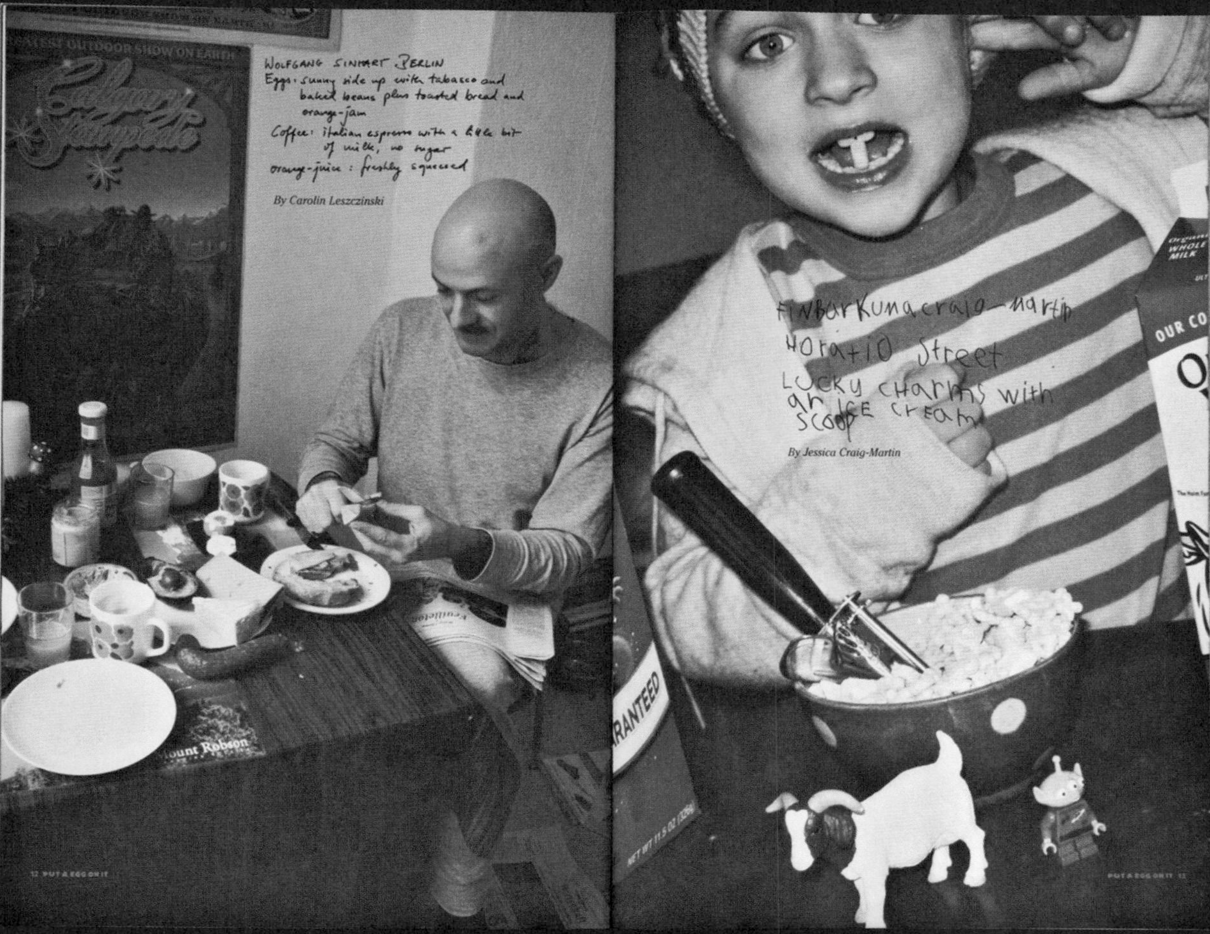

Put A Egg On It
USA, Issue 3, Winter/Spring 2011 (140 × 215mm, 5½ × 8½ inches)
The green paper stock lends an alternative feel to this food magazine, highlighting its approach to its subject: no stylized glossy food photography here.
Editors and creative directors *Sarah Forbes Keough and Ralph McGinnis*

'The art of making a magazine is editing. You have to make a choice, stick with it, then it's out in the world and it's done. That's why I don't believe print is dead.'

RALPH McGINNIS
CO-FOUNDER
PUT A EGG ON IT

Put A Egg On It (USA)

EDITORS AND CREATIVE DIRECTORS
RALPH McGINNIS AND SARAH FORBES KEOUGH

Put A Egg On It is a Brooklyn-based fanzine about food – or 'Tasty Zine' as its creators describe it. It was first published as an eight-page zine in 2008, but Ralph McGinnis and Sarah Forbes Keough waited two years before getting round to a second issue, and are now just about maintaining a regular biannual schedule. Although deliberately zine-like in most physical and design respects – the A5 page size, green paper stock and design aesthetic – it has attracted plenty of attention for its sophisticated editorial approach to food.

While it does carry some traditional food content in the form of recipes and tips, *Put A Egg On It*'s main focus is the way people relate to food in terms of visual culture and the communal enjoyment of food. I interviewed Sarah and Ralph in Manhattan as Issue 5 was about to go to press.

Describe how *Put A Egg On It* came about.
RALPH: Sarah and I have been friends for so long. We were at college together and worked on our school magazine and a dance magazine project. We've worked at mainstream magazines together too. We were like, 'when are we gonna do a zine together', and so in 2008 we did the eight-page first issue using one of those printers you just upload everything to remotely. We just did it all ourselves, I didn't care if it was perfect, but I still like the issue.

What is the magazine about?
RALPH: We tell writers and photographers it's not just about the food. We look at it as a dinner conversation. A dinner party isn't just food, the point is to hang out together.
SARAH: It's about storytelling. The best writers that we've had have been fiction writers or musicians, people that don't usually write about food.
RALPH: It's a good way to explore culture in the broader sense. With food we can be idiosyncratic and appeal broadly at the same time. Even people's grandmothers like our magazine because it's cute.

How do you describe your zine to people who don't know it?
SARAH: We say it's an art magazine about food, because if you say it's a food magazine people get the wrong idea. But if you couch it as an art project then it at least makes it something different. That's the easy, fast way.
RALPH: It's easier to just give them a copy.

There seem to be a lot of small food magazines around. Have you thought why?
RALPH: It's just that everyone likes food!
SARAH: Suddenly everyone I know is cooking – for barbecues, dinner parties. People are realizing it doesn't take much to make amazing things. And that culture combines well with the culture of people making magazines about what they like.
RALPH: There are lots of photocopied/stapled food zines and cookbooks. Our favourite NY zine is *Slice Harvester*. He's on a mission to taste every piece of pizza in NY. Each issue is about a different area of Manhattan and he finished recently. He's great, he's a good writer too. He compared a slice of pizza to the Ramones, with each ingredient one of the band.

Why a print publication and not a website?
RALPH: I've been blogging since 1999 so I'm neither one nor the other. But there is a difference. Magazines are about editing and choice, while the Internet is about immediacy. The art of making a magazine is editing. You have to make a choice, stick with it, then it's out in the world and it's done. That's why I don't believe print is dead. It's not just old people, it's young people too. A 20-year-old photographer doesn't care if their photograph is posted online. But

A PROVIDENCE TRADITION
Haven Bros. Diner
SINCE 1888
Clockwise: Haven Brothers Diner, Dorrance and Fulton Streets, Providence. Chili dog $2. Jamaican Dutchy, 51st Street and 7th Avenue, Manhattan, thejamaicandutchy.net. Curry goat mini meal $7. Little Mexico, Maria and Alejandro Martinez, The Woods 48 S. 4th Street, Brooklyn. Chicken burrito $5. The Border Cart, Jose O.
Martinez and Luanne Romero, 50th Street and 6th Avenue, Manhattan. Taco Salad $6. Rockaway Taco, Andrew Field and Parker Shipp, 95-19 Rockaway Beach Blvd., Queens, rockawaytaco.com. Fish taco $3.

Put a Egg On It
Issue 2, Summer 2010
Two typical photo spreads: THIS PAGE, a set of images of street-food vendors and customers records both the choice of food available and the vernacular style of the outlets (photographs *Sarah Keough*); and, OPPOSITE, the photographer's family in Plainview, NY, celebrate Valentine's day with meatballs, lasagne and garlic bread (photographs *Laura Jane Kirsch*)

if that photo gets in a magazine, they love it. They understand it's a big deal.

Where did the name come from?
SARAH: A friend's brother used to say it. He would eye your leftovers, no matter how small, and say no, don't throw that away, I'll take it home and put a egg on it!
RALPH: So many magazines have one word in their title and it's kind of fun to have something a little longer. We like absurd titles.
SARAH: We have fun thinking up long magazine names.
RALPH: We want to do a fashion magazine and call it *A Room Full of Awesome Clothes*.

Why A egg instead of AN egg?
SARAH: That's just the way we say it!
RALPH: People still email us saying 'You know it's AN egg not A egg ...'. And they're not joking! I think you shouldn't take yourself too seriously. It's *Put A Egg On It* – it's supposed to be fun, a little childish.

Describe the visual sense of the magazine. Why green paper?
RALPH: Coloured paper abstracts everything a little and makes it playful. I like mistakes, and that I don't always know how the pictures are going to look. I like that in other magazines, when I see they took a chance.
SARAH: We're not trying to sell food so we don't have to make it look perfect. Real life isn't always pretty.
RALPH: I wanted the magazine to look like ads from comic books from when I was a kid, so the two typefaces we use are eighties advertising fonts, Barmeno and Cantoria.

Is *Put A Egg On It* a zine or a magazine?
SARAH: I've been thinking about this because of our scheduling problems. If you're going to put out an issue once it's finished, whether that's once a year or three times a year, then that's more a ziney way of things. Deciding you're going to make a magazine means working to schedules.
RALPH: To me, a zine means you love the subject, not that you're trying to make money. We want to make money, but that's great after the fact. The whole point of making it is you're interested in the subject. People working on magazines are also fans but I feel like they get lost in the business of it.

Do you see a time when you might become business-led?
RALPH: I would end it before that. When I think of my favourite magazines they all ended. The only one that's kept going is *i-D*.

What is the future of magazines?
RALPH: I hate to say it, but I look forward to a time when all the big, corporate magazines are gone. They don't add anything to culture. Yeah, I wish people all have jobs, but I've worked there and I don't see why money is wasted printing that stuff. What the big publishers should do instead is invest in people like us, people making small magazines on tiny budgets. Even if we paid everybody involved, the money it takes for us to put out our magazine would be infinitesimal, and they would make a profit. Instead of one big stupid magazine, they could have twenty small magazines with two- or three-person teams. That should be the future of magazines.

And the future of *Put A Egg On It*?
SARAH: Going quarterly and getting bigger. But we need help – it's so much hard work.
RALPH: Just doing it twice a year, sometimes I can't believe the time it takes. We plan in advance and explain everything to contributors, but we still run late. But it's gotta be good. Our new issue is cool: the titles are food packaging, actual boxes and bottles.
SARAH: He designed them, then I made them all and shot them.
RALPH: It looks great. That's why I'm so frustrated how late it all is!

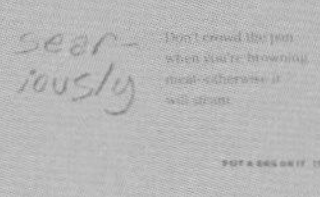

Put a Egg On It

TOP: *Issue 3, Winter/Spring 2011*
Examples of commercial sign painting by Lester Carey in New Orleans.

CENTRE, BOTTOM: *Issue 5, Spring 2012*
Text pages showing the *Put A Egg On It* branded food packaging created by McGinnis for column headlines.

MENU

VEGETABLES

VEGETABLE LASAGNE
Govinda's, Hare Krishna Temple, 17 St Andrews Rd, Rondebosch. 074 134 2585. Open Friday – Sunday 11am – 6pm. Rice, dahl and one dish R25, add R10 per extra dish.

MATIR PANEER
Govinda's, Hare Krishna Temple, 17 St Andrews Rd, Rondebosch. 074 134 2585. Open Friday – Sunday 11am – 6pm. Rice, dahl and one dish R25, add R10 per dish extra.

POTATO SALAD
Potato and mayonnaise salad (vegetarian option) or potato, bacon and onion salad with vinegar oil dressing.

Raith Gourmet, Shop no 38, Gardens Centre, Mill St, Gardens. 021 465 2729/6396. Open Monday – Thursday 8:30am – 7pm, Friday 8am – 7pm, Saturday 8am – 5pm and Sunday and public holidays 9am – 2pm. R42.50 – R49.95/kg.

BEYEAYNETU
A combination of Ethiopian vegetable dishes and green salad. Bring your own booze.

Little Ethiopia, 76 Shortmarket St, CBD. 021 424 8254. Open Monday – Sunday 12pm – 10pm. R30

VEGETARIAN BUFFET
Selection of three fresh vegetarian meals daily.

The Cookshop, 117 Hatfield St, Gardens. 021 461 7868. Open Monday – Friday 7am – 4pm. Vegetarian plate small R35, large R45.

SHERPA STEW
Steamed lentil balls on a bed of mashed potato with braised onion, fresh tomato sauce and sesame seed garnish.

Tibetan Teahouse at Sophea Gallery, 2 Harrington Rd, Seaforth, Simon's Town. 021 786 1544. Open Tuesday – Sunday 10am – 5pm. R58

SWEET POTATO CURRY
Sakarkhanda Ko Tarkari – Nepalese sweet potato curry on brown rice with dhanja, organic yogurt and chutney.

Tibetan Teahouse at Sophea Gallery, 2 Harrington Rd, Seaforth, Simon's Town. 021 786 1544. Open Tuesday – Sunday 10am – 5pm. R58

Soup Kitchen

1. Scalabrini Centre of Cape Town
47 Commercial Street, Cape Town
Soup with bread or pap served daily at 9am and hot meals are served Tuesday and Thursday from 9am – 1pm. Meals are not served to just anyone. There are strict requirements which include a South-African ID and a neat appearance. A development programme is planned for each morning. The programme incorporates raising awareness about HIV/AIDS, TB and drug addiction. Art therapy sessions, drumming sessions and movies are incorporated. Scalabrini also offers a welfare desk, health clinic, trauma counselling and various workshop programmes. Call 021 465 6433 for more information or to make a donation.

2. The Service Dining Room
In July 1935 Dorothy Syfret founded The Service Dining Rooms and its function became to provide a substantial and nourishing midday meal to the poor. It has been going successfully ever since then. "The meals served at The Service Dining Rooms consist of bread, soup, meat, fish and spicy soya served with rice or samp, fruit in season, cake, tea and products nearing expiry dates – all subject to availability, of course," says manager Desmond Billings. "We serve soup as a starter every day as it seems to be the only way to get people to eat their vegetables," he adds. Meals served Monday – Friday 11:30am - 12:30pm at 5c each. Call Des Billings at 021 465 2390 to make a donation.

3. Soup Clinic currently serves meals consisting of homemade soup and bread on weekdays in Wineberg and Ysterplaat. They are funded from own pocket and meals are made at the homes of volunteers. For more detail or donations contact Sonja at 083 294 6393.

-22-

Menu
South Africa, Issue 1, 2011 (170 × 238mm, 6¾ × 9½ inches)
This guide to the street food of Cape Town seeks to record the food and its vendors as they face the challenge presented by international chain outlets. Photography shows the reality, good and bad, of street food: the colourful, welcoming environments and the mess of food dropped on the street.
Creative director *Peet Pienaar*; Photography *Paul Ward*

Meatpaper

USA (205 × 255mm, 8 × 10 inches)

'Your Journal of Meat Culture' uses meat to examine our relationship with food in a more general sense. Claiming to be neither pro- nor anti-meat, these end-papers sum up the magazine's approach – some will love these images of plenty, others will be repulsed.

Editor-in-chief and art director *Sasha Wizansky*

OPPOSITE

Yummy

France (213 × 275mm, 8½ × 11 inches)

A celebration of fast food and related ephemera, *Yummy*'s book-like issues are packed with collections of international confectionery packaging, fast-food outlet signage and creative musings on the subject by photographers and illustrators. Made all the more powerful for being created in Paris, home of haute cuisine.

Creative director *Pascal Monfort*; Design director *Alexandra Jean*

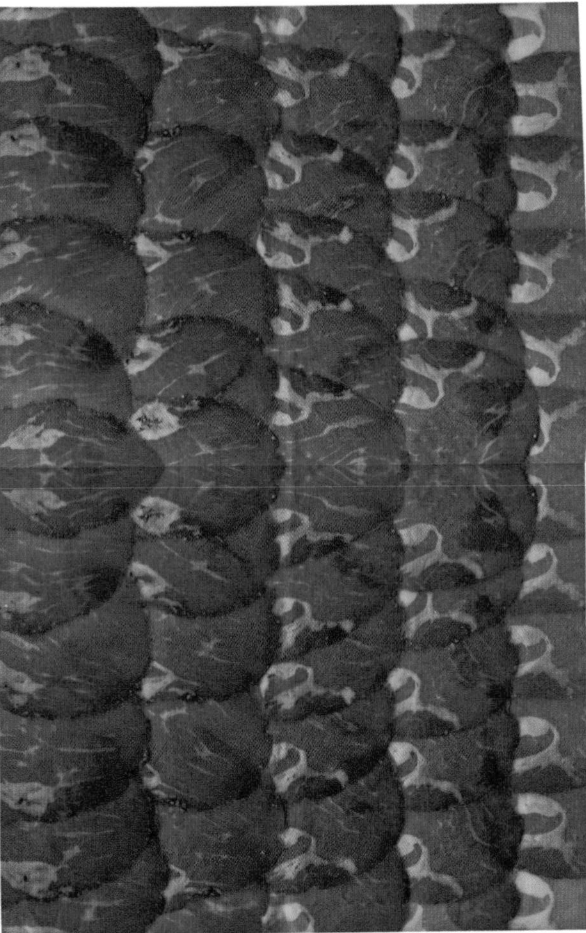

Issue 6, Winter 2008

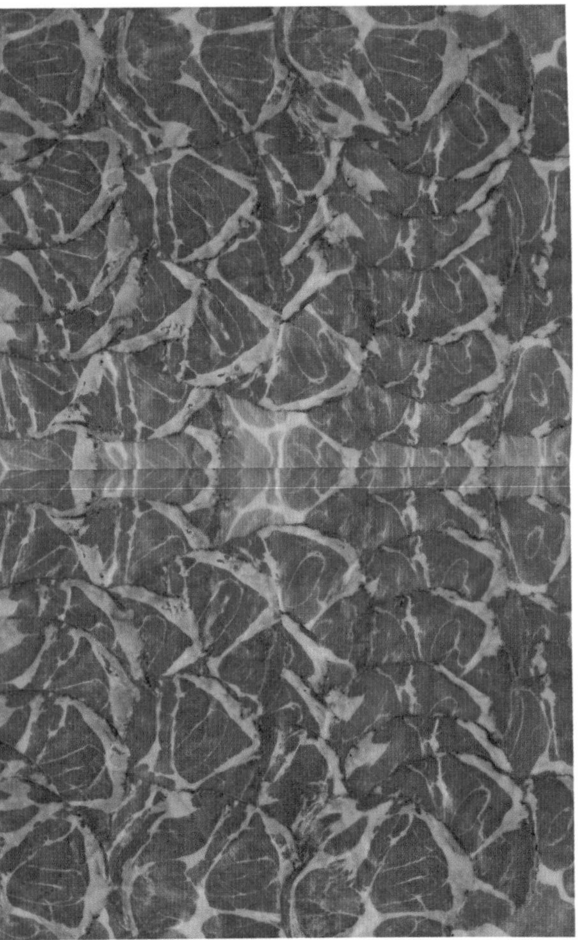

Issue 12, Summer 2010

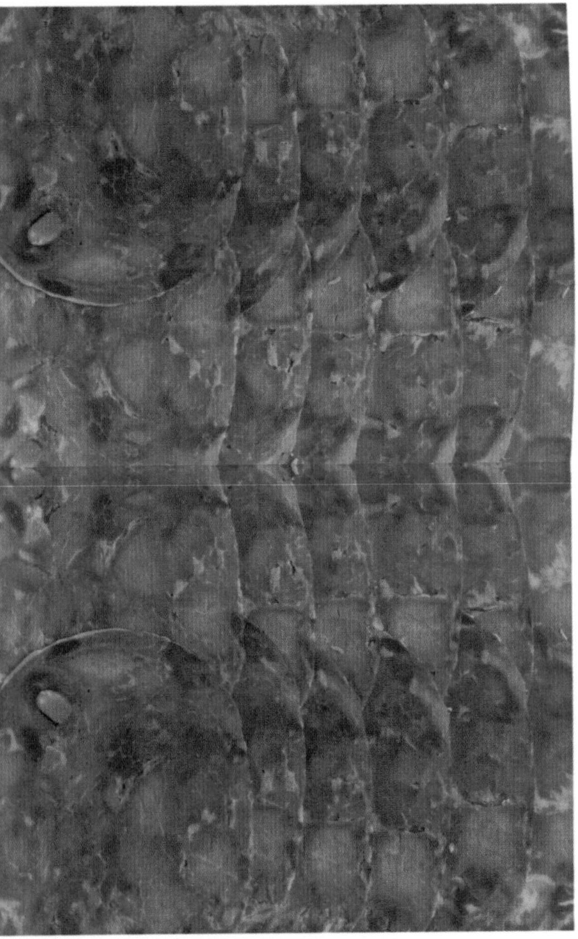

Issue 7, Spring 2009

Issue 2, September 2006

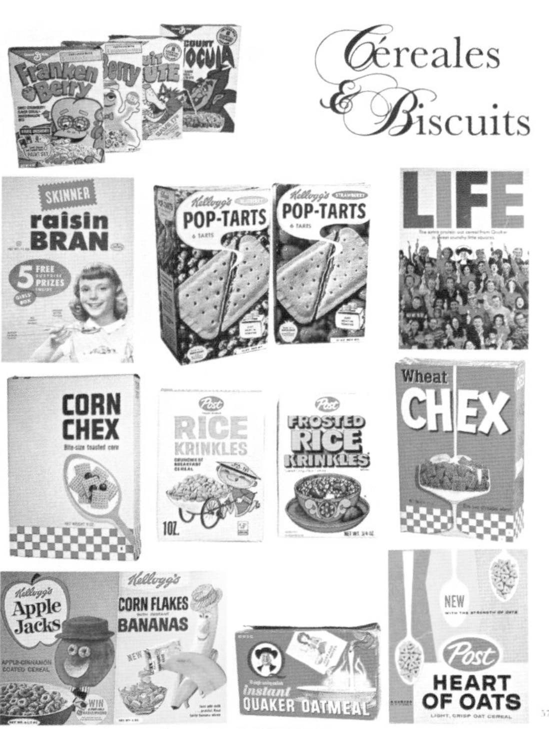

Issue 1, January 2005

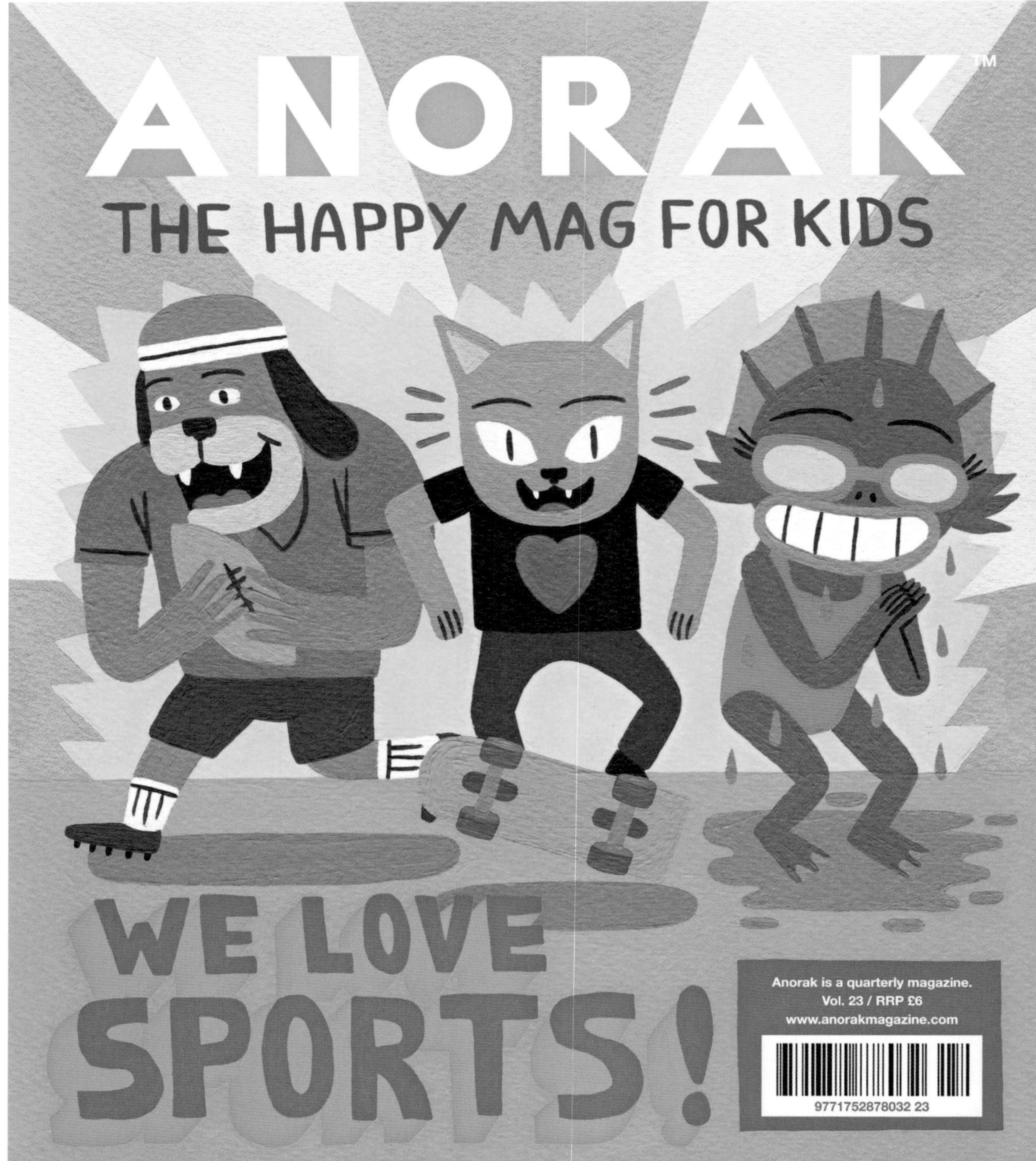
ANORAK™
THE HAPPY MAG FOR KIDS
WE LOVE SPORTS!
Anorak is a quarterly magazine.
Vol. 23 / RRP £6
www.anorakmagazine.com
9771752878032 23

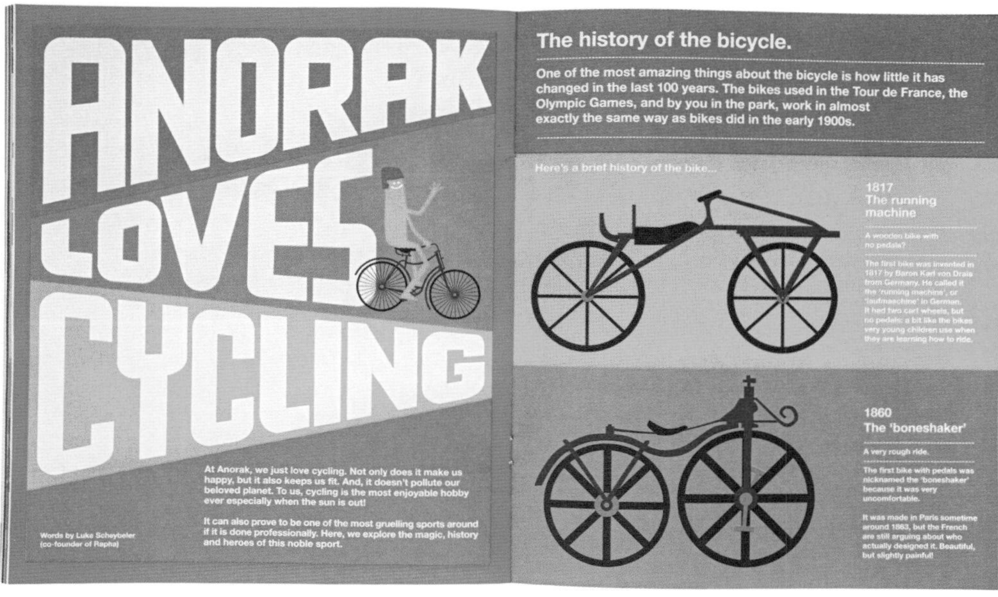

ANORAK LOVES CYCLING
At Anorak, we just love cycling. Not only does it make us happy, but it also keeps us fit. And, it doesn't pollute our beloved planet. To us, cycling is the most enjoyable hobby ever especially when the sun is out!
It can also prove to be one of the most gruelling sports around if it is done professionally. Here, we explore the magic, history and heroes of this noble sport.
Words by Luke Scheybeler (co-founder of Rapha)
The history of the bicycle.
One of the most amazing things about the bicycle is how little it has changed in the last 100 years. The bikes used in the Tour de France, the Olympic Games, and by you in the park, work in almost exactly the same way as bikes did in the early 1900s.
Here's a brief history of the bike...
1817 The running machine
A wooden bike with no pedals?
The first bike was invented in 1817 by Baron Karl von Drais from Germany. He called it the 'running machine', or 'laufmaschine' in German. It had two cart wheels, but no pedals: a bit like the bikes very young children use when they are learning how to ride.
1860 The 'boneshaker'
A very rough ride.
The first bike with pedals was nicknamed the 'boneshaker' because it was very uncomfortable.
It was made in Paris sometime around 1863, but the French are still arguing about who actually designed it. Beautiful, but slightly painful!

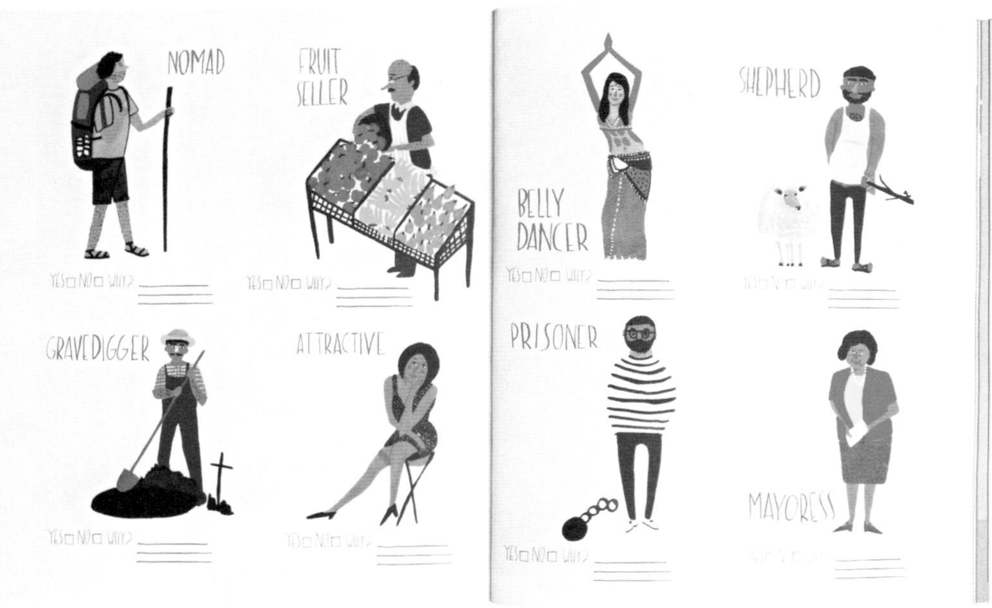

My extraordinary friend.
"Don't go any further than the trees at the edge of the park," said my Mum as I got ready to take the dog for a walk. She also told me to take my coat because it was raining.
"Yes, Mum!" I said, as I kissed her goodbye. Rosie was really pulling me as she was excited to be going out for a walk, so I let her off the lead when we got near the park.
Words by Ellen Blackah
Pictures by Supermundane
Normally, I would take a ball with us, but this time I forgot, and so instead I threw sticks for her. She was running after the sticks and bringing them back, but then all of a sudden she stopped. She put her head up in the air and I could see that she was sniffing.
She then ran off towards the other side of the park and near the trees that my Mum had told me not to go past.
I ran as fast as I could, and as I got closer to the trees I saw her in the distance, running into a shabby little black hut.
I was scared because my friends had told me that a witch lived in the hut, and that she made horrible brews and spells using fish heads and puppy dog tails. I thought maybe Rosie had smelt this in the air. I was scared that the witch might do something terrible to her.

Anorak
UK (220 × 260mm, 8¾ × 10¼ inches)
Designed as an interactive, creative experience for kids aged 6–12. *Anorak* features new stories and colourful artwork by contemporary illustrators, a fresh alternative to the many TV/movie tie-ins produced for this market. Editor *Cathy Olmedillas*

TOP, BOTTOM *No. 11, The Cycling Issue, Summer 2009*
Art director *Rob Lowe*

CENTRE, OPPOSITE *No. 23, The Sports Issue, June 2012*
Chief designer/illustrator *Matthew Bromley*

an everyday life interiors magazine – issue #09

apartamento

Featuring: Tierney Gearon, Duncan Fallowell, Yrjö Kukkapuro, Conor Donlon, Nanos Valaoritis, Tomás Nervi, Annabelle Dexter-Jones, Jean Abou, Li Edelkoort, Wolfgang Tillmans, Nic & Jackie Harrison, Gonzalo Milà, Jordi Labanda, Jem Goulding, Ramdane Touhami, Chris Johanson & Jo Jackson, BOPBAA, José León Cerrillo, India Salvor Menuez, Nicolas Congé & Camille Berthomier, Henry Roy, Jeff Rian, Max Lamb, Reg Mombassa
Plus: a **fiction supplement** by Jocko Weyland and Amanda Maxwell

36

Brazilian born Marcelo Krasilcic is a passionate man. He loves fun, friends, hosting parties, family, travel, Rio, New York City, interior design, open floor plans, tropical plants, abstract ceramics, colorful pillows, balance, beauty, bodies, sex, his boyfriend, his two cats, yoga, vegetarian cooking, collaborating and making art. He also loves love. Marcelo has created an enviable life where all these passions are explored daily in his work, and then that joy is shared with the rest of the world through his images. Marcelo is a photographer. When he graduated college in the early '90s he had the good fortune to be starting his professional life when a new generation of magazines was emerging, looking for new talent and new ways to showcase art and fashion.

MARCELO KRASILCIC
Brazilian Sunshine on the Lower East Side

INTERVIEW BY MICHAEL BULLOCK
PHOTOGRAPHY BY MARCELO KRASILCIC

As an early contributor Marcelo helped set the visual tone for such influential magazines as *Visionare, Purple, Purple Sex, Dazed & Confused, Self Service* (and later *BUTT, PIN-UP, Candy* and *ElectricYouth*). Since these exciting beginnings, Marcelo has worked non-stop creating an amazing body of work that includes everything from ceramics, to video, to sculpture, to his own line of conceptual products (Krazy Chic) – but photography always remains at the core of his practice. Marcelo's distinct images are filled with a bold Brazilian vision of the world where everything is playful, colorful, open and dripping with a happy, dynamic sexuality. The same principles are also at play in his two apartments: one in one of the dirtiest neighbourhoods in New York (the Lower East Side), and the other in the cleanest neighbourhood in São Paulo (Higienópolis).

apartamento - New York City

Apartamento
Spain, Issue 8, Autumn/Winter 2011–12 (170 × 240mm, 6¾ × 9½ inches)
A typical opening spread leads with a portrait of the inhabitant of the living space the magazine is featuring, along with his name as the headline.
Editor-in-chief *Marco Velardi*; Creative director *Nacho Alegre*; Art director *Omar Sosa*

'The magazine has been evolving from its first day and is driven by our curiosity to explore new worlds, meet new people and most of all share our finds and excitement through its pages for our readers.'

MARCO VELARDI
EDITOR-IN-CHIEF
APARTAMENTO

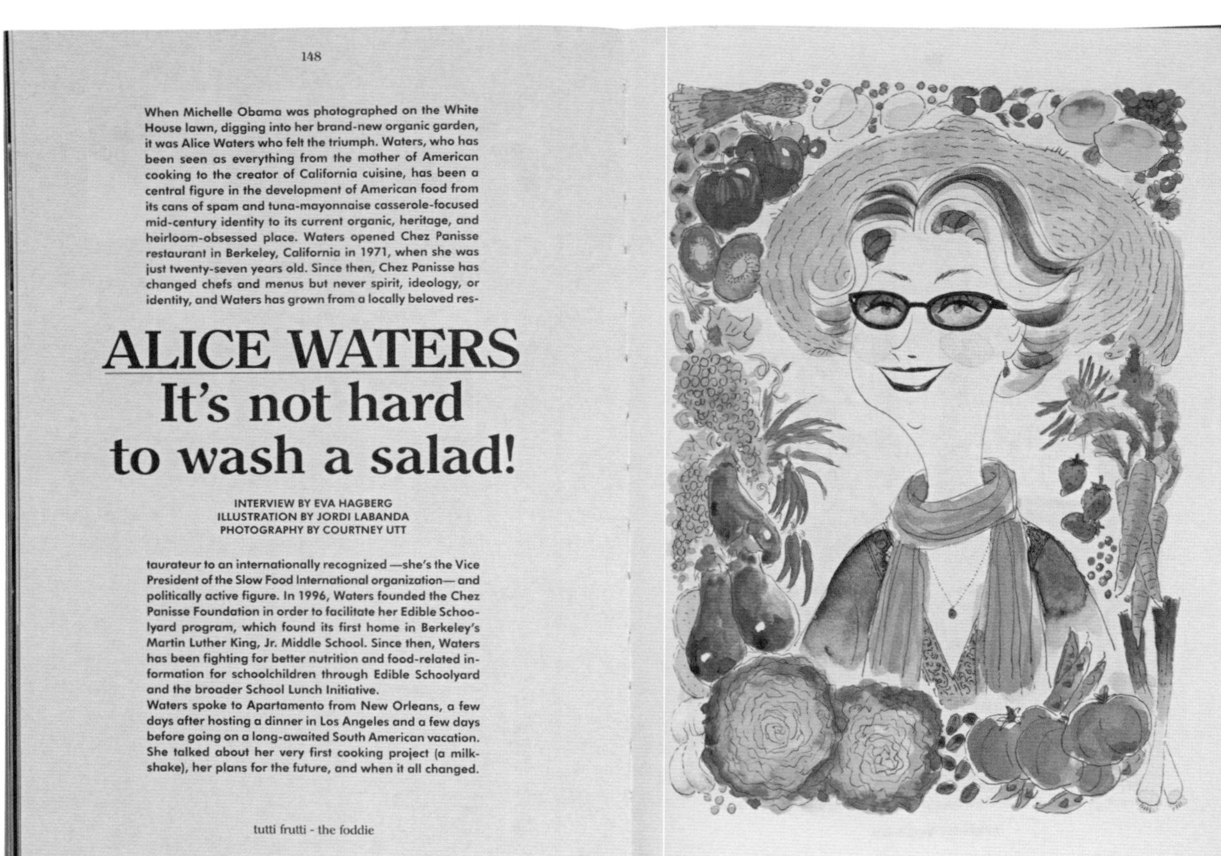
148

When Michelle Obama was photographed on the White House lawn, digging into her brand-new organic garden, it was Alice Waters who felt the triumph. Waters, who has been seen as everything from the mother of American cooking to the creator of California cuisine, has been a central figure in the development of American food from its cans of spam and tuna-mayonnaise casserole-focused mid-century identity to its current organic, heritage, and heirloom-obsessed place. Waters opened Chez Panisse restaurant in Berkeley, California in 1971, when she was just twenty-seven years old. Since then, Chez Panisse has changed chefs and menus but never spirit, ideology, or identity, and Waters has grown from a locally beloved res-

ALICE WATERS
It's not hard to wash a salad!

INTERVIEW BY EVA HAGBERG
ILLUSTRATION BY JORDI LABANDA
PHOTOGRAPHY BY COURTNEY UTT

taurateur to an internationally recognized —she's the Vice President of the Slow Food International organization— and politically active figure. In 1996, Waters founded the Chez Panisse Foundation in order to facilitate her Edible Schoolyard program, which found its first home in Berkeley's Martin Luther King, Jr. Middle School. Since then, Waters has been fighting for better nutrition and food-related information for schoolchildren through Edible Schoolyard and the broader School Lunch Initiative.
Waters spoke to Apartamento from New Orleans, a few days after hosting a dinner in Los Angeles and a few days before going on a long-awaited South American vacation. She talked about her very first cooking project (a milkshake), her plans for the future, and when it all changed.

tutti frutti - the foddie

Apartamento (Spain)

EDITOR-IN-CHIEF MARCO VELARDI

Interiors magazines have developed an aspirational language based around collecting objects to place in your newly renovated 'perfect home'. They follow a template set by high fashion: photo shoots are glamorously styled and all the items are listed with prices and stockists. The assumptions behind such content are many, the primary one being that you own a property. In 2007 Omar Sosa, Nacho Alegre and Marco Velardi decided they wanted to create a different type of interiors magazine, one that reflected the way they lived, and a year later the first edition of *Apartamento* appeared.

Everything about the new magazine spoke of a different approach to interiors coverage. The name set it apart from most interiors titles' reference to houses and homes – a point emphasized by its tagline, 'An everyday life interiors magazine', and further still by the format of the magazine. Bookishly small, and printed on uncoated paper, *Apartamento* didn't have the page size or gloss finish to match most interiors magazines even if it had wanted to.

The trio behind the magazine lived in apartment-orientated European cities: Sosa was art-directing various magazines at the Folch Studio in Barcelona, where photographer Alegre was also based. These two brought in Milan-based editor–consultant Velardi and launched the magazine as a side venture to their main activities, using their own money and relying on email and Skype to communicate as a team. 'In fact, I never met Omar in person until the launch in April 2008 in Milan,' says Velardi.

Such lack of personal contact is remarkable given the unified tone of the magazine. 'We were each inspired by many different sources, magazines, photographers, artists, books,' says Velardi, 'but overall, it was the lack of a publication satisfying our desire to see interiors in a way we felt was relevant.' In short, they published the interiors magazine they wanted to see. 'We were our own readers,' admits Velardi, 'but we soon realized there were a lot of us out there.' They found they no longer had to explain their magazine: 'people already knew what it was about and even had their opinions on it and could quote or tell you about a specific picture or story they remembered'. His initial ambition simply to reach a second issue was replaced by a more focused target for the magazine to be perceived as 'a serious effort to put out a publication which we wanted to last – a voice for our views on interiors and people'.

Note that 'interiors *and* people'. People play a key part in *Apartamento*. Like many contemporary independent magazines, the foreground subject is an excuse to examine people, their lives and relationships. The magazine features plenty of interiors shoots, but all avoid the afore-mentioned clichés of the form. Instead, we're invited inside the smaller, cluttered living spaces of a young, international creative milieu – people rather like the magazine's founders. We see real living spaces, shot as they are found and with the tell-tale signs of real life very present: laundry is drying, friends are visiting and the houseplants need some care.

What we do not see are selected items highlighted with price tags. *Apartamento* presents a very specific aesthetic – lofts and repurposed older buildings often figure, and London's Hoxton and New York's East Village are regular addresses – but it is not selling it piece by piece from the page. It is surely the first interiors magazine to acknowledge the old adage that it's people that make a house (or apartment) a home. As a nod towards this, most interiors features in the magazine lead with the inhabitants' names.

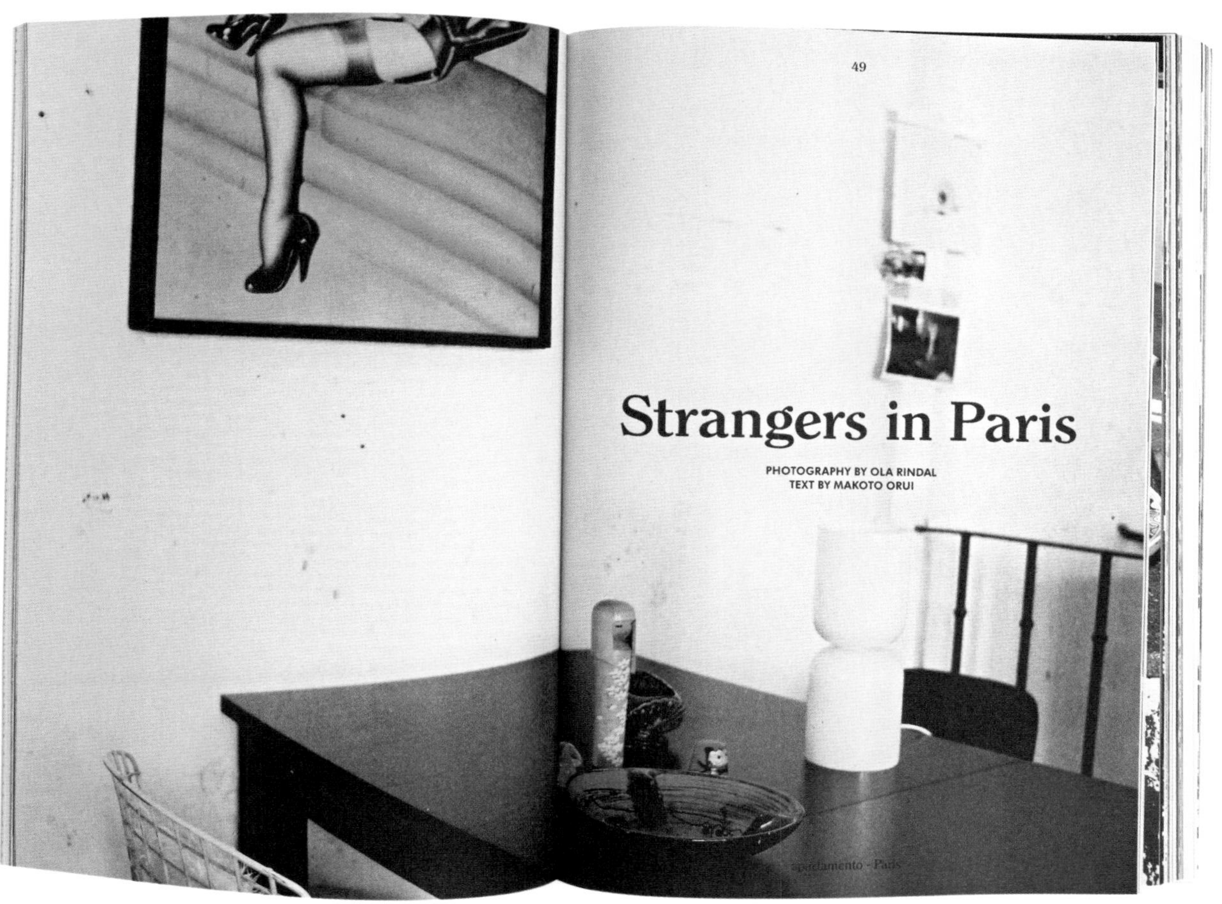

Velardi points to issue four as the point at which he and his colleagues felt the magazine truly became itself. It's certainly the issue where they seemed to discover a confidence in what they were doing and realise the potential of their publication. Chloë Sevigny talks us through her history of eight New York apartments, culminating in her current one; there's a guide to making your own potato-print wallpaper; there is the first of several children's supplements, with pages to colour in and artist–illustrator Geoff McFetteridge talking about the furniture he builds for his six-year-old daughter; we meet Sonic Youth's Kim Gordon and Thurston Moore at home in Massachusetts; plus insight into living in Beijing and Tokyo and a dissertation-level piece about architecture. 'We find people we are intrigued by and dig into their lives and spaces in an intimate way, but without trying to expose,' explains Velardi. 'It's about creating a personal relationship.'

They take great care in compiling each issue, but the fun had mixing the many different elements is evident to the reader – something that has only increased as more collaborators get space to participate and new content (food, poetry, illustration) is added.

The page design has to hold all this disparate content together, and Sosa's layouts achieve this effortlessly. A clear grid and set of type styles are applied throughout, but these are subtle and always let the images take centre stage. It is an informal design, with the only decorative detail the thin red underscores used as a highlighter throughout, and no headlines larger than about 60 point. The small page size means there are fewer options available, or needed. Use of different paper stocks is exaggerated through the use of pale background tints, and new typographic devices appear as necessary. A series of roundtable discussions has used multiple colours to highlight each participant's words, and in issue nine their first pieces of short fiction used a paperback-style single-column design with no further detail.

The magazine is successful enough – they printed 36,000 copies of the tenth issue – to cover its production costs, and according to Velardi the aim is 'to get better and better and one day be able to live on it'. But if that's to happen it will be on their own terms. 'The magazine has been evolving from its first day and is driven by our curiosity to explore new worlds, meet new people and most of all share our finds and excitement through its pages for our readers.'

Apartamento
A deceptively simple grid and set of type styles provides a clear identity and ties together images ranging from colourful illustration to full-bleed interiors shots.

Issue 8, Autumn/Winter 2011–12
Photograph *Ola Rinde*

OPPOSITE *Issue 7, Spring/Summer 2007*
Illustrated portrait *Jordi Lananda*

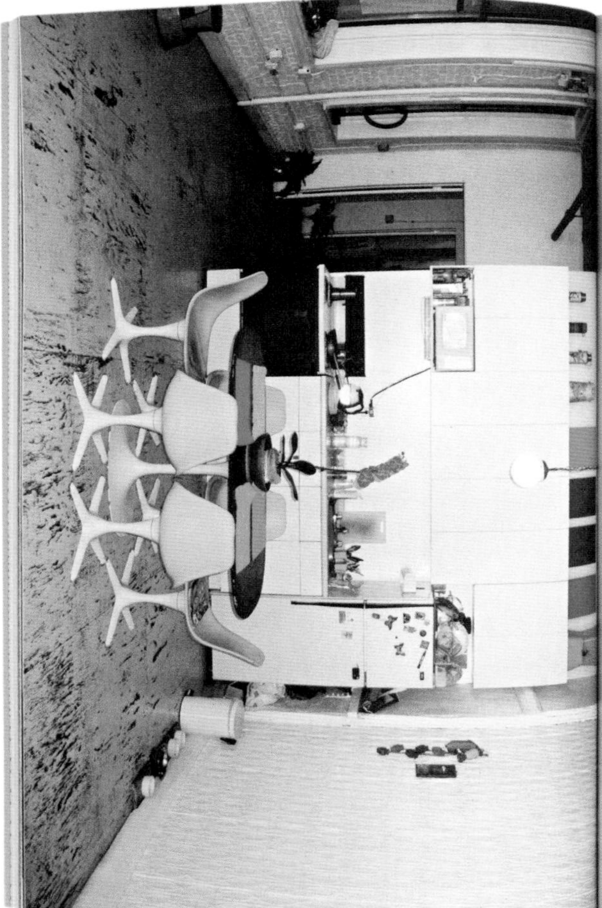

47

Most of the images are still-lifes you've made and photographed?
Yeah. It's the Krazy Chic logos and still-lifes, and some designs using the pillows. I'm a big fan of the design with the number 69 made out of many key chains.
I inherited that key chain collection from my parents. '69 is the year I was born, the erotic year and it all makes sense. I'll get you a 69 T-shirt.

What are you working on right now that you are overjoyed about?
I'm really excited because I'm going to have a book out next year. It's all work from the '90s. Right now it's titled *20s in the '90s*. It's about being in my 20s in the '90s. It's also very much about being loving. I moved here in 1990 and I finished college in '92. At that time there was so much openness in photography and all these new magazines –*Purple, Visionaire, Self-Service* and *Dazed*– were looking for new, passionate ways of showing work. Being more conceptual with fashion was celebrated then.

You were shooting for all of them?
Yeah, that's right. When I finished school I went from doing more conceptual work to being really passionate about fashion. So the book is all '90s and film photography, which is part of what shaped me. I used to spend months in the lab printing my own photographs and loving every second of it. I was beyond broke, my credit card bills were ridiculous, but I was passionate about the work. My life was work and work was life. It was one thing.

What were you focused on at that time?
Coming from Brazil the whole concept of gay pride was new and very exciting to me. It was a time when I was longing for love and longing for intimacy. My graduation work in college was different men in bed with me. It was passionate but very hard because I had no money. So the book's all about loving and being accepted. On one page there are pictures of me with somebody in bed, then the next page is my parents being affectionate with each other, and the next is my mom being affectionate with me. As much freedom as we have in America, and nowadays as much freedom as people have in Brazil, the idea of being gay and having a committed relationship is still foreign to a lot of people. It's still a crime in some countries (looking through the book mock up).

Leaf table in Marcelo's house in São Paolo

And are there many interiors?
Yeah, I've always been interested in shooting interiors because they tell a lot about a person. I was really interested in chance and choice and how you make so many choices within a limited array of possibilities of things you can get with the money you have. At the time I asked, 'How much am I in charge of it all? Am I really responsible for how this living room is?' I have my choices but I have limited money, time and options for what I can put in this living room. I was curious about that challenge.

So do you have a conclusion on chance and choice? It seems both have been good to you?
Yeah, I love my everyday experience of working with creative people to make images that go out into the world and influence people in one way or another. It's wonderful. And when you can do that and make money it's really exciting. Putting the book together I learned that back then, even though I was as excited as I was, there was a lot of angst because everything was so uncertain. Every exciting moment seemed fleeting. It made me see how precious that time was and it makes me realise how precious time is today. In the sense that every experience, every photograph, every kiss is so profound and nourishing in itself. The idea is to enjoy whatever's happening, because it's great.

apartamento - Marcelo Krasilcic

REINVENTING GENRES

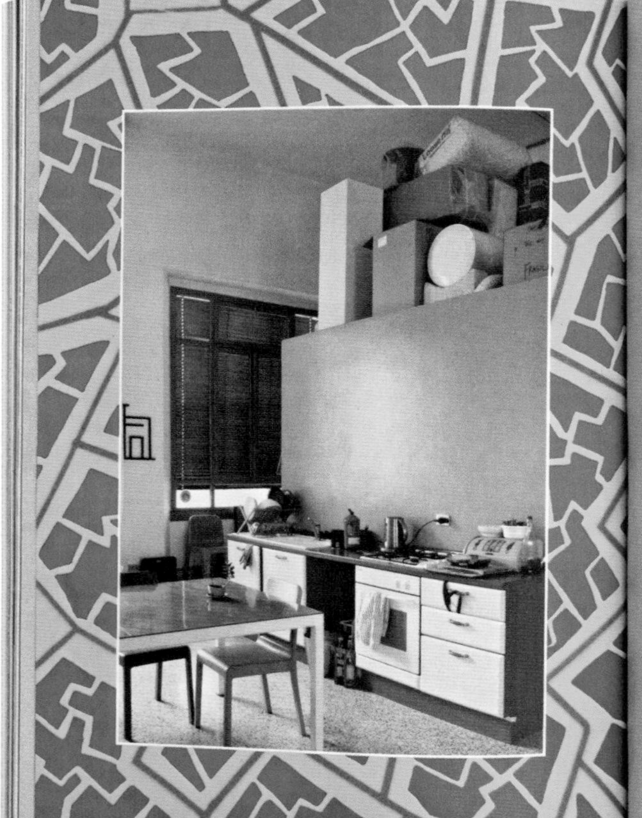

123

fashion in six months. I've always tried to do my best for the moment, and whether things last or disappear doesn't depend on you, on the decisions you as the designer make. I think if you do something very seriously and sincerely, then there's always something that remains even if it's not fashionable anymore. It's only things that are done without the heart that don't last.

What's your view on kitsch?
I'm not interested in kitsch; it's a genre I don't understand. I think there's a certain cynicism in kitsch which doesn't belong to me.

Why do you think the Memphis group dissolved? What made you go your separate ways?
I think it was over. By the end of the '80s it'd become quite well known; it was just time to stop. For me Memphis had been a special experience. It wasn't like working for a company. By that time I'd also realised I didn't want to be a designer, so I started painting.

I guess that must have meant quite a change in your work routines?
Well, my work routines had always been very independent anyway. Apart from the six months I worked in the Fiorucci studio, which I didn't like, I've always worked on my own. First from the kitchen table, and then George and I had a little studio next to where we were living. But I didn't like the life in the studio. What I like basically is to be on my own and do what I want (laughs). When you have a design studio it's a completely different kind of life. I like to do things myself, I don't like to tell somebody what to do. When you have a studio that's what happens; you spend all your time in meetings or on the phone, correcting what other people do. I didn't want that, it's not for me.

Where do you draw the line between art and design?
Nowadays I don't draw a line. For many years I drew a very precise line and I didn't want things to mix. Now I think most designers do art, and a lot of artists work like designers, so I don't know why I should put myself on a line in between. But still, my work as an artist takes 95 per cent of my time, design maybe 5 per cent.

'Bricks and Orange', 2005, Oil on canvas

I'd like to ask you about your early paintings. They seem so full of movement, people, landscapes and animals, quite opposite from what you paint now. Why's that?
I think when I decided to move away from design I wanted to fill my life completely with other things than just objects. That's why I made these narrative works with elements inside, probably to capture deep emotions. But soon I realised that painting very simple things that were all around me, and concentrating on what they were, was enough. One always moves forward, otherwise what's life?

apartamento - Nathalie Du Pasquier

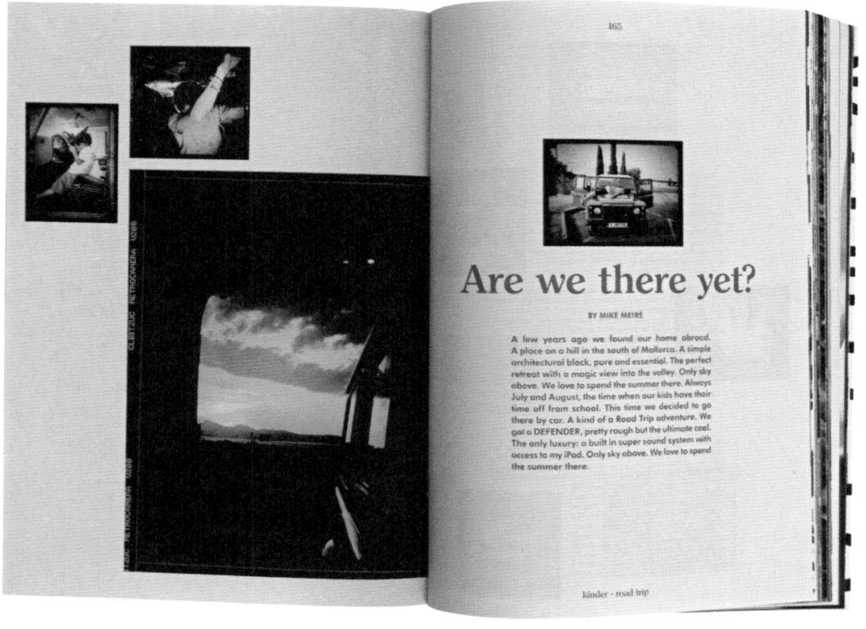

165

Are we there yet?

BY MIKE MEIRÉ

A few years ago we found our home abroad. A place on a hill in the south of Mallorca. A simple architectural block, pure and essential. The perfect retreat with a magic view into the valley. Only sky above. We love to spend the summer there. Always July and August, the time when our kids have their time off from school. This time we decided to go there by car. A kind of a Road Trip adventure. We got a DEFENDER, pretty rough but the ultimate cool. The only luxury: a built in super sound system with access to my iPod. Only sky above. We love to spend the summer there.

kinder - road trip

Apartamento

TOP: *Issue 8, Autumn/Winter 2011–12*
Colleagues from other magazines often contribute or feature, such as this travel story by *032c* art director Mike Meiré.

CENTRE: *Issue 7, Spring/Summer 2011*
An example of what has become a signature still-life style in the magazine, conceived by Omar Sosa and Ana Dominguez and shot by Nacho Alegre.

BOTTOM: *Issue 3, Spring/Summer 2009*
Text in the now familiar two-column grid is colour-coded to define contributions from different participants in a roundtable discussion.

OPPOSITE TOP: *Issue 8, Autumn/Winter 2011–12*
Examples of how the magazine adapts to suit content: if an image needs to be landscape it might run vertically, and if text doesn't fill the final column it's left empty

BOTTOM : *Issue 8, Autumn/Winter 2011–12*
A piece about artist Nathalie Du Pasquier reproduces some of the patterns she created for the furniture collective Memphis as borders to Alice Fiorilli's photographs.

Wilder Quarterly
US, Volume 1, Issue 3, Summer 2012 (166 × 242mm, 6½ × 9½inches)
Primarily a gardening magazine, *Wilder Quarterly* also covers the natural world in a broader sense and so includes camping, the science of horticulture and the sounds plants make.
Founder and publisher *Celestine Maddy*; Art director *Monica Nelson*

OPPOSITE **'Sup Magazine**
USA (198 × 274mm, 7¾ × 10¾ inches)
Documenting all types of contemporary music, *'Sup* provides space for long Q&A sessions with musicians and works closely with them on the accompanying photography to produce a magazine that looks as good as the music sounds
Publisher and editor *Marisa Brickman*; Creative director *Brendan Dugan*; Art director *Eric Wrenn*
MORE 'SUP p127

WILDER QUARTERLY Summer 2012
PURE CAMP
All the Gear That's Fit to Pack

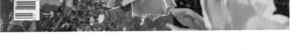

In 1885, like many well-off New Yorkers of the time, Thomas and Sarah Newbold bought a second home. Located in the town of Hyde Park, New York, Bellefield commanded views of the expansive waters of the Hudson River. In 1912, when they hired the firm that had recently designed the nearby Vanderbilt mansion to enlarge the house, they asked Thomas's cousin, Beatrix Jones, to design a new garden. Jones, who married the following year, taking the name Beatrix Farrand, was to become one of the most important landscape architects of her time.

Few of her gardens survive today, but fortunately the garden at Bellefield, Farrand's earliest residential design, lives on. It was created nearly two decades into her professional career, in the same year that she designed the campus landscape of Princeton University and just prior to designing gardens for the White House. Farrand created gardens for many influential individuals, public institutions and universities, and was a founding member—the only woman—of the Association of American Landscape Architects.

Her plant selections were rooted in childhood summers spent in Maine and formative years of study at Harvard University's Arnold Arboretum. Farrand was part of a vanguard movement in garden design that departed from elaborate Victorian bedding schemes. Her approach drew upon classical as well as natural landscapes; she incorporated shrubs, hardy perennials and many native plants into her designs.

One special plant that worked its way into many of Farrand's designs, particularly in the Bellefield garden, is the peony. Known in China as far back as 1000 BC, where they were prized for their medicinal virtues, peonies were later introduced to Japan, in the eighth century, and to Europe in the eighteenth. European immigrants brought peonies with them to North America, where their sturdy varieties were a treasured element in pioneer gardens. The breeding of peonies has flourished in nearly every part of the world where they have been cultivated. Chinese, Japanese, European (particularly French and British) and American breeders have all contributed to the dazzling array of peony varieties we enjoy today.

In the 1970s, Newbold descendants donated the Bellefield house along with 20 landscaped acres to the National Park Service. In an attempt to discourage weeds, the Park Service covered the garden beds with black plastic sheeting. In 1994, a nonprofit organization formed to restore the garden, as its original plantings had all but disappeared, leaving scarcely more than weeds and stone edgings behind. Newly hired horticulturist, Anne Cleves Symmes, and a crew of volunteers rolled back the plastic in the spring of 1997—and with astonishment discovered that some stalwart peonies had survived. Peonies have a reputation for being tough, but that they withstood decades of dry shade, crowding from competitive weeds, stifling heat and darkness for numerous seasons says it all.

Although peonies require little special care, they will not grow where winters are too warm; research indicates that they must be exposed to approximately 600 hours of temperatures below freezing. Peonies prefer rich, well-drained soil with good sun exposure. They are remarkably drought-resistant and do not interest browsing deer. When planting peonies, make sure that the crowns are planted no deeper than they previously were as planting too deep can prevent bloom. Peonies make spectacular cut flowers, but cut only one or two stems per plant, leaving plenty of foliage to nourish the plant. When older, previously flowering peonies stop blooming, it may be time to divide them.

Today, many spectacular peonies bloom within Bellefield's walls. A Bellefield classic is "Festiva Maxima," splendid with a profusion of lush white petals flecked with crimson; this variety exudes the finest peony perfume. Some of Bellefield's peonies are original survivors, and others were donated by Reverend Eliot Lindsley, who collected old-fashioned specimens from numerous gardens around Hyde Park, including at least one from the previous Bellefield garden beds. One of the oldest varieties, still commercially available, is "Edulis Superba," which was cultivated in 1824 and sports pink, rose-scented blooms that are excellent for cutting. This year, on June 2, the Beatrix Farrand Garden at Bellefield celebrates its 100th anniversary with a special garden party.

To learn more, go to **beatrixfarrandgarden.org**.

23

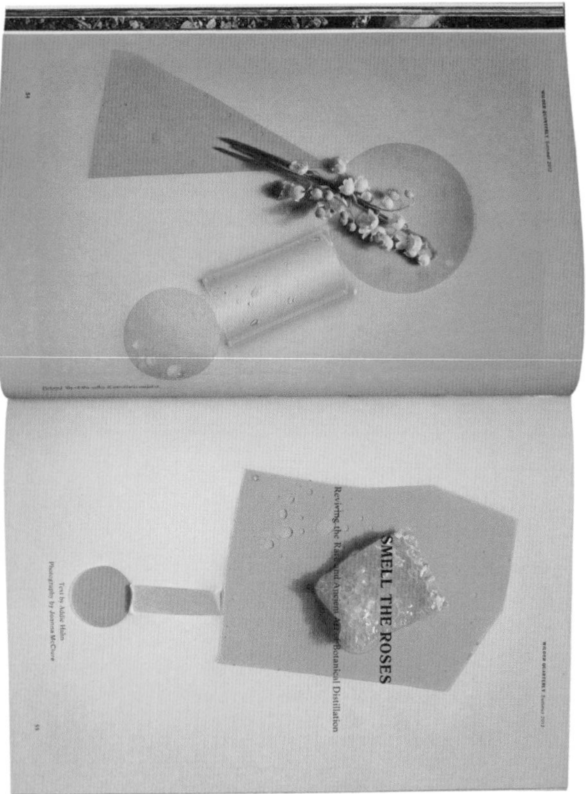

WILDER QUARTERLY Summer 2012
SMELL THE ROSES
Reviving the Rare and Ancient Art of Botanical Distillation
Text by Addie Hahn
Photography by Joanna McClure

Issue 22, 2010

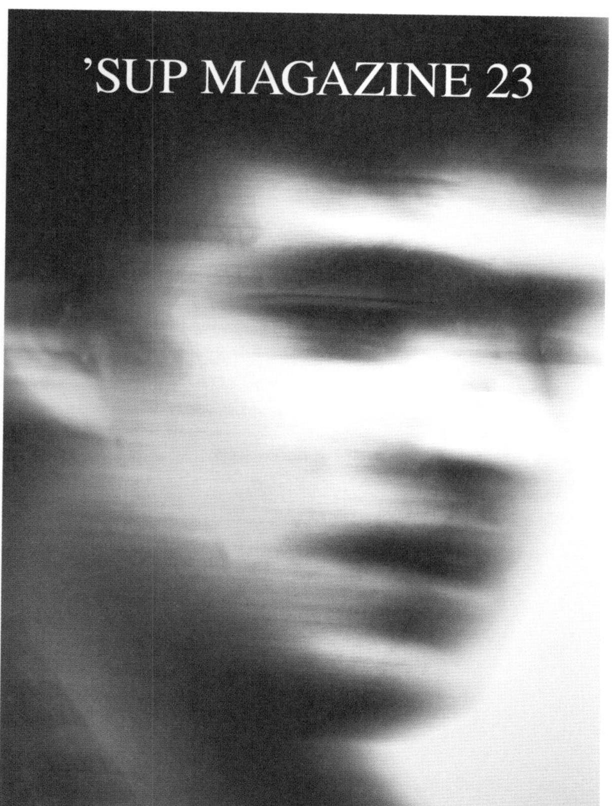

Issue 23, 2010

Issue 24, 2011

Issue 25, 2012

Little White Lies

UK (200 × 245mm, 8 × 9¾ inches)

Each issue of this magazine about 'Truth and Movies' leads with a single new film release, the whole features section taking its lead from that movie, providing cultural context as well as critique and interview(s). The front cover always leads with a commisioned artwork relating to this movie, helping establish the unique character of the magazine and building up an impressive gallery of cover designs.

Editor *Matt Bochenski*; Creative director *Paul Willoughby*; Various illustrators as listed

MORE LITTLE WHITE LIES p203

Issue 37, September/October 2011. Michael Gillette

Issue 1, March/April 2005. Paul Willoughby

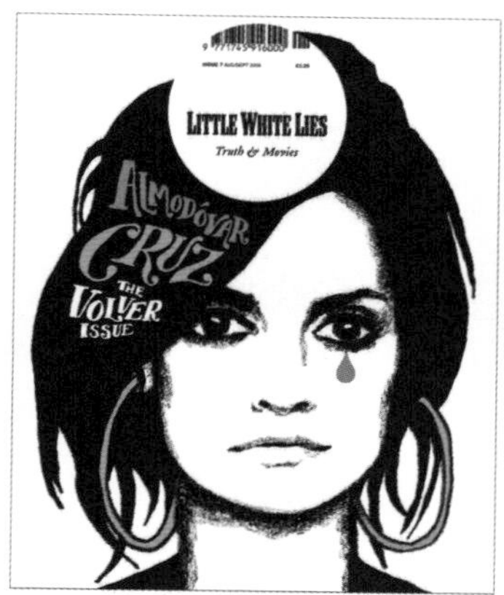

Issue 7, Aug/Sept 2006. Paul Willoughby

Issue 23, May/June 2009. Siggi Eggertsson

Issue 25, Sept/Oct 2009. Michael Gillette

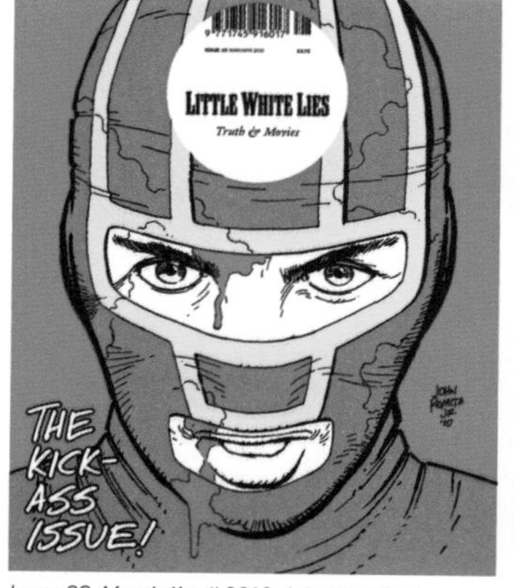

Issue 28, March/April 2010. John Romita Jr

Issue 31, Sept/Oct 2010. Steve Wilson

Issue 32, Nov/Dec 2010. Paul Willoughby

Issue 33, Jan/Feb 2011. David Carson

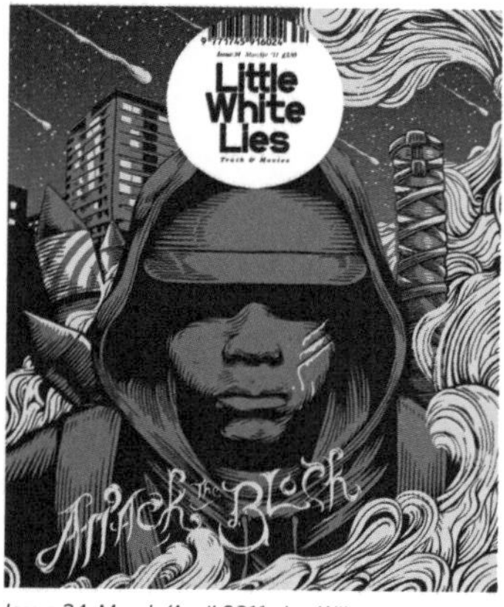

Issue 34, March/April 2011. Joe Wilson

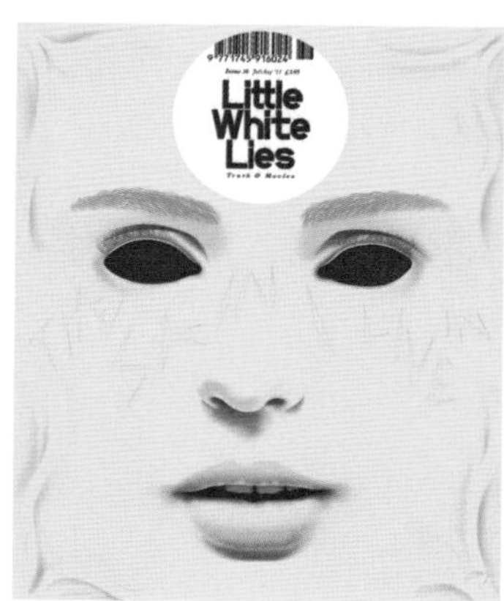

Issue 36, July/August 2011. Jesse Auersalo

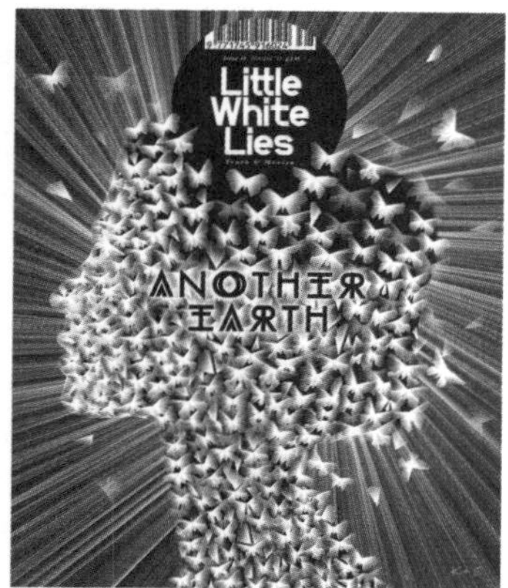

Issue 38, Nov/Dec 2011. Kai and Sunny

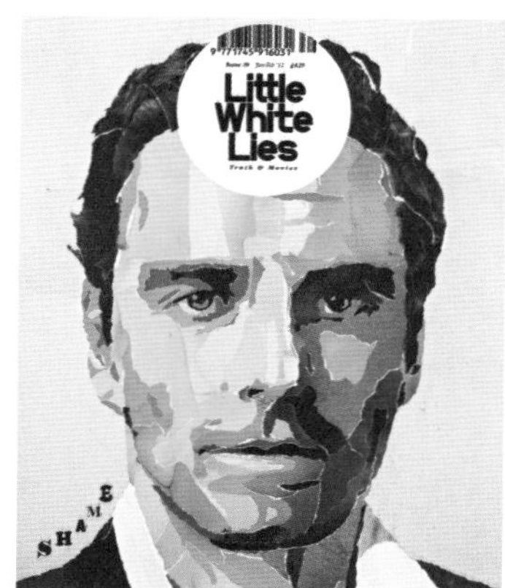

Issue 39, Jan/Feb 2012. Paul Willoughby

Issue 40, March/April 2012. Jean Jullien

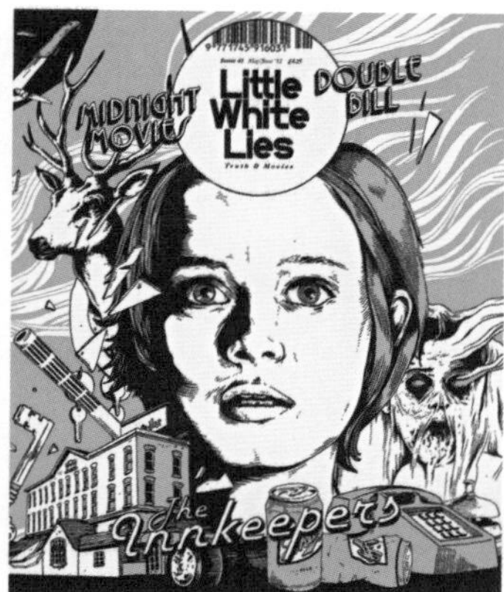

Issue 41, May/June 2012. Joe Wilson

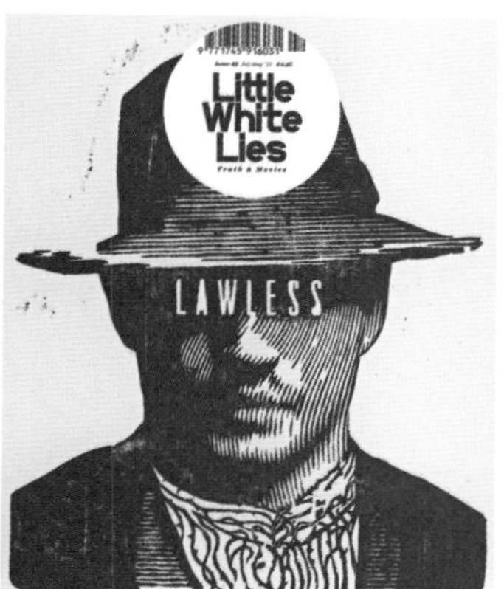

Issue 42, July/August 2012. Paul Willoughby

Issue 43, Sept/Oct 2012. Paul X Johnson

Butt

The Netherlands (165 × 235mm, 6½ × 9¼ inches)
A prime example of a niche magazine covering its subject with such refeshing honesty that it broke out of that niche to reach a wider audience. *Butt* was a gay porn magazine that featured real people rather than the glossy porn stereotypes. The monochrome, stripped-back design was a precursor to the same team's later *Fantastic Man*.
Editors and designers Gert Jonkers and Jop van Bennekom

Issue 3, Spring 2002

OPPOSITE *Issue 2, Autumn 2001*

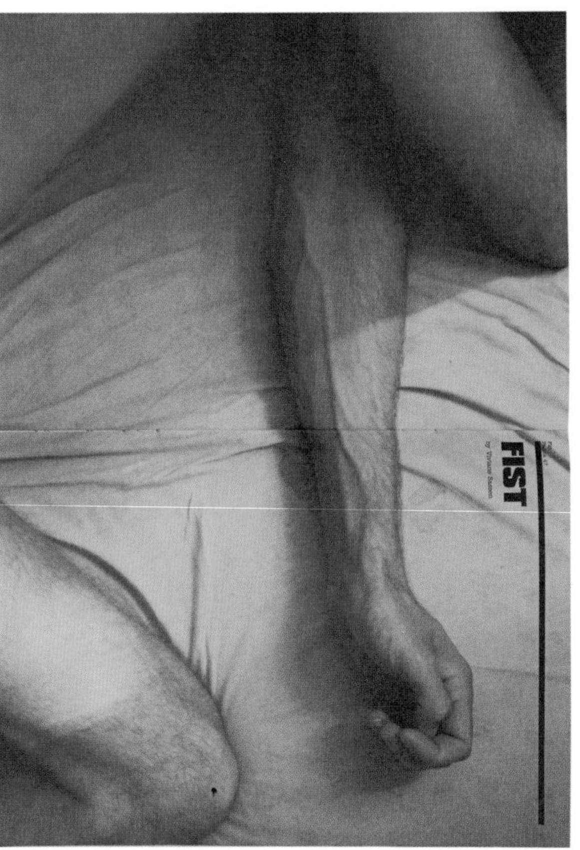

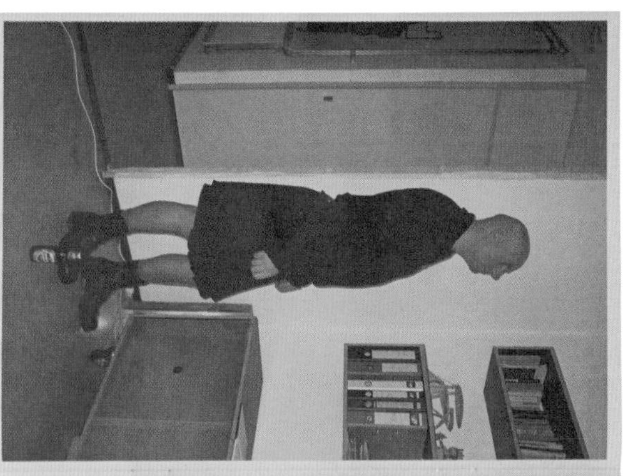

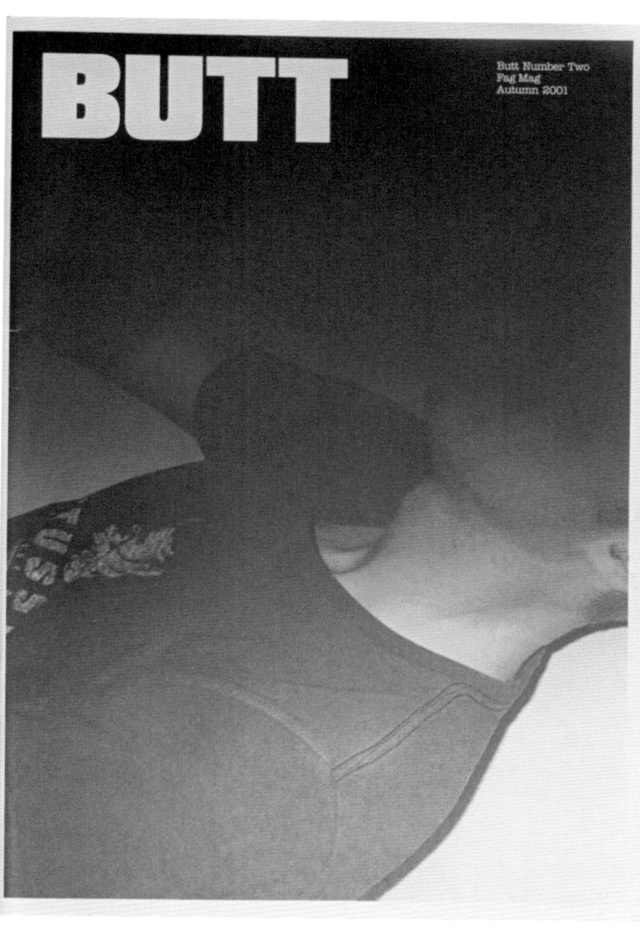

Wolfgang
Pagina 56

SOME THINGS WOLFGANG TILLMANS SAW AND LIKED

by Wolfgang Tillmans

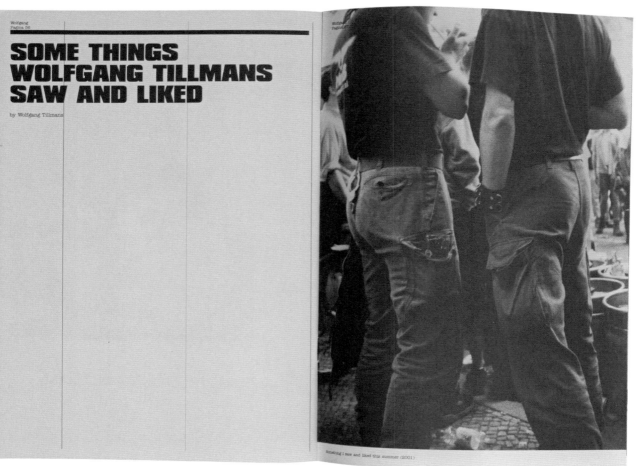

Something I saw and liked this summer (2001)

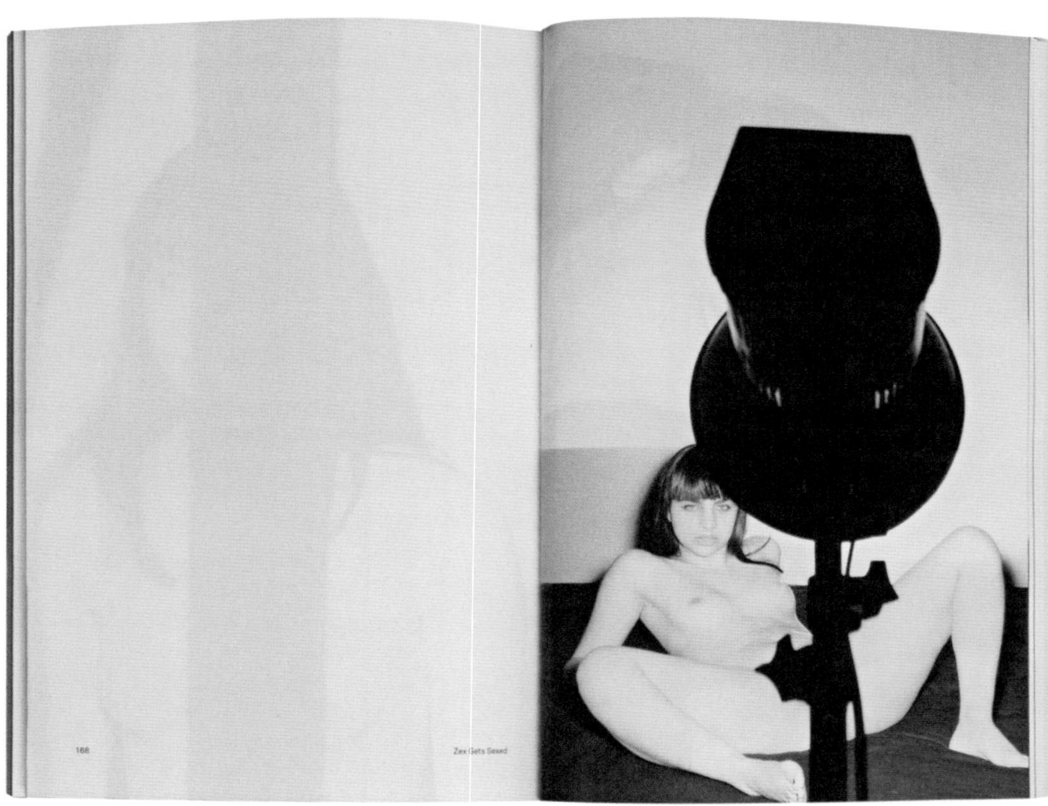
168
Zex Gets Sexed

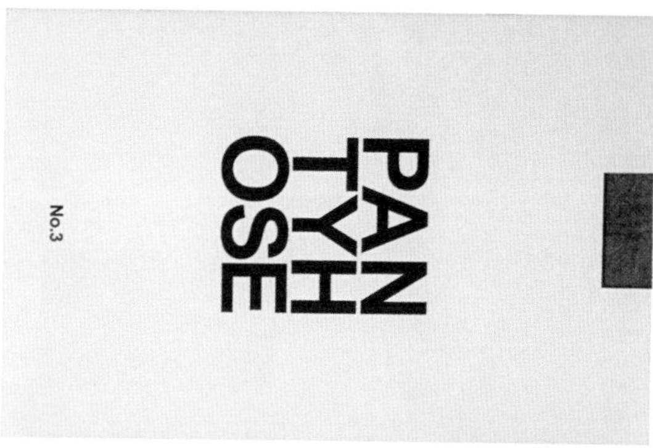

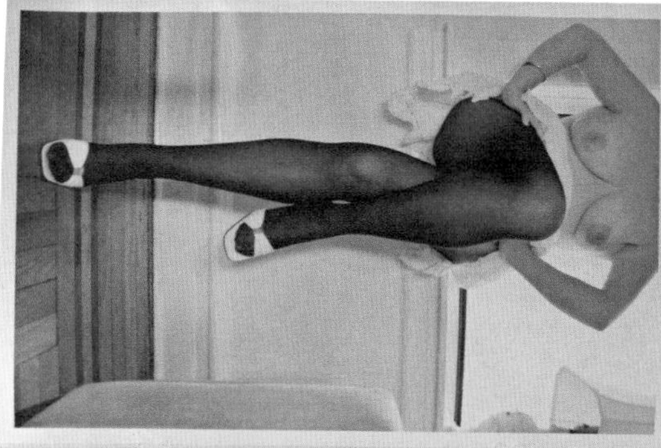

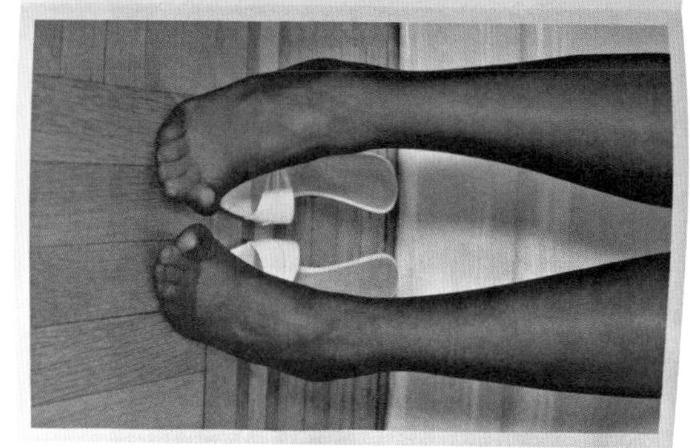

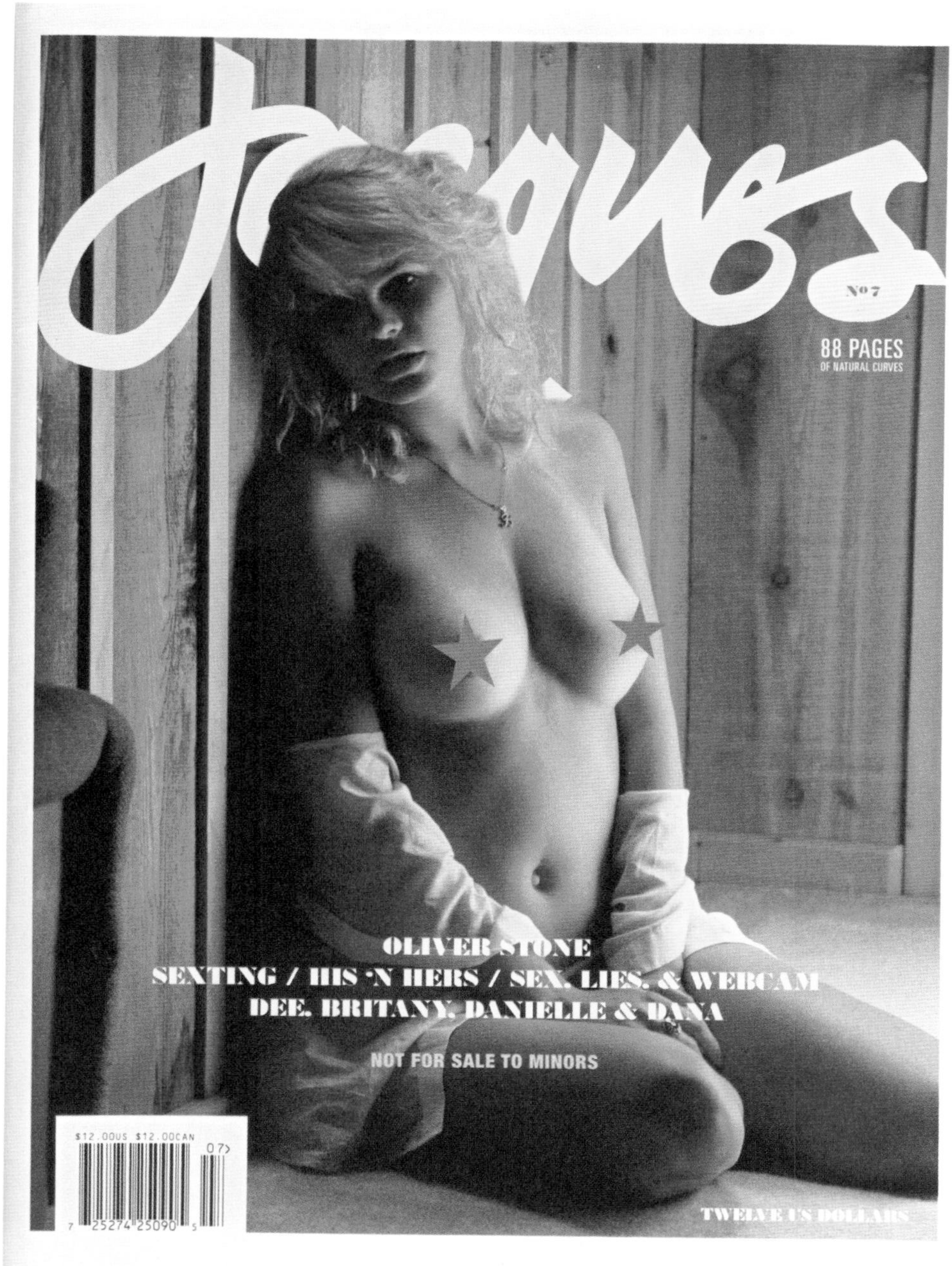

Pantyhose
USA, Issue 3, 2010 (168 × 260mm, 6¼ × 10¼ inches)
Creative director *Howard Chu*

Jacques
USA, Issue 7, Winter 2011 (228 × 305mm, 9 × 12¼ inches)
Editor *Danielle Leder*; Creative director *Jonathan Leder*

OPPOSITE **Baron**
UK, Issue 1, 2012 (110 × 165mm, 4½ × 6½ inches)
Editor *Jonanthon Baron*; Creative director *Matthew Holroyd*

New erotic magazines have stepped into the space left by the mainstream pornography industry as it has retreated online. *Pantyhose* specializes in underwear fetishism and arrives packaged in the style of women's tights; *Jacques* is a retro-styled magazine featuring softcore imagery of real women rather than established porn models; *Baron* is a pocket-sized 196-page 'Erotic Paperback' featuring photography and fiction.

www.brandeins.de brand eins 12. Jahrgang Heft 10 Oktober 2010 7,60 Euro C 50777

brand eins

Wirtschaftsmagazin

WISSEN, WAS GUT IST.

4 195069 807601 10

Schwerpunkt Qualität

Verbrechen, gut organisiert

Facebook fürs Büro
Vor 41 Jahren wurde die E-Mail erfunden. In den meisten Unternehmen ist sie das wichtigste Kommunikationsmittel – und längst keine reine Freude mehr.
Dabei gibt es ein Leben ohne Mail-Pingpong und überfüllte Postfächer.
Text: Christoph Koch
Illustration: Manu Burghart
Vom Geniestreich zur Plage: E-Mails

Die Matrix
Die US-Fondsgesellschaft Pimco ist eine der erfolg- und einflussreichsten Finanzfirmen weltweit. Und das dank einer scheinbar banalen Frage, die sich die Geldexperten bei allem, was sie tun, unermüdlich stellen: Ist es wichtig – oder nur dringend?
Text: Patricia Döhle Foto: © Getty Images

Brand Eins
Germany (214 × 280mm, 8½ × 11 inches)
Since 1999 this business monthly has been using challenging design and art direction in a market not usually known for creative experiment. A boldly simple typographic structure houses strong photography, illustration and design. Editor *Gabriele Fischer*; Art director *Mike Meiré*

TOP: *March 2001*
The subject in a stock image has his face obscured for a story about the mafia. Photograph *Daniel Josefsohn*

CENTRE, BOTTOM: *March 2012*
Two feature opening spreads show how graphic and illustrated elements are used. Illustration (centre) *Manu Burghart*

OPPOSITE *October 2010*
A typically bold use of colour and typography on the cover.

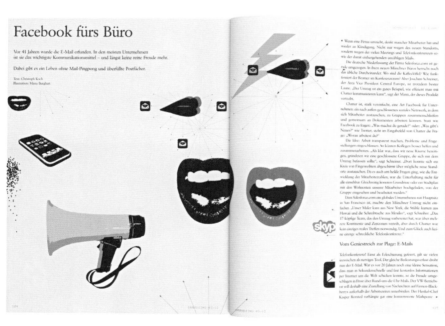

092

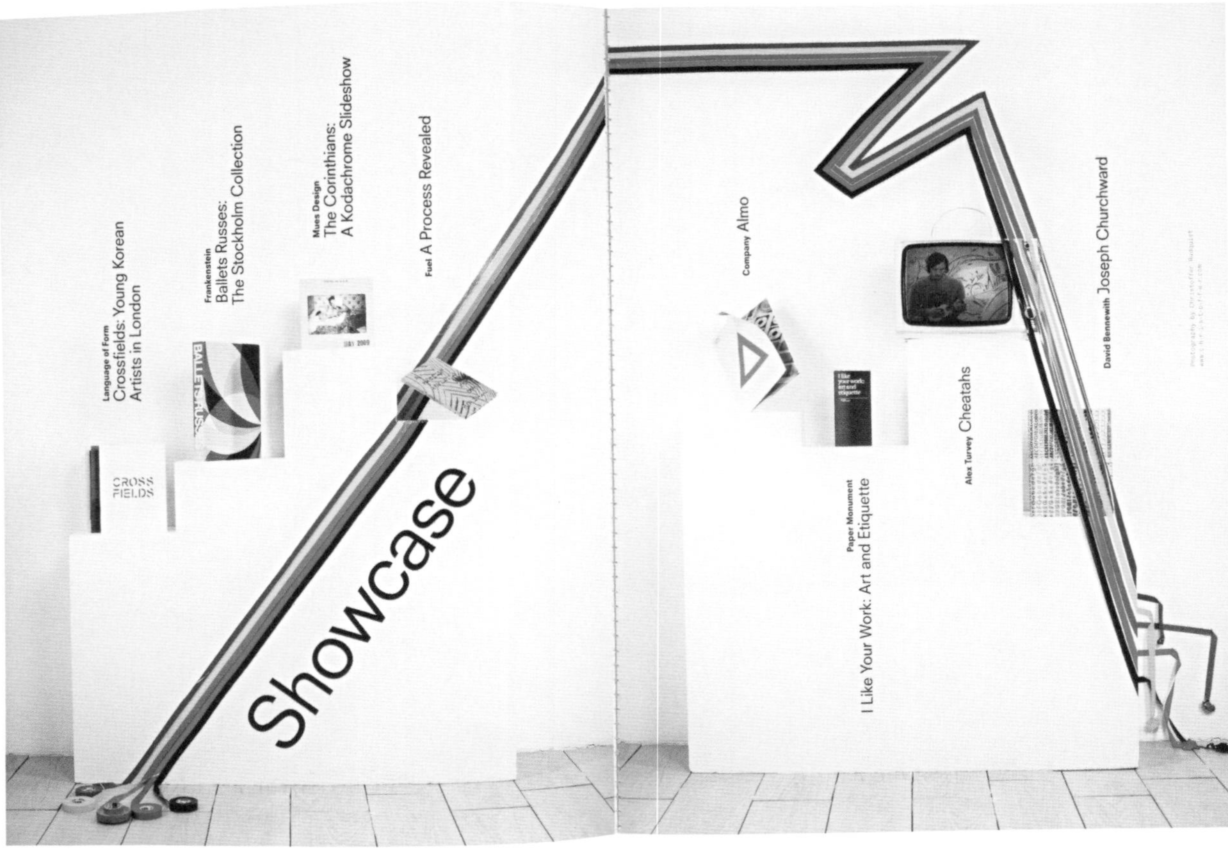

Grafik 115 Review 46

Review.
Books.
What is Packaging Design?
Classic Cafés
I'll Keep Thinking
Animation Unlimited
Identity Design Sourcebook
History of Modern Design
Size Matters
Art Directors Annual 82

What Is Packaging Design?
By Giles Calver
Published by RotoVision (£24.99)

The third in RotoVision's What Is series starts (as many of our parents did in the 1950s) with an egg. Surely the classic grey egg box is the ultimate in great packaging design? Practical, cheap and made from recycled material, the humble egg box has stayed pretty much the same for years. It's never going to win any design prizes, falling as it does into the Trellick Tower school of beauty, and only gets a mention here as having inspired the packaging for some rather expensive-looking organic shampoo. Mr Newark set the standard with the first in this series, and Calver has certainly taken up the challenge. This is a thoughtful and thorough book with some inspiring work—great for students and anyone taking their first step into the heady world of packaging design.

Classic Cafés
By Adrian Maddox
Published by Black Dog (£19.95)

A timely, if nostalgic look into the caff—a phenomenon that only hit Britain in the 1950s and has all but disappeared thanks to the likes of Starbucks. OK, so the coffee's bigger and frothier, but the decor's horrible and you can pay nearly three quid for a drink. It's time to fight back against the blandardisation of the high street and start using these 'little gems of British vernacular high street design' as Mr Maddox describes them. Each is an oasis of Formica and PVC, selling, according to a certain Mr Raymond Blanc, who is clearly not a fan, 'something disgusting' to eat, which we love because according to him it endorses our working-class status. Mr Blanc is surely missing the point here—going to the caff has never been about quality food. It's about omelette and chips, apple pie and custard and lashings of slightly stewed tea, is it not? A lovely little book, straight from the heart and worthy of a place on your bookshelf. Up yours, Monsieur Blanc.

I'll Keep Thinking
By Nick Crosbie, Inflate
Published by Black Dog (£13.95)

This is the latest book in the small but perfectly formed Serial series on contemporary product and furniture designers. It's an honest and extremely interesting account of the trials and tribulations of setting up a business based (in the beginning) on inflatable objects. While all the various Inflate products are featured here, Crosbie lets us in on the stories behind the designs, starting with his very first inflatable design created at college in an effort to stop him being thrown off the course. It worked—and the rest, as they say, is history. Whatever you think of Inflate products, this book makes a refreshing change from yer average ego-inflated designer monograph and is essential reading for anyone thinking of trying to make it in the business of making things.

Animation Unlimited
By Liz Faber and Helen Walters
Published by Laurence King (£28.00)

This book takes a look at 'Innovative Short Films since 1940' and rather sensibly comes with its very own DVD showing a selection of the films featured. There's something for everyone and some of the most interesting stuff stems from the pre-digital era. Divided into chapters covering Form, Sound, Words and Character, it contains a diverse and interesting selection. The wheels of publishing turn very slowly so nothing from the last two years is featured, which is a shame—the short film as a medium is developing at an ever-increasing pace as the technology becomes more widely available. Which begs the question—why bother with the book? Looking at stills from films is never satisfactory and, while the text is informative, you would be hard-pushed to describe the book as being visually stunning. Instead of a book with a free DVD, why not make it a DVD with an accompanying brochure?

Grafik 115 Review 47

Identity Design Sourcebook
By Clay Andres, Catharine Fishel and Pat Matson Knapp
Published by Rockport (£27.50)

Hmmm. A graphic design book that uses barcodes as graphic devices in this day and age—and not in an ironic way (but then irony has never been big Stateside, I guess). Pardon me for being so picky, but surely if you're going to create a book showing great examples of work, shouldn't the way that the work is displayed be given a bit more thought? Actually, it doesn't really matter, since most of the work on show here is fairly pedestrian—at best. Maybe it's because corporate identities (like cheap French wine) rarely travel well, being as they are so intrinsic to the social and cultural context in which they are created. It's saying something when one of the most interesting pieces in here is the Wolff Olins' rebrand of Powwow. One for the bargain bin.

History of Modern Design
By David Raizman
Published by Laurence King (£24.95)

A scholarly look at product and graphic design since the Industrial Revolution, starting with the first textile factories in 1770, right the way through to Jonathan Ive's candy-coloured iMacs of the late Nineties. With nearly three hundred years' worth of modern design to choose from, this book—while not unattractive—is hardly the visual treat that it could be given the wealth of fantastic source material available. There are some great examples here, just not enough of them. Rather than working together, the images serve really to illustrate the text (large chunks of which will no doubt be forming part of many a student thesis in years to come). While the book features almost exclusively manufactured goods, it lets itself down right at the end, with a rather questionable section on craft and an extremely dodgy Fish Lamp courtesy of one Mr Frank Gehry.

Size Matters
By Lakshmi Bhaskaran
Published by RotoVision (£29.99)

This book covers everything from Holocaust memorials to phone books—anything in fact where designers are faced with huge amounts of copy or images. Some of the projects featured veer more towards the information-design side of things (bills for British Gas, signage for Bristol, Quickmap's Journey Planners), others towards the whimsical (Sagmeister's mammoth AIGA poster, Paula Scher's hand-painted maps). Whether there's really anything new to say about Harry Beck's Underground map is debatable and the least interesting stuff here (with a couple of exceptions such as the Book of Common Prayer) is the examples of book design, a discipline where organising large amounts of information is generally par for the course. It's always nice to see some of the more idiosyncratic examples, though, such as the Struktur calendar, Plumb Design's Visual Thesaurus and the classic Point It by Graf Editions—a multi-million-seller which really should have been awarded some kind of design effectiveness award by now...

Art Directors Annual 82
Published by RotoVision (£44.99)

This, for the uninitiated, is the annual tome published by the Art Directors' Club of New York showcasing the winning entries from its design awards. It's a bit like the D&AD Annual, but without the irritating yellow cover or Michael Johnson. Same cheesy pictures of judges, though. It's nicely produced, and there's some interesting work in here if you look closely enough. But like any awards scheme, it's only going to be as good as the stuff that's entered. Yup, in the words of the great, underrated Eamonn Holmes: "You've gotta be in it to win it," and not all the best stuff gets entered in the first place, let alone picked by the (sometimes) stingy judges. Mildly diverting.

REINVENTING GENRES

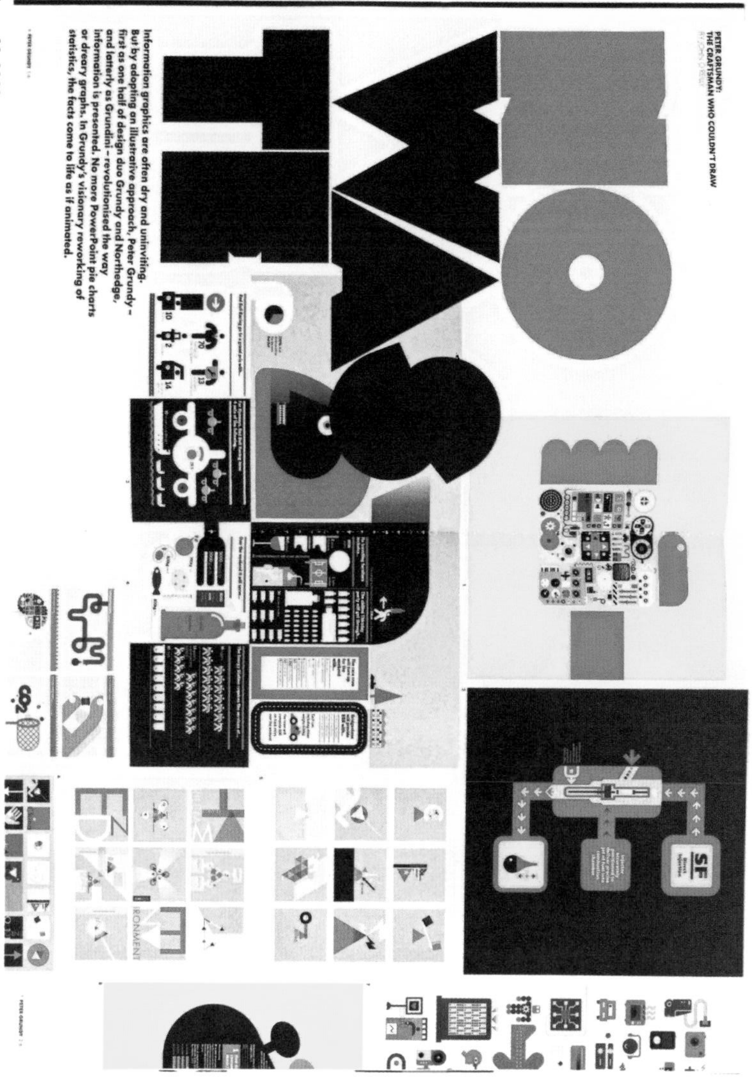

Issue 09, 2009

Issue 02, 2006

Varoom
UK (210 × 297mm, 8¼ × 11¾ inches)
A magazine about illustration will always have many reproductions in its pages. Non-Format developed a typically strong typographic approach that provided a very clear visual identity for the publication but was also abstract enough not to distract from the illustration work.
Editor *Adrian Shaughnessy*; Art direction *Non-Format*

OPPOSITE **Grafik**
UK (225 × 310mm, 9 × 12½ inches)
Design magazines present a particular problem to the designer: how to impose an identity without overwhelming the work you are presenting. *Grafik* worked with several art directors but always maintained a layered approach with images built into the page structure rather than carefully defined as objects in their own right.

TOP: *Issue 168, October 2009*
Editor *Caroline Roberts*; Art director *Matilda Saxow*

BOTTOM: *Issue 115, March 2004*
Editor *Caroline Roberts*; Art direction *Madethought*

Gratuitous Type

USA, Issue 2, March 2012 (190 × 253mm, 7½ × 10 inches)
This 'Pamphlet of Typographic Smut' relishes its obsession with letters and lettering, featuring work and practices that catch the eye of Brooklyn-based designer Schlenker.
Editor and art director *Elana Schlenker*

OPPOSITE **Eye**

UK (238 × 295mm, 9½ × 11¾ inches)
Graphic design review *Eye* has established a highly recognizable cover identity using overlaid and often abstracted details of work from within the issue.
Editor *John L Walters*; Art director *Simon Esterson*; Art editor *Jay Prynne*

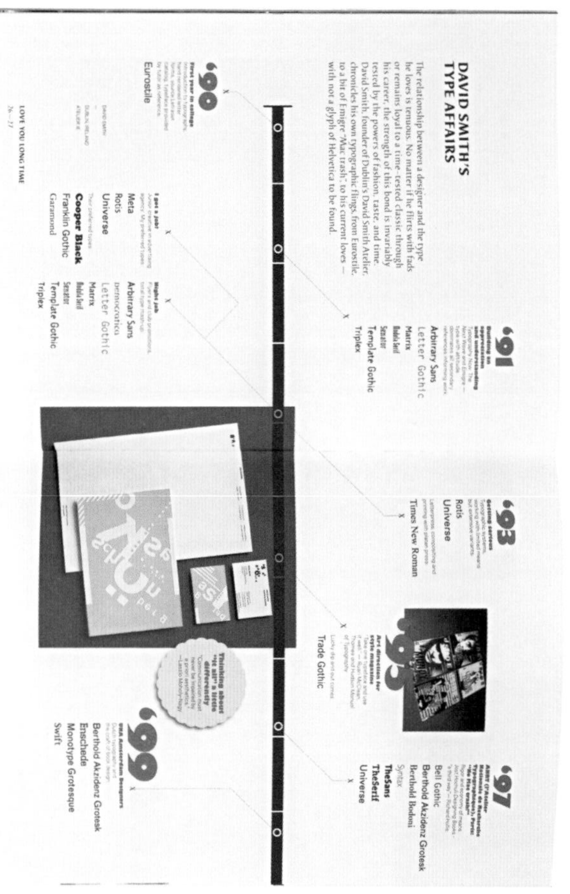

Issue 75, Spring 2010
Calligraphy (detail) *Niels Shoe Meulman* across an image of Anthony Burrill's notebooks

Issue 76, Summer 2010
Record sleeve for 'Blues by Basie' (detail) *Alex Steinweiss*

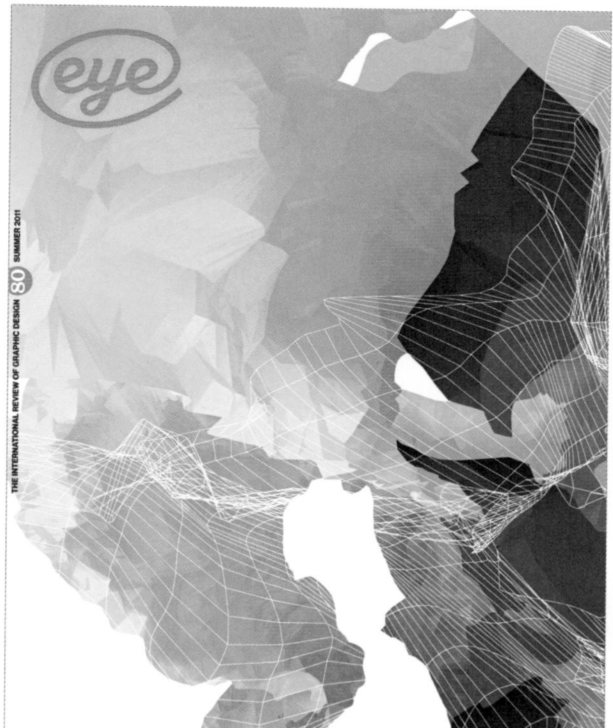

Issue 80, Summer 2011
Generative illustrations (detail and wireframe) *Field* for paper sample brochure *SEA*.

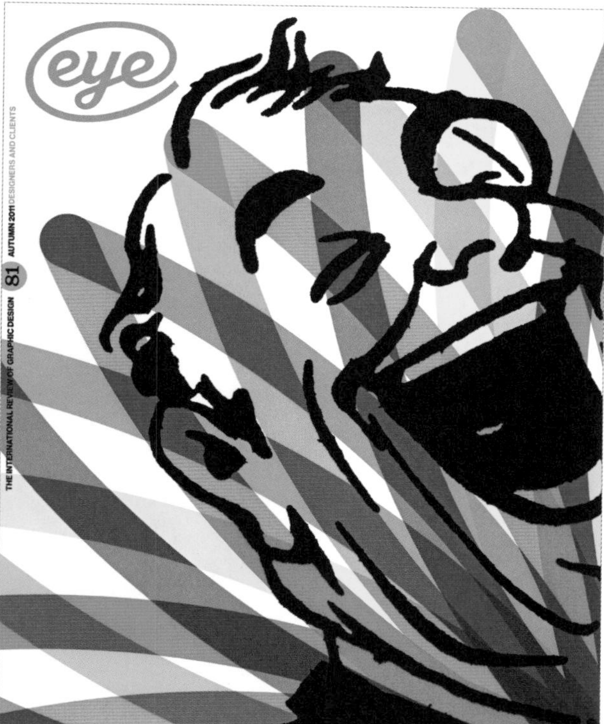

Issue 81, Autumn 2011
Illustration (detail) *Helmo* across 1990 D&AD Annual cover (detail) *John McConnell*

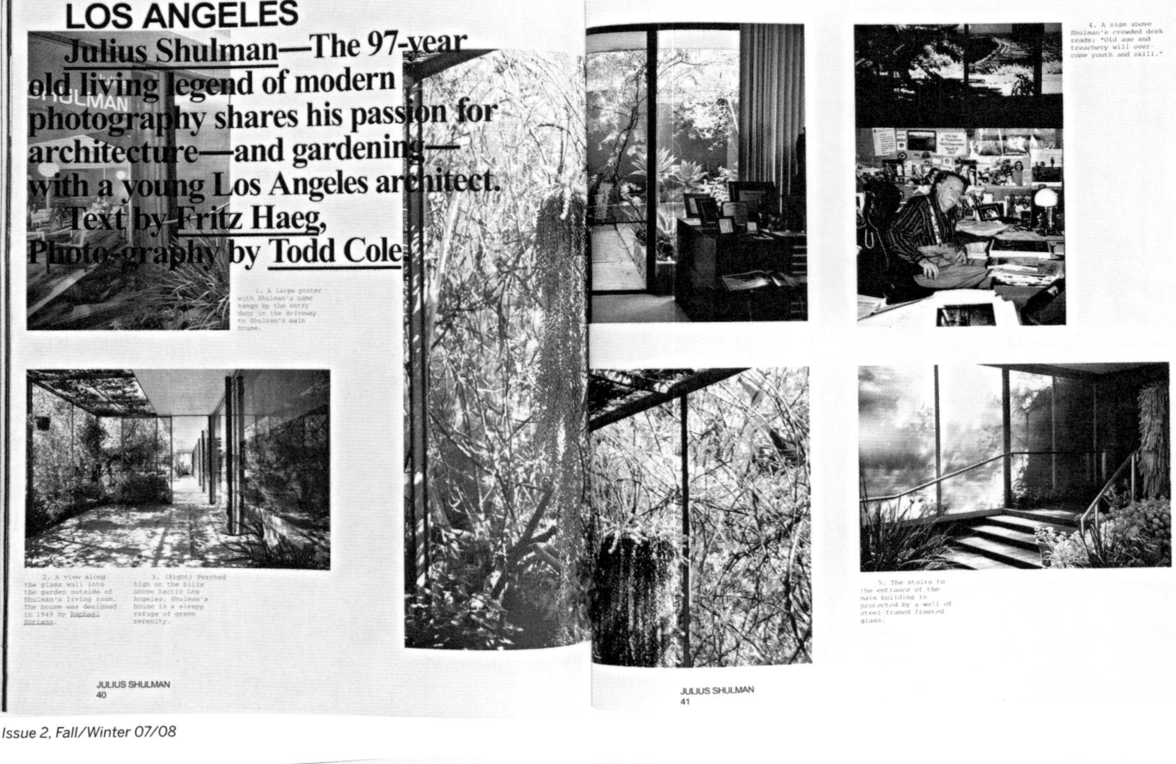

LOS ANGELES

Julius Shulman—The 97-year old living legend of modern photography shares his passion for architecture—and gardening—with a young Los Angeles architect. Text by Fritz Haeg, Photo-graphy by Todd Cole

1. A large poster with Shulman's name hangs by the entry door in the driveway to Shulman's main house.

2. A view along the glass wall into the garden outside of Shulman's living room. The house was designed in 1949 by Raphael Soriano.

3. (Right) Perched high on the hills above hectic Los Angeles. Shulman's house is a sleepy refuge of green serenity.

4. A sign above Shulman's crowded desk reads: "Old age and treachery will over-come youth and skill."

5. The stairs to the entrance of the main building is protected by a wall of steel-framed frosted glass.

JULIUS SHULMAN
40

JULIUS SHULMAN
41

Issue 2, Fall/Winter 07/08

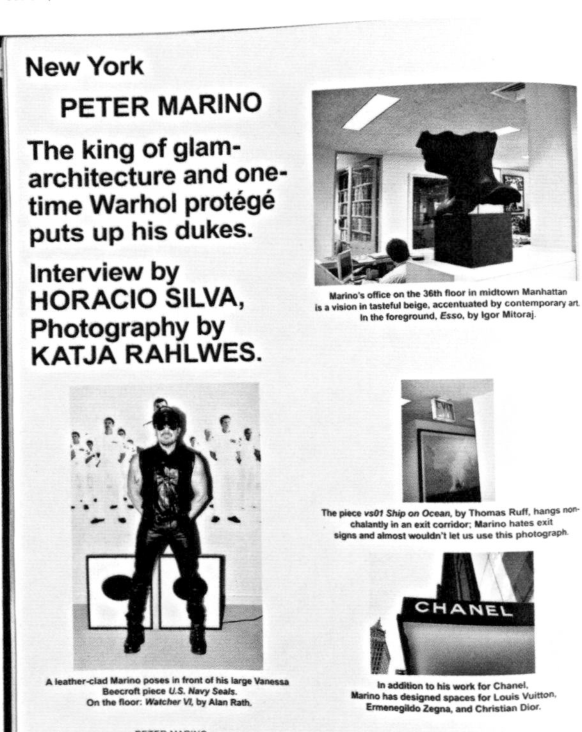

New York

PETER MARINO

The king of glam-architecture and one-time Warhol protégé puts up his dukes.

Interview by HORACIO SILVA, Photography by KATJA RAHLWES.

Marino's office on the 36th floor in midtown Manhattan is a vision in tasteful beige, accentuated by contemporary art. In the foreground, *Esso*, by Igor Mitoraj.

A leather-clad Marino poses in front of his large Vanessa Beecroft piece *U.S. Navy Seals*. On the floor: *Watcher VI*, by Alan Rath.

The piece *vs01 Ship on Ocean*, by Thomas Ruff, hangs non-chalantly in an exit corridor; Marino hates exit signs and almost wouldn't let us use this photograph.

In addition to his work for Chanel, Marino has designed spaces for Louis Vuitton, Ermenegildo Zegna, and Christian Dior.

PETER MARINO 22

Marino, standing in front of an LED-encrusted staircase of his own design, prepares for a cruise on his Triumph in the middle of the Chanel store on 57th Street.

Issue 5, Fall/Winter 08/09

Pin–Up

USA (233 × 284mm, 9¼ × 11¼ inches)

Turning away from the earnestness of most architecture magazines, *Pin–Up* celebrates the contemporary spirit of collaboration between architects, designers and artists. The bold contemporary design aesthetic imposes itself across the pages to hold together text and images about many disparate subjects – high and low culture, old and new, slick and rough.

Editor and creative director *Felix Burrichterz*

PIN–UP

Clémence Seilles, p. 77
"In Berlin you find a huge range of creators with many different ways of working."

Francis Kéré, p. 118
"I wanted to see how Berlin was built."

Magazine BERLIN **for**

SPECIAL

David Chipperfield, p. 24
"The city is coming to terms with its own identity, which I think is fascinating."

Jürgen Mayer H., p. 58
"Berlin is the producer, the lab, the studio — ideas get condensed somewhere else."

Architectural

Andro Wekua, p. 199
"I like that you can have lots of space and quiet here."

Entertainment **Issue 12**

Spring Summer 2012 **USD 15.00**

Issue 12, Spring/Summer 2012

Issue 1, June/July 2010

Issue 2, September/October 2010

Issue 5, March/April 2011

Issue 6, June/July 2011

Issue 7, September/October 2011

Issue 8, Winter 2011/12

Issue 9, March/April 2012

Issue 11, August/September 2012

Issue 12, October/November 2012

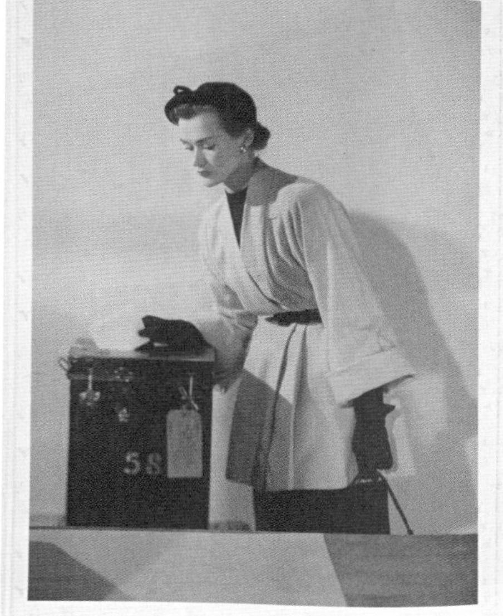

HOW WE GOT THE VOTE

bloomers, blackmail and ballots all played a part in australian women's suffrage. words georgia frances king

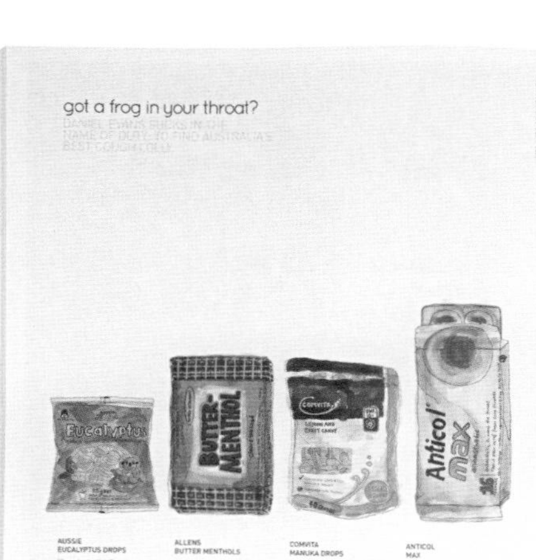

Frankie

Australia, Issue 48, July/August 2012 (210 × 274mm, 8¼ × 10¾ inches)

Launched by a pair of friends uninspired by the mainstream women's magazines, *Frankie* has set a warmer, more approachable agenda covering things they thought readers might enjoy: realistic fashion, art, design and travel. They have created their own world and aesthetic that succesfully engages a significant readership and has grown to include books, calendars and recently a men's magazine, *Smith Journal*.

Editor *Jo Walker*; Creative director *Lara Burke*

OPPOSITE **Oh Comely**

UK (210 × 274mm, 8¼ × 10¾ inches)

A magazine for women that seeks to inspire readers to be creative, with a warm, welcoming outlook summed up by these front cover designs. Each one features a different logo hand-drawn by the editor's mother.

Editor-in-chief *Des Tan*; Art directors *Rosanna Durham and Dani Lurie*

Manzine
UK/Germany, Issue 5, Second half, 2011 (210 × 297mm, 8¼ × 11¾ inches)
Editor *Kevin Braddock*; Creative director *Warren Jackson*

OPPOSITE **Port**
UK (230 × 290mm, 9 × 11½ inches)
Editor *Dan Crowe*; Creative directors *Kuchar Swara and Matt Willey*

Two very different approaches to reinventing the men's magazine. *Manzine* applies a sureal humour to the genre, using the creative team's direct experience of working for mainstream titles to parody magazines of all types verbally and visually. Design and production standards are deliberately anti-glossy. *Port* takes a more serious approach, looking back to the early years of men's magazines to produce a highly art-directed and designed publication based on commissioning of high-quality writing, photography and illustration

MORE MANZINE p131
MORE PORT p142

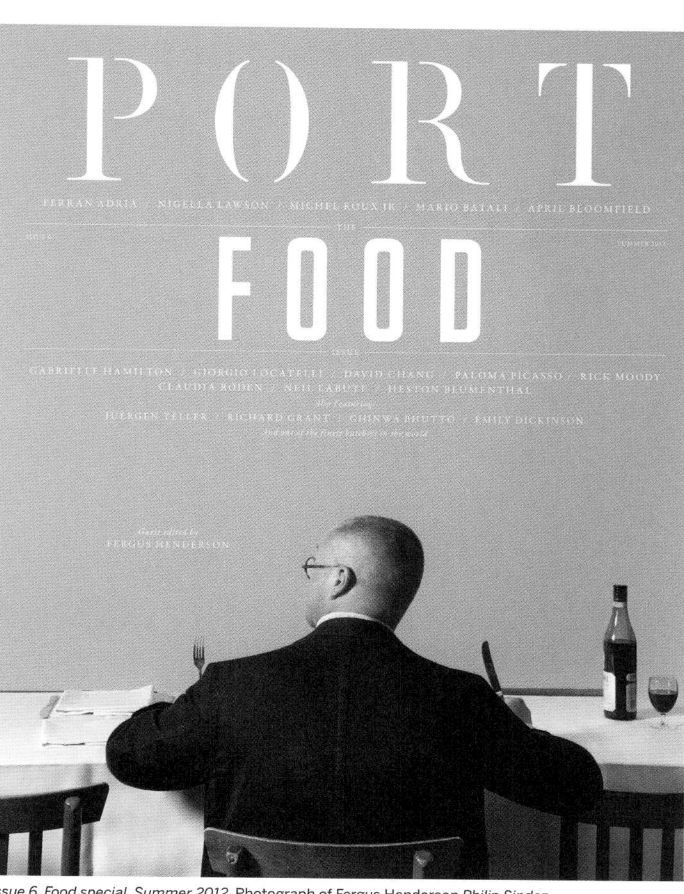

Issue 6, Food special, Summer 2012. Photograph of Fergus Henderson *Philip Sinden*

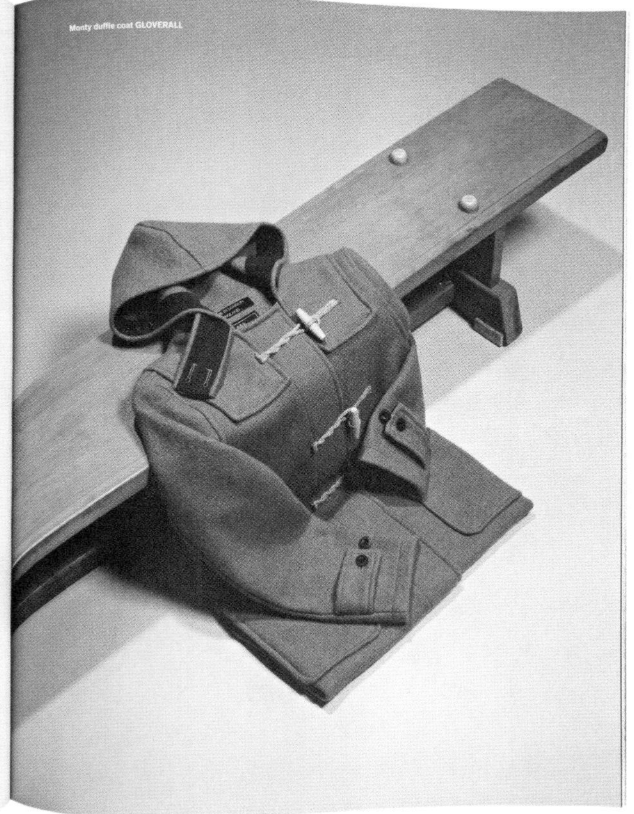

Observations
Margaret Howell

Duffle Coat

The clothing designer Margaret Howell pays homage to a classic British coat that's popular with schoolgirls and Naval officers alike

No one knows for sure who invented the duffle coat.

Like Ironbridge, the Anglepoise lamp and the pylons of the UK National Grid, its success as a design icon depends as much on what is left out as on what is included. Like them it is inspired in its use of materials, it is minimal, and it evolved from a practical need.

In this case the need was for an overcoat in the truest sense of the word: protecting British Navy uniforms against the elements. Two large patch pockets held equipment, toggles could be fastened by gloved hands, oversized hoods covered peaked caps and dense wool resisted freezing spray.

It's ironic that such a tough, functional garment should still be so appealing, and to women as well as to men. My first duffle coat covered my school uniform on wintery mornings, withstanding snowball fights and cold waits at bus stops. Even then I loved the windproof warmth, the protective hood, the tactile wooden toggles. I still do, but it's become more than that: I love the simplicity, and I love the adaptability.

The duffle coat's exact origin might be unknown – but whoever came up with it came up with a classic.

70

Monty duffle coat GLOVERALL

STYLE BRIEFING . PHOTOGRAPHY THOMAS BROWN

Issue 1, Spring 2011. Photograph *Thomas Brown*

FANTASTIC MAN

€7.50 / £5.00 / $10.95

Furthermore in this eleventh issue of THE GENTLEMAN'S STYLE JOURNAL for Spring and Summer 2010... The esteemed New York journalist Mr. BOB COLACELLO, the HOT CHIP singer Mr. ALEXIS TAYLOR, the world-famous icon of masculinity FABIO, plus so much more to enjoy while travelling or at home in the garden.

Issue 11, Spring/Summer 2010

FANTASTIC MAN

PROFILE

Mr.
McGREGOR

The handsome actor Mr. EWAN McGREGOR and his new wave of fantastic films...

Text .... Paul Flynn
Photography .... Alasdair McLellan
Styling .... Olivier Rizzo

Issue 10, Autumn/Winter 2009

Fantastic Man
The Netherlands (235 × 300mm, 9¼ × 12 inches)
From its first issue this magazine had a very clear confidence in its tone and direction, combining high-quality commissioned content with an assured sense of ironic respect for its subjects.
Editor *Gert Jonkers*; Art director *Jop van Bennekom*

An early contender for the name was *Sexy Man*, but they 'decided that was exactly what we didn't want ... to sexualize men. That's what's wrong with so many men's magazines.'

JOP VAN BENNEKOM
CO-EDITOR
FANTASTIC MAN

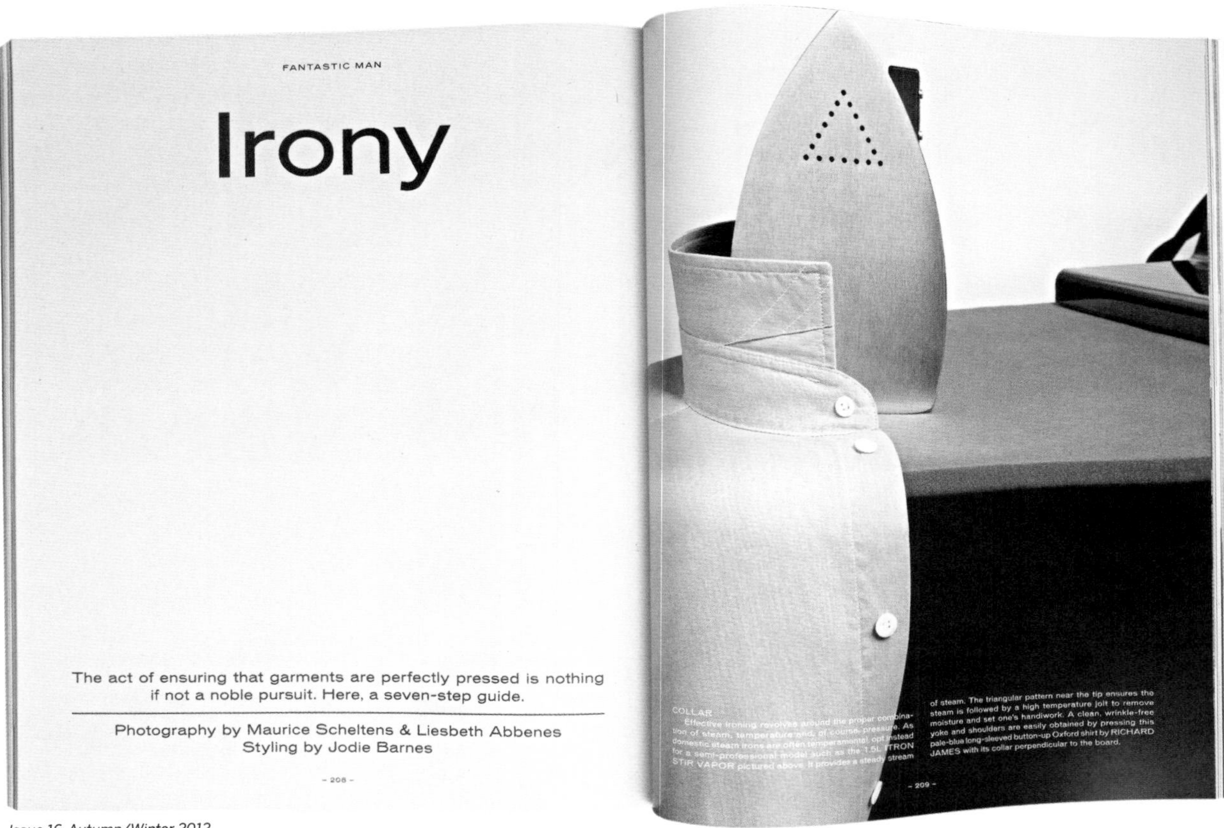
FANTASTIC MAN

Irony

The act of ensuring that garments are perfectly pressed is nothing if not a noble pursuit. Here, a seven-step guide.

Photography by Maurice Scheltens & Liesbeth Abbenes
Styling by Jodie Barnes

- 208 -

COLLAR
Effective ironing revolves around the proper combination of steam, temperature and, of course, pressure. As domestic steam irons are often temperamental, opt instead for a semi-professional model such as the 1.5L ITRON STIR VAPOR pictured above. It provides a steady stream of steam. The triangular pattern near the tip ensures the steam is followed by a high temperature jolt to remove moisture and set one's handiwork. A clean, wrinkle-free yoke and shoulders are easily obtained by pressing this pale-blue long-sleeved button-up Oxford shirt by RICHARD JAMES with its collar perpendicular to the board.

- 209 -

Issue 16, Autumn/Winter 2012

REINVENTING GENRES

Fantastic Man (The Netherlands)

CO-EDITOR JOP VAN BENNEKOM

Rarely does a new magazine arrive with such a fully formed visual and linguistic character as when *Fantastic Man* first appeared in 2005. With its tongue firmly in cheek, it set out to reinvent the men's fashion magazine and quickly established itself as an influential part of the fashion world.

Founders Jop van Bennekom and Gert Jonkers had already collaborated for several years on *Butt* magazine (see page 086), and before that van Bennekom had created and self-published the experimental *Re-Magazine*. *Re-* started life as a graduate project examining the minutiae of everyday life via the language of magazines. Regular components – headlines, lists, photo shoots – were used to make pages that defied definition, as each issue adapted to a different theme. Was it serious? Ironic? By turns fascinating and frustrating, *Re-* set the visual and editorial tone for van Bennekom's future projects.

Re- led to a design job at *Blvd* magazine, where he met Jonkers and the two began to develop thoughts for a 'reality' gay porn magazine. *Butt* set out to redefine the gay market, featuring real people in their day-to-day lives rather than glossy models in studios. Printed on uncoated pink paper in a small format, it helped redefine independent publishing in a broader sense, showing what was possible through careful development and planning. It was a highly coherent piece of editorial invention that reached beyond its natural constituency and appealed to people simply interested in other people.

Graphically there were distinct similarities with *Re-* and the soon-to-follow *Fantastic Man*. Control and when to lose it are the central tenets. All three magazines use a tight grid system, highlighted by the use of printed rules and an almost exclusively monochrome colour palette applied to a limited set of typefaces. Column rules in *Butt* would appear across photos and texts as one part of this rigid design scheme clashed with another. This ability to set tight guidelines and then knowingly break them reflects the wit of the content.

The links between the highly developed design language and the written content are vital, and start with the magazine names. The name *Butt* perfectly reflects the magazine's attitude towards its subject matter. Direct, honest and no-nonsense, it has a knowing irony to it too. Who would ever call a magazine *Butt*?

A similar irony was to be a cornerstone of *Fantastic Man*. 'We felt we needed to expand our world and take on a magazine that wasn't a gay project,' explains van Bennekom. 'We thought we should try to make a men's fashion magazine on our own terms.' They spent a year developing the first issue and working through various names for the new project. An early contender was *Sexy Man*, but they 'decided that was exactly what we didn't want ... to sexualize men. That's what's wrong with so many men's magazines.'

The proposition for the magazine can be traced directly back to *Butt*, though – real people wearing their own clothes. The definition of 'real' can be tested here, as the majority of people featured are celebrated in one way or another for what they do, but they're not the usual fashion models. Van Bennekom: 'We just wanted to feature men we thought were fantastic. Of course the name *Fantastic Man* is ridiculous, but we couldn't get it out of our heads. We felt it was a good title.'

The name reflects the slightly outsider nature of the magazine, which retains the sense of formal experimentation

THE
MODERNIST

PHOTOGRAPHED AT THE RIETVELD SCHRODER HOUSE IN UTRECHT, THE NETHERLANDS

MR. CROUWEL — THE GRAND MASTER OF 60s MODERNIST DESIGN IS HOLLAND'S ONE AND ONLY GENTLEMAN...

PHOTOGRAPHY—VIVIANE SASSEN · STYLIST—JOFF
TEXT—EMILY KING

Issue 3, Spring/Summer 2006

first seen in *Re-*, albeit adapted to a more commercial arena. Fashion magazines are almost by definition highly serious enterprises, yet *Fantastic Man* gently mocks the often pompous nature of the genre by appearing to question it. From the magazine's name to the section titles, headlines and standfirsts, the language used is so unusually respectful it can be seen as parody. Every interviewee is referred to by their surname and with the prefix 'Mr' (there aren't any Mrs). Most are 'Legendary' or 'Amazing'. Footnotes provide intricate background details to the main text, and the 'Recommendations' section veers from picnic blankets to the colour green, via living without ambition and fluffy towels. It's serious, but funny.

The magazine is produced partly in Amsterdam and partly in London, and Van Bennekom sees elements of both cities in his magazine: 'The way it's set up is super-Dutch – its attention to detail and the super-straightforwardness of it. And it has a Dutch humour, but I don't think it looks that Dutch. The typefaces I use are British – Gill Sans and Times New Roman.'

After 16 issues, its success is such that it is inevitably being copied. Is that frustrating? 'A text-only black-and-white page in a magazine was a no-go five years ago, and that's changed quite a bit now, but there's a lot that can't be copied. Most of our time goes into choosing the subjects, doing research, discussing the angle of a piece. We concentrate on getting really good content.'

The choice of cover subjects has been a clever mix of the cool and the popular. For issue one they were able to leverage their *Butt* contacts to get actor Rupert Everett. By issue 13 David Beckham was asking to be the cover star. 'We thought about it for a week and then realized we should just do it. I'm not a big fan but I find him very interesting as an icon,' says Van Bennekom, who accepts that such a famous figure might alienate the core reader. 'We needed to come up with a pretty obscure personality for the next cover.' Have they ever said no to anyone? 'We've said no to quite a few famous men – Kanye West for example. You need a good reason for wanting to feature someone, and I think a good reason is because you think they're fantastic.'

Van Bennekom and Jonkers are having their cake and eating it – you can read *Fantastic Man* as a definitive fashion bible or as a clever critique of definitive fashion bibles. Either way, you get a good-looking, well-produced and entertaining magazine.

Their latest challenge is a women's fashion magazine. *The Gentlewoman* launched in 2010, and has had a bumpier ride than its brother title as it seeks to apply a similar aesthetic and wit to the far more competitive women's market. Some thought the launch issue too masculine – criticism van Bennekom, Jonkers and editor Penny Martin have taken on board. 'With the first issue we were really trying to figure out how much fashion should there be? Can we feature people we love without being too camp?' says van Bennekom, while Martin asserts she wanted the first issue to be 'quite dry and then insert sexuality, sensuality and fun later. Looking back you can see it was a pilot issue.'

They've softened their approach slightly now, the uncompromisingly different early front covers replaced by the warmer presences of singer Adele, supermodel Christy Turlington and octogenarian actress Angela Lansbury. Issue by issue, you sense the confidence rising in the pages, and there's no reason to think the team can't do as much for the women's market as it has done for the men's.

Fantastic Man
The tight, monochrome design lets the knowing editorial attitude jump off the page. The magazine often uses self-referencing headlines.

FANTASTIC
MAN

MR. MALC

McLAREN

INTERVIEW JOP VAN BENNEKOM & GERT JONKERS
PORTRAIT BY SLAVICA ZIENER

THE QUINTESSENTIA
PARIS MIGHT TAKE
AND MILAN BY STO
BLOODY INTERESTI

— 34 —

COLM

ENGLISHMAN IN
LLYWOOD, BERLIN
M WITH SOME
NEW PROJECTS...

– 35 –

Fantastic Man
Issue 1, Spring/Summer 2005
A defining example from the launch issue of the written and visual language used to flatter its subjects.

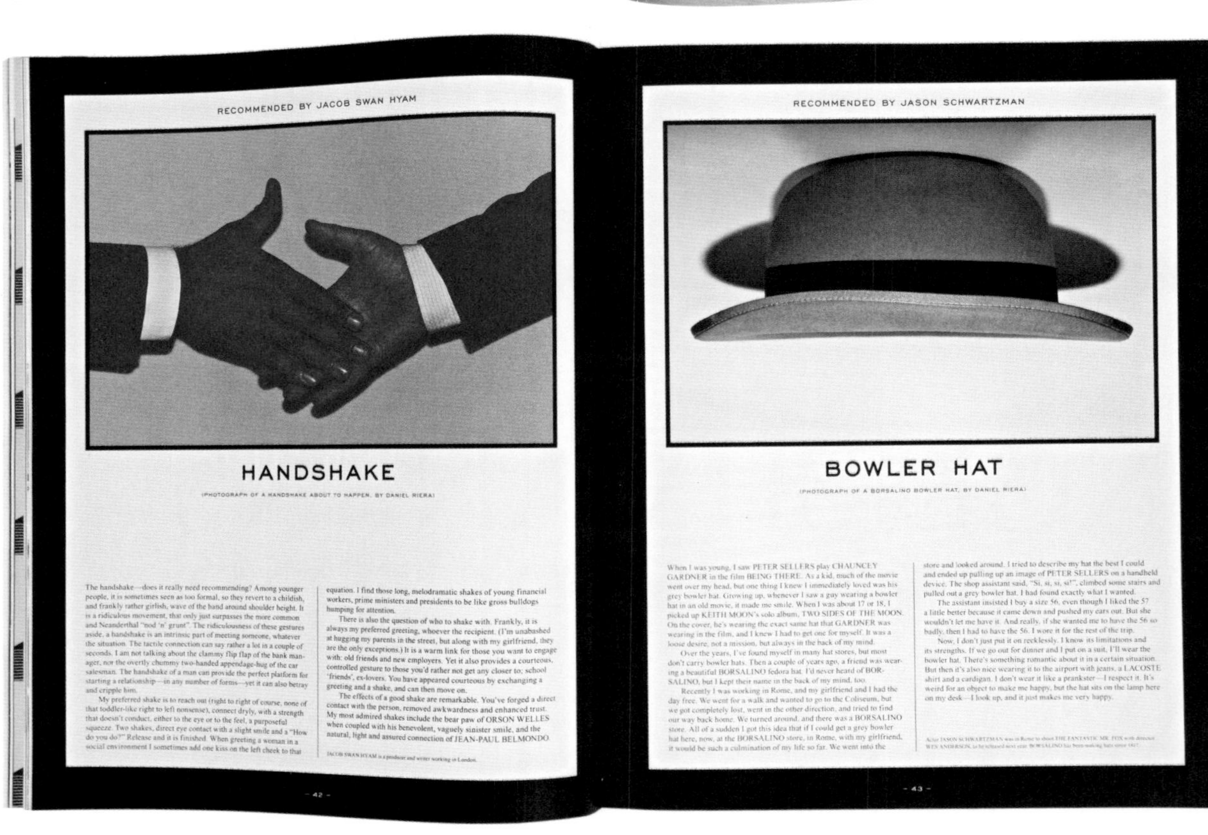

Fantastic Man

TOP: *Issue 11, Spring/Summer 2010*
A summer fashion shoot featuring the season's nude colours, set on a Spanish nudist beach. Photography *Benjamin Alexander Huseby*

BOTTOM: *Issue 8, Autumn/Winter 2008*
Examples of the magazine's 'Recommendations': each is accompanied by a stylized image and several hundred words of detailed justification.

the gentlewoman

Fabulous women's magazine, issue n° 3
Spring and Summer 2011

9 771879 869005 01

UK £5.00

A new voice

USA $10.95

The Gentlewoman
The Netherlands. Issue 3, Spring/Summer 2011 (235 × 300mm, 9¼ × 12 inches)
The name for the sister title to *Fantastic Man* was taken from a seventeenth-century British publication.
Editor *Penny Martin*; Creative director *Jop van Bennekom*; Photograph *Alasdair McLellan*

The Gentlewoman

The magazine combines profiles of strong role models with humorous fashion stories to achieve the same combination of respect and wit as *Fantastic Man*.

TOP: *Issue 1, Spring/Summer 2010*
A fashion story featuring different-sized models.
Photography *Daniel Riera*

BOTTOM: *Issue 5, Spring/Summer 2012*
Christy Turlington interview, featuring a handwritten headline. The magazine regularly uses handwriting to soften the monochrome page designs.
Portrait *Inez & Vinoodh*

OPPOSITE TOP: *Issue 5, Spring/Summer 2012*
Leading photography agents are profiled while at the petrol station filling their cars, permitting puns about 'well-oiled machines'.
Photography *Daniel Riera*

BOTTOM: *Issue 5, Spring/Summer 2012*
Maria Sharapova interview and on-court fashion shoot.
Photography *Zoë Ghertner*

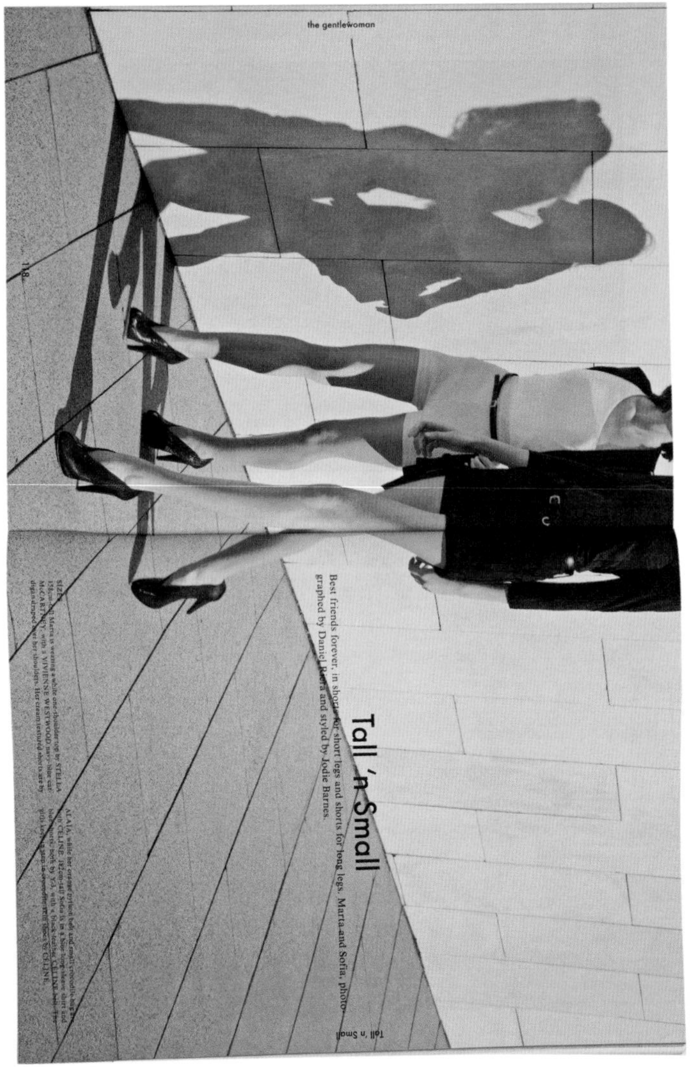

the gentlewoman

Tall 'n Small

Best friends forever, in shorts for short legs and shorts for long legs. Marta and Sofia, photographed by Daniel Riera and styled by Jodie Barnes.

The campaigning supermodel who everybody loves
Christy Turlington
Christy
Portraits
by
Inez & Vinoodh
Styling
by
Carlyne Cerf de Dudzeele
Text
by
Lynn Yaeger
176
177

Ayesha

Art Partner

The business of fashion photography is a well-oiled machine, and these are the powerful women who negotiate the deals and keep the engine humming. Six London agents make a brief pit stop to refill. Photography by Daniel Riera, styling by Jonathan Kaye.

Power Pump

Over in London for the day from Art Partner's Paris office, British-born Ayesha Arefin makes the most of having a car. "I'd never drive in Paris," she says. "It's crazy – no lanes, weird rules about turning right, even when it's a red light. So I cycle. But I'd never do that in London – it's too big." Here, Ayesha is taking full advantage of a splendid Mercedes-Benz SLS AMG Gullwing. Its flip-up doors are dramatic yet practical, particularly if one is inclined towards large headwear or big hairstyles.

Ayesha wears her own white silk CÉLINE shirt and jeans from TOPSHOP.

144

145

The Competitor

Russian tennis star Maria Sharapova is the glamorous sportswoman who wins her tournaments on mental strength as much as an astonishing long-armed reach, then gets the hell out of the locker room to fight another day. She'd rather go home and play Scrabble with her 6-foot-7 basketball-player boyfriend than make friends with her on-court foe. Now, the world's highest-earning female athlete is setting her sights on the Wimbledon title, which she aims to win for the second time.

Photography by Zoë Ghertner, styling by Lester Garcia
Text by Guy Adams

206

The amazing $25-million tennis star
Maria Sharapova

207

REINVENTING
GENRES

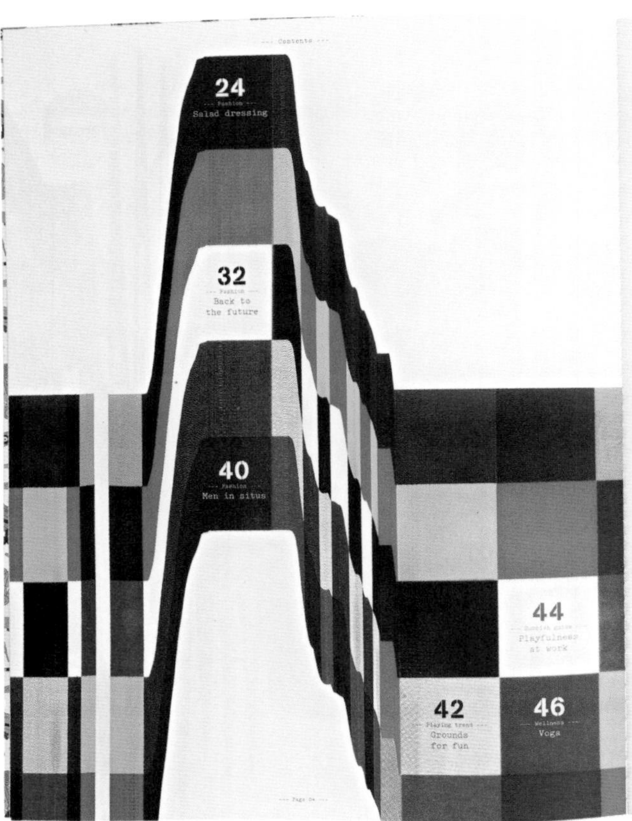

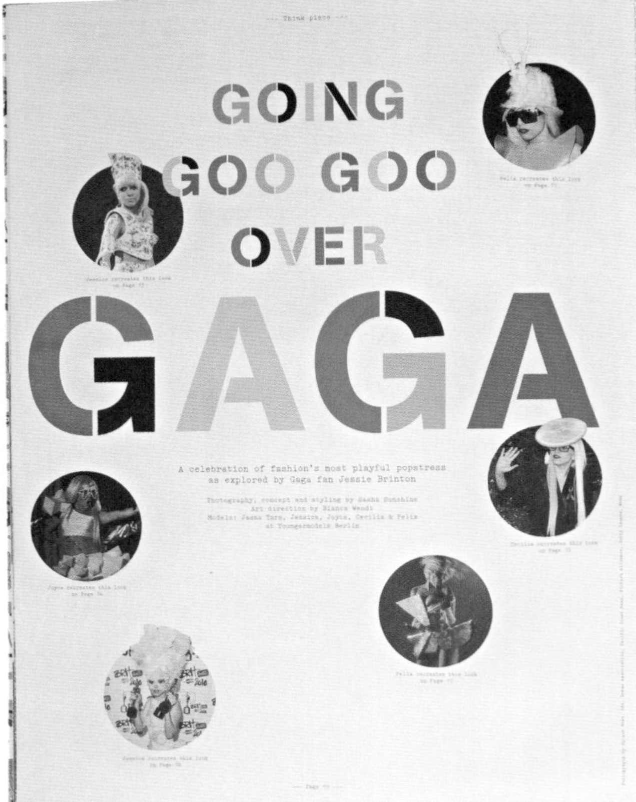

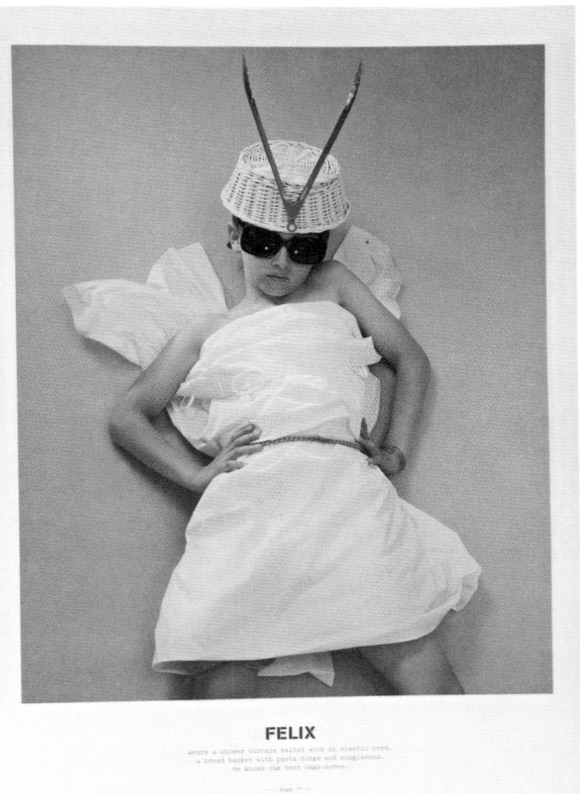

REINVENTING GENRES

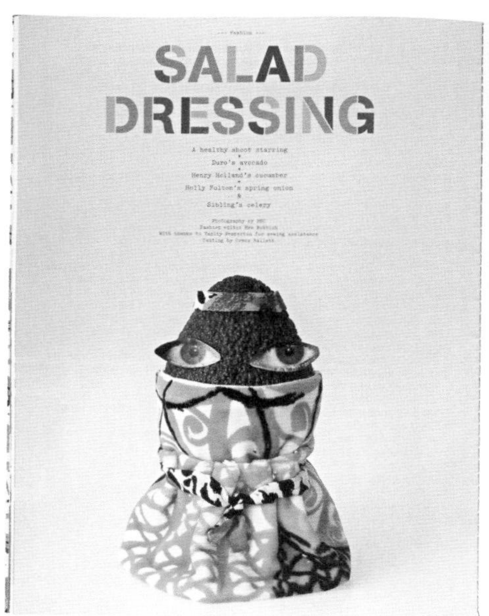

SALAD
DRESSING
A healthy shoot starring
Duro's avocado
Henry Holland's cucumber
Holly Fulton's spring onion
&
Sibling's celery

Rubbish

UK, Issue 2.5, December 2010 (300 × 395mm, 12 × 15¾ inches)

Acknowledging in its editor's letter that fashion is often 'snooty and elitist', this occasional magazine uses its fashion connections to poke fun at its subject, with contributors often taking part under pseudonyms. The issue number is a typical example of its gently iconoclastic attitude.
Editor *Jenny Dyson*; Art director *Bianca Wendt*

Fashion designers dress vegetables (each credited as 'model'), from top:
Duro Oluwo, Henry Holland, Holly Fulton.
Photography *PSC*

OPPOSITE TOP: A pastiche set of news stories set the tone with their large drop capitals.

BOTTOM: Children recreate some of Lady Gaga's signature fashion statements.
Photography *Sasha Sunshine*

DESIGN × CONTENT

The raw material from which magazines are made is content – words and images. Responsibility for these lies traditionally with different parts of the creative team – the words with the editor, images with the art director. Once the elements are ready to be assembled on a page, a process of consultation and compromise between these two principals (and their teams) ensues before a finished layout is signed off.

Design has two crucial and interrelated roles to play in the production of that layout. The first and most basic expectation of design is that it presents the content in a clear and legible manner, just as the editor must ensure the words are factually and grammatically correct. Design should help the reader, and rules have developed over many years to achieve this goal. Early navigational devices were borrowed from books – contents lists and page numbers, for instance – while others have developed unique to the format, such as turn arrows at the bottom of pages and end marks at the end of long articles.

Even the most pared-back example of magazine design is more complicated than most books because the content is so varied. Section headings announce different parts of the magazine, some of which will have multiple stories on a single page, while features may last for long runs of pages. In the case of American magazines, a long feature may be split into two, with a jump to a more text-heavy layout at the back of the magazine. The pace and variety of the layout from page to page needs consideration to encourage movement through the pages and provide highs and lows of visual intensity. Along the way, running heads, usually at the top of the page, and keep the reader informed.

On each of those individual pages a hierarchy of information exists. The headline attracts the reader's attention, the sell or deck explains more and the text carries the story. This will be presented in columns at a size and line length calculated to be easily legible, with devices such as drop capitals, subheads and pull quotes added to break the visual uniformity of the page and provide entry points for the reader to engage, or remain engaged, with the story. There will also be images – often the first element to catch the reader's eye – along with associated captions, diagrams, sidebars and authors' credits.

Such conventions are just the beginning of the design process. If there were an agreed perfect way to design a layout, each page of every magazine would be identical. But magazines aspire to have their own unique character, and to help achieve this the designer must balance the need to help the reader with the choices of scale, colour and relationship between elements that provide the magazine's personality. This is part of what defines a publication as a magazine rather than a book, and today this process has been extended by computerization, bringing almost limitless options to the computer desktop. On one machine we can design typography, edit photography, create illustrations and combine all the resulting files into a single layout.

But it doesn't matter how stunning the designs are if they don't reflect the tone of the written content. This is where the relationship between editor and art director is an ever more vital one. It has always been the case that a good editor must have a working knowledge of design and the art director must understand writing, but today this is truer than ever. The two must work together to create a synthesis of design and content that adds up to more than the sum of its parts – they must collaborate as visual journalists.

It is no longer enough merely to pay lip service to this long-discussed idea, as all the interviewees in the following section of this book emphasize. In a world full of easily accessible content, one of the virtues of printed magazines is their ability to combine multiple story-telling methods – text, photography, infographics and illustration – to create strong narratives with distinct character. Editors Adam Moss and Josh Tylangiel each point out that to achieve this, written content needs to adapt to design as much as design does to the words.

Moss's relaunch of *New York* (USA) magazine continues to be a defining project of the recent era, but for several years in the mid-noughties the US edition of *Wired* magazine held a similar position. Overseen by creative director Scott Dadich, the magazine established a hi-tech graphic language that reflected its content while bringing to visual life what might otherwise be quite dry science and technology content. 'I built the design on the simplest of building blocks, the pixel. Everything was related to the square: the grid, the slab serifs in the "Test" section were squares, and everything beyond that had some relationship to the Golden Mean or the Pythogorean theorem,' explains Dadich. 'We built the pages using math and science.'

He uses an apposite analogy to describe his revamp of the magazine. 'The new iMac had just come out at the time of my interview for the job at *Wired*, and I compared the original *Wired* to the Blueberry iMac. It was breakout, it was something the world had never seen before, it was boundary breaking. And yet Apple had gone and done this next thing that was even more of its time, sleeker and more modern. I said I wanted to perform the same moves on the magazine, make it much more about what's on the screen than the box it's put in.'

Dadich was lucky to be working with another editor, Chris Anderson, who sees the edit–design relationship as a partnership. In his current role as Vice-President of Editorial Platforms and Design at Condé Nast, Dadich works with many editors. 'Being in this position now, where I get to have a front-row seat to some of the greatest magazines in the world, I can see there are two classes of editor. There are clearly those that get it and those that fight it. It's partly generational, but it also depends on the kind of content they're working with. There's no hard and fast rule how and why.'

New York (USA) and *Bloomberg Businessweek* (USA) have both made a speciality of applying monthly design standards to a weekly production routine, and use intelligent combinations of templated regular pages and bespoke feature designs to achieve this. They share a love of devices and diagrams – details that can be added as a second layer to bring visual variety to otherwise tightly structured pages.

Such work relies on modern design software to achieve the detailing and quality of typography and layouts. But some magazines react against the possibilities provided by the software. London-based creative magazine *Marmalade* (UK) refused to use the usual layout software. Instead they created pages as physical tableaux, complete with headlines, text and imagery, to be photographed and printed as single images. This attempt to circumvent software was visually effective, despite the irony that the final photographs had to be laid out as pages using the very software the magazine sought to avoid.

More recently, culture magazine *032c* (Germany) has experimented with definitions of what is ugly and beautiful, deliberately subverting ideas of 'good' design to reflect the edgy nature of the written content. Such an experiment could only be successful given the shared vision of editor and designer.

In all these cases it can be argued that the design has *become* content.

Design also informs and directs the physical nature of a magazine. In part a response to the challenge of the Internet, publishers have looked to special printing finishes to emphasize their engagement with multiple senses (touch and smell, as well as sight) and exaggerate their physical presence. *Wallpaper** (UK) has made a speciality of this, inviting guest creatives to contribute ideas – such as when Zaha Hadid created laser-cut paper sculptures based on one of her building designs. *Amelia's Magazine* (UK) used the same laser technique to execute Rob Ryan's intricate cover design.

Other magazines use special fluorescent and metallic inks to help their covers demand the attention of readers. For smaller print runs, foil blocking can add drama to a cover. British *Harper's Bazaar* went further, embellishing its logo with Swarovski crystals for a limited-edition special cover.

Magazines also develop new ideas from their production processes. It has long been possible for publishers to vary the front cover content of different editions of their magazines. *UK Elle* is one of several magazines that has adopted a clever strategy to make their subscriber issues special and therefore more desirable. Every month they now produce entirely different front-cover designs for their newsstand and subscriber issues. With no need to sell the content to the subscriber, their covers can be more creative rather than commercial.

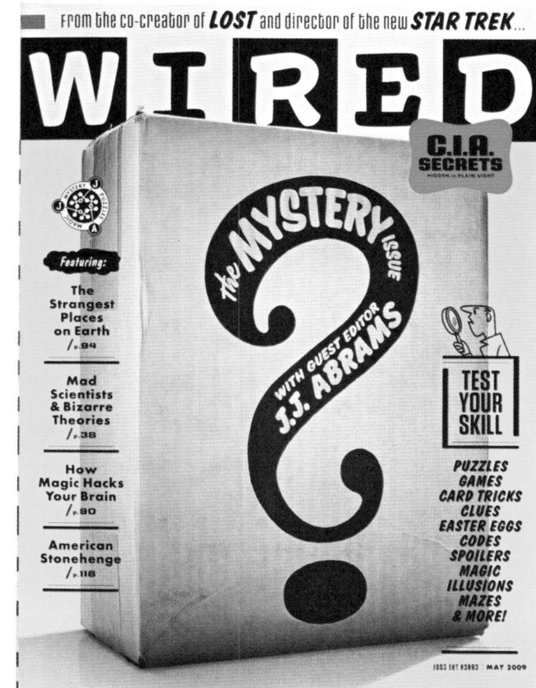

Wired
USA, May 2009 (203 × 276mm, 8 × 11 inches)
This special 'mystery' issue was guest-edited by film/TV writer J.J. Abrams, who worked closely with creative director Dadich to redesign the magazine using visual puzzles, optical illusions and 1950s-style typography. Even the logo was adapted for the occasion. Editor-in-chief *Chris Anderson*; Creative director *Scott Dadich*

Surreal Estate

Turning a Manhattan apartment into a puzzle palace.

The first hint that something was up came in a letter stamped LOST POST. It was addressed to the family of six who had recently moved into the sprawling Fifth Avenue apartment—and was apparently written by a former occupant who had died decades earlier. Inside the envelope was a poem full of riddles, the solutions to which were all around them: The home was filled with puzzles that had been covertly installed during an extensive renovation. ¶ The letter led the family down a rabbit hole of hidden keys, secret compartments, and glowing boxes. Today, more than three years after they settled into their magic kingdom, they still haven't solved everything—even with the book of clues that architectural designer Eric Clough planted in a wall to guide them. ¶ The elaborate project started with a casual aside. "Can we do something for the kids?" Clough asked his client, the CEO of a private equity firm, when he began work on the $1 million–plus job. Nothing complicated at first, just a few hidden lines of verse. But soon the carpenters were carving ciphers into radiator covers and adding secret compartments to the credenza. "I kept sneaking back into the apartment and hiding a few more clues," Clough says. ¶ Even after the family decodes the last brainteaser, the game won't really be over: Someday the special keys for the secret compartments will be lost. The veneer will begin to warp. Someone new will move in, and they'll be enthralled by the enigmas around them. "Then," Clough says, "they'll find these clues in the archives of WIRED." —ANDREW BLUM

The apartment was once part of a 54-room penthouse atop this 1925 building on New York's Upper East Side (1). In 2005, an architectural designer retrofitted it with a treasure trove of puzzles and mysteries, unbeknownst to the new residents. Encrypted verses were carved into radiator covers (2) and elaborate Rubik's Cube–like toys (3) were hidden in a secret cabinet.

The apartment's elegance (4) belies its cunning accoutrements. A cherry tree mural in the kids' bedroom (5) doubles as a map of Central Park. Starburst chandeliers (6) figure in a riddle on Galileo. A Japanese wood puzzle (7), when assembled, becomes the key to unlock a hidden compartment. A poem written by the father (8) is revealed when panels are released by a special magnet.

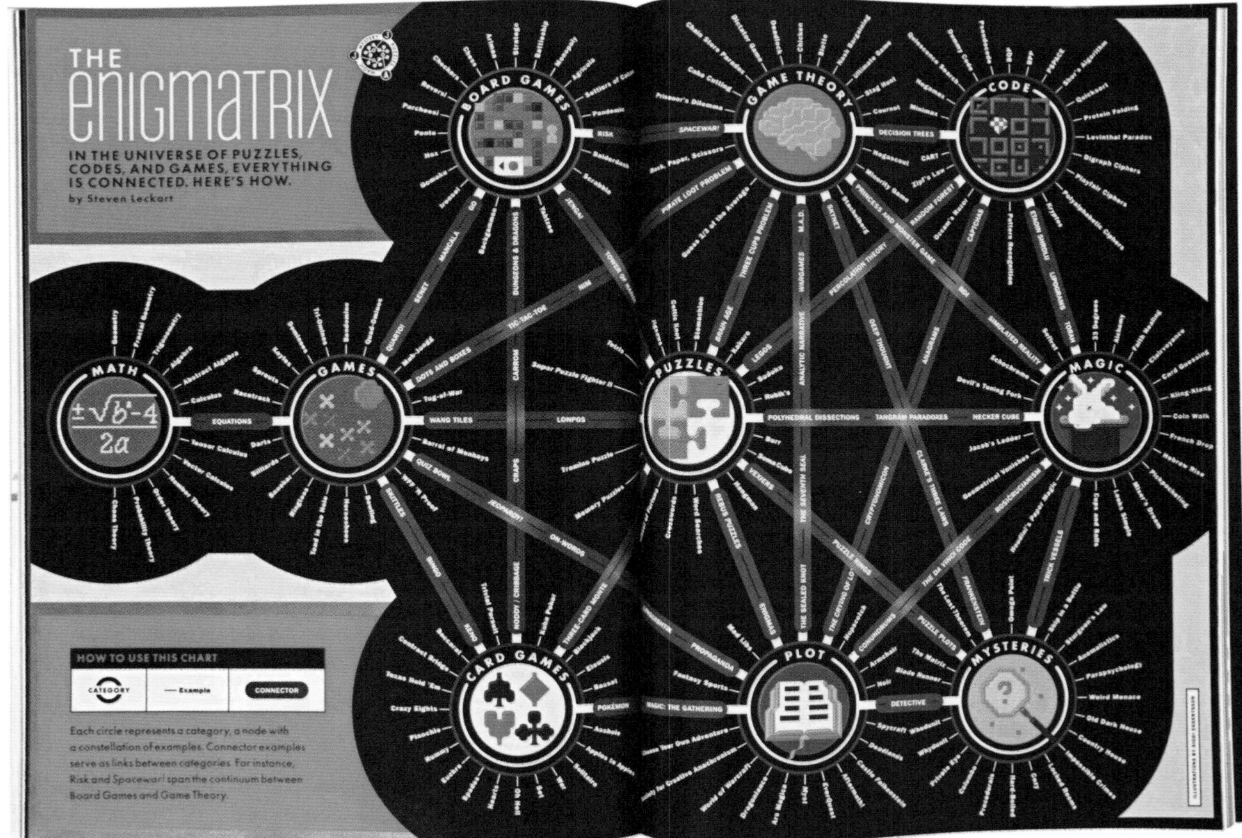

THE enigmatrix

IN THE UNIVERSE OF PUZZLES, CODES, AND GAMES, EVERYTHING IS CONNECTED. HERE'S HOW.

by Steven Leckart

HOW TO USE THIS CHART

CATEGORY	— Example	CONNECTOR

Each circle represents a category, a node with a constellation of examples. Connector examples serve as links between categories. For instance, Risk and Spacewar! span the continuum between Board Games and Game Theory.

DESIGN × CONTENT

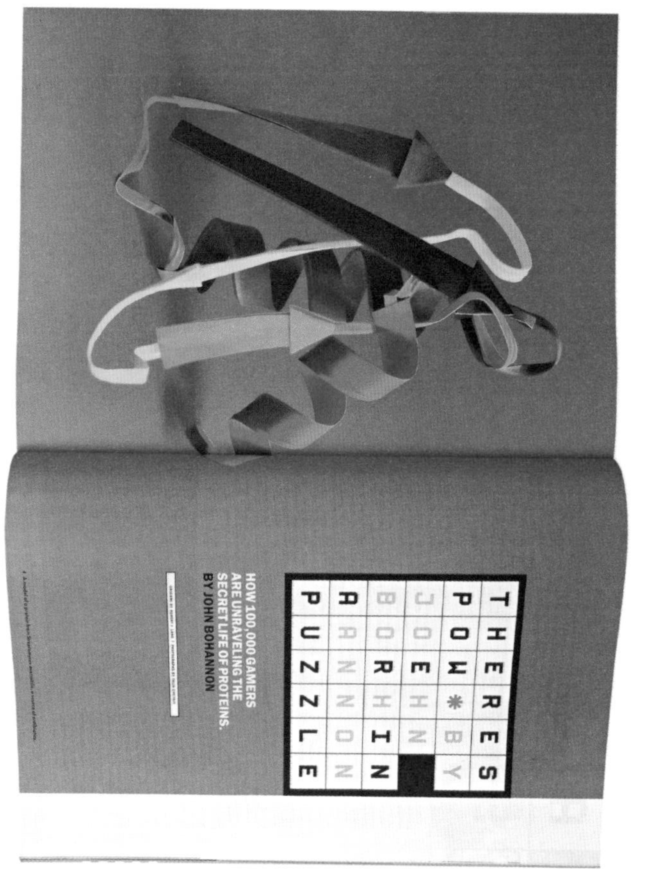

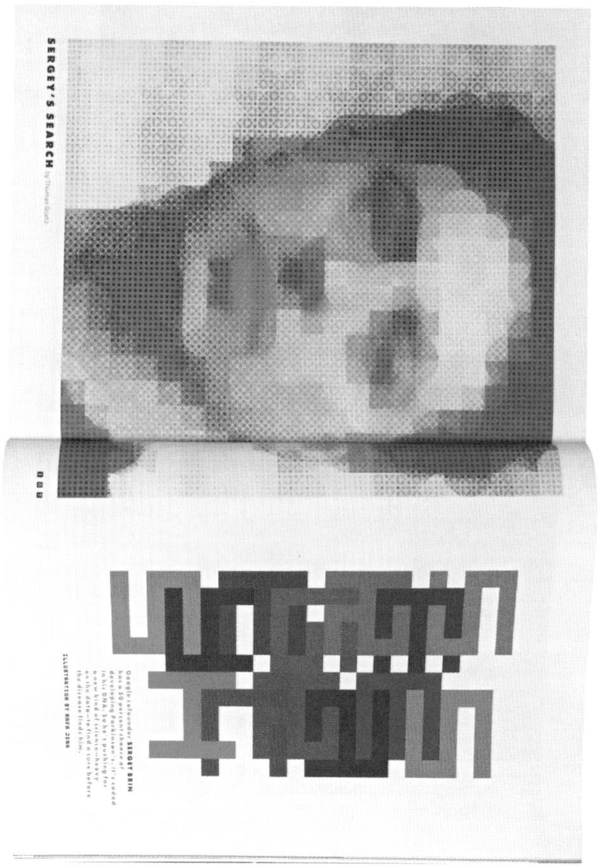

Wired

USA (203 × 276mm, 8 × 11 inches)
Editor-in-chief *Chris Anderson*; Creative director *Scott Dadich*

OPPOSITE & THIS PAGE, TOP *May 2009*
Three spreads from the special 'Mystery' issue. OPPOSITE, TOP: the front section revamped to fit the theme; OPPOSITE, BOTTOM: an infographic linking the many forms of puzzles, codes and games; THIS PAGE, TOP: a feature opener with the headline in the form of a letter puzzle.

THIS PAGE, CENTRE & BOTTOM *July 2010, March 2012*
Two typographically powerful feature openers, one the start of a feature about Sergey Brin, the other a piece about a crop fungus.

MORE WIRED p143

IT'S WHAT YOUR RIGHT ARM'S FOR
WE KEEP YOUR PROMISES
WE'RE NUMBER TWO. WE TRY HARDER

WE DO IT YOUR WAY
HEAD FOR THE BORDER
ONE LEG AT A TIME
WOT A LOT I GOT

FINGER-LICKIN' GOOD
WHILE IN EUROPE, PICK UP AN UGLY EUROPEAN
A LITTLE DAB'LL DO YA

CLEANS ROUND THE BEND
JUST IMAGINE
STOPS HALITOSIS!
TASTE AS GOOD AS IT SMELLS

GEE, I WISH I HAD A NICKEL
LIVE TODAY. TOMORROW WILL COST MORE
ONLY 1 OUT OF 25 MEN IS COLOR BLIND. THE OTHER 24 JUST DRESS THAT WAY
MAKE YOURSELF HEARD

WE SELL MORE CARS THAN FORD, CHRYSLER, CHEVROLET, AND BUICK COMBINED
LIMITED EDITION OF UNLIMITED IDEAS

PURE GENIUS
SOFT, STRONG AND VERY LONG
IT'S SO BIG, YOU'VE GOTTA GRIN TO GET IT IN
HELLO BOYS
THE GENUINE ARTICLE

IT IS. ARE YOU?
PREPARE TO WANT ONE
THINK DIFFERENT
BLOW SOME MY WAY
COME TO WHERE THE FLAVOR IS

Futu
Poland, Issue 6, July–September 2008 (230 × 280mm, 9¼ × 11 inches)
A typographic front cover made up from advertising slogans, for an issue themed 'Label'.
Editor-in-chief *Martyna Bednarska-Cwiek*; Art director *Matt Willey*
MORE FUTU p176

OPPOSITE **Blender**
USA, November 2008 (197 × 275mm, 7¾ × 11 inches)
Strong typography is used to great effect in combination with photography, the two elements working together rather than fighting each other.
Editor *Joe Levy*; Creative director *Dirk Barnett*

BY ROB SHEFFIELD

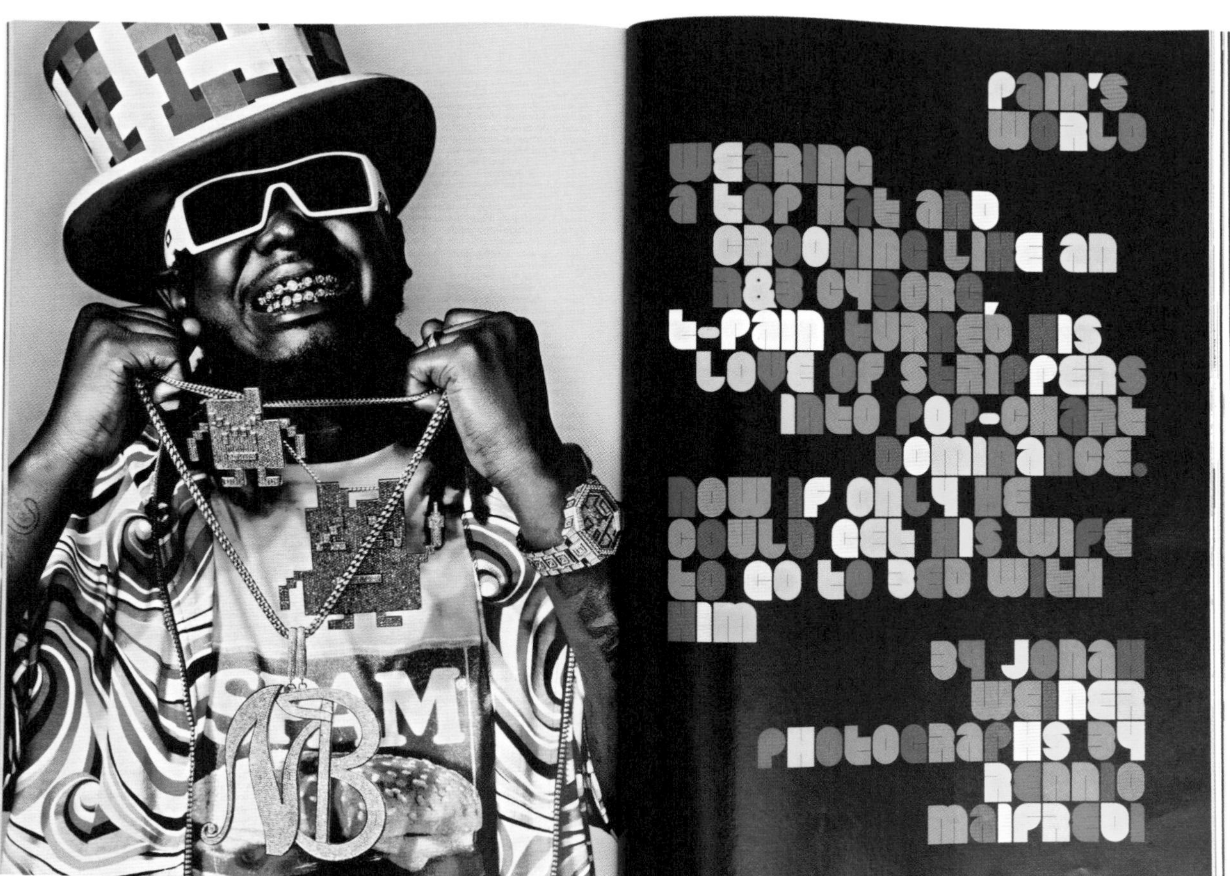
PAIN'S WORLD
WEARING A TOP HAT AND CROONING LIKE AN R&B CYBORG, T-PAIN TURNED HIS LOVE OF STRIPPERS INTO POP-CHART DOMINANCE. NOW IF ONLY HE COULD GET HIS WIFE TO GO TO BED WITH HIM
BY JONAH WEINER PHOTOGRAPHS BY RENNIO MAIFREDI

Three-headed babies!
ELVIS LIVES!
EXCLUSIVE! JOHN EDWARDS'S LOVE CHILD!
And...a Pulitzer?! (WELL, ALMOST.)

June 2010 • GQ.COM • 185

ALEX PAPPADEMAS EMBEDS WITH THE BADASS REPORTERS AT THE

NATIONAL ENQUIRER

to find out how this onetime SCANDAL SHEET has become

THE RESPECTED PAPER OF RECORD WHEN IT COMES TO HARD-NOSED REPORTING AND BREAKING THE BIG SCOOPS OTHER PAPERS CAN'T

ALL THE DIRT THAT'S FIT TO PRINT

GQ © Condé Nast

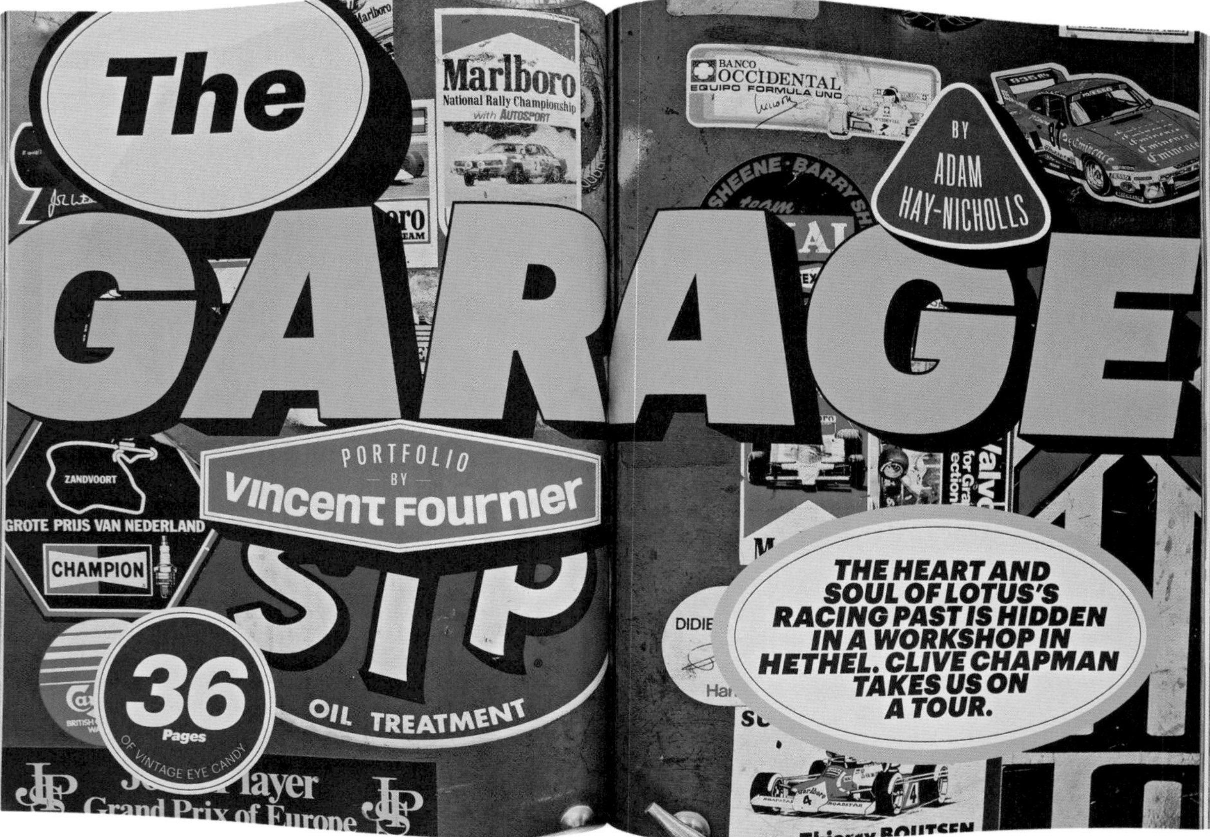

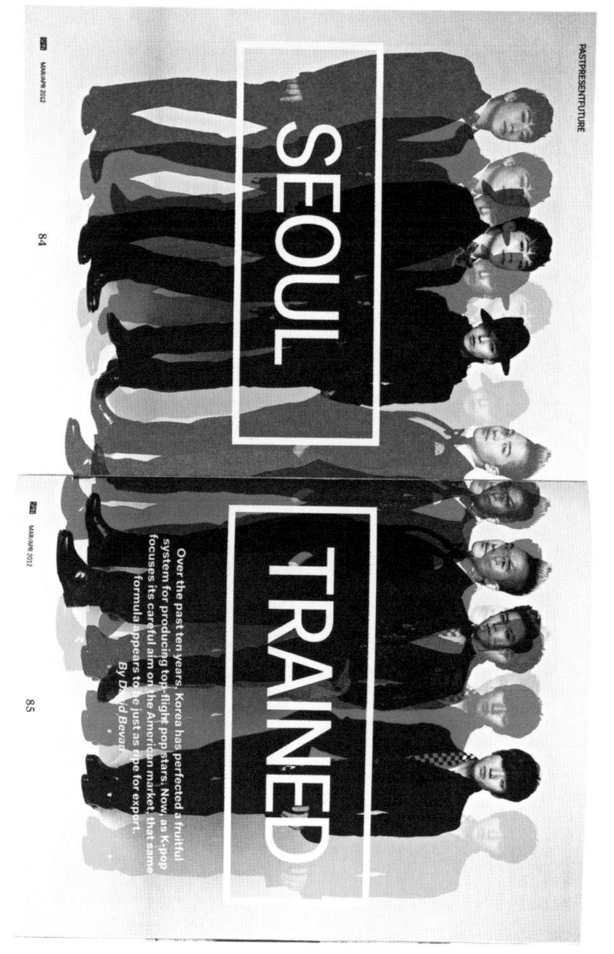

PASTPRESENTFUTURE
SEOUL
TRAINED
Over the past ten years, Korea has perfected a fruitful system for producing top-flight pop stars. Now, as K-pop focuses its careful aim on the American market, that same formula appears to be just as ripe for export.
By David Bevan
MAR/APR 2012 84
MAR/APR 2012 85

HIPPY
TOP.DAWG
ENT
GOTTA HAVE IT
Kendrick Lamar, Section.80; Schoolboy Q, Habits & Contradictions
KINDA REMINDS YOU OF
Souls of Mischief with older souls, Freestyle Fellowship wearing Death Row chains, when rap groups were great
MAR/APR 2012 73

Sleigh Bells' hit debut was relentlessly modern and oddly unrevealing. For the follow-up, they drew on hair metal and a personal tragedy. Then came the hard part.
By David Marchese
Photographs by Nick Haymes
HEART-
BREAK
55

Spin
USA, March/April 2012 (242 × 303mm, 9½ × 12 inches)
The redesign of this music magazine by Everything Type Company brought a bold, no-nonsense approach to typography that makes a hero of the photography.
Editor *Steve Kandell*; Design director *Ian Robinson*

OPPOSITE, TOP **GQ**
USA, June 2010 (203 × 275mm, 8 × 11 inches)
Idealized versions of tabloid newspaper typography is used to open a story about US tabloid, *National Enquirer*.
Editor-in-chief *Jim Nelson*; Design director *Fred Woodward*
MORE GQ p166

OPPOSITE, BOTTOM **Lotus**
USA, Issue 4, Winter 2011 (245 × 315mm, 9¾ × 12½ inches)
Headline typography is designed to meld with the background photograph of an archive packing case covered with events/sponsors' stickers.
Editor *Christian Kaemmerling*; Creative director *Anton Ioukhnovets*

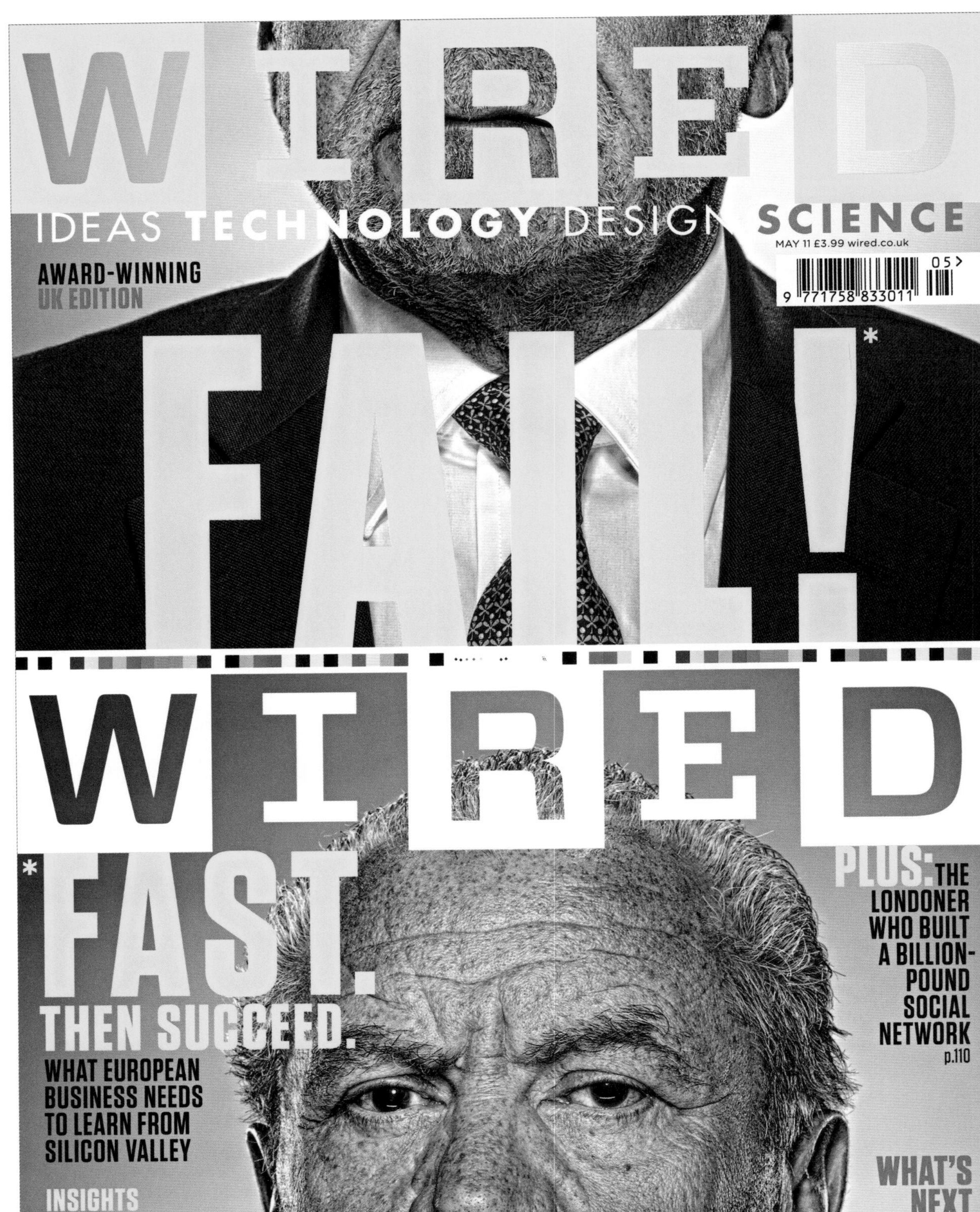

Wired
UK, May 2011 (204 × 276mm, 8 × 11 inches)
This design pulls out all the graphic stops to make a strong concept cover about failure. A mock printing error highlights the theme and lets Alan Sugar star while acknowledging that he is probably not a natural *Wired* subject.
Editor *David Rowan*; Art director *Andrew Diprose*; Photograph *Peter Beavis*

Mark
The Netherlands, Issue 1, Winter 2005/2006 (240 × 320mm, 9½ × 12½ inches)
Photography and headline merge as one, emphasizing the meaning of the headline.
Editor *Robert Thiemann*; Graphic design *Machine*

The New York Times Magazine
USA, February 12, 2012 (228 × 276mm, 9 × 11 inches)
A quirky use of upper- and lower-case headline typography provided a unifying identity to this special travel edition of the magazine and holds this opening spread together in the absence of a single 'lead' image.
Editor-in-chief *Robert Hugo Lindgren*; Design director *Arem Duplessis*

Six examples of how typographic rule-breaking and playfulness can be highly effective at bringing to life otherwise simple page layouts.

Framer

Finland, Issue 2, 2011 (200 × 250mm, 8 × 10 inches)
A simple sans serif is artifically italicized to create visual patterns in this magazine published by a Finnish art fund.
Creative director *Pekka Toivonen*; Editor-in-chief *Laura Köönikkä*; Editorial co-ordinator Paivi Mustola; Content director *Jonathan Mander*; Editor Tero *Kartastenpää*

Kaleidoscope

Italy, Issue 14, Spring 2012 (220 × 288mm, 8¾ × 11½ inches)
Bold, stark typography provides this contemporary art magazine with a strong structure against which the many images stand out.
Editor-in-chief *Alessio Ascari*; Art direction and design *OK-RM*
MORE KALEIDOSCOPE p178

Slanted

Germany, Issue 7, Spring 2009 (210 × 270mm, 8½ × 10¾ inches)
This typography magazine regularly features challenging display fonts.
Editor *Lars Harmsen*; Art director *Flo Gaertner*

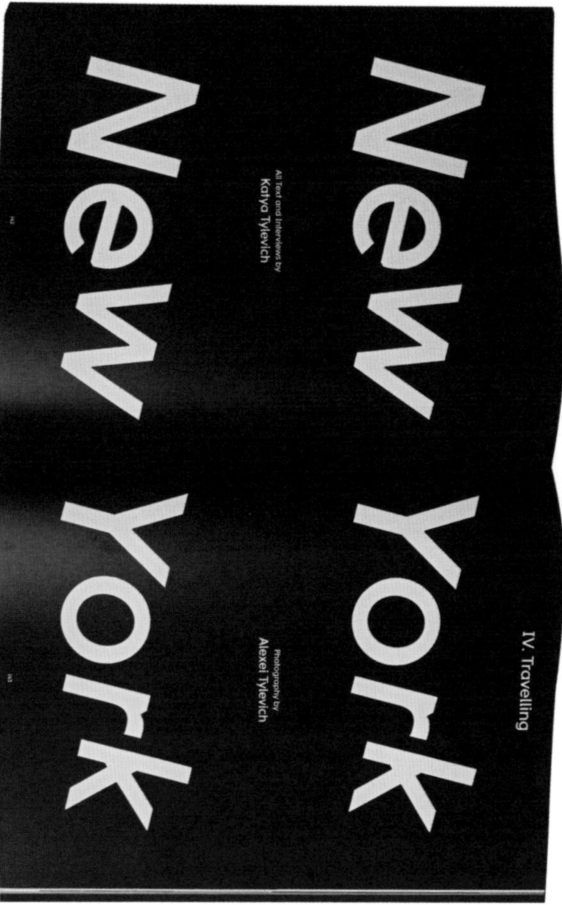

Waw

Poland, Issue 1, Spring 2010 (220 × 270mm, 8¾ × 10¾ inches)
A combination of strong Grotesk type, bespoke headline font and graphic pattern throughout this art and culture title make it visually exciting even to non-Polish readers.
Editor-in-chief *Mike Urbaniak*; Art director *Edgar Bak*

Elephant

UK, Issue 7, Spring 2011 (220 × 280mm, 8¾ × 11 inches)
Tilting individual characters just a few degrees makes an otherwise simple design feel surprisingly unnerving.
Editor-in-chief *Marc Valli*; Art direction and design *Julia*

Arc

UK, Issue 15, Summer 2011 (170 × 238mm, 6¾ × 9½ inches)
A custom headline font run unintuitively upwards both fills space and gives simple character to the page of this annual publication from the Royal College of Art.
Editor *Charmian Griffin*; Art direction and design *Hannah Montague*

Op basis van Bas Oudt
Chris Reinewald

Op basis van Bas Oudt

Het oeuvre van de Amsterdamse grafisch ontwerper Bas Oudt (1956), is fijnzinnig, vindingrijk en doordacht. Als basisjaardocent op de Gerrit Rietveld Academie in Amsterdam bracht Oudt zijn onconventionele ontwerpmentaliteit over op zijn studenten. Enkele van hen – Jozee Brouwer, Katja van Stiphout, Yolanda Huntelaar & Pieter Boddaert (Werkplaats Amsterdam), Harmen Liemburg, Esther de Vries en Richard Niessen en ex-stagiair Ron Faas (Dietwee), bewijzen nu, versterkt door grafisch vormgeefster Claudi Kessels en fotografe Uta Eisenreich, in een opmerkelijk kunstenaarsboek eer aan hun oud-docent. Titel: *Op basis van Bas Oudt / Based on Bas Oudt*

De basis vormt Oudts werk en zijn 'canon' met helden, rolmodellen en kunstwerken. Foto's van rampen, Jo Spiers elegante illustraties, het mysterie van de bijna niet te reproduceren kleur groen, Monsieur Bibendum (het Michelin-mannetje), de rake zang van Frank Sinatra, experimenteren op de drukpers. Bas Oudt verbindt zijn fascinaties binnen en buiten de grafische vormgeving aan zijn stellingname ten opzichte van het vak. "Eigenlijk wilde ik de Willem Elsschot van de Nederlandse vormgeving worden: spijkerhard in de analyse, mild in het oordeel", vertelt hij.
Na zijn eindexamen aan de Gerrit Rietveld Academie ging Bas Oudt werken bij de Vrije Drukkers, een autonome belangengroep van linkse drukkers. Oudt: "We drukten onder andere voor actiegroepen. Vaak slecht drukwerk, maar je kon wel fijn rare experimenten uitvoeren. Als je iets laat drukken bij een drukkertje om de hoek, kan je namelijk vragen eens iets anders te doen. Alles live op de pers proberen. Pregen op een offsetpers door papier op de tegendrukcilinder te plakken. Nat in nat drukken. Dekwit over zwart. Drukken op grijsbord, zilveren fond, verschillende formaten tekstpagina's erin, spiraal er doorheen. Zo krijgt het iets fysieks, dus authentieks."

Voor W139, het Amsterdamse kunstenaarscentrum aan de Warmoesstraat 139 ontwierp hij uitnodigingen, tentoonstellingsinrichtingen en catalogi. Minder interessante teksten van kunstenaars pareerde hij door ze simpelweg zwart op zwart te drukken. Voor twee gefuseerde welzijnsorganisaties ontwikkelde hij een voordelige doe-het-zelf huisstijl. Telkens weer onttrok Oudt zich aan conventies: "Spelregels bestaan alleen voor mensen die er niet met hun hart bij kunnen." Deze filosofie bleek geknipt voor de praktijk van het lesgeven. "Ontwerpers moet je leren zich persoonlijk te verhouden tot het eindproduct dat ze ontwikkelen. In het basisjaar gaf ik de studenten opdracht om iets aan zichzelf te verbeteren om zo het individuele te stimuleren. Daar kwamen dan heel verrassende dingen uit."
Zijn afnemend gezichtsvermogen dwong Oudt enkele jaren geleden te stoppen met werken en lesgeven. Zijn studenten, inmiddels collega's, hebben zijn dwarse liefde voor de grafische vormgeving overgenomen. "Zakelijk gezien doen zij het beter dan ik. Werken voor zichzelf, niet voor een bureau waar al het leuke en afwijkende wordt weggenivelleerd. Ze zijn hun eigen eieren gaan leggen." •

Chris Reinewald is freelance journalist op het gebied van design en beeldende kunst en hoofdredacteur van *Museumvisie*.

Verhuisdozen met daarin Bas Oudt's verzameling groen glas en aardewerk

Verzameling 'Bibendums'

Welcome Stranger, Poster, 1994

Portfolio Aldo Bakker
Peter van Kester

Ik trek me weinig aan van de tijdgeest

"De dag dat ik met mijn vader een tentoonstelling bezocht van Leerdams glas staat in mijn geheugen gegrift. Er ging een wereld open." Kort na die dag ontwierp Aldo Bakker zijn eerste glas, een verstild, esthetisch champagneglas.

Hij was net zestien, maar distantieerde zich van de uitbundigheid van het toen heersende Memphis-virus. Ook het huidige populaire concept-design benadert hij kritisch. Interessante concepten leiden niet automatisch tot interessante vormen, vindt hij. De beheersing van esthetiek is minstens zo essentieel.
Praten over vormgeving met de bevlogen Aldo Bakker (1971) wordt al snel abstract. Hij is gefascineerd door het gebruik, hoe je bijvoorbeeld wijn drinkt. In glazen met een zware kristallen voet mist hij een direct contact met de vloeistof. Daarom werkt hij met het flinterdunne borosilicaatglas, alsof je de drank bijna direct op de tafel schenkt. De beste modellen uit zijn Glass Line bevatten een enkele 'facet' die de geur vasthoudt en spannende vormen genereert. "Het gebruik is niet mijn enige inspiratie", zegt Bakker. "Elk ontwerp ontstaat uit vele facetten, zoals vorm, materiaal, betekenis, kleur en dergelijke. Zo ontstaat er een complexiteit die zich goed verhoudt tot de mens." Als autodidact onderzocht hij al doende de cirkel, het vierkant en de driehoek. "Glass Line no. 1 ontstond door lijnen te trekken tussen referentiepunten. In de S/M/L verdelen facetten het glas in ringen. Alsof de vloeistof als een druppel aan de bovenring hangt."

Zoektocht

De Glass Line herinnert aan waterglazen van de Fin Kaj Franck, maar ook aan de sieraden van zijn moeder Emmy van Leersum (1930-1984). In haar aluminium armbanden uit de late jaren zestig veroorzaken minieme ingrepen interessante vormveranderingen. Het persbericht dat Aldo Bakker onlangs verspreidde naar aanleiding van de Triennale van Hasselt suggereert dat het werk van zijn moeder van grotere invloed is dan dat van zijn vader Gijs Bakker, boegbeeld van het conceptuele design. Is hier sprake van vadermoord, een uitgesteld Oedipusconflict? "Dat is te sterk uitgedrukt", zegt Bakker, "mijn manier van werken lijkt meer op die van mijn moeder. Ik trek me weinig aan van de tijdgeest, ik zoek rijping. Mijn vader kan veel beter met de tijdgeest overweg."
Met plezier denkt hij terug aan de lange uren die hij knutselend doorbracht in de ouderlijke ateliers. En aan de vele exposities die hij met hen bezocht. Zijn moeder overleed op zijn dertiende en eenzame jaren van moeizaam zoeken volgden. Diep in zijn hart wilde hij als iedereen zijn, maar alleen al het moderne interieur waarin hij opgroeide, was niet doorsnee. Na een periode van de nodige verwarring vond hij in de vriendenkring van zijn ouders een inspirerend spoor. Zijn afkomst wekte verwachtingen die hem zwaar drukten. Dat leidde onder meer tot een heftig conflict met zijn vader toen Bakker na drie maanden edelsmeden, drie maanden Rietveld en twaalf maanden Academie Industriële Vormgeving Eindhoven een punt achter zijn opleiding zette. Het was 1994 en hij begon voor zichzelf. Enkele dagen per week assisteerde hij zilversmid Willem Noyons en leerde sieraden, modellen en maquettes maken. Ondertussen werkte hij aan een eigen oeuvre. Toen het Amsterdamse restaurant Zuid Zeeland hem in 1999 vroeg voor het ontwerp van een nieuwe inrichting, kon hij op eigen benen staan. Een jaar later voelde hij zich zeker genoeg voor een solopresentatie in galerie BINNEN. Twee jaar later werd hij docent aan de Design Academy Eindhoven.

Ziel

Architectuur is een constante inspiratiebron. De Esdoornbank verwijst naar de Beurs van Berlage. Bakker: "Die blokachtige massa wordt onderbroken door sculpturen. Deze zijn afgeleid van de hoekige basisvorm en bewaren zo een relatie tot het geheel. Zo werken ook de rondingen in de Esdoornbank: ze komen het lichaam tegemoet (beschermen tegen stoten), maar hebben ook een visuele functie." Ook beeldende kunst inspireert hem. Hij bewondert Giorgio Morandi, Luc Tuymans en David Claerbout die met weinig middelen geabstraheerde beelden tot leven brengen. "Vanuit puur visuele parameters durven zij nieuwe vormen te ontwikkelen. Wij ontwerpen vaak zo theoretisch. Kunstenaars werken veel intuitiever. Hun werk is tijdlozer."
Aldo Bakker gelooft dat voorwerpen, net als muziek, film en beeldende kunst,

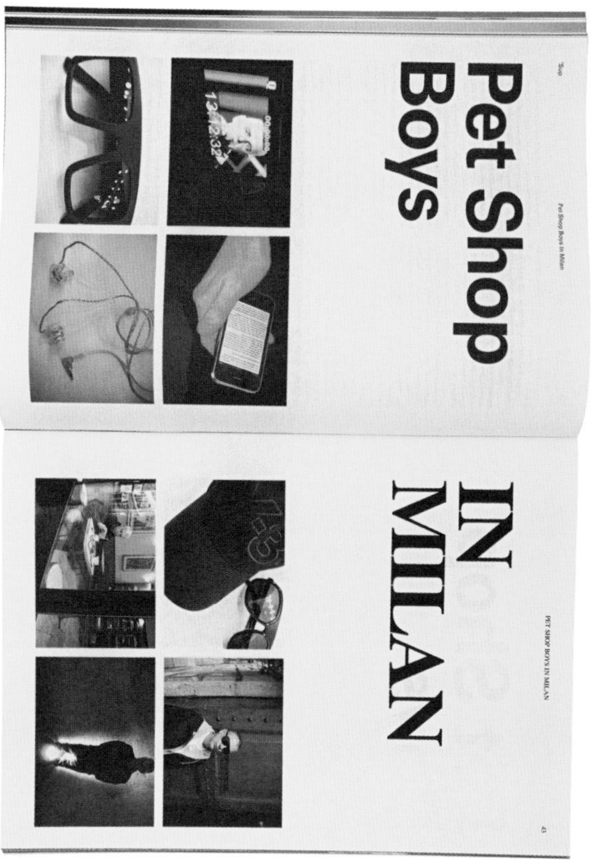

Issue 20, 2009

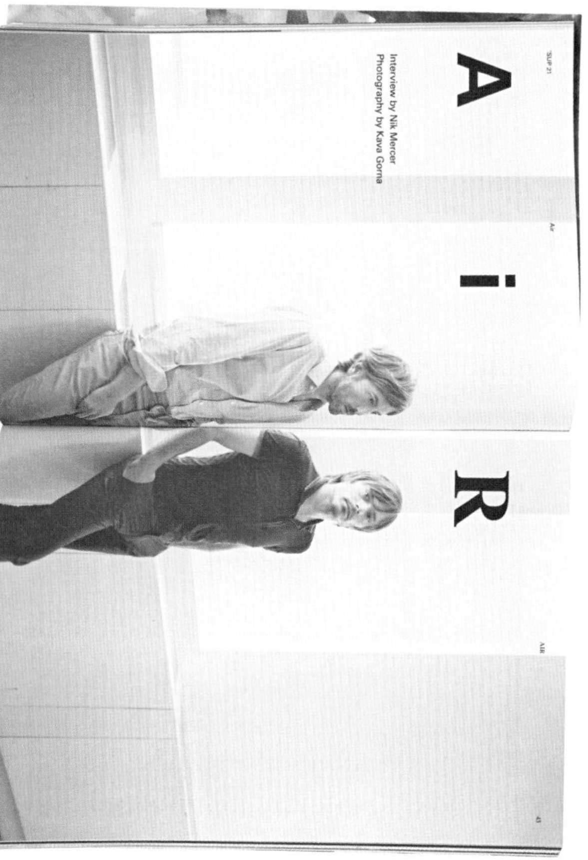

Issue 21, 2009

Issue 20, 2009

'Sup Magazine

USA (198 × 274mm, 7¾ × 10¾ inches)

This music magazine applies systematic design rules. In these examples all type on the left-hand page appears in sentence-case bold sans serif, while that on the right-hand page uses a capitalized serif. This is applied to all elements, including headlines that run across spreads and to long-form text.

Publisher and editor *Marisa Brickman*; Creative director *Brendan Dugan*; Art director *Eric Wrenn*

OPPOSITE **Items**

The Netherlands, Issue 3, 2009 (210 × 275mm, 8½ × 11 inches)

This Dutch design magazine splits its headlines through an imaginary 'filter' which renders the words in two typefaces, the complete headline only legible when the two parts are combined. The effect references the process of designing pages using the grid and text boxes.

Editor-in-chief *Max Bruinsma*; Art direction *Thonik*

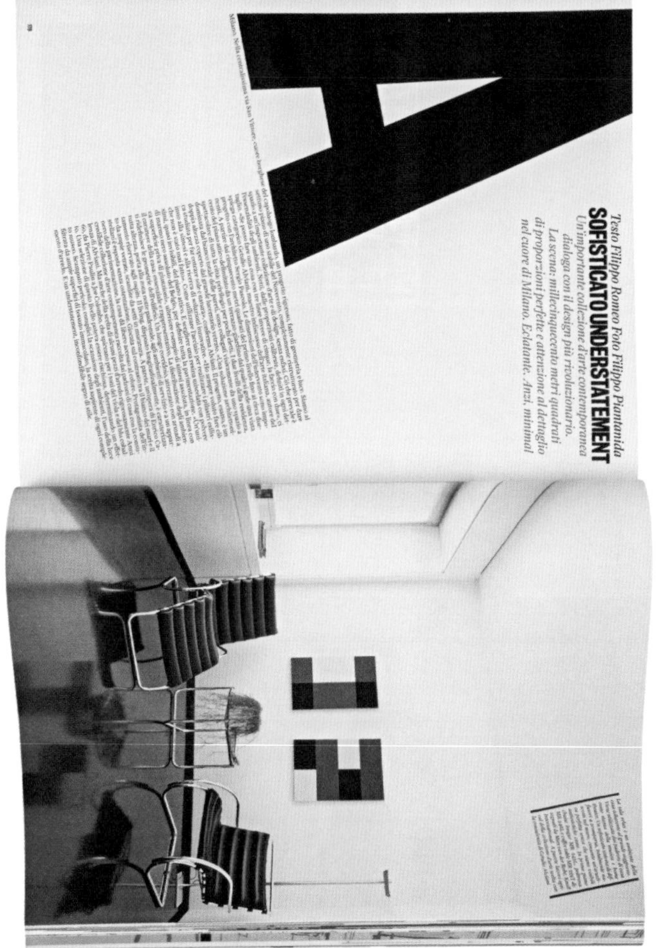

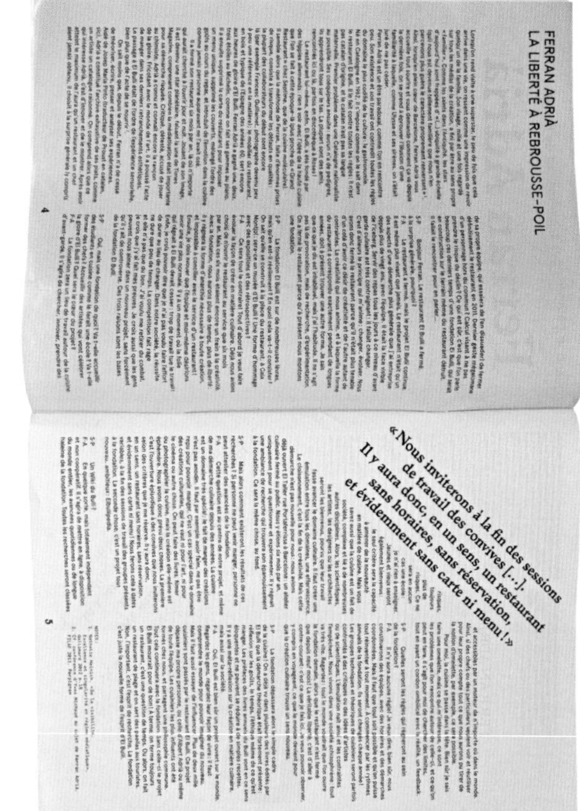

Six examples of how the basic building-block of magazine content, the text column, can be broken up to create visual variety across the page.

Case da Abitare
Italy, Issue 122, November 2008 (227 × 287mm, 9 × 11½ inches)
An interiors magazine that uses a classic combination of bold Grotesk headlines and serif text face, applying bold shapes and use of white space to impart drama.
Editor *Francesca Taroni*; Art director *Kuchar Swara*
MORE CASA DA ABITARE p181

Figure
France, Issue 1, June 2012 (240 × 320mm, 12½ × 11½ inches)
Four solid columns of text broken by an angled pull-quote.
Editors and creative directors *Côme de Bouchony and Vincent de Hoÿm*

A Guide Magazine
Austria, Issue 1, Autumn/Winter 09/10 (215 × 297mm, 8½ × 11¾ inches)
Columns of text rise from the bottom of the page to seemingly random heights in this listing guide to Vienna.
Editors-in-chief *Ulrike Tschabitzer-Handler, Doris Rothauer and Albert Handler*; Art director *Albert Handler*

The Shelf
France, Issue 1, 2012 (210 × 310mm, 8¼ × 12¼ inches)
The text columns in the magazine about book design are regularly broken into by spaces containing bold graphic 'shelf' icons.
Editorial director *Morgane Rébulard*; Design *The Shelf Company*

The Modernist
UK, Issue 5, 2012 (170 × 240mm, 6¾ × 9½ inches)
Featuring an appropriately modernist design, this magazine about twentieth-century design regularly breaks its text columns with oblong 'holes' containing details such as authors' credits.
Editors *Jack Hale and Maureen Ward*; Graphic design *Des Lloyd Behari*

mono.kultur
Germany, Issue 32, Summer 2012 (150 × 200mm, 6 × 8 inches)
Redesigned to suit the subject of each issue, this one about furniture designer Martino Gamper features shapes from his designs breaking up the text. The reader must read across the gaps in each line.
Publisher and creative director *Kai von Rabenau*

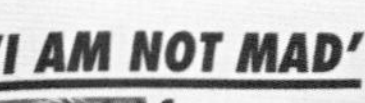

FRENCH CANDIDATES DENY TRYING TO WIN OVER FAR-RIGHT VOTE

'Shaken judges' scandal grows

CAMERON EMPLOYS AUSSIE NANNY

GNOME 24 — THE PAGE YOU CAN READ 24 HOURS A DAY

BBC Radio 3

POETRY CORNER

'I AM NOT MAD' Screams Brown

Those Rebekah Brooks Xmas Party Games in Full

New Oxford Dictionary

the guardian angel — Dirty Devil Flies In

Spot the balls competition!!!!

TV Highlights

the PREMIERSH*TS

Little black jacket

NAILING IT

WATCH THIS

MUSE OF THE MOMENT

IN LANVIN WE TRUST

TOP GEAR

Garance and Kate's GIRL GANG

KUSAMA CRAZY

HAPPY BIRTHDAY SMYTHSON

MATCH POINT

ENGLISH ROSE

OH LA LA

NATIONAL ANTHEM

ROCK SOLID

HOVER YOUR DEVICE OVER EACH IMAGE TO SEE THEM COME TO LIFE

TELEVISION

'MAD MEN' AND WORKING WOMEN

BY ELEANOR CLIFT

PHOTOGRAPHS BY ART STREIBER

It was the era of the philandering Don Draper and stay-at-home Betty. Author Eleanor Clift saw it all at Newsweek.

38 Newsweek March 26 & April 2, 2012 39

Private Eye
UK, Issue 1313, May 4, 2012 (210 × 297mm, 8½ × 11¾ inches)
Despite the introduction of colour and computer production, this fortnightly satirical magazine has carefully retained the loose, hand-made layout it launched with in the early 1960s.
Editor *Ian Hislop*; Art director *Tony Rushton*

O:
UK, Autumn/Winter 2012 (233 × 294mm, 9¼ × 11¾ inches)
The news pages of this seasonal fashion magazine distributed with *The Observer* newspaper make graphic reference to 1950s classified ads.
Editor-in-chief *Caroline Issa*; Creative director *Liz Muller*

Newsweek
USA, March 26, 2012 (200 × 265mm, 8 × 10½ inches)
A one-off edition of the news magazine reverted to a careful pastiche of its 1960s design to celebrate the new season of TV's *Mad Men*. As well as *Mad Men*-related content, the regular news sections were redesigned for the occasion too.
Editor-in-chief *Tina Brown*; Creative director *Dirk Burnett*

BALLARDIAN ITEM

WESTFIELD: IT'S WEIRD

A psycheographic shopping/dining meditation

BY ALEX BILMES

Last autumn, a spaceship landed in our back garden. Just like in the movies, it seemed to hover above the earth before settling, improbably gently, on wasteland near the A40. Also like in the movies, it was illuminated from within. And it seemed to pulse and thrum. It was scary but also somehow seductive, otherworldly and yet reassuring. It occurred to me – rightly or wrongly – that no harm, no physical harm anyhow, was likely to come to us if we entered it.

So we flocked to it and wandered around it. Tardis-like, it appeared bigger inside than out, though still warm and womb-like. Un-Tardis-like, it sold Prada and served Pho noodles. Still does, last time I checked.

Westfield is in Shepherd's Bush but not of it. Or perhaps it's not in Shepherd's Bush *nor of* it. Perhaps it's nowhere. I think this is more likely. I suspect that Westfield occupies an alternative space or zone, in the same way that motorway service stations and high-security prisons do. It seems untethered from the humdrum and the concrete, liberated from the quotidian, and removed from the humble inner London suburb in which it purports to exist.

In this way, entering it is equivalent to stepping off the earth into... where? Westfield World? Westworld, perhaps. Like in the Michael Crichton film, where robots pretending to be humans "populate" an adult-oriented theme park. Is that what Westfield is: a theme park? A lot of right-on adults – especially the ones who live round my way – got a bit steamed up about it. It's the end of civilisation, they reckoned – and the traffic'll be murder. Less critical types were excited: it's got a Waitrose! And a Niketown! Mind you, the traffic'll be murder...

In the Michael Crichton film the robots malfunction and, led by Yul Brynner's cowboy android, wreak havoc, killing the schlubbish tourists they were supposed to entertain. All very Ballardian. Still more Ballardian is "Kingdom Come", in which the great man imagines an ultra-modern shopping complex, the Metro-Centre, which orbits London off the M25, a petri dish in which to grow a fascistic culture where racism, violence, football, fundamentalism and consumerism collide and cross-pollinate.

I am not as highly attuned as the Seer of Shepperton, and I don't sense that seething terror at Westfield – the piped music sounds less than martial to me. The shoppers seem benumbed, sure, maybe even so supine as to be dangerously suggestible. But maybe the credit crunch has put the kibosh on the link between consumerism and ultraviolence?

I hope so, because on my last visit there – Foyles, Uniqlo, The Real Greek and Waitrose then home – I rather enjoyed myself.

The centre was developed by the Westfield Group, at a cost of £1.6bn, on a site bounded by the West Cross Route (A3220), the Westway (A40) and Wood Lane (A219), and opened on 30 October 2008.

It was a Monday lunchtime. In the Food Court, young mums had gathered with their infants, presumably taking a break from the Early Learning Centre. They were sitting and chatting. The kids were playing or sleeping or bawling. It felt comfortable and sheltered and human. Ballard thought that shopping centres have taken the place of town squares, and that that was a bad thing. This has become the bien-pensant orthodoxy. I'm not so sure. I just know it's weird, and not in an altogether bad way, that within a five-minute walk from my front door there is another world. A world that is cleaner, brighter and more productive than Shepherd's Bush.

I Have Slept With All The Girls In Berlin

Shake me down again
Shake me down and then
Shake me down again
I can wake up in this zoo

I've been used and abused
I've been chased and I've been bruised
I can take what I've been to
I've been naked on the news
I've been debased and disabused
Just leave me downtown when you're through
Turn me over
Turn me in
I have slept with all the girls in Berlin

Girls on smoke and girls on weed
Girls on coke and girls on speed
Girls who choke and girls who smile
Girls who swallow in denial
Girls in crisis, ultra-hipped
Weird as Isis, wide as Egypt
Girls in cars and girls on ships
Girls in bars and girls on strips
Girls on journeys, girls on trips
Girls on gurneys, girls on drips
And a girl too far with pale blue lips so shake me down again

Girls like you with poison tips
Girls like you like pistol whips
Girls in over-zealous green
With a third degree in jealousy so
Turn me over
Turn me in
I have slept with all the girls in Berlin

– Andrew Eldritch*

* "We're not here for conversation, so just keep it quiet"

10

SEIZE THE BREEZE

A TAXONOMY OF SUMMER SHORTS-WEARING

With summer here and global warming being so enjoyable, many readers are eagerly asking, what are the options for showing a bit of leg while working, commuting, being recreational and drinking to excess? So many options, but so little guidance now that Maxim and Arena are no longer with us. Permit Manzine to enlighten you with this handy guide to getting your pins out, yeah?

TYPE + HEIGHT	BEST FOR	WHAT IT SAYS ABOUT YOU
Turns-ups & Birkies, 2" above heel	Thurs drinking, Clerkenwell 1998	You are a junior creative @ Mother
Turn-ups, plimoses, no socks, 3"	Poolside, Shoreditch House	You're channelling Tintin
Turn ups + brogues, 3.5"	Hanover Square, lunchtimes	You want to be on The Sartorialist
Thom Browne turn ups + brogues, 4.5"	Hanover Square, brunchtimes	You are The Sartorialist
Reebok/FCUK "Longs", 6"	Blackpool/Magaluf	You are suburban/Northern
Green & pink plus-fours, 8"	The tobacconist on Jermyn Street	You edit *The Chap*
Hawaiian Beach shorts, 10"	Festivals on Clapham Common	You're are an Aussie, it is winter
Sawn-off camo shorts, 11"	On the piss in Thailand/Laos/'Nam	Your'e not as hard as you think you are
Rolled-up black Nudies, below knee	Dalston/Haggerston	You ride Fixed, couriers laugh at you
Seersucker suit shorts, knee-height	Saturday shopping Zara, Westfield	You take Homme+ far too seriously
Footy shorts, knee-height	The Highbury Barn	You just lost 35-19 to the other pub team
Villebrequin florals, waist minus 14"	St Trop./Wimbledon	You are Tony Blair/Duncan Bannatyne
Cycling shorts, waist minus 12"	Hanging round Condor Cycles	You are "Focused"/tedious
Perv shorts, waist minus 9"	Parks, public toilets etc	You are under arrest
Daniel Craig walnut-bag Speedos	Mustique/Pinewood	Sean Connery was better
Speedo briefs (red)	Porchester Baths	You are a gay MP
Kilt	Burns night/weddings/ceilidhs etc	Stop trying so hard

Notes
Q: Is it okay to look at other men's legs?
A: YES. Provided no-one sees you doing it.

Q: I would quite like to shave/clipper my legs. Is that acceptable?
A: YES. Many style journalists have experimented this way – but be warned, people might mistake you for a cyclist and immediately call the police.

Q: Is it uncool to wear those OrlebarBrown/Monocle ltd edition shorts?
A: NOT REALLY. But it would help if you live in Zurich.

11

Hip Hop Home Help - with Sir Fix-A-Lot

There's not a problem that he can't fix – 'cos can do it in the mix. Manzine's resident rap-based agony uncle has got the hot lyric for every domestic upset.

Q: Dear Sir Fix-A-Lot, I would like to collect rainwater from the roof of my verandah. What type and size of water receptacle would you recommend?
A: *I like big butts, and I cannot lie.*

Q: I am trying tried to keep fuel bills down by diverting gas from the mains using a complex system of pipework. Now I'm worried I'll gas myself. Could you have a look at it for me?
A: *It was you who chose your due, you built the maze you can't get thru/ but I'll try to help you all I can, cos I'm a qualified Corgi engineer, man. HomeBase for your place!*

Q: To Sir Fix-A-Lot: how can I stop my rock cakes keep from sticking to the baking tray?
A: *Join with us and use the b-b-b-b-butter wrap!*

Q: I recently started learning to drive but I can never remember what order the pedals are in. Can you help?
A: *Sure: These Are The Brakes.*

Q: Yo Fix! I been havin' trouble with urban foxes getting at my garbage, partly because our rubbish collection has been erratic recently, yo? Can y'all recommend a course a action?
A: *Don't put your bins out until Tuesday night/ Cos you might find that your council is tight.*

Q: Hi Fix-A-Lot. I'm worried about my carbon footprint. Any advice for a greener lifestyle?
A: *Switch off the power!*

Q: Help! I just dropped a crystal vase and it's shattered across the kitchen floor. What should I do?
A: *Broken glass – everywhere! Hmm, that's a tricky one. Use a hoover but be careful not to miss any tiny shards. Try shining a torch across the floor, as any remaining glass will sparkle in the light. Hope that helps, aiiight. FIX*

Next issue: Sir Fix-A-Lot tackles relationship issues. (MH/PL)

Things I'm Bored of Hearing About from People

+ Thing that are done "with a twist"
+ Things that are "quirky"
+ Things that are "deleterious"
+ Views that are said to be "stunning" when all they really are, are views
+ People who wish to "touch base"
+ People who are said to a "safe pair of hands"
+ People who go on about "wellness"
+ People refer to the "[insert-word-here] side of things"
+ People who go on about "leveraging"
+ People who are said to "opine" about stuff
+ People who go on about "social media" the whole time
+ People who affix "über" to the beginning of words, and for that matter, people who go on about a such-and-such "-fest"
+ People who refer to French musicians as "Gallic"
+ People who go on about "watering holes" and "drinking establishments"

MANZINE MUSIK KLUB

SELLING BERLIN BY THE BUNDESLIGA

4th OFFICIAL ALBUM REVIEWS

ISSUE 3'S GUEST REVIEWER IS
MR DIAGO RIVIERA

This expressive and synthetic art has become in their hands a vacuous stylistic exercise, a jumble of ill-mixed formulae to disguise a run-of-the-mill traditionalist box of bricks and stone as a modern building.

The vegetating schools, conservatories and academies act as snares for youth and art alike. In these hot-beds of impotence, masters and professors combat any effort to widen the musical field.

All those Maxim Gorkys, Krupins, Bloks, Sologubs, Remizovs, Averchenkos, Chornys, Kuzmins, Bunins, etc. need only a dacha on the river. Such is the reward fate gives tailors.

An electric iron, its white steel gleaming clean as a whistle, delights the eye more than a nude statuette, stuck on a pedestal hideously tinted for the occasion. A typewriter is more architectural than all those building projects.

Next issue: Ed Ruscha assesses the 12" dub of Nena's 99 Luftballons

MIDNIGHT BULLETIN

EARLY EVIDENCE OF SOCIAL MEDIA DISCOVERED IN ENGLISH LITERATURE

- "It was all over for her. The sheet was stretched and the bed narrow. She had gone up to the tower and left them blackberrying in the sun" – Virginia Woolf, Mrs Dalloway
- "With the birdlike freshness of the very aged, she still twittered, 'give me your hand and let me opress is gently'" – Virginia Woolf, Mrs Dalloway
- "Let Rome in Tiber melt, and the wide arch/Of the rang'd empire fall! Here is my space" – William Shakespeare, Anthony & Cleopatra

- LITERARY INVESTIGATION BY PAUL SULLIVAN

Acht und Zwanzig

GRAPHIC DESIGN SEX *ETIQUETTE* QUIZ

Learnings in lust for the Modern Man

No.14

SCENARIO: It has been a long night clubbing in a Berlin and dawn is breaking. You have spent hours in conversation with an attractive woman who suggests you both go back to hers for a cup of herbal tea. On several occasions she has pointedly mentioned that she has a BOYFRIEND. Upon gaining her flat, she unlocks the door and gestures to the large 1mx2m poster on the wall. It reads:

FUCK ME LIKE THE WHORE I AM

DO YOU:

A: Go for broke, say "Okay then," and start taking your trousers off.

B: Play it cool, saying "What, now? I didn't have you down as that kind of girl..."

C: Come over all hip, saying "That poster's wicked yeah, I'm well into graphic design."

D: Pretend you're not interested, aloofly saying "Cool, which way's the bathroom."

E: Sit on the sofa with the girl, drink the tea, talk about stuff, ignore the sex thing and try to stay awake for another 20 minutes before accepting the inevitable and getting a cab home.

OUTCOMES
A: you are not going to get laid tonight.
B: you are not going to get laid tonight.
C: you are not going to get laid tonight.
D: you might get laid tonight.
E: you are not going to get laid tonight.

MANZINE COMMENT:
"Don't be taken in by appearances — some women may look, act, drink, talk and decorate their appartments as if they were prostitutes, but the reality is that few of them actually are."
Poster by www.paul-snowden.com

MANZINE CREATIVE PITCH

Four new home-furnishing products lines brainstormed **FREE OF CHARGE** by Manzine's Creative Solutions department – suitable for any large Swedish furniture retailer with an international presence.

CONSUMER PROFILE
SINGLE ADULT MALES, 30-55, ABCD12, HEAVY INTERNET USERS, MODEST DISPOSABLE INCOME, GSOH/WLTM WOMEN, 18-27 YO.

PRODUCT RANGE:

Tössä
Quirky but useful wall-mounted bathroom facilities suitable for housing tubs of Rohypnol etc. Forms an attractive addition to the Komplett Tössä modular wet-room suite.
Code MZ4710

Wåankå
Ceiling-mounted smoked mirror installation (36m2) for the master bedroom PLUS **Schlbåddt**: handy cleaning product suited to wiping up sticky substances from laptop keyboards.
Code MZ2130 / MZ 2113

Clårksünn
Easy-to-assemble sofa-side DVD rack/coffee table, perfect for storing *Top Gear* box sets, Piers Morgan autobiographies etc. For the commited bachelor who enjoys TV.
Code MZ0666

Aåshølle
Bauhaus-inspired bedside shelving system for managing hairgel and aftershave products. Comes with storage facilities for skin-tight silver meggings – a must for young, wild at heart men.
Code MZ90210

NOTE to product managers of large Swedish interiors brands: if you would like to work with Manzine's creative department on a retained or project basis, our fees start at no more than €20,000 per day. Please contact brian.storm@themanzine.com in the first instance.

Maxims & Meditations from the Wise Old Barbour Jacket

In this world there is no satisfaction in the instant and ephemeral – apart from Sambucca shots and Burger King.

THE SPORTING LIFE

I went to softball training this afternoon. During the winter we do it in a sports hall. Lots more running around than normal summer training. Near the end we were having a break and I laid down on the floor for a couple of minutes. When I got up, there was a Turin Shroud of my Yankee t-shirt on the floor, where the sweat didn't go through the name and number on the back. Aside from it meaning I was a disgusting sweaty boy, it was kinda beautiful (CR)

29

Manzine
UK/Germany, Issue 3, Dritte ausgabe (210 × 297mm, 8¼ × 11¾ inches)
Starting as a parody of men's magazines – the principals on the project have all worked for big-name men's titles – *Manzine* has established a surreal, satirical voice that is aimed at broader targets; examples here include, TOP, a visual pastiche of *The New Yorker* and, BOTTOM, a parody of IKEA furniture.
Editor *Kevin Braddock*; Creative director *Warren Jackson*

032c

CONTEMPORARY CULTURE
15th Issue Berlin Summer 2008
D €10 EU €12 US $20 www.032c.com

REM KOOLHAAS, HERZOG & DE MEURON, and HUO on
HAUS DER KUNST
MÜNCHEN

From NAZI TEMPLE to
ART LABORATORY
Page 41-80

LUXURY MARKETING (the New York way), 20 Years of MAISON MARTIN MARGIELA, COLLIER SCHORR vs THOMAS DEMAND

Issue 15, Summer 2008

032c
Germany, Issue 15, Summer 2008 (200 × 270mm, 8 × 10¾ inches)
This contemporary culture magazine has regularly reinvented itself as it strives to maintain an aesthetic as challenging as its content.
Editor *Joerg Koch*; Art director *Mike Meiré*

‘It got called the new ugly, but ugly was never, ever in my mind. I wanted to create a doubt in people’s minds about what is beautiful’.

MIKE MIERÉ
ART DIRECTOR
032c

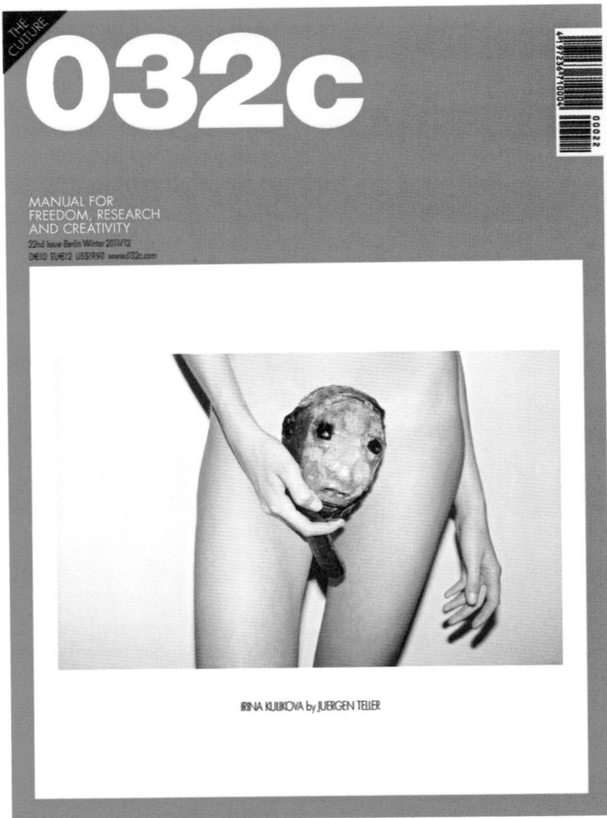

Issue 22, Winter 2011/2012. Art director *Mike Meiré*

Issue 19, Winter 2007/2008. Art director *Mike Meiré*

032c (Germany)

EDITOR JOERG KOCH
ART DIRECTOR MIKE MEIRÉ

Berlin-based culture magazine *032c* provides the perfect example of how today's magazines must reinvent themselves as they develop. Since first appearing in late 2000, it has gone through several distinct phases. Each one has seen a clear shift in editorial stance reflected by a similarly definite visual rethink.

The first three editions consisted of 48 pages of unbound newsprint printed in two colours – black and Pantone 032c red ink – hence the magazine's name. It had an outsider, samizdat appeal, with large, capitalized Franklin Gothic headlines in red and black reflecting an aggressive editorial stance that invited responses to themes such as 'Destruction' and 'What's Next?' Founder-editor Joerg Koch described it at the time as a 'punk fanzine designed by Dieter Rams'.

Like many projects that start life as outsiders, the magazine soon found itself courted as an insider, and Koch realized his fanzine had to establish a more serious aesthetic. From issue four it became a magazine: perfect-bound with a glossy cover, different paper stocks and full-colour printing. It retained a strong visual identity but shifted to a calmer, Modernist approach under new art director Petra Langhammer, which better reflected a more journal-like approach to art, culture and fashion. It dropped the red visual reference to its name, and saw the arrival of brand advertising in its pages. *032c* was now an intelligent, directional magazine that challenged editorial norms from within a smart, but rather conservative, minimalist package.

Too conservative, perhaps? Koch felt so: 'Everybody knows now how to design a magazine in a tasteful, aspirational manner. It has become such a cliché,' he said in 2007. So for issue 13 of *032c* he asked German art director Mike Meiré to reinvent the magazine. Meiré had built a strong

Issue 1, Winter 2000/01. Art director *Vladimir Llovet Casademont*

Issue 12, Winter 2006/2007. Art director *Petra Langhammer*

reputation within his home country with *Apart*, *Econy*, *Brand Eins* and other magazines, but Koch felt he remained an unknown quantity outside Germany. *032c* is published in English and has an international readership.

The resulting redesign caused quite a stir. The new issue revived the bright 032c-red cover, and introduced screaming, artificially stretched Helvetica and Times headlines, clashing reds and greens (see page 138) and sections on pastel green paper. At a basic level it functioned, the text was largely legible and you could sense the hand of design on the pages. But it was hard to avoid the word ugly – so extreme was this *volte face*.

My first reaction at the time was confusion. I emailed Koch to say so, to which he replied, 'Your message made me incredibly happy! This is exactly what we wanted to achieve, this sort of engagement with a magazine where you question yourself if it makes sense, if it is really brilliant or simply daft.'

The redesign became more than just a story of magazine design, it was a story of beauty versus ugliness, Europe versus the USA, even Germany versus the UK. The arguments raged in what was perhaps one of the last design blog comment-fests before Twitter took over. *Creative Review* termed it part of the 'New Ugly' trend, and Pentagram partner Michael Beirut attacked the redesign on *Design Observer*, asking of the stretched type, 'Dear God in heaven: at long last, is nothing sacred?'

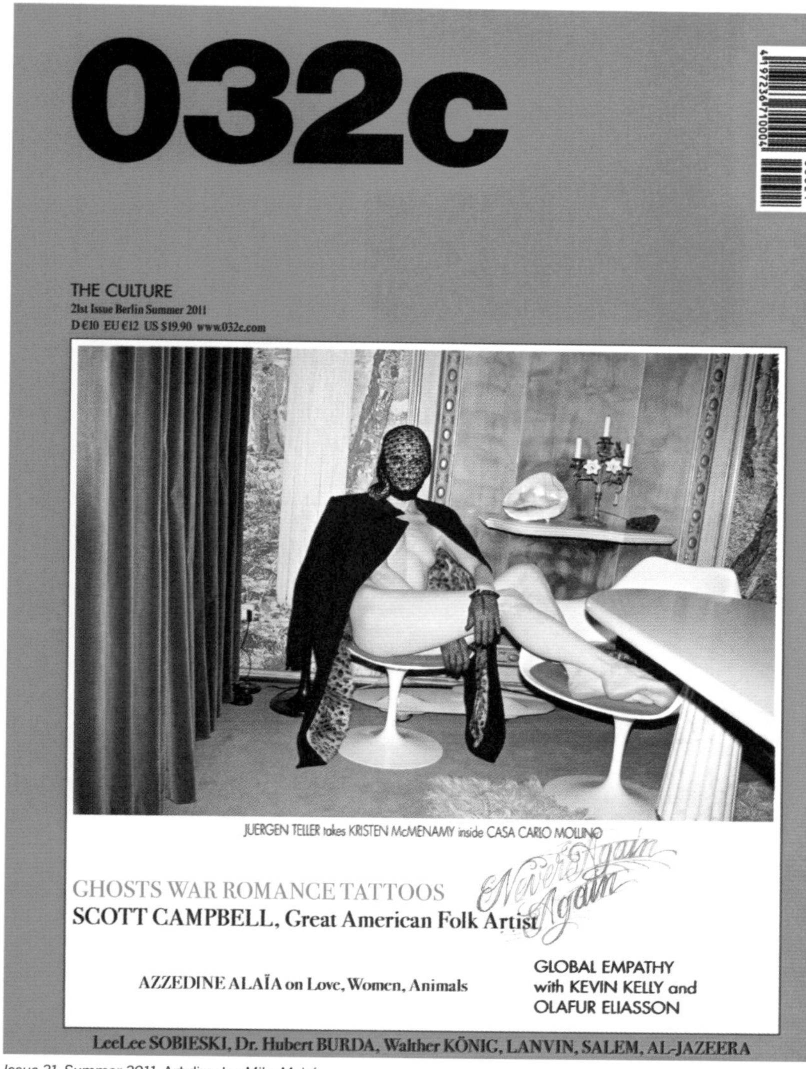

Issue 21, Summer 2011. Art director *Mike Meiré*

Koch and Meiré saw things differently, of course. They preferred to talk of brutalism rather than ugliness. 'It was about creating clashes between images, type and content, brutalizing minimalism to save it,' says Koch, while Meiré goes further: 'Ugly was never, ever in my mind. I wanted to create a doubt in people's minds about what's beautiful. Too many magazines today are just technically immaculate design and styling, empty formats for advertising. You must also share some emotion.'

In this respect he sees his approach as more genuine than most and, listening to him, it's hard to disagree: '*032c* has great content and needs to stand apart from this "good taste" and get people's attention, make them go "ooh what is this?"'

It took them just 30 minutes to agree the direction of the redesign. Koch recalls he thought Meiré was disappointed: 'Mike wanted to explain his direction, but I just said, "let's do it" – I could already feel the energy from him. The design of *032c* has always happened by talking and referencing of atmospheres, ideas, architecture, music and art. Mike seemed to be the perfect counterpart for that process.'

Meiré and designer Tim Geisen spent three months on the first issue, working late nights, drinking too much and checking pornography for colour references. 'I remember Peter Saville buying things under the counter, and I thought, this is an idea. How should a culture magazine look if it is a bit "under the counter"?'

Despite working remotely from different cities – *032c* is based in Berlin, Meiré in Cologne – editor and art director have a very smooth working relationship. 'There is a lot of prototyping of pages and discussions and there is almost always a consensus on the direction,' says Koch. 'There is total trust in the work of Mike and Tim, our reference systems are synchronized. And if unsynchronized moments happen, it actually produces irrational effects that we cherish. Happy end!'

The problem now, of course, is what to do next. How far do you go? Publishing content that challenges the distinctions between art, fashion and politics – 'The Culture', as *032c* covers now announce – demands a unique approach, and Meiré has provided that. A knowing marriage between content and design has been perfected – the reversed-out reproduction of a *New Yorker* interview is perhaps the key example: spontaneous yet coolly referencing the context within which *032c* operates and to which it aspires (see page 136).

The design has continued to develop, issue by issue, but even in the context of *032c* there appears to be limits. The magazine has now spent just about half its 12-year existence with the Meiré design, and there are already signs that the hardline aesthetic is softening, with gentler typefaces and calmer designs. Watch this space for phase four.

032c
Germany, Issue 14, Winter 2007/2008
(240 × 315mm, 9½ × 12½ inches)
The 2000 launch issue featured a square of PMS 032c colour on the cover; for a period that colour was dropped (OPPOSITE, BOTTOM) before being reintroduced with Meiré's 2007 redesign (OPPOSITE, TOP RIGHT).
Editor *Joerg Koch*; Art director *Various as listed*

THE ANTI-GRAVITY MEN
Cecil Balmond and the structural engineers of Arup
by David Owen, reproduced from
THE NEW YORKER
— June 25, 2007

Collaboration is a key concept at Arup and central to the way Balmond works. Rem Koolhaas says that he and Balmond are

was educated mainly in Germany and Denmark. ("Ove" rhymes with "rove"; the stressed syllable in "Arup" is the first.) In 1938, back in England, Ove and his cousin Arne went into business as Arup & Arup, Ltd., Civil Engineers and Contractors, and after the war Ove struck out on his own, creating the firm that exists today. His biography—"Ove Arup: Masterbuilder of the Twentieth Cen-

ern architectural masterpieces, sits on a promontory in Sydney Harbor and resembles an opening white blossom, or a jumbled cascade of cockle shells. It was designed by Jørn Utzon, a young, visionary, temperamental architect from Denmark, who won the design competition, in 1957, despite having submitted little more than dazzling sketches. The judges were concerned about Ut-

technical challenges posed by the roof shells—the most recognizable and structurally audacious feature of the design—the firm built a computer center in the basement of its London offices. Even then, completing the calculations and testing the designs took four years. Balmond, who had joined the firm as a new university graduate in 1966, wasn't involved in the project,

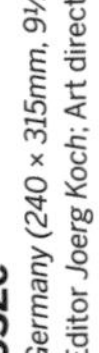

032c
Germany (240 × 315mm, 9½ × 12½ inches)
Editor *Joerg Koch*; Art director *Mike Meiré*

Issue 14, Winter 2007/08
Wolfgang Tillmans's photo essay about structural engineer Cecil Balmond was accompanied by the text of an interview with Balmond from *The New Yorker* presented in the form of reversed-out reproductions of that magazine's actual pages, complete with page furniture and cartoons.

OPPOSITE TOP: *Issue 13, Summer 2007*
A self-portrait by Cyprien Gaillard announces the anti-Modernist outlook of the newly redesigned magazine, the headline typeface clumsily stretched.

BOTTOM: *Issue 14, Winter 2007/08*
The red crosses from the front cover onto the contents page, which features unusual combinations of typefaces, a semi-structured layout and the main headline bleeding off the top of the page.

THE ANTIMODERNIST

CECIL BALMOND

032c
Berlin Winter 2007/08
14th Issue "Cecil Balmond"
www.032c.com

Cecil Balmond Wolfgang Tillmans 37
The Anti-Gravity Men David Owen 44
Interview with Cecil Balmond Hans Ulrich Obrist 60

GLOBAL BRIEFINGS 16
Kiev Paris Moscow Rome Berlin-Dahlem
London Isfahan India Scotland Ticino

The Berlin Review 225

Life Winter 2007/08

Beda Achermann Joachim Bessing 86
Sarah Morris Alex de Looz 96
Taryn Simon Christopher Bollen 112
Oscar Niemeyer Todd Eberle 1W22
Phantasie Fotostudio Esthacus Teichwynd 124
Balenciaga Todd Cole 132
Idea Magazine Nick Currie 140
Stefano Tonchi Payam Sharifi 146
Havisham David Armstrong 152
Odile/Tulles Paul Wetherell 164
America Clang 176
Homo Novum Roger Deckker 186
Limi Yamamoto Estelle Hanania 220

EDITORIAL	06
MASTHEAD	08
CONTRIBUTORS	10
STOCKISTS	224

Cover photography by Paul Wetherell
Rachel wears coat by Martin Margiela Couture

ONE HALF-REVOLUTION AND EVERYTHING TURNS RED

The Axis of Evil

With Andreas Gursky in North Korea

Issue 23, Summer 2007

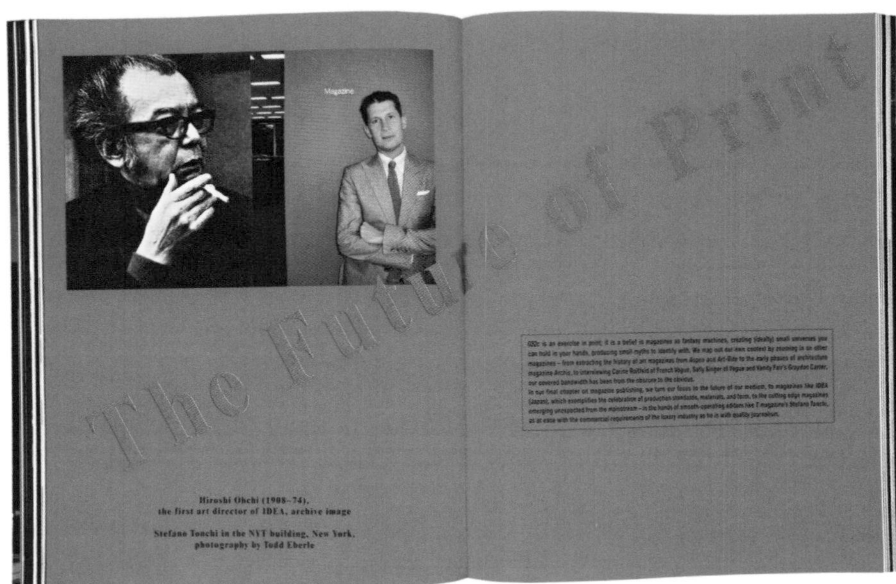

The Future of Print
Hiroshi Ohchi (1908–74),
the first art director of IDEA, archive image
Stefano Tonchi in the NYT building, New York,
photography by Todd Eberle

Issue 14, Winter 2007/08

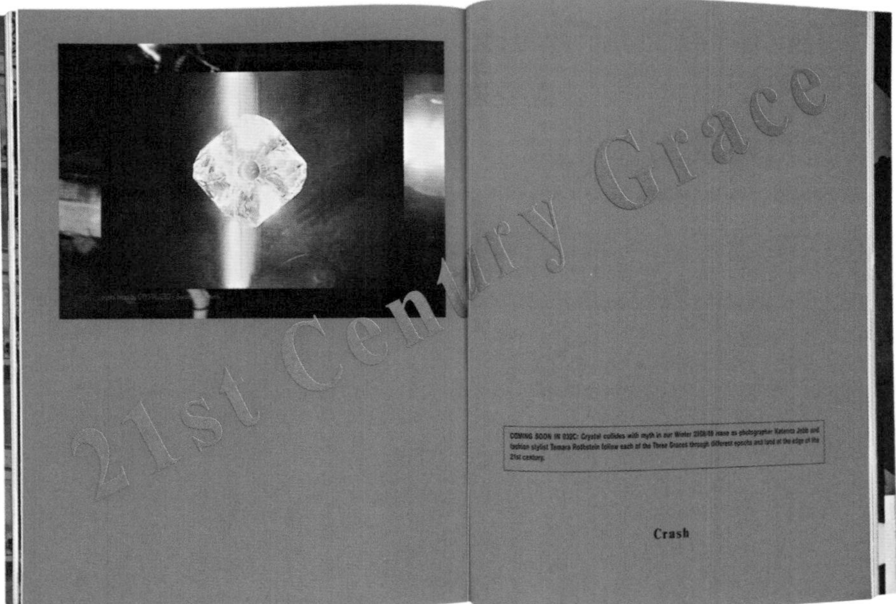

Issue 15, Summer 2008

032c
Germany (240 × 315mm, 9½ × 12½ inches)
A series of opening spreads using a repeating design that appeared in consecutive issues following the 2007 redesign. The clash of colours, uncomfortably formatted typography and apparently self-referencing headlines became the defining image of the redesign.
Editor *Joerg Koch*; Art director *Mike Meiré*

THE teenagers

The Teenagers' Homecoming 7" is out now on Merok

QUENTIN

DORIAN

IN TRUE KEVIN AND PERRY STYLE, THE TEENAGERS ARE A BAND OF FEW WORDS, WITH ONE HECK OF A PETER PAN COMPLEX TO BOOT, BUT BOY OH BOY IS EVERYONE FALLING HEAD OVER HEALS IN PUPPY LOVE WITH THEM...

If Larry Clark were directing a movie of The Virgin Suicides right about now then Air would so not be the band he'd be ringing up to score the soundtrack – The Teenagers would most definitely be the boys for the job. Leading man Quentin Delafon and his supporting cast of Dorian Dumont and Michael Szpiner make up The Teenagers. They come on all soft focus lusting, adolescent romance, dirrrty words, hanging out, falling out, making it up and getting it on. In lay mans terma they're 'totally awesome'. But hang on a seismic second aren't they all French?

We put on our clubbing clogs and trotted along to their show at the Digitalism hosted Chalk club night to investigate. 'In the beginning we were trying to hide our French accents', confesses Michael shockingly – we knew it they are French seeeee! 'We really thought nobody would think we were French. Turns out we got busted quite quickly', adds Quentin with a wink and a nudge, 'but our lyrics are pretty much how we speak everyday.'

Faux Americana sure hasn't stopped them cranking up a whopping 37924 myspazz friends and a hefty 747970 plays (we can say that at least 70 of those were blasted from the SuperHQ – we literally haven't loved anything French quite this much since we heard Jentina's, Cathy Dennis penned song French Kisses).

So maybe that's the secret to their appeal – their Frenchiness !!! We could be onto something here. What could be cooler than a hawt boy talking filthy in a French accent over some lo-fi indie noise! NOT VERY MUCH!

Now we've figured that out lets get back to the boys and find out where it's all going. Rumour has it they've been using their popularity to encourage lady fans to scribble 'I LOVE THE TEENAGERS' on various parts of their anatomy! Michael explains, 'It was a joke at the beginning, we just started it on myspace and erm 'things' came back.'

'But we stopped it now', adds Quentin, 'it got out of control – you don't want to see what we saw I'm telling you!'

We would've liked to have seen really, but moving along swiftly, the 'power of myspace' effect seems to have blasted The Teenagers from zero to hero faster than greased lightening. 'With myspace we managed to avoid all of the playing in a tiny bar to five of your friends stuff, now we have a real ready made audience to play to already', says Dorian.

But the boys aren't getting to big for their boots by any means, 'We're not claiming to be the most sophisticated musicians, we started a band together because we were friends', tells Quentin. They've already be lambasted for making two-chord lo-fi indie that's 'a bit thin for a while career' – we say who needs more than three chords if they're the best ones, you go boys!

Whatever the reason the boys got it on and made some sweet music, we should all be thanking our lucky stars. Their first release, a 7" single of their Homecoming track on Merok records, is the sort of effortless cool most bands would sell their grannies for. It's also not the kind of stuff you'll be hearing on the likes of Radio1 anytime soon, with its defiantly catchy chorus of 'I fucked my American cunt... just like I like it she's got nice tits'. Smut if ever we heard, but you can't argue when it's in a French accent, its just cultured and sophisticated!

Right now our favourite Teenagers' track is the aptly named Scarlett Johansson, but has the lady in question heard it yet? 'I don't know if she heard it yet', says Quentin, 'BUT she will one day and she will love it. Its a tribute to her hotness and our love for her; if we could meet her we would sing our song to her acapella whooooo!'

It's just like Lindsay Lohan in Mean Girls, you join a click, become popular, date a hot boy, great! So what happens when The Teenagers grow up? 'Haha, we can be teenagers forever if we want to!', exclaims Quentin with the glint of a man with a plan in his eye, 'we're 25 but suddenly we're teenagers again, we don't have to grow up we can be young forever!'

myspace.com/theteenagers

Dorian & Michael Photographed by Matthew Brindle Quentin Photographed by Billa Interview by RussellDeanStone

"Our sound is totally awesome!"

MICHAEL

SUPER*MUSIC*
The hot new sounds coming to a rave/catwalk/bus stop/shop near you...

86 87

GET THE LOOK! (FOR MORE!!!)

with

Alice Diamanté

In the future girls like Alice Diamonte will rule the world for sure. She's a hot girl on a one-woman Xanadu revival [Olivia Newton-John never looked this good, not even in that black skintight number at the end of Grease]. Sometime assistant to fashion design superstar Gareth Pugh, she's set to graduate from fashion design/marketing at St Martin's this year so watch this space, man!

"*When you're a proper lady there is nothing better than a trip back to the country to join in the hunt! We have to use rags now because of the fox laws, but the foxes can still be used for fur if they're neatly discarded of, but not if they're all mangled with teeth bites!...*

The Hunt (above)
THE FOX: The fox is called Suz and my friend Dominic gave me her to wear to the Christmas Pop [Magazine] Party. She came home with her head ripped in two, a tail missing and my boyfriend found one of her paws in his jean pocket!
FENDI SCARF: My friend Tanja and Alaxe gave this to me. I was convinced it was real until they informed me they found it on Mare Street in Hackney in a puddle. No one would treat a real Fendi so badly!'
LACE BODY: Barnardos, Nottingham £1.50. I got two of these, they remind me of something Britney would have worn before she lost it.
JACKET: I hope no one's gonna see this and claim it, my housemate Chris gave it to me after finding it. I've had it for long enough to have squatter's rights on it though.
RABBIT FUR BOOTS: Oxfam, Chesterfield £3. Chesterfield is the best place for charity shopping as there's a hell of a lot of old folk there and in the winter, when there are twice as many funerals, there are twice as many beauties in the stock shelves!
SHOE HORN/RIDING WHIP: When I moved into my old house in Hackney there was this lady at the top of the road that was one of these compulsive borders. I think shed had to clear loads out cos there was a lifetime supply of mad shit in her garden and she lent me her shopping trolley to fill so I could help her clear it. A few journeys later my bedroom looked much the same as hers!
HORSE MASK: Present from Chris (again!).

...And of course you must be prepaired for a good old knees up with champagne and canapes! (see right)
SILVER BALLGOWN: My friend Gemma has left this at my house for a very long time, and I'm hoping she has forgotten about it.
NECKLACE AND RINGS: Soho wholesalers
SWAROVSKI EARINGS: These are a present form Gareth Pugh, he made them for me out of some scraps we found in the Gina Shoes skip!
SHOES: I acquired these at the Giles for New Look launch party.
SILVER CLUTCH: Also from the mad lassey who used to live up the road.

And when I have some spare time there's nothing I like more than to jet down to St. Tropez for a tan top-up and a massage on the beach... (see left)
D&G SWIMMING COSTUME: I won this in a very tense bidding war on eBay – finally it was mine for a mere 25 pounds. Paris was very disappointed!
T-SHIRT: Before they got rid of it, every Sunday you could find me head-first in the £1 pound bin at the back of East End vintage haven Beyond Retro. Once you dug through all the vile curtain print size 16 dresses you could often find a treasure. This did have loads of beads on the tassels but I had to cut them off because they would flick around and hurt me when I danced.
SUNGLASSES: Westmorland Rd Market, Camberwell, £2.
DIOR BAG: I actually paid £10 for this thinking it was real from a charity shop in Hackney but everyone pointed out that Dior would NOT put a velcro fastening on anything.
PONYTAIL: Dalston, where else?!

Photography by Simian Coates

myspace.com/alicekirkpatrick

SUPER*STYLE*

42 43

Super Super
UK, June 2007 (245 × 343mm, 9¾ × 13½ inches)
This youth-culture magazine was as consciously anti-Modernist in its design as 032c but in a far less knowing manner. Seemingly designed using PhotoShop rather than a layout programme, the result is a chaotic, multi-coloured mix of multiple typefaces on gridless pages.
Editor *Russell Dean Stone*; Creative director *Super Steve*

TV DINNER PARTY
Glenn O'Brien

Memory fades. Videotape too. Memory fades to black. Video fades to white. Sometimes *TV Dinner Party* looks like ghosts emerging from fog or smoke, but on close inspection, most of the characters still exist, but older, whiter, foggier.

In 1978, I started a public access cable television show called *Glenn O'Brien's TV Party* and over the next four years we made about eighty or ninety shows. It was "the TV show that's a cocktail party, but which could be a political party." It went on at midnight and was seen by New Yorkers lucky enough to be wired for cable and wired enough to still be awake. Today you can get some moments from *TV Party* on DVD and more will come.

We did *TV Party* almost every week, sometimes we would re-run a show when we were short of funds, and we began doing theme shows. Usually the show was recorded and went out live on cable, but sometimes we shot on videotape in a nightclub. In the spring of 1979 we decided to do a *TV Dinner Party* on location at One University (so called after its address, aka Chinese Chance, its corporate name), the current and final restaurant operated by Mickey Ruskin of Max's Kansas City fame. Mickey Ruskin also operated the Ninth Circle, Max's Terre Haute, the Longview Country Club (later known as Levine's—a Canadian-Jewish deli in collaboration with the artists Les Levin), the Lower Manhattan Ocean Club on Chambers Street (where bands such as the Patti Smith Group and the Talking Heads played early gigs), and the Locale, in a basement on Waverly Place.

One University was less of club atmosphere than Max's and it had a more evolved menu. At one point Julian Schnabel worked there as a cook. It had art on the walls and a jukebox curated by painter Stephen Mueller (recently deceased). Having been fed TV dinners as a child (a fact my mother still denies), I thought it would be fun to have a *TV Dinner Party*, or a *TV Party* where dinner would be served. Mickey Ruskin was a friend and he agreed to host the show, which was plagued with technical difficulties. This episode was definitely directed by Amos Poe, who is visible on camera through much of the show, wearing my Wayfarer sunglasses and green dinner jacket, and generally acting as my double. He opens the show impersonating me.

Guests included Tim Wright of the band DNA, who performs an extraordinary solo guitar piece with bird tween accompaniment David Byrne, and the TV Party Orchestra—Walter Steding, Lenny Ferrari, Catherine Ruby (now Rebennack), and the Scottish actor Robbie Coltrane. This was just before Robbie became one of the most well known actors in cinema—in films from *European Vacation* to *Caravaggio, Mona Lisa, Absolute Beginners, Nuns on the Run, The Pope Must Die, The World is Not Enough*, and the entire *Harry Potter* series). On *TV Dinner Party*, Robbie guested as a Don Luigi Caponato, a record company executive who resembled some of the heavies he'd play later.

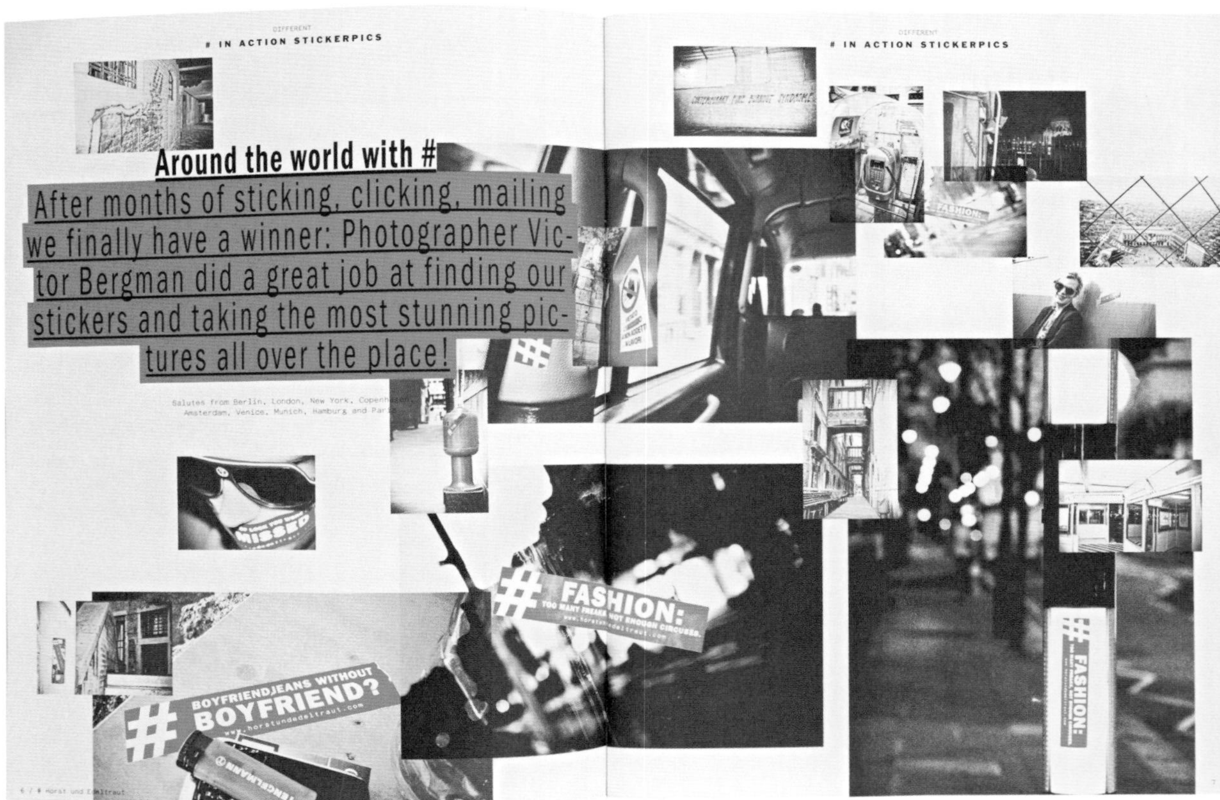

DIFFERENT
IN ACTION STICKERPICS

Around the world with #

After months of sticking, clicking, mailing we finally have a winner: Photographer Victor Bergman did a great job at finding our stickers and taking the most stunning pictures all over the place!

Salutes from Berlin, London, New York, Copenhagen, Amsterdam, Venice, Munich, Hamburg and Paris

YOUR SPIRIT ANIMAL

RANDOM AFTERNOON WHEREABOUTS

Seth Clark is either a Frog, Otter or Spider

From houses to steel mills, artist Seth Clark is inspired by Pittsburgh's industrial past and the abandoned structures left in its wake. A collector at heart—Clark recently began what he calls a "lifelong project" of collecting unique envelope swatches—it is no surprise that Clark's work relies heavily on materials scavenged from his daily life in Pittsburgh. In his own words, "just about anything that is flat and clean enough to be adhered to paper is layered to create a dimensional foundation." The result is awesomely complex and energetic, much like Clark's muse, the Steel City herself.

CREATE

OUTPOST JOURNAL

21

ISSUE 01 / FALL 2011

ART/DESIGN/ACTION FROM THE FRINGES

PITTSBURGH, PA

Lenka Clayton's Optimistic Mythology

Lenka Clayton's conceptual work is often about structure, reorganization and exaggeration, taking an everyday idea or question and seeing it through to its (il)logical end. The tasks she sets up for herself—photographing 613 people mentioned in a German newspaper; collecting, hand-numbering and redistributing 7000 stones; sending handwritten letters to every household in the world with writer Michael Crowe; or re-editing President Bush's famous "Axis of Evil" speech so every word comes out in alphabetical order (the result is a mesmerizing, audible word-cloud)—often involve laborious processes and a cheery commitment to what Clayton describes as her "optimistic mythology."

HOBBIES

HOW LONG HAVE YOU LIVED IN PITTSBURGH

22

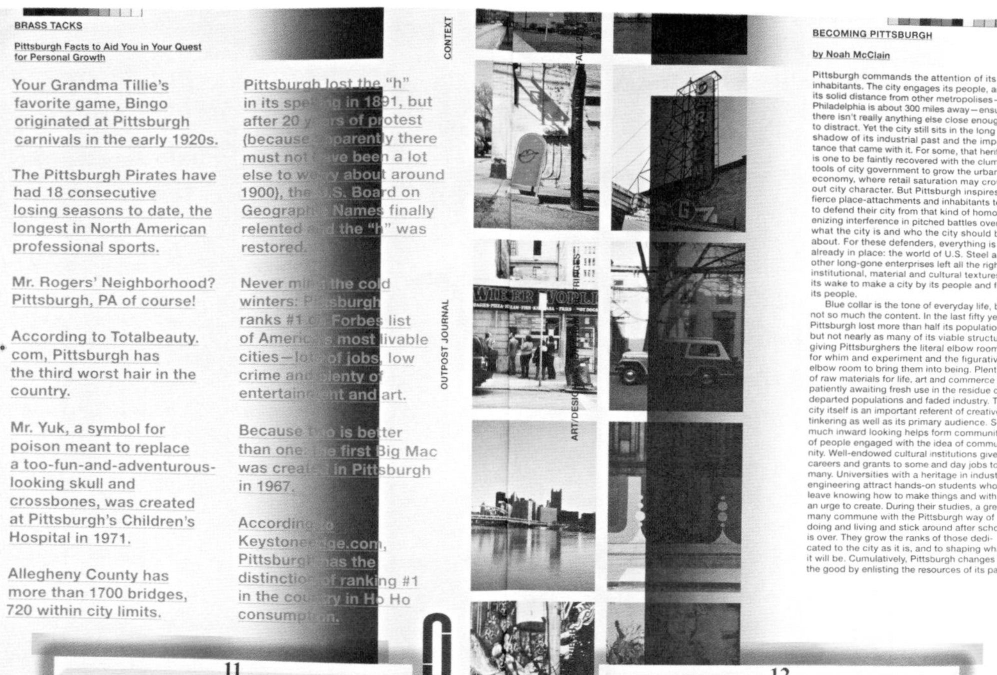

BRASS TACKS

Pittsburgh Facts to Aid You in Your Quest for Personal Growth

Your Grandma Tillie's favorite game, Bingo originated at Pittsburgh carnivals in the early 1920s.

The Pittsburgh Pirates have had 18 consecutive losing seasons to date, the longest in North American professional sports.

Mr. Rogers' Neighborhood? Pittsburgh, PA of course!

According to Totalbeauty.com, Pittsburgh has the third worst hair in the country.

Mr. Yuk, a symbol for poison meant to replace a too-fun-and-adventurous-looking skull and crossbones, was created at Pittsburgh's Children's Hospital in 1971.

Allegheny County has more than 1700 bridges, 720 within city limits.

Pittsburgh lost the "h" in its spe[illegible]g in 1891, but after 20 y[illegible]rs of protest (because [illegible]parently there must not [illegible]ve been a lot else to w[illegible]y about around 1900), the [illegible].S. Board on Geograph[illegible] Names finally relented [illegible] the "h" was restored.

Never mi[illegible] the cold winters: P[illegible]sburgh ranks #1 o[illegible] Forbes list of Americ[illegible] most livable cities—lo[illegible] of jobs, low crime and plenty of entertainment and art.

Because two is better than one: the first Big Mac was created in Pittsburgh in 1967.

According to Keystone[illegible]ge.com, Pittsburgh has the distinction of ranking #1 in the country in Ho Ho consumption.

CONTEXT

OUTPOST JOURNAL

11

BECOMING PITTSBURGH

by Noah McClain

Pittsburgh commands the attention of its inhabitants. The city engages its people, and its solid distance from other metropolises—Philadelphia is about 300 miles away—ensures there isn't really anything else close enough to distract. Yet the city still sits in the long shadow of its industrial past and the importance that came with it. For some, that heritage is one to be faintly recovered with the clumsy tools of city government to grow the urban economy, where retail saturation may crowd out city character. But Pittsburgh inspires fierce place-attachments and inhabitants tend to defend their city from that kind of homogenizing interference in pitched battles over what the city is and who the city should be about. For these defenders, everything is already in place: the world of U.S. Steel and other long-gone enterprises left all the right institutional, material and cultural textures in its wake to make a city by its people and for its people.

Blue collar is the tone of everyday life, but not so much the content. In the last fifty years, Pittsburgh lost more than half its population but not nearly as many of its viable structures, giving Pittsburghers the literal elbow room for whim and experiment and the figurative elbow room to bring them into being. Plenty of raw materials for life, art and commerce are patiently awaiting fresh use in the residue of departed populations and faded industry. The city itself is an important referent of creative tinkering as well as its primary audience. So much inward looking helps form communities of people engaged with the idea of community. Well-endowed cultural institutions give careers and grants to some and day jobs to many. Universities with a heritage in industrial engineering attract hands-on students who leave knowing how to make things and with an urge to create. During their studies, a great many commune with the Pittsburgh way of doing and living and stick around after school is over. They grow the ranks of those dedicated to the city as it is, and to shaping what it will be. Cumulatively, Pittsburgh changes for the good by enlisting the resources of its past.

12

Outpost Journal

USA, Issue 1, Pittsburgh, Fall 2011 (230 × 305mm, 9 × 12 inches)

Each issue of this biannual magazine shares culture from a lesser-known city – an outpost. A strong visual structure gives it the appearance of a report or catalogue, while printing guides and gradient fades add to a layered aesthetic. Editors *Manya K. Rubinstein and Pete Oyler*; Design director *Jay Peter Salvas*

OPPOSITE, TOP

White Zinfandel

USA, Issue 2, TV Dinners, Fall/Winter 2012 (230 × 330mm, 9 × 13 inches)

A food magazine named after a wine grape, most pages are monochrome and feature a highly structured grid and full-page gradient fades. Editor and creative director *Jiminie Ha*

OPPOSITE, BOTTOM

Horst und Edeltraut

Germany, Issue 2, 2010 (230 × 300mm, 9¼ × 12 inches)

An annual magazine spin-off from an online publishing project that uses different paper stocks, fluoro inks and an often dense, layered design. Editors *Johanna Moers and Cosima Bucarelli*; Art director *Pascal Schöning*

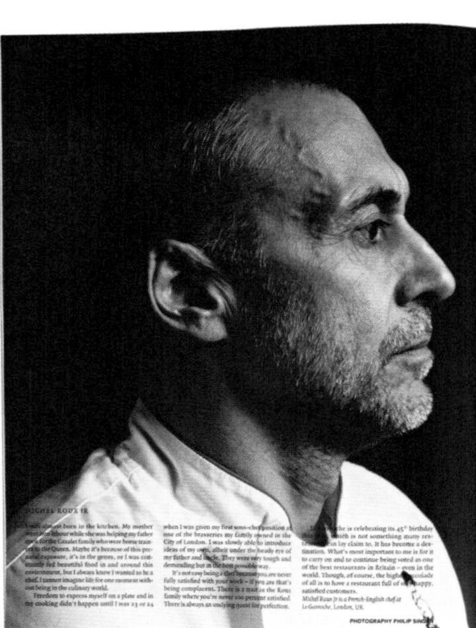

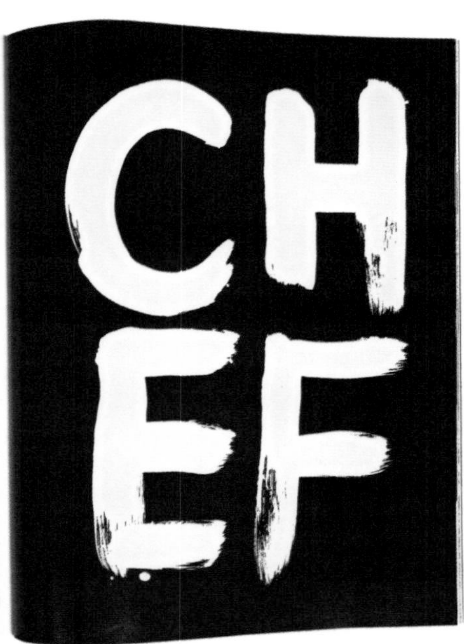

Port

UK, Issue 6, Summer 2012 (230 × 290mm, 9¼ × 11½ inches)

The crisp, hard-line Modernism of the page layouts of this men's magazine is both emphasized and opposed by full-page handpainted headlines.

Editor *Dan Crowe*; Creative directors *Kuchar Swara and Matt Willey*; Hand-lettering *Sara Cwynar*

MORE PORT p178

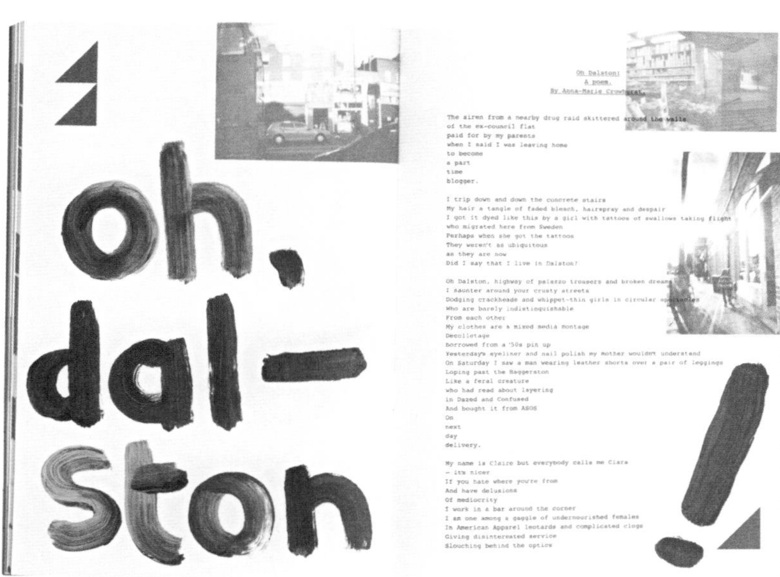

Cagoule
UK, Issue 1, Winter 2011 (180 × 260mm, 9½ × 12½ inches)
A handpainted headline adds colour and personality to the page.
Editor *Cathy Olmedillas*; Art director *Rob Lowe*

Wired
USA, July 2010 (203 × 276mm, 8 × 11 inches)
Photograph, headline and standfirst become a single entity.
Editor-in-chief *Chris Anderson*; Creative director *Scott Dadich*; Illustrations *Sarah King*; Photography *Eric Ray Davidson*
MORD WIRED ON p000 / digital

Man About Town
UK, Issue 9, Autumn/Winter 2011 (230 × 300mm, 9¼ × 12 inches)
Photography and styling credits are repeated in large, hand-drawn characters to fill the entire spread.
Editor-in-chief *Philip Utz*; Creative direction *M/M (Paris)*

BENJAMIN BRUNO JAMIE HAW KESWORTH HA WORTH A JNUMAN WILL IAOJDSON

Issue 3

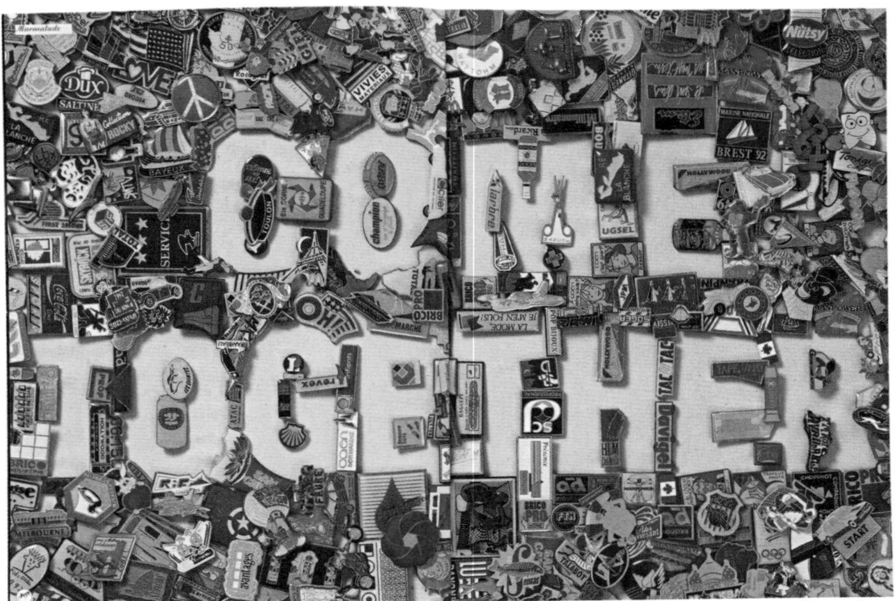

Issue 2

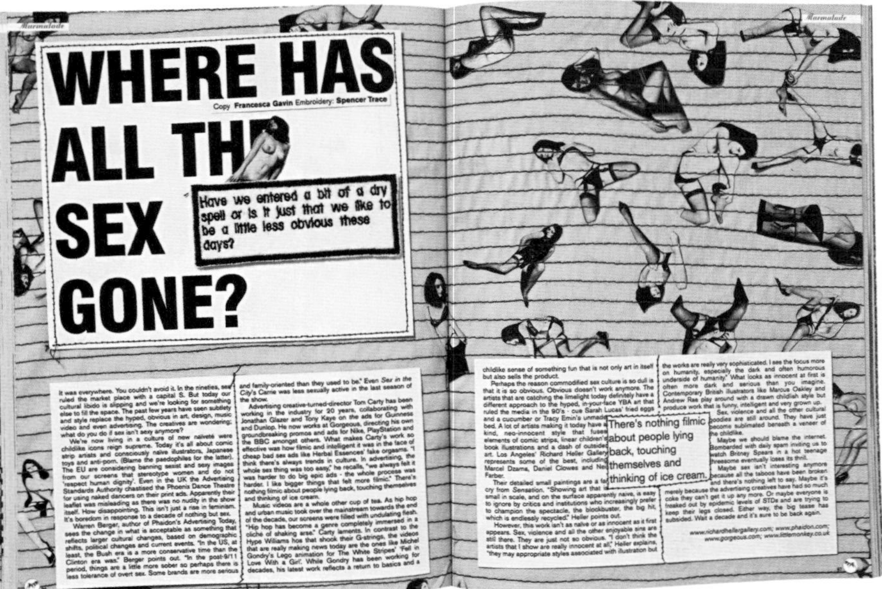

Issue 2

Marmalade
UK (187 × 252mm, 7½ × 10 inches)
Subtitled 'The Creative Spread', *Marmalade* covered young ad creatives, designers and musicians. It used a hand-made aesthetic: each page was created as a live tableau that was photographed to be included in the magazine. Headlines were cut out of paper, shaped out of lapel-pins or printed out and machine-sewn onto a decorated background.
Editor *Kirsty Robinson*; Art director *Sacha Spencer Trace*

CUT'N'
HAND AUFS HERZ: HAST DU SCHON
EINMAL JEMANDEN IMITIERT? ODER DICH
GEÄRGERT, DASS EIN ANDERER DICH KOPIERT?
IN DER MODE PASSIERT DAS STÄNDIG
UND ES LIEGT IN DER NATUR DER DINGE. WENN
ES DABEI NUR NICHT UM SO VIEL GELD
UND EHRE GINGE.
TEXT KERSTIN GÜNTZEL

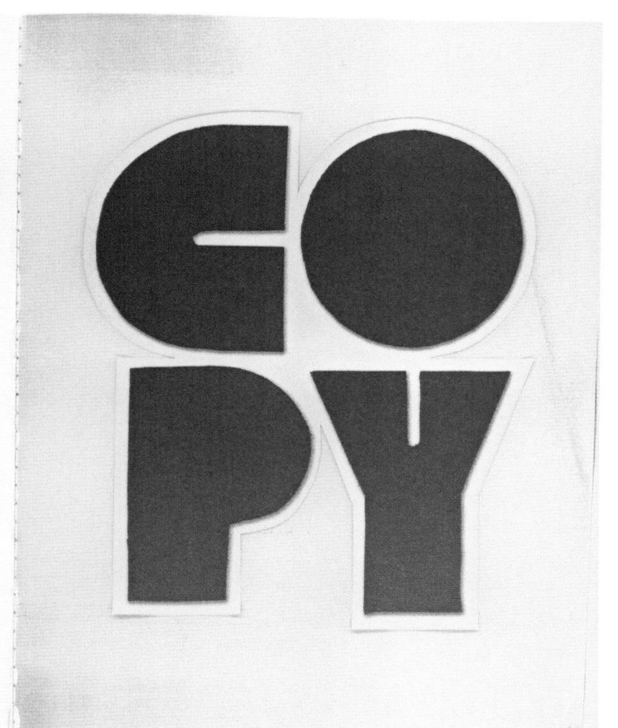

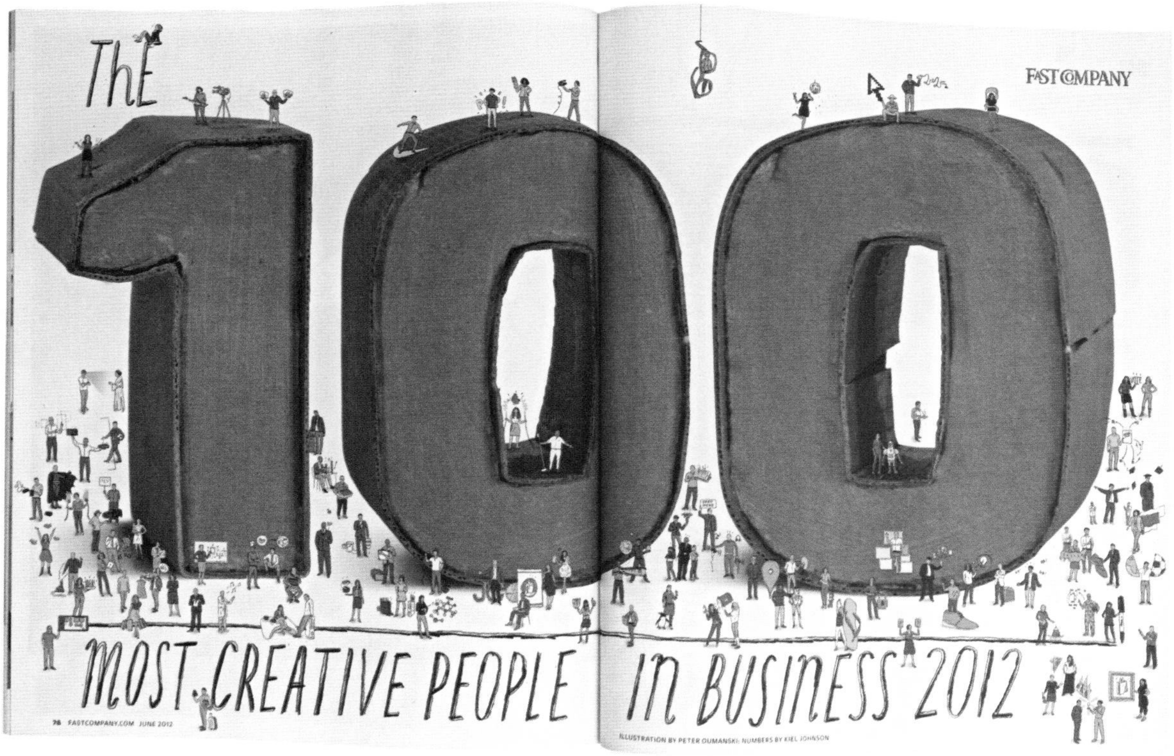

THE
100
MOST CREATIVE PEOPLE IN BUSINESS 2012
FAST COMPANY
78 FASTCOMPANY.COM JUNE 2012
ILLUSTRATION BY PETER OUMANSKI; NUMBERS BY KIEL JOHNSON

CUT – leute machen kleider
Germany, February 2009 (210 × 270mm, 8¼ × 10¾ inches)
This magazine celebrates making your own clothes. The design reflects this DIY outlook with hand-made lettering and details sewn onto the page.
Publisher Horst Moser; Editor-in-chief *Anja Kellner*; Art directors *Lucie Heselich and Marta Olésniewicz*

Fast Company
USA, June 2012 (223 × 275mm, 9 × 11 inches)
The opening spread to a list of the '100 Most Creative People in Business' has a cardboard '100' peopled by drawn characters representing the following 100 entries.
Editor *Robert Safian*; Creative director *Florian Bachleda*; Art director *Alice Alves*; Illustration *Peter Oumanskiz*

Paris (Fading Like a Childhood Memory)
South Africa, Issue 1, 2012 (168 × 240mm, 6¾ × 9½ inches)
Palindromic (they can be viewed either way up) images of heads and hats set against images of Antarctica.
Editor and creative director *Peet Pienaar*; Portraits *Paul Ward*; Landscapes *US Antarctica Program*

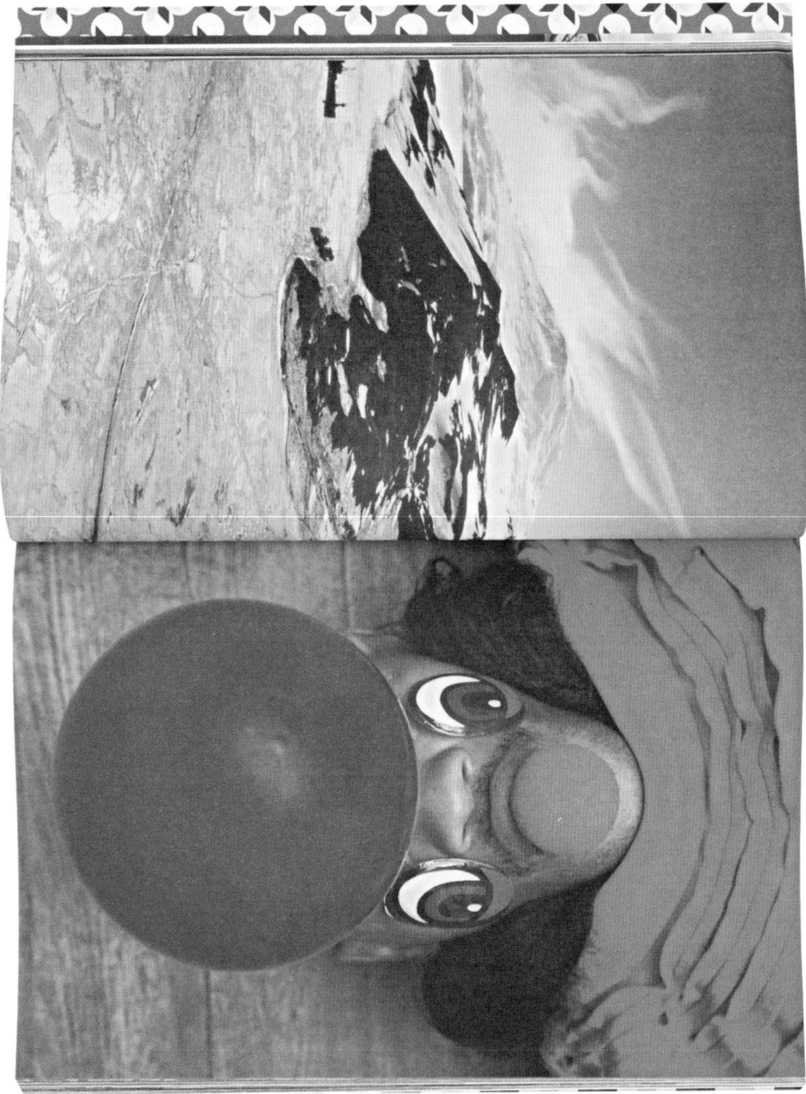

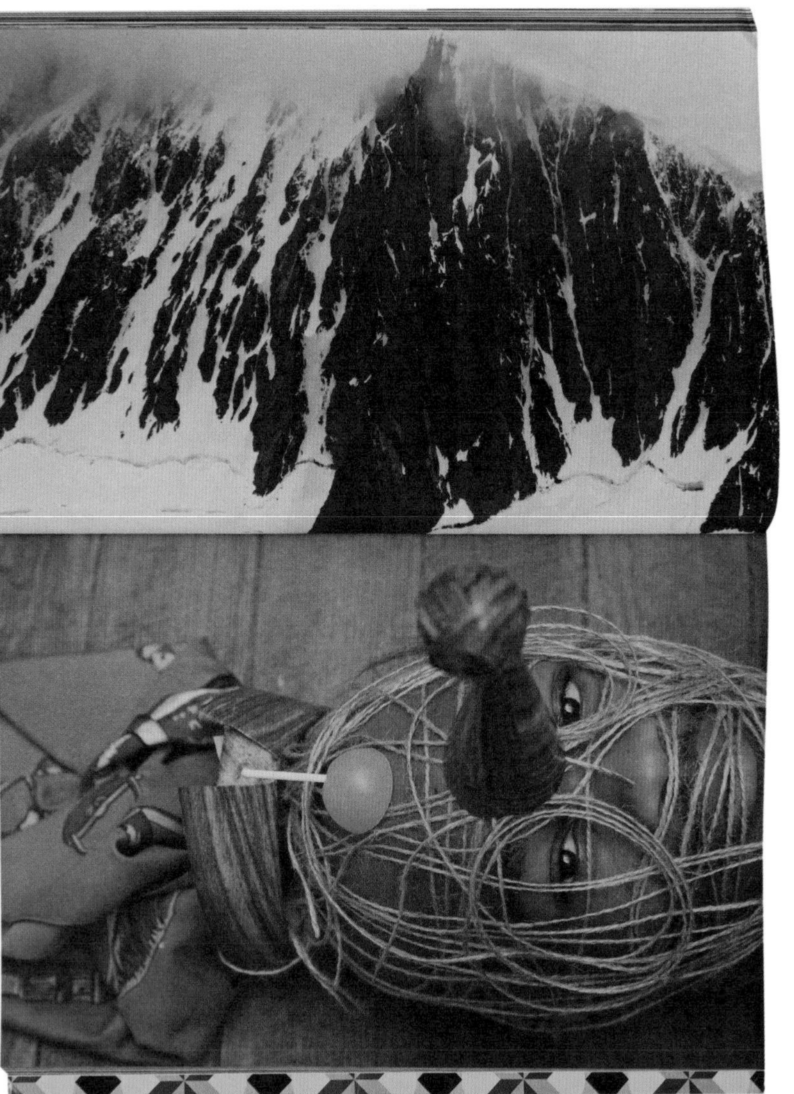

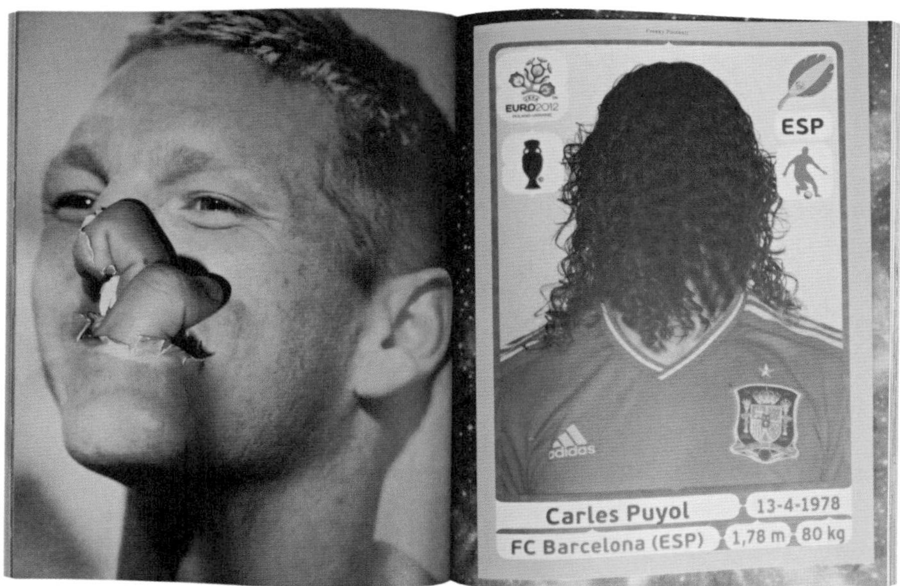

Sepp
Germany, Issue 6, Euro 2012 (235 × 308mm, 9¼ × 12 inches)
'Freaky football' is the headline to this set of absurdist photomontages that question the perfect images of our footballing heroes.
Editor-in-chief *Godfrey Deeny*; Creative director *Beda Achermann*; Artwork *Beni Bischof*

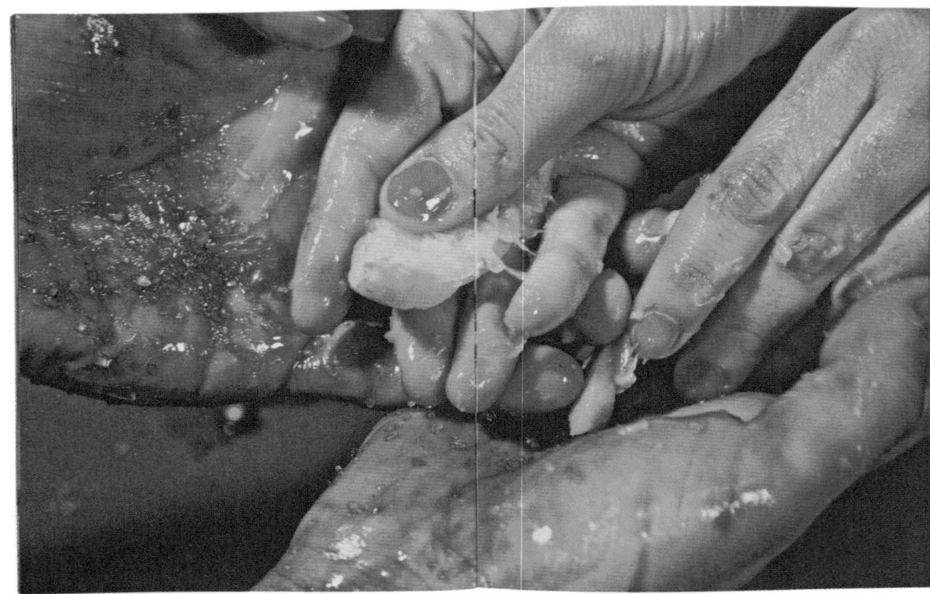

Permanent Food

Italy, Issue 14 (170 × 230mm, 6½ × 9 inches)
Each issue is a collection of appropriated items – photographs, magazine pages and advertisements – collated by artist Cattelan and advertising art director Manfrin into a run of images without any attribution or captioning. Some pairings of images echo each other visually, but all interpretation is left to the reader.
Editors *Maurizio Cattelan and Paola Manfrin*

OPPOSITE **Toiletpaper**

Italy, February 2012 (225 × 290mm, 9 × 11½ inches)
A similarly configured series of full-page-sized bled images, this time Cattelan collaborates with photographer Ferrari and numerous models and stylists to create images that subvert advertising and lifestyle photography.
Editors *Maurizio Cattelan and Pierpaolo Ferrari*

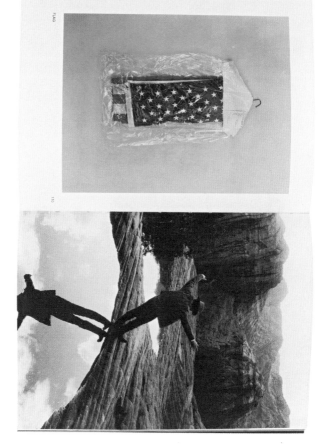

ELLE
Lady don't fall backwards
OCTOBER 2009
£3.60
Popeye the sailor man
Lives in a caravan
Popeye the sailor man
It's strange what we recall
& odd what we forget
Broken love song
We are the goon squad & we're coming to town
(meep meep)

OH YES
i'M FiNE EVERYTHiNG'S
JUST WONDERFUL
i'M HAVING THE TIME OF MY LiFE

Lurex socks by Topshop. Suede boots by Camilla Skovgaard. Gold bracelet, worn throughout, Lily's own. Taffeta and metal dress by
Luella
Lily Allen: the voice of a generation. Matthew d'Ancona meets her,
& London's hottest designers create one-off pieces for our controversial cover star
Photographs by RANKIN
Fashion by ANNE-MARIE CURTIS

Elle
UK, October 2009 (220 × 284mm, 8¾ × 11¼ inches)
Elle often uses a handwritten font as warm contrast to the Baskerville used elsewhere in the magazine. For this interview with Lily Allen a personal quote from the singer is reversed out of the portrait (ABOVE). This front cover (OPPOSITE), also featuring Allen, is from the special subscription edition and combines Rankin's portraiture with lettering from another feature in the issue by Peter Docherty (see page 152 for the newsstand cover). Editor-in-chief *Lorraine Candy*; Creative director *Marissa Bourke*

'I'm not interested in the questions around format. Print and digital have their place and do very different things. I'm much more interested in great ideas and producing inspiring, surprising and innovative content.'

MARISSA BOURKE
CREATIVE DIRECTOR
ELLE

October 2009, newsstand cover. Photography *Rankin*

Spring/Summer 2012

Elle, Elle Collections (UK)

CREATIVE DIRECTOR MARISSA BOURKE

An international magazine brand such as *Elle* presents a particular challenge to the designer. Now the largest-circulation fashion title in the world, *Elle* first launched in France in 1945 with a brief to be the local version of *Harper's Bazaar* (USA) – something it quickly achieved under art director Peter Knapp. It now has 42 international editions, spin-off publications, including *Elle Decoration* and *Elle Girl*, and a series of 27 websites.

Produced by different publishers in different territories, the many creative teams are linked by a loose network that aims to maintain a united approach to the content and design of the magazines. In reality, each local edition has to operate within its own context and, as with many such global publishing brands, the editions vary enormously. Other, more niche titles can be better templated and repeated, but fashion brands such as *Elle* have to adapt to the local fashion landscape. A quick comparison of the UK and French versions of *Elle* demonstrates this very clearly – for a start, the French edition is weekly while in the UK the magazine is published monthly. As a result, the common features between the editions tend to boil down to easy-to-enforce features such as a particular typeface, and for over 25 years all editions of *Elle* have been dominated by the typeface Futura.

When Marissa Bourke was recruited by new *UK Elle* editor Lorraine Candy in 2004, arriving from *British Vogue* after previous roles at *The Face*, *Arena*, *Vogue Russia* and *Allure*, she felt 'there was room for improvement, that everything looked very dated'. People had warned her about the Futura aspect, but she hadn't really taken it in. 'It was their thing: "this magazine, across the world, will be designed in one font and you will not do anything else". Now, I don't really like to be told what to do, so after a couple of years of

struggling, I said: "something's gotta go, either me or this font"'.

Luckily, her timing was right, coinciding with the strategic decision to shift the magazine to the higher end of the mid-market, verging on the upmarket. 'The mid-market was floundering at the time, and it felt like the natural position for the brand', explains Bourke. 'I had grown up in Australia reading *UK Elle*, and it seemed to have strayed too far from its original proposition.' She suggested replacing Futura with Baskerville and dropping the reliance on warm reds and pinks, instead using monochrome typography throughout. 'I wanted a font template that worked with the photography rather than against or around it. It was also a very big magazine – up to 450 pages a month – so I needed a simple template that could withstand the worst a bad freelancer could throw at it.' She was not the only *Elle* creative director who felt it was time for a change: 'The redesign was subsequently picked up by a lot of other editions around the world.'

The *Elle* production schedule means that Bourke now spends most of her time working on photography for the magazine. 'Having time to focus on type and design has become a luxury, but if you have bad pictures it doesn't matter what fonts are used.' She designs the cover and cover feature, and sees every page of the magazine as it goes through the studio. But she enjoys the speed of making magazines: 'I can't bear looking at things forever. I like to do it well and quickly, then move on.'

Elle was not the first magazine to produce less commercial, more esoteric subscriber-only covers for its subscribers, but it has developed the idea beyond gimmickry and made the split print-run between newsstand and subscriptions a feature of its creative positioning.

The same can be said of *Elle Collections*, the biannual fashion catwalk special. It was originally published in a larger format to distinguish it from the monthly edition, but other titles began to copy that. 'I felt we needed to establish a point of difference by focusing more on editorial content rather than pure catwalk coverage,' explains Bourke. Reducing the page size produced financial savings that were invested in better (and varied) paper stocks and more commissioned content.

The overriding experience of the reinvented *Elle Collections* is fun. It takes full advantage of digital production to build up complex montages of images, and is often playful in its use of cut-outs and graphic devices. It is a great example of the way the fun of making a piece of editorial can shine through on the pages. 'Fashion can be an intimidating and overly serious subject. I tried to make something inclusive and celebratory, rather than exclusive for the sake of being clever,' says Bourke, who is very clear on the different roles of the two publications. 'The creative freedom of *Collections* has definitely informed the main edition, but we need to maintain the commercial positioning and identity of *Elle*, so I have to steer my team away from the more indulgent aspects of *Collections* when they sometimes appear in the main magazine.'

Bourke has a clear vision of the future for magazines: 'I'm not interested in the questions around format. Print and digital have their place and do very different things. I'm much more interested in great ideas and producing inspiring, surprising and innovative content.' Something she'll be applying to her new role as design director at the British edition of *Harper's Bazaar*. 'I'm very excited about the move. Fabien Baron's *Bazaars* were to my mind some of the best magazines ever printed, so it's very exciting to be working on a brand with such an extraordinary heritage.'

TOP & OVERLEAF
Elle Collections
UK, Spring/Summer 2011 (230 × 300mm, 9 × 12 inches)
A typical cover and series of spreads from the fashion biannual uses multiple images to create an inclusive, celebratory look at the season. Editor-in-chief *Lorraine Candy*; Creative director *Marissa Bourke*

OPPOSITE, BOTTOM
Elle
UK, June 2010 (220 × 284mm, 8¾ × 11¼ inches)
Two covers are published for each issue: a harder-working version for the newsstand and a more esoteric one for subscribers. This pair features photographs of Kylie Minogue by David Slijper. Editor-in-chief *Lorraine Candy*; Creative director *Marissa Bourke*

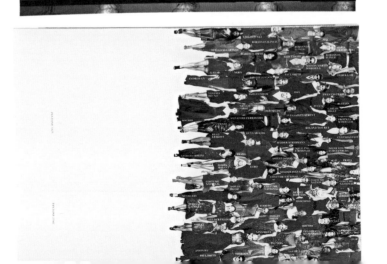

Elle Collections

UK (230 × 300mm, 9 × 12 inches)

THIS PAGE, BOTTOM Detailed street-style photographs by blogger Tommy Ton fill a spread.

OPPOSITE, BOTTOM Accessories are montaged together to create comical style portraits.

Spring/Summer 2010

Spring/Summer 2012

Photograph by JEAN-BAPTISTE MONDINO
ONE VISION
In 1985, there were two aspiring designers, and there was a black bra. The rest, as they say, is fashion history. ELLE's Lorraine Candy interviews Domenico Dolce and Stefano Gabbana. Girl meets boys!

October 2011. Photograph Jean-Baptiste Mondino

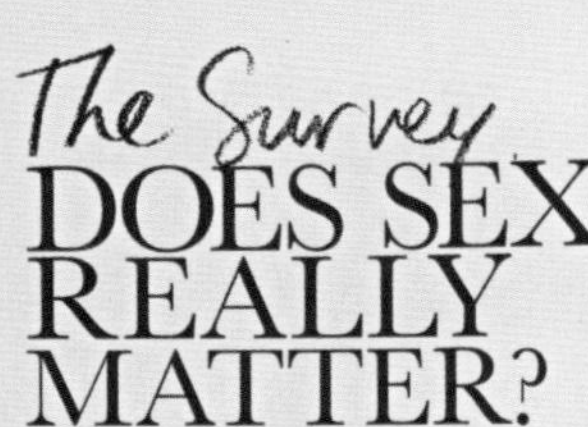

The Survey DOES SEX REALLY MATTER?

Books, TV & films all insist relationships live or die on how much SEX *we have, but are we just being talked into it? We asked you all to be* HONEST *about your libidos and you didn't let us down. Hephzibah Anderson investigates*

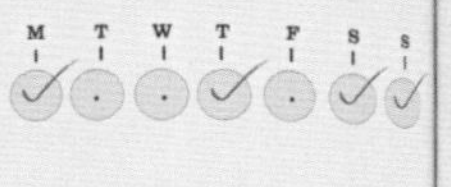

58%

of you have sex to emotionally bond with your partner

When it comes to sex, it can feel, in our regular dissection and discussion of the subject, like we have left no stone unturned, no nook or cranny unexplored, either physically, mentally or conversationally. But there's still one question that carries a *frisson* of the forbidden: how much does sex really matter?

Well, *of course* it matters, you scoff – but then you would say that, because don't we all agree that a woman who says she doesn't care about sex is either an uptight prude or a terrifying matron? Even worse are the *men* who say women don't care about sex, as though we only daydream about holding hands during sunsets and 'give in' to sex out of obligation, or as a thank you for doing the washing up.

66%

of you have had a one-night stand

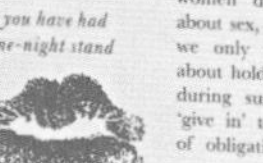

You certainly wouldn't expect a poised, worldly Parisian fashion writer and critic like Sophie Fontanel to say she actually doesn't care that much about sex. But in her autobiographical novel *L'Envie* ('Desire'), she does just that, lustily advocating celibacy and causing perfectly plucked eyebrows across France to rise as a result. To say 'non' to sex? Whatever next? In essence, it seems that for Fontanel her desire for sex is outweighed by her desire not to go on any more bad dates, or be let down by any more flighty boyfriends. Sex doesn't matter enough for her to take the chance.

Having written a similar book myself about spending a year without having sex (*Chastened*, Chatto & Windus), I can relate. I had just turned 30 and broken up with a man who hadn't loved me back. The sex had been amazing – a physical connection so powerful I simply couldn't believe it didn't mean something. Yet there he was, telling me that, yes, it was sensational, but that's all it was – simply pleasurable physical sensations. I decided if that's how we were defining sex, then I wanted none of it. Especially as it seemed sex was frustrating my desires – the deeper, emotional ones – rather than fulfilling them.

It's not exactly front-page news: mind-blowing sex does not necessarily equal emotional connection. But I'd argue even good sex can complicate relationships, and not always in a good way. And if you decide, for whatever reason, to bow out of sex for a bit, I can confirm that people look at you like you have two heads. It's taken as read that we all want sex, no matter what.

But there *are* those who willingly turn away from great sex and live to tell the tale, and even find it has a happier ending. Take a lawyer friend of mine who has contentedly accepted that, these days, affection overrules attraction. 'My early twenties were spent having great sex in toxic relationships where I tended to feel like crap. I think I got turned on by the threat of rejection. I just don't find commitment sexy. Then I fell in love – properly – and after a while sex stopped mattering, but I really don't care. Yes, I know I can go to therapy and unravel my screwed-up psyche, but I don't want to. Why risk unravelling everything else as well? I'm happy and sex just isn't that important to me.'

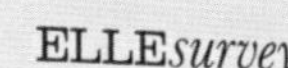

12%

of you want to have sex every day

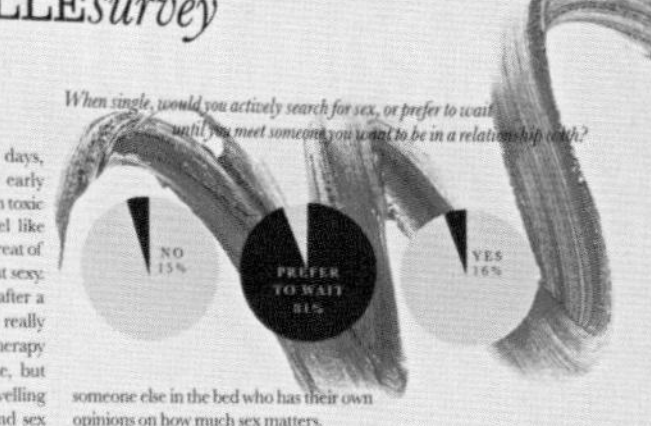

Just not that important. Really? It's not what we're led to believe. Agony aunts insist that sex is the 'glue' in any functional relationship; diminishing sex being seen as a fail-safe sign that a couple are heading for Break-Up City. But what about all the happy couples who gel just fine without it, and the miserable ones who can only connect between the sheets?

60%

of you instigate sex equally as often as your partner

We tend to feel that wanting-needing-passionate orgasmic sex is natural, normal and expected. But the brutal – and unerotic – truth is that fashion plays a much greater part in our love lives than we give it credit for. Once upon a time, it was 'natural' for women to have no interest in sex at all. Our ideas of what's sexy change all the time – and very quickly. Right now (and for the past 50 years, it seems, with ever-intensifying pressure to experiment, explore and exploit it for all it's worth) sex is having 'a moment'. It's hot to be hot. No wonder it can be hard to admit when we think we'd really rather… not.

But does it matter? Sex is, after all, a uniquely social activity. You might spend a year – as I did – analysing your desires and come up with the perfect formula for you: twice a night, twice a week, month, year… And then you remember there's someone else in the bed who has their own opinions on how much sex matters.

In a frank conversation, four of my female friends recently agreed that none of them – and no one they know – has levels of desire that match that of their boyfriends once the first six months' nightly marathon of lovemaking had burned itself out. Two of the women wanted way more sex than their boyfriends were willing to give – one because she just loves sex, the other because she needs the reassurance of being desired. The remaining two had boyfriends who wanted sex too often for them. One woman effectively limits her boyfriend to the times when she is in the mood (about twice a week). The other has sex twice a week, too, but even that was more than she really wants. She does it 'because I love him and I don't want him going elsewhere'.

How much sex matters begs us to define what it is that we LOOK *to sex to provide*

The thing is, though, none of them cared that they weren't getting exactly what they wanted in purely sexual terms because they'd all found a way to make their sex lives work in the context of their relationships. And figuring out how much sex matters also begs us to define exactly what it is that we look to sex to provide. There's the pure physical sensation, of course – sex for sex's sake. (And let's not underestimate the ➤

When in a relationship, how often do you turn down your partner for sex?

ALWAYS 2% · NEVER 23% · HALF THE TIME 14% · OCCASIONALLY 60% · OTHER 1%

ELLEUK.COM **243**

March 2012

July 2012. Photography *Doug Inglish*; Handwriting *Frank Stanley*

February 2008. Photographs *Matthias Vriens*

Elle
UK (220 × 284mm, 8¾ × 11¼ inches)
These spreads show how the magazine's strong typographic identity is combined with photography, handwriting and subtle infographics.

YEAR-END DOUBLE ISSUE

NEW YORK®

DECEMBER 22–29, 2008

REASONS TO LOVE NEW YORK (Especially Right Now)

$4.99 USA/CANADA

0 74808 01912 0 01

NYMAG.COM

December 22–29, 2008

New York

LAST MONTH, Michael Bloomberg said that he wants to leave office "having a reputation as ... maybe the greatest mayor ever." Better than Fiorello La Guardia? Well, who *was* New York's greatest mayor? Or athlete? Or gangster? Or burlesque beauty? True to the spirit of the city, this is an issue of such arguments: about New York's greatest musical, and New York's greatest bouncer, and New York's greatest mistake. About its greatest novel. And rock show. And gossip item. Our arguers include such legendarily milquetoast individuals as Al Sharpton, Frank Rich, Nora Ephron, Robert A.M. Stern, Thurston Moore, and our magazine's own critics. And you get to play, too, by choosing (on page 26) the single best day ever. Let the shouting begin.

The GREATEST NEW YORK EVER

THIRTY PAGES OF ARGUMENTS, BEGINNING WITH THE SINGLE BEST YEAR TO HAVE LIVED IN THIS TOWN.

1898
When the City Came Together

by PHILLIP LOPATE

WHAT BETTER TIME to have been a New Yorker? On January 1, 1898, the consolidation plan went into effect, joining the largest city in the nation (Manhattan) with the fourth-largest (Brooklyn) and throwing in Queens, Staten Island, and the Bronx for good measure. A huge crowd gathered in Union Square and marched down to City Hall, celebrating with fireworks and floats. Though some Brooklynites mourned their loss of municipal identity, the amalgamation had been inevitable ever since the opening of the Brooklyn Bridge, in 1883. Expansion was the order of the day: That same year, the United States annexed the Philippines, Guam, Puerto Rico, and Hawaii. A beefed-up New York was now primed to become America's imperial city, dazzling the world.

In keeping with this self-conscious sense of global destiny, the city was now awash in institutions of neoclassical Roman grandeur: The Metropolitan Museum of Art, the New York Public Library, the Brooklyn Museum, and Columbia University were in various stages of construction. It was a great time for the wealthy, the so-called Four Hundred who could fit into Mrs. Astor's ballroom. The city had finally recovered from the 1893 recession, and the economy was on the rise.

If you went down into the streets, you would see that clash of ugliness and beauty, comfort and inconvenience, elegance and grit that would become the New York aesthetic and that Alfred Stieglitz was documenting in photographs. Immigrants, especially Italians and Jews, were pouring in, bringing a cosmopolitan flavor to street life and alarming Anglo-Saxon nativists. Realist writers such as Stephen Crane and William Dean Howells were injecting harsh truths into the decorous minds of middle-class readers.

The era came to be called the Gay Nineties because of its ostentatious emphasis on fun; it was called the Mauve Decade because of its Wildean "decadence" and openness to license. There was plenty of entertainment, as New York City had begun marketing itself as America's show-business and media capital. You could go to vaudeville shows or see Edison's movies at kinetoscope parlors; you could watch Lillian Russell in operettas by Victor Herbert, when she was not being squired around by Diamond Jim Brady; you could root for prizefighters like Bob Fitzsimmons, Gentleman Jim Corbett, and James Jeffries. A popular song like "Sidewalks of New York" sold millions of sheet-music copies.

New York's port was in the midst of an ambitious improvement project. J.P. Morgan ruled the financial world; Tammany's canny boss Richard Croker ran the city's politics. Smooth going all around. Of course, there was vast misery in the tenements and sweatshops; tuberculosis, syphilis, and alcoholism were rampant, the rivers polluted with sewage. But even this gave rise to the reformist activism of Emma Goldman and Jacob Riis. So in the end, everyone was happy in 1898 New York City, and you'd have been too.

PHOTOGRAPH: GETTY IMAGES

Fifth Avenue in front of the Plaza, 1898.

1947
Because It All Seemed to Work

by DANIEL OKRENT

BRANDO ON Broadway in *Streetcar*, the same year *All My Sons*, *Brigadoon*, and *Finian's Rainbow* opened for business. Miles and Bird and Billie on 52nd Street. Bruno Walter at Carnegie in front of the New York Phil, Toscanini over at Rockefeller Center leading the NBC Symphony,

22 NEW YORK | JANUARY 17–24, 2011

JANUARY 17–24, 2011 | NEW YORK 23

January 17–24, 2011

New York
USA, January 17–24, 2011 (200 × 265mm, 8 × 10½ inches)
This front cover is an elegant reworking of Milton Glaser's famous 'I ♥ NY' identity for the city, created in collaboration with book designer and photographer Rodrigo Corral; the spread has a typically strong typographic treatment, drawing on the magazine's heritage. Editor-in-chief *Adam Moss*; Design director *Chris Dixon*

'You cross the road here to the magazine store and you'll see a gazillion stunning 10,000-circulation fashion magazines from Europe. Beautiful paper. You don't want to read a word, but you flick through the pages and it's so ... exciting as a canvas. But that's not what this magazine is. This magazine is about content.'

ADAM MOSS
EDITOR
NEW YORK

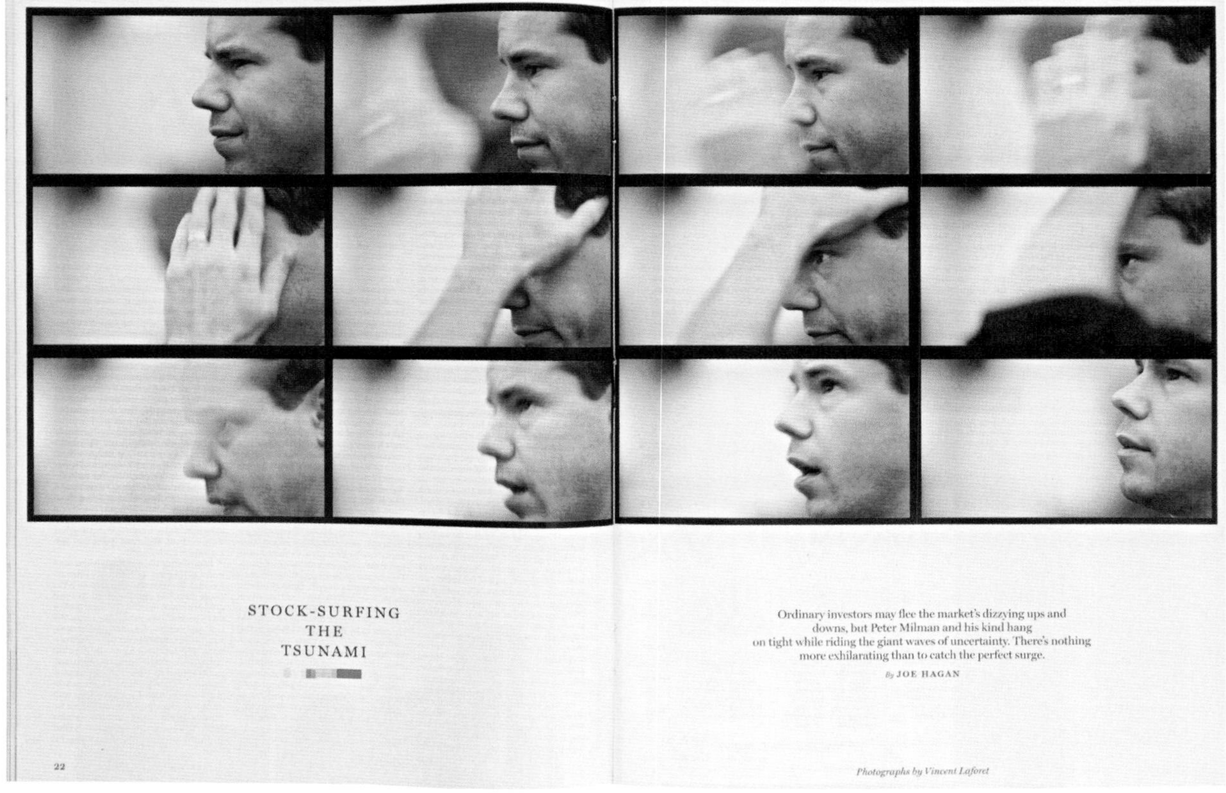
STOCK-SURFING
THE
TSUNAMI

Ordinary investors may flee the market's dizzying ups and downs, but Peter Milman and his kind hang on tight while riding the giant waves of uncertainty. There's nothing more exhilarating than to catch the perfect surge.

By JOE HAGAN

22

Photographs by Vincent Laforet

New York
February 2, 2009
As well as a strong art department, the magazine benefits from strong photography overseen by photography director Jody Quon. Photography *Vincent Laforet*

OPPOSITE Front covers switch week to week between photography (previous page), photomontage, typographic treatments and illustration.

New York (USA)

EDITOR ADAM MOSS
AND DESIGN DIRECTORS LUKE HAYMAN AND CHRIS DIXON

Usually published to be as current as possible, magazines also have the role of recording their times for future generations to look back at. Despite other more literal measures of success – sales, profit – most editors and designers like to think their magazine will one day be lauded as 'of its time', to have had a 'golden age'. Few magazines achieve such status, and even fewer manage to do so twice. *New York* magazine is one of those select few.

Originally a supplement to the *New York Herald Tribune* newspaper, *New York* launched as a stand-alone magazine in April 1968 following the closure of the newspaper. Under the editorship of Clay Felker, and with Milton Glaser as designer, the new magazine was the first city magazine – a spiky young newcomer that reflected the energy of its home city. For several years it both drove and recorded Manhattan politics, art and life, and was hugely influential on editorial design. This was the title's initial golden age. But Rupert Murdoch's takeover of the magazine in 1976 was the first in several changes of ownership that caused the title to lose its way.

In March 2004, editor Adam Moss was appointed from *The New York Times* magazine to reinvigorate the magazine. 'It wasn't a reinvention but a restoration,' explains Moss. 'We were going back to the principles of the 1968 magazine. Massively modernized, both visually and in content terms, but borrowing heavily from the original magazine.' Completed in six months, it proved to be one of the most influential redesigns of the noughties, and heralded the second golden age of the magazine.

Moss first put together a new creative team, hiring photo editor Jody Quon whom he'd worked with at *The New York Times Magazine*, and then creative director Luke Hayman. 'I'd never hired a designer before. I made him spend a lot of time with me in a way that I'd be embarrassed to do now. Drawing, working, testing our relationship. It gave me a sense of confidence that we wanted the same thing.' Hayman recalls attending five meetings with Moss: 'I remember telling my wife if I didn't get offered the job in that last meeting I was going to tell him to shove it!' But he was offered the job and in turn brought in Chris Dixon as art director.

The redesign process was intense. From day one they were producing two magazines a week. 'We had to put a magazine out every week so we did that during the daytime, then at nighttime and weekends we would imagine the new magazine,' recalls Moss. Dixon produced the actual weekly issue, while Hayman led the redesign. 'It wasn't just a visual project, we were rethinking everything about the magazine,' says Moss. 'We had competing groups trying to answer the same issues – "how do we solve the problem of food?", "how do we solve the question of politics?" – these sorts of things.'

For Hayman, the first stage was a research job. 'Growing up in Long Island, Adam had been a passionate fan of the magazine. He talked about his excitement as the magazine arrived at his parents' home, and wanted a connection with that "golden era".' Hayman describes Moss as a 'great collaborator. He had an intuitive feel for typography and layout. He pushed us all to be creative', and it is clear talking to Moss that he enjoys the process of design and sees it as more important than ever to magazines today. 'A magazine is an organism, it has certain characteristics, and those are best communicated through design.' He's seen his editorial colleagues pick this up. 'All the editors were so enthusiastic about the redesign that they all became quite literate in design. Design and editorial became partners.'

The team went through the magazine's archives looking for visual directions. 'We had all the old issues out,' remembers Dixon. There was a shared desire to produce a magazine that looked like it had always been that way. 'The graphic language of cut-outs, charts and graphs was developed over several months. It was important to me that the result was rich, slightly off and not slick,' says Hayman. 'I craved the immediacy and rough edges of an old-school weekly like *The Village Voice*, where you could feel the human hand of paste-up.'

The masthead was redrawn by Ed Benguiat, based on the magazine's very first logo – a logo with several claimed designers including George Lois. A year later they had Benguiat redraw it again: 'A photographer had scanned it to superimpose on a potential cover image. The scanning and Photoshop manipulation made the logo look skinnier', according to Hayman. 'Adam saw it on my wall and thought it elegant, so we asked Ed to slim it further. That's the current logo.'

Other influences were evident too. Moss refers to contemporary British newspapers and their 'big, bold, graphic use of type', while both he and Hayman mention *Spy*, the 1980s US satire magazine that pioneered the use of diagrams, charts and devices to enhance and often lead its stories. The most famous (and copied) of these remains the 'Approval Matrix', devised by editor Emily Nussbaum and based on a small one-off device she saw in *Wired* magazine. Hayman recalls, 'Half of the office (those below 40 years old) loved the device and half (above 40) didn't really get it, including Adam. I (being around 40 at the time) was on the fence. To Adam's credit he tried it and then it became a "thing".'

'Words and photographs are important but diagrams provide a breakdown of information in ways that are highly effective, visceral and also quite beautiful,' says Moss. 'I wanted to make the magazine feel like New York City – the abundance, the ambition, the optimism. New York isn't a second- or third-tier city; the magazine had to feel visually modern. I wanted to prove you could be smart and fun at the same time.' For Hayman it was important not to be too slick: 'I pushed back against beauty, elegance and designiness. I wanted *New York* raw with some rudeness, not a Condé Nast sheen.' Nonetheless, a major feature of the new design was the detail. From a European standpoint the magazine had (and has) the finish of a monthly rather than weekly production – a result of the US-sized creative team available to Hayman and Moss.

Instead of withholding the redesign until the whole project was ready, each section was published as it was completed. 'We had this strange Frankenstein-like magazine for a while, with the old design and the new design at the same time. We were able to see what worked and didn't work,' says Moss. 'It was like putting a beta version of a digital product out there.'

Moss doesn't see an end to the print edition of *New York*. 'I don't think print is dead, and I wouldn't imagine it's going be dead in ten years,' he states. The recession saw a drop in print sales, while digital revenue held strong. 'We thought we'd be OK as a company because we could just become a digital company and we were poised to do that. But print got strong again.' Not in the same way as before, though. 'Subscriptions are growing, as single-copy sales decrease,' Moss explains.

The magazine posts all content from every issue on its website. 'My theory is that any single article you want, which you used to have to buy a whole magazine for, that's the kind of thing you'll read on the web. You don't have to pay the $5.95', says Moss. 'But if you actually want a relationship with a magazine, you buy a subscription.'

Hayman left the magazine in 2007, handing over to Dixon – a smooth transition that means the same design ethos continues. Another magazine might have succumbed to a further redesign project, but as Moss points out: 'If you have to redesign a magazine again after three years you really did a bad job in the first place.'

Some parts that they didn't get right first time have been updated, and others dropped. The 'High Priority' illustrations that opened the Strategist section went. 'It was a great way to show off design but you had to really work hard to figure out what the five important things to do that week were,' says Moss, who accepts design can sometimes become too dominant. 'There's a place for design for design's sake. You cross the road here to the magazine store and you'll see a gazillion stunning 10,000-circulation fashion magazines from Europe. Beautiful paper. You don't want to read a word, but you flick through the pages and it's so ... exciting as a canvas. But that's not what this magazine is. This magazine is about content.'

November 12, 2007

April 19, 2010

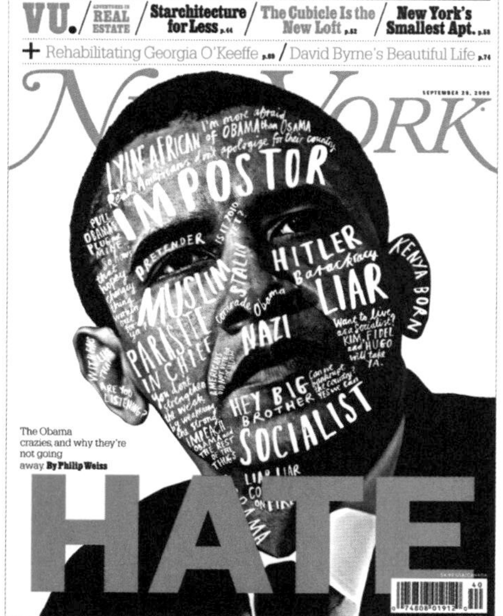

September 28, 2009

New York

A highlight of the 2004 redesign was the typographic detail and photography of the 'Strategist' and 'The Week' sections. 'Strategist' featured regular elements such as this full-length portrait of a New Yorker as well as highly styled food photography.
Photography director *Jody Quon*

OPPOSITE *November 12, 2007*
A hugely popular and much-copied innovation was 'The Approval Matrix', a weekly SWOT analysis-style breakdown of the city's cultural news and events that helped define the magazine's love of high- and low-brow culture.

December 6, 2004. Design director *Luke Hayman*; Photograph *Jake Chessum*

February 2, 2009. Design director *Chris Dixon*; Photograph *Tom Schierlitz*

THE APPROVAL MATRIX

Our deliberately oversimplified guide to who falls where on our taste hierarchies.

HIGHBROW

DESPICABLE

BRILLIANT

LOWBROW

Les Misérables won't die.

***None of the Above* at the Lion Theatre** takes a ripe subject (Upper East Side SAT tutors) and goes nowhere with it.

JFK rounds up stray cats; likely destination, a "farm" in the "country."

A program called **Lost Book of Nostradamus** shows up on the "History" Channel.

Seinfeld **bullies an unknown cookbook author** on *Letterman* and **peppers NBC with dull *Bee* "minisodes."**

Morrissey overdoes it with the passionate shirt removal at **Hammerstein.**

The absurd prevalence of simultaneous orgasm on *Tell Me You Love Me.*

The Botanical Garden's "Kiku" exhibition of **Japanese floral elegance.**

Pianist Angela Hewitt performs Books One and Two of *The Well-Tempered Clavier*—**almost five straight hours of virtuosity**—at Carnegie Hall.

Benjamin Millepied and Nico Muhly's electric ***From Here On Out* at American Ballet Theatre.**

Naomi Klein's indictment of Chicago-school economics, *The Shock Doctrine.*

The **Muji store** arrives.

This "**condominium for birds**" floating off Long Island City.

The Federal Reserve Bank weighs in on Hannah Montana ticket prices.

Hack turned professor Graham Russell Gao Hodges's cabdriver history, **Taxi.**

Rob Lowe's tan in *Brothers & Sisters.*

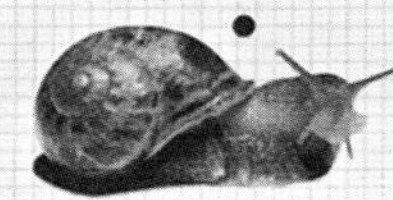

The M23, **slowest bus in the metropolis** (four mph).

After a *Friday Night Lights* episode about covering up a murder, **NBC's PSA** warns kids about the danger of ... unsafe driving?

A **shoe-donation program** inflicts Crocs on already-suffering Dominican children.

Meta-cannibalism: The plotlines on *Nip/Tuck*'s show-within-a-show **are taken from previous episodes of *Nip/Tuck*.**

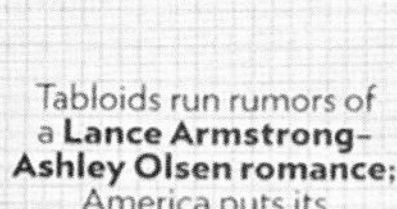

Tabloids run rumors of a **Lance Armstrong–Ashley Olsen romance;** America puts its fingers in its ears and yells "I can't hear you!"

The guest on *Regis and Kelly in 3D* was Dr. Phil. Way to ruin an amusingly pointless stunt, guys!

Joe Hollywood.

Old-school rap gets the coffee-table-book treatment with *The Breaks* and *Born in the Bronx.*

The Violent Femmes' Gordon Gano joins the New Pornographers for an encore at Webster Hall.

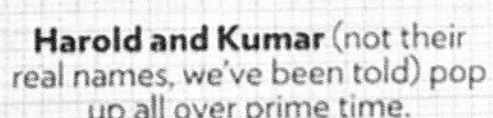

Clarence Williams III, so lovably paternal as kingpin "Bumpy" Johnson in *American Gangster* that you'll want your kids to grow up to be heroin dealers.

Harold and Kumar (not their real names, we've been told) pop up all over prime time.

Chelsea Peretti's hilarious *faux*-reportorial online video series **All My Exes.**

The riff-riffic lineup of **Guitar Hero III songs.**

PHOTOGRAPHS: KEVIN ESTRADA/RETNA (MORRISSEY); LAURENT BOURLIER/COURTESY OF THE HISTORY CHANNEL (NOSTRADAMUS); DOUG HYUN/COURTESY OF HBO (TELL ME YOU LOVE ME); SUPERSTOCK (3-D GLASSES); PATRICK MCMULLAN (ARMSTRONG, OLSEN); DAVID LEE/UNIVERSAL PICTURES (AMERICAN GANGSTER); GENE SCHIAVONE/COURTESY OF ABT (DANCERS); RICHARD J. TERMINE (HEWITT); JOHN STANTON/WIREIMAGE (GANO); ADAM TAYLOR/COURTESY OF FOX (HOUSE); COURTESY OF NYBG (KIKU ARRANGEMENT); JOAN MARCUS/COURTESY OF THE PUBLICITY OFFICE (LES MISÉRABLES) MICHAEL DESMOND/COURTESY OF ABC (LOWE); MICHAEL BECKER/COURTESY OF FX (NIP/TUCK); CLARENCE ELIE-RIVERA/GETTY IMAGES (TORRE); GIDEON SHAPIRO/COURTESY OF ARW (A TREE FOR ANABLE BASIN)

Movies...94 / Theater...97 / Art...101 / Music...105 / Nightlife...106 / The Word...107 / Restaurants...108 / Kids...112

THE WEEK

MOVIES

EDITED BY SARA CARDACE

NEW THIS WEEK

NYMETRO.COM FOR MOVIE-THEATER LISTINGS, SHOWTIMES, AND EXPANDED REVIEWS, VISIT NEW YORK MAGAZINE ON THE WEB.

94 NEW YORK | MARCH 28, 2005

Typography by Michael Bierut

March 28, 2005. Illustration *Michael Bierut*

Movies...168 / Theater...173 / Art...178 / Music...184 / Nightlife...185 / TheWord...186 / Kids...187 / Restaurants...188

THE WEEK

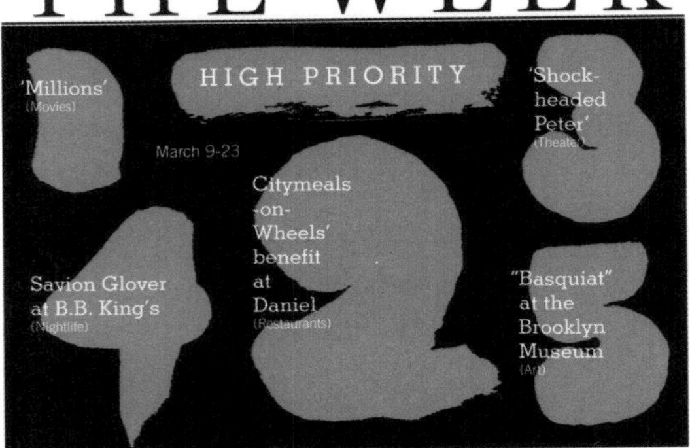

MOVIES

EDITED BY SARA CARDACE

NEW THIS WEEK

NYMETRO.COM FOR MOVIE-THEATER LISTINGS, SHOWTIMES, AND EXPANDED REVIEWS, VISIT NEW YORK MAGAZINE ON THE WEB.

168 NEW YORK | MARCH 14–21, 2005

Typography by Milton Glaser

March 14, 2005. Typography *Milton Glaser*

Movies...136 / Theater...139 / Art...142 / Music...147 / The Word...148 / Nightlife...149 / Kids...150 / Restaurants...151

MOVIES

EDITED BY SARA CARDACE

NEW THIS WEEK

NOW PLAYING

NYMAG.COM FOR MOVIE-THEATER LISTINGS, SHOWTIMES, AND EXPANDED REVIEWS, VISIT NEW YORK MAGAZINE ON THE WEB.

136 NEW YORK | NOVEMBER 7, 2005

Typography by Michael Ian Kaye

November 7, 2005. Typography *Michael Ian Kaye*

Movies...109 / Theater...114 / Art...116 / Music...121 / Nightlife...122 / TheWord...123 / Kids...124 / Restaurants...125

THE WEEK

MOVIES

EDITED BY SARA CARDACE

NEW THIS WEEK

NYMAG.COM FOR MOVIE-THEATER LISTINGS, SHOWTIMES, AND EXPANDED REVIEWS, VISIT NEW YORK MAGAZINE ON THE WEB.

Typography by Christoph Niemann

OCTOBER 24, 2005 | NEW YORK 109

March 24, 2005. Illustration *Christoph Niemann*

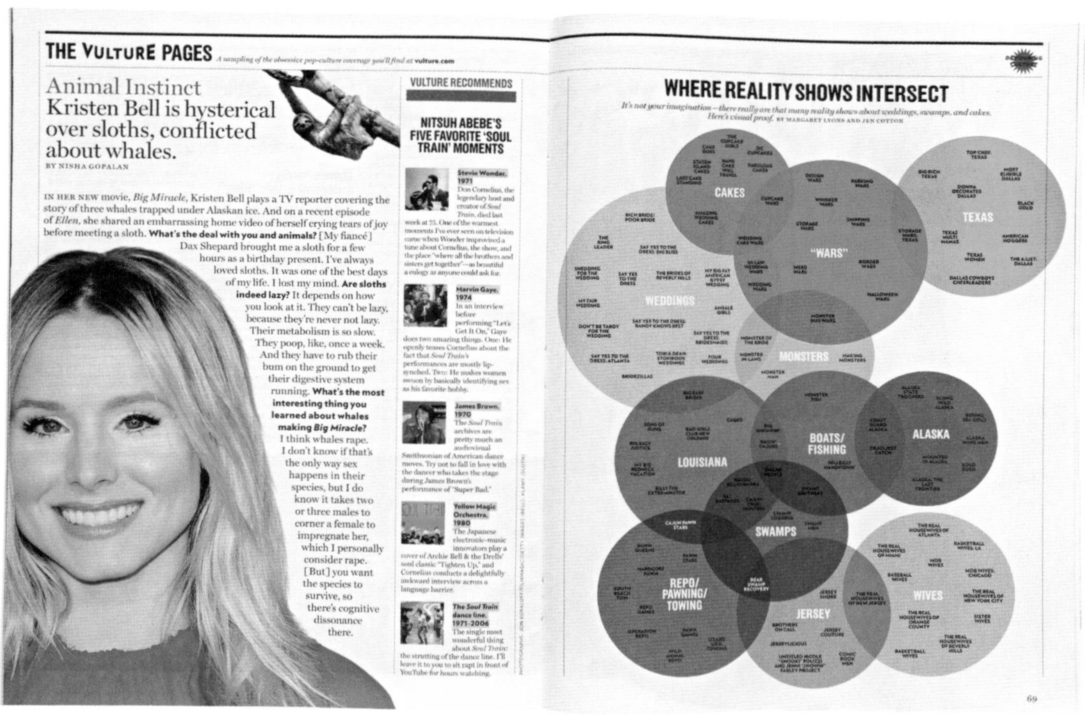
THE VULTURE PAGES *A sampling of the obsessive pop-culture coverage you'll find at vulture.com*

Animal Instinct
Kristen Bell is hysterical over sloths, conflicted about whales.

BY NISHA GOPALAN

IN HER NEW movie, *Big Miracle*, Kristen Bell plays a TV reporter covering the story of three whales trapped under Alaskan ice. And on a recent episode of *Ellen*, she shared an embarrassing home video of herself crying tears of joy before meeting a sloth. **What's the deal with you and animals?** [My fiancé] Dax Shepard brought me a sloth for a few hours as a birthday present. I've always loved sloths. It was one of the best days of my life. I lost my mind. **Are sloths indeed lazy?** It depends on how you look at it. They can't be lazy, because they're never not lazy. Their metabolism is so slow. They poop, like, once a week. And they have to rub their bum on the ground to get their digestive system running. **What's the most interesting thing you learned about whales making *Big Miracle*?** I think whales rape. I don't know if that's the only way sex happens in their species, but I do know it takes two or three males to corner a female to impregnate her, which I personally consider rape. [But] you want the species to survive, so there's cognitive dissonance there.

VULTURE RECOMMENDS

NITSUH ABEBE'S FIVE FAVORITE 'SOUL TRAIN' MOMENTS

WHERE REALITY SHOWS INTERSECT

February 13, 2012

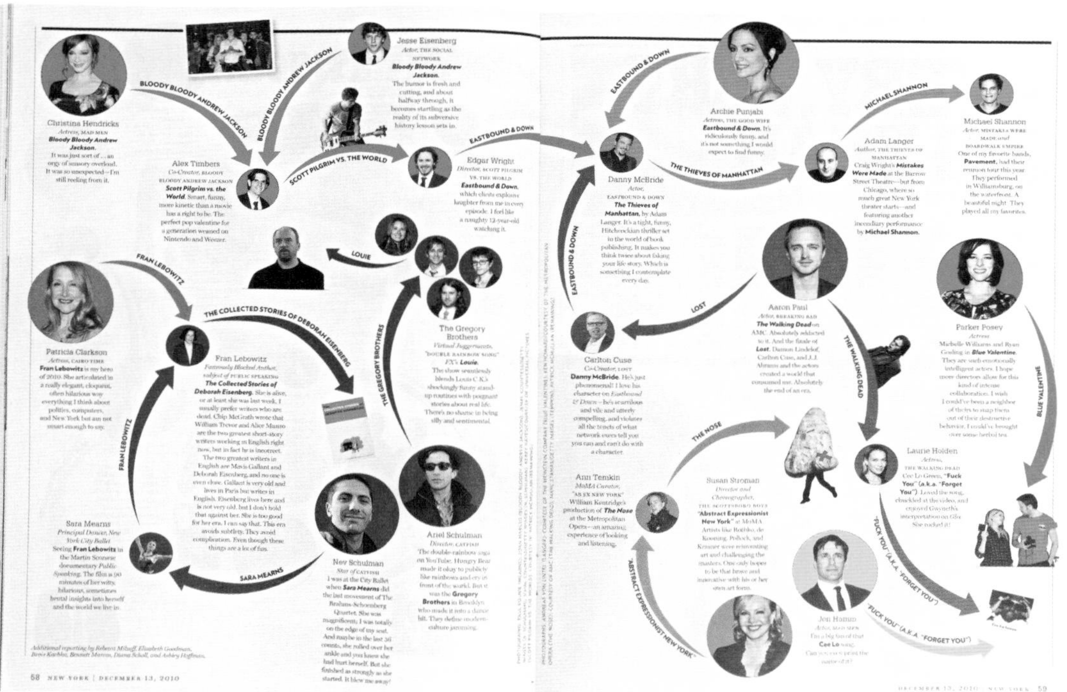
December 13, 2010

New York
The magazine remains known for its sophisticated and influential combination of cut-out photography, design devices, diagrams and infographics.

OPPOSITE 'The Week' is the magazine's art and culture listings section. Rather than open with a single event, five key events were selected each week and given to a different illustrator, designer or typographer to create an opening image listing these five 'High Priority' events. The feature was later dropped.
Editor-in-chief *Adam Moss*; Design director *Luke Hayman*;
Various artists as listed

THE TALKIES

A bunch of immature guys sitting around arguing about this and that, especially pop culture . . . Thanks to *Diner* acolytes such as Richard Linklater, Quentin Tarantino, and Judd Apatow, the template has spread from genre to genre

banter ("Who do you make out to, Sinatra or Mathis?") tossed about by men over drinks, behind the wheel, in front of a cooling plate of French fries—and made it central.

Of course, kitchen-sink films had been made before, featuring snippets of halting, realistic dialogue, as epitomized by Paddy Chayefsky's *Marty*. And in 1981, Louis Malle's *My Dinner with Andre* elevated one long conversation into an art-house hit. But producers and editors mostly found the imperatives of plot and pacing best served by verbal ping-pong matches where nobody is at a loss for words—snappy *His Girl Friday* lines that keep the viewer awake until the next thing happens. When making the 1973 Robert Redford–Barbra Streisand hit, *The Way We Were*, director Sydney Pollack had to argue furiously with producers to keep a scene where Redford and his friend Bradford Dillman lounge on a boat, trying to top each other by ranking the best city, day, and year. But it ended up saying far more about time and regret than did Streisand crooning about memories.

During postproduction on *Diner*, MGM/UA executive David Chasman complained to Levinson about one of its most famous set pieces, when Guttenberg's Eddie and Reiser's Modell argue ownership ("You gonna finish that?") of a roast-beef sandwich. Chasman wanted it cut because it didn't advance the story. "You don't understand," Levinson explained: between the lines about roast beef lies all you need to know about their fear, their competitiveness, their friendship. The roast beef *is* the story.

"I wanted the piece to be without any flourish, without anything other than basically saying, 'This is all it was,'" Levinson says. "These conversations that can go on endlessly through the night—bets over the stupid fucking things that you can bet on—is it. Without gimmicks: nothing. Without gimmicks. This is it. Period." John Wells, the executive producer of the kaleidoscopic 90s hospital series, *ER*—nominated for a record 122 Emmys during its 15-year run—and former president of the Writers Guild of America, West, was a graduate student at the U.S.C. film school when *Diner* came out. Mesmerized by Levinson's "tremendous empathy for those characters even when they were being idiots," Wells estimates he saw it 30 times in 1982 alone. He still makes a point of watching *Diner* once a year.

"It influenced a whole generation of writers," Wells says, "revolutionizing the way characters talk and how realistic we were going to be. And it was particularly influential with actors—this notion that you could play someone who was extremely real and at the same time be humorous and emotional. It had a complexity that not a lot of movies at the time had—they tended to be tremendously dramatic or broadly comic—and this was landing in a territory between, where somebody could be entertaining and humorous and also make you cry."

And do so in a vocabulary at once familiar and new. Because, while movie audiences lived in an outside world cluttered with names and faces from newspapers, TV, politics, and the products of the Hollywood machine, movies themselves didn't much reflect popular culture. There was, beyond plot, a practical reason: TV was still viewed by movie executives as the enemy, and to acknowledge its omnipresence must have seemed like free—and suicidal—advertising. So even movies set in the here and now played out in a hermetically sealed universe: the bank robbery, the romance, or the bankrupt farm was the only story to tell.

There were occasional references here and there, and, at the time, Steven Spielberg was spelling out TV's place in suburbia like never before. But *Diner* threw open the windows to a constant flow of brand-name appliances and soda, TV shows from soap operas to *Bonanza* to *GE College Bowl*, Bergman films, President Eisenhower, newscasts, real N.F.L. players like Alan Ameche, and real actors like Troy Donahue. Levinson even playfully mixed his own dialogue with that of a background TV.

But, while *Seinfeld* mass-marketed Levinson's focus on minutiae, the ultimate film geek made it cool. In 1994, Quentin Tarantino's *Pulp Fiction* won praise for its ultra-stylized, ultra-violent take on the L.A. underworld. But what made the movie click were the jazzy back-and-forths between hit men John Travolta and Samuel L. Jackson about Big Macs, foot massages, and the virtues of eating pork like "that Arnold on *Green Acres*." Tarantino's genius, first demonstrated in 1990's *Reservoir Dogs*, sprang from the decision to make his reprehensible characters sympathetic—to make the audience laugh in recognition while wincing at the blood—through dialogue that any truck-driver would recognize. Guy talk. *Diner* talk.

Pulp Fiction became, arguably, the most influential movie of the 1990s, but Levinson's reach didn't end there. Between the release of writer-actor Jon Favreau's *Swingers*—with its dinner-table riff on *Reservoir Dogs*, no less—in 1996, and the debut of HBO's *Entourage*, in 2004, comics Ricky Gervais and Stephen Merchant began dreaming up a BBC series, fated to reboot in a still-running American version, that all but assaulted the viewer with hilariously dead-end dialogue. "Ricky and I often talked about how, in *The Office*, we featured life's boring bits—the bits other shows would cut out," Merchant says. "That's something *Diner* taught me: that there is charm and interest and value in capturing the way real people behave. You don't have to have 90 minutes of shouting or fist-fights or blue aliens. Eavesdropping on the people who drink in your local bar can be just as interesting."

But, at heart, *Diner* is, as *I Love You, Man* director John Hamburg says, "the Cadillac of male-bonding movies," and no one has tapped that vein better in recent years than director Judd Apatow. With *The 40-Year-Old Virgin* and *Knocked Up*, Apatow was credited with creating the "bromance," one of the few genres capable of luring the increasingly elusive male audience into theaters. When Apatow was asked in the spring of 2009 to speak at the U.S.C. film school and screen his favorite movie, the choice couldn't have been easier.

At 14, Apatow sneaked in alone to see the R-rated *Diner* in a Huntington, Long Island, theater, then pestered his mother to take him again. Ever since, he's been trying to match the shaggy, improvised dialogue that Levinson encouraged during his tabletop scenes. The part in *Knocked Up* when Seth Rogen and his pals are talking about the vengeance-seeking Eric Bana in *Munich*? "That was my version of a Barry Levinson run from *Diner*: finally they're letting Jews kill people," Apatow says.

But, really, he adds, "anytime I have four or more people sitting around a table, I think about *Diner*. It's a different spin and more my experience, but the naturalness and the humor that he created—that's the bar I've always tried to reach. Whether it's in *The 40-Year-Old Virgin*, where everybody's sitting around talking about sex and you realize [Steve Carell] doesn't know what he's talking about, or 'You know how I know you're gay?,' or any of the scenes with Adam Sandler and Seth Rogen in *Funny People*—they're all at some level influenced by the dialogue style that Barry Levinson is the master at."

"Influence" can be a tricky word. "When people talk about influential movies, what did they influence?," Nick Hornby asks. "It's a very good question. Come on, then, what did *Raging Bull* influence? What did *Blue Velvet* influence? Can you see it anywhere else? It seems to me those movies were so *sui generis*—you can't see their 'influence' anymore. People just mean that they were really good movies. Whereas *Diner* did start a way of thinking about writing about popular culture. It did create a mind-set where people like me and Jerry Seinfeld and all sorts of others thought, Oh, I can see how to do this stuff now."

ELLEN BARKIN HAD TO BE CONVINCED. "IF YOU DON'T DO THIS MOVIE," HER AGENT TOLD HER, "I WILL KILL YOU."

No Concept

In *Diner*'s early days, though, it was easy to miss the point. Forget high-concept; this script was nearly no-concept: A half-dozen young guys talk over a table; one fears getting married; one's semi-girlfriend is pregnant; one worships his record collection. There was oldies music and a plot geared to culminate in the stands at the '59 Colts championship-winning game—except the game-day payoff never ended up being filmed. Levinson had been an Emmy-winning comedy writer for Carol Burnett and Mel Brooks, and, with co-writer and then wife Valerie Curtin, had received an Academy Award nomination for the screen-

334 | VANITY FAIR | www.vanityfair.com MARCH 2012

MARCH 2012 www.vanityfair.com | VANITY FAIR | 335

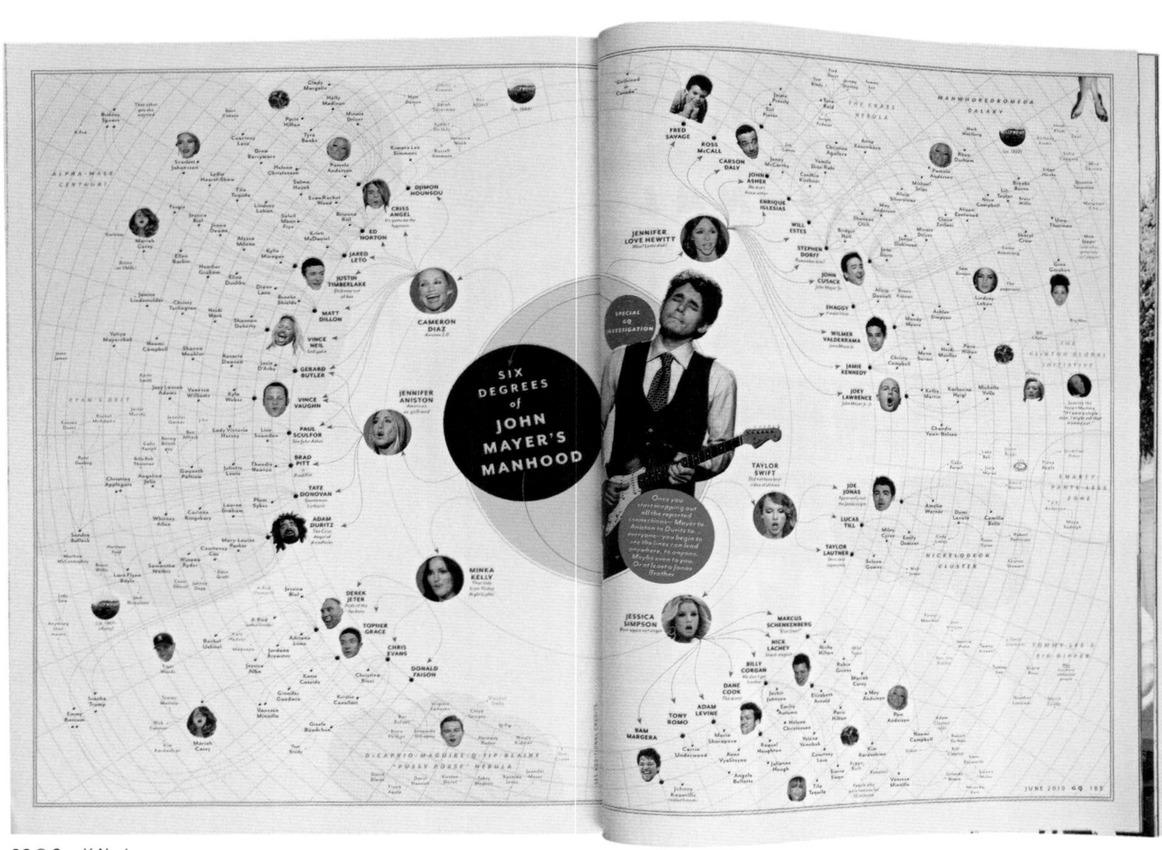

DESIGN × CONTENT

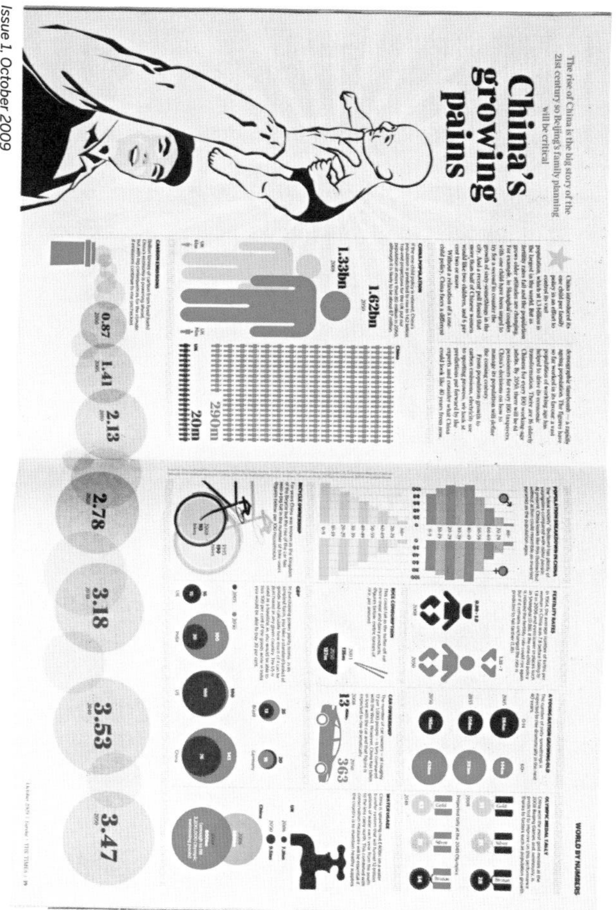

Issue 1, October 2009

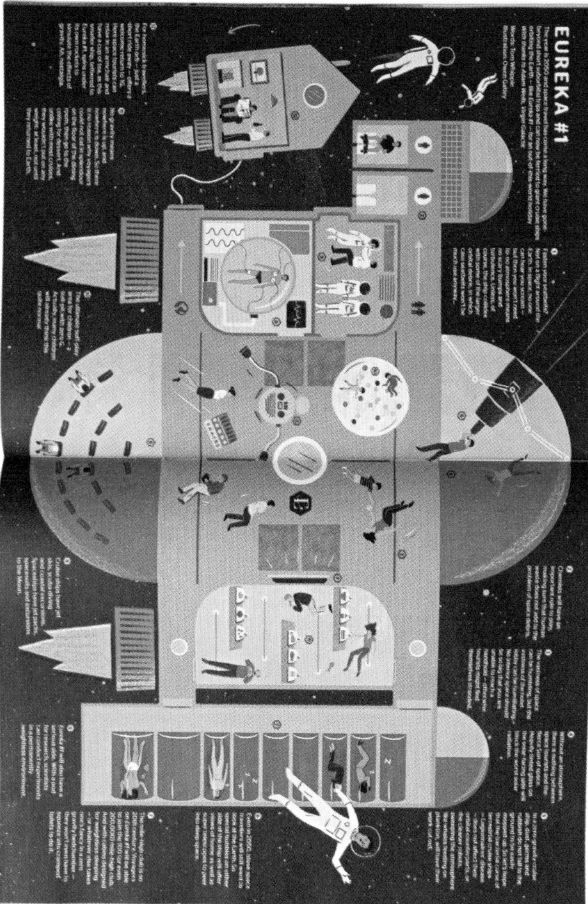

Issue 21, June 2011. Illustration *Owen Gatley*

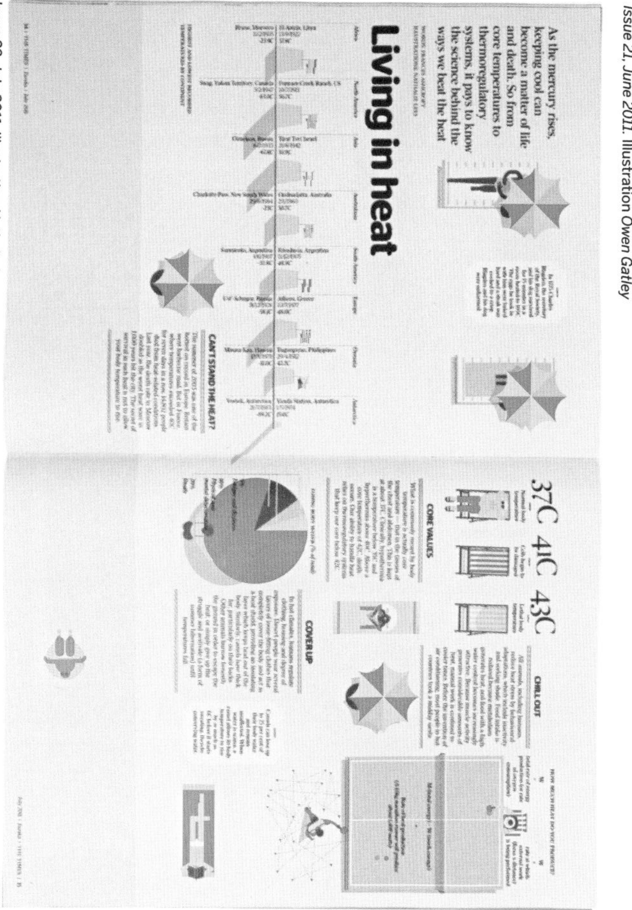

Issue 22, July 2011. Illustration *Nathalie Lees*

Eureka

UK (222 × 295mm, 8¾ × 11¾ inches)

A monthly magazine published (2009–12) with *The Times* newspaper that specialized in detailed editorial infographics about science, technology and the environment, with generous space given over to illustrated exposition. The magazine helped inspire a new interest in infographics.

Editor *David Edwards*; Art director *Matt Curtis*

OPPOSITE, TOP

Vanity Fair

USA, March 2012 (203 × 277mm, 8 × 11 inches)

Editor *Graydon Carter*; Design director *Chris Dixon*

OPPOSITE, BOTTOM

GQ

USA, June 2010 (203 × 276mm, 8 × 11 inches)

Editor-in-chief *Jim Nelson*; Creative director *Jim Moore*

MORE GQ P211

Science and techonology have always relied on infographics and diagrams to help describe complex ideas. Inspired by *New York*'s 'Approval Matrix', other magazines have now picked up these forms of graphic explanation as alternative ways to present arts and culture stories. Here, *Vanity Fair* grades a common movie scene in a manner more visually engaging than a written list, while *GQ* takes an entire spread to map the cultural links around musician John Mayer. The information in this example is almost irrelevant; it's the absurdist complexity that makes it compelling.

LO STATO DELL'ITALIA

Come siamo, come potremmo essere e soprattutto come vorremmo essere
Inchiesta ottimista sul futuro del nostro Paese

Issue 44, September 2012

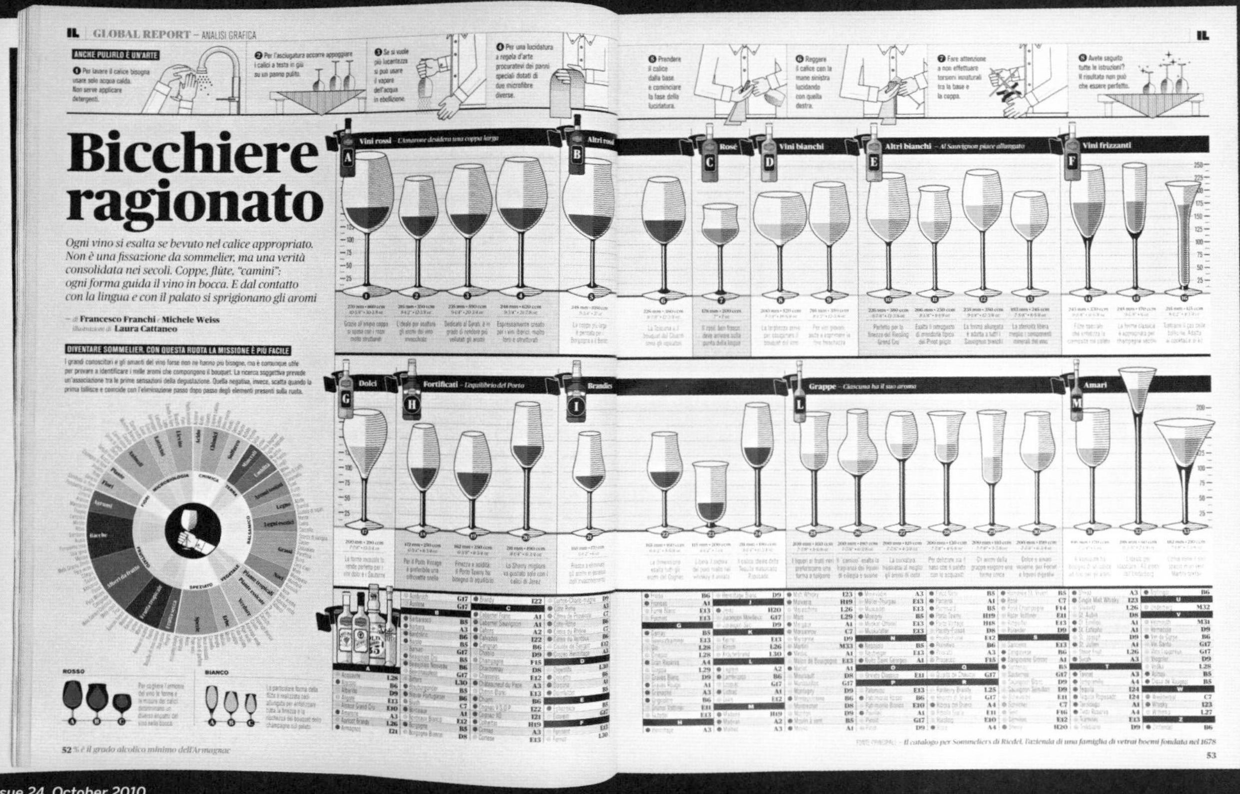
IL GLOBAL REPORT – ANALISI GRAFICA

Bicchiere ragionato

Ogni vino si esalta se bevuto nel calice appropriato. Non è una fissazione da sommelier, ma una verità consolidata nei secoli. Coppe, flûte, "camini": ogni forma guida il vino in bocca. E dal contatto con la lingua e con il palato si sprigionano gli aromi

di Francesco Franchi / Michele Weiss
illustrazioni di Laura Cattaneo

Vini rossi – Altri rossi – Rosé – Vini bianchi – Altri bianchi – Vini frizzanti

Dolci – Fortificati – Brandies – Grappe – Amari

Issue 24, October 2010

IL
Italy (235 × 290mm, 9¼ × 11½ inches)
This monthly newspaper supplement uses beautiful typography throughout its pages, but it's the reliance on infographics as its primary storytelling device that has won it attention. This spread (ABOVE) is a typically detailed example, looking at which shape of glass to use with which wine. Even this front cover (OPPOSITE) includes excerpts from the infographics inside the issue.
Editor *Walter Mariotti*; Art director *Francesco Franchi*

'Our editor-in-chief calls it a functional hierarchy, within which everyone can collaborate. We think about the graphics together, starting from a journalistic idea.'

FRANCESCO FRANCHI
CREATIVE DIRECTOR
IL: INTELLIGENT LIFESTYLE

Strategie fatali

Ikea da New York al Giappone
Nel 2011 il gruppo Ikea ha aperto sette nuovi negozi in sette Paesi. Al 31 agosto 2011, il gruppo contava 287 negozi in 26 Paesi. Nel 2011 i siti web del gruppo svedese hanno registrato 870 milioni di visite, mentre sono state 655 milioni le visite fisiche ai negozi del gruppo.

Ikea non è solo mobili da montare a casa: nelle foto di questa pagina gli spazi dedicati alle lampade, agli accessori da cucina e l'area DecoVerde destinata a balconi e giardini. **01** — Per GIACOMO: giubbino in pelle con tasche applicate, *Gucci*; felpa girocollo tinta unita, *Woolrich*; pantaloni in cotone a cinque tasche, *Incotex*. **02** — Per SANGIL: giacca in maglia intrecciata con collo in rafia colorata doppiopetto con tasche applicate, *Burberry Prorsum*; camicia in cotone effetto jeans, *Càrrel*. **03** — Per THEO: k-way in tessuto tecnico con cappuccio estraibile, *K-Way*; pull in lana girocollo, *Ermenegildo Zegna*; camicia in cotone, *Mash*.

112 113

Issue 38, February 2012

IL (Italy)

ART DIRECTOR FRANCESCO FRANCHI

IL (Intelligent Lifestyle) is a monthly magazine published as a supplement to Italian financial newspaper *Il Sole 24 Ore*. Originally conceived as a glossy lifestyle accompaniment to the newspaper, since its 2008 launch it has developed a unique graphic identity based around the ideas of its young art director, Francesco Franchi.

Franchi studied graphics in London before returning to Italy to complete a Master's degree in industrial design. Dividing his time between working for editorial design studio Leftloft and completing his degree, he began to develop his concept of the modern newsroom, writing his dissertation on newspaper design. He worked on several Italian newspapers, including *Corriere della Sera* and sports daily *Dieci*, before being invited to join the *IL* team.

'The publishers wanted a glossy consumer magazine, like the FT's *How To Spend It* – a magazine connected to the advertising,' Franchi explains. The pre-launch dummy issue stuck to that brief more tightly than the eventual

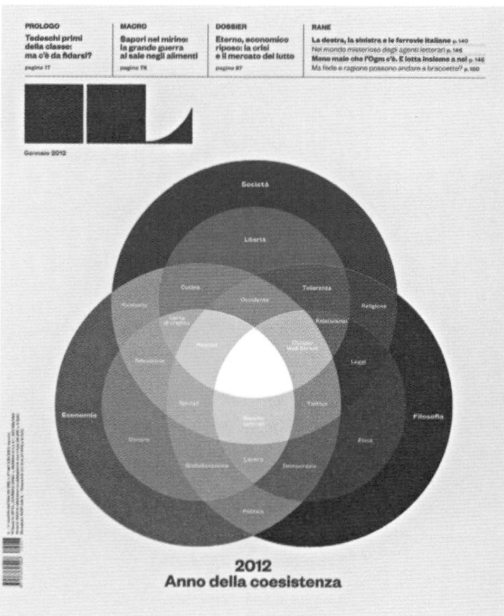
PROLOGO
Tedeschi primi della classe: ma c'è da fidarsi?
pagina 17

MACRO
Sapori nel mirino: la grande guerra al sale negli alimenti
pagina 78

DOSSIER
Eterno, economico riposo: la crisi e il mercato del lutto
pagina 87

RANE
La destra, la sinistra e le ferrovie italiane p. 140
Nel mondo misterioso degli agenti letterari p. 144
Meno male che l'Ogm c'è. E lotta insieme a noi p. 146
Ma fede e ragione possono andare a braccetto? p. 150

Gennaio 2012

2012
Anno della coesistenza

Issue 37, January 2012

MACRO
Aldilà digitale: chi gestirà il mio profilo Internet?

REPORTAGE
Scorie di vita: Fukushima dopo la grande paura

RARE
La nuova sezione di cultura: 23 pagine d'idee e di sfide

E=boh?
A colpi di neutrini crollano le nostre ultime certezze. Politica e religione, società e finanza: inchiesta sulla crisi dell'Occidente

Issue 34, October 2011

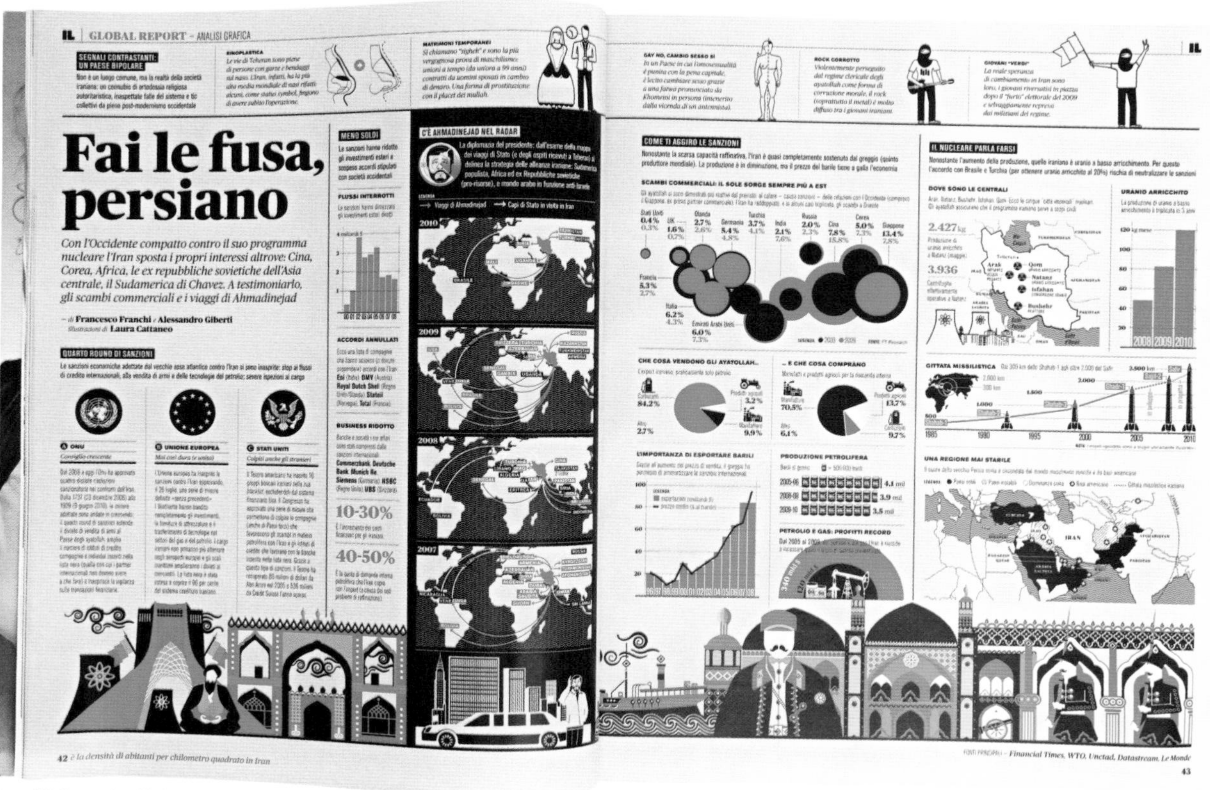

IL | GLOBAL REPORT – ANALISI GRAFICA

SEGNALI CONTRASTANTI: UN PAESE BIPOLARE

Non è un luogo comune, ma la realtà della società iraniana: un connubio di ortodossia religiosa autoritaristica, inaspettate falle del sistema e tic collettivi da pieno post-modernismo occidentale

RINOPLASTICA

Le vie di Teheran sono piene di persone con garze e bendaggi sul naso. L'Iran, infatti, ha la più alta media mondiale di nasi rifatti: alcuni, come status symbol, fingono di avere subito l'operazione.

Fai le fusa, persiano

Con l'Occidente compatto contro il suo programma nucleare l'Iran sposta i propri interessi altrove: Cina, Corea, Africa, le ex repubbliche sovietiche dell'Asia centrale, il Sudamerica di Chavez. A testimoniarlo, gli scambi commerciali e i viaggi di Ahmadinejad

– di **Francesco Franchi** e **Alessandro Giberti**
Illustrazioni di **Laura Cattaneo**

QUARTO ROUND DI SANZIONI

Le sanzioni economiche adottate dal vecchio asse atlantico contro l'Iran si sono inasprite: stop ai flussi di credito internazionali, alla vendita di armi e delle tecnologie del petrolio; severe ispezioni ai cargo

MENO SOLDI

C'È AHMADINEJAD NEL RADAR

COME TI AGGIRO LE SANZIONI

IL NUCLEARE PARLA FARSI

Issue 22, September 2010. Illustrations *Laura Cattaneo*

171

launch edition. Editor-in-chief Walter Mariotti, creative director Luca Pitoni and Franchi wanted to produce a harder news magazine, so they changed the magazine before its launch. 'The actual first issue was a surprise for everybody. Luckily, the publishers trusted the new formula.'

The new concept for the magazine was a brave but effective one: to apply hard news techniques to the telling of softer, lifestyle stories. A fashion story was shot in the country's largest branch of IKEA, allowing the shoot to be accompanied by a written and graphic analysis of the company's business strategy. Another fashion shoot was combined with a report on independent film-making and included a guide to budget film-making equipment.

While such editorial concepts help the magazine stand apart from immediate competitors, the Italian language limits the international understanding of much of the detail. But Franchi's designs have attracted the wider world's attention, not only for their obvious graphic flair but for the way they represent his thoughts on the very process of making magazines.

'My dissertation reflected the situation in Italian newsrooms, how they are organized in a very traditional, vertical manner where designers can only do what the editor-in-chief tells them to do,' he explains. His dissertation proposed a new paradigm for the newsroom, one with a more collaborative system. This is how the *IL* team – ten people including Franchi, three designers and the editorial and picture staff – work day to day. 'Our editor-in-chief calls it a functional hierarchy, within which everyone can collaborate. We think about the graphics together, starting from a journalistic idea.' The aim is to merge form and content and create a new visual language. 'Design is content. You can't develop a design without having an editorial direction. For a recent redesign we started with a new concept and structure and then we designed the graphics.' The alternative results in pages that might look beautiful but are 'not functional'.

A solid sense of editorial structure and a powerful typographic palette provide the basis for this collaborative approach. The design aesthetic is very different to most Italian magazines. While we talk, Franchi often refers to magazines from northern Europe and the USA, and it is no surprise to hear *Bloomberg Businessweek* is high on his list of likes. 'You can see from their weekly videos on the iPad app how closely the editor and design director cooperate.'

If such cooperation helps the written stories and front covers, it comes into its own for *IL*'s trademark infographics. At launch Franchi was responsible for them, but now the magazine has a dedicated three-person team – a designer, an illustrator and a journalist – which specializes in using data and graphic visualisation as an alternative to long-form writing. 'Together we've developed a visual language – a shared, infographic way of thinking,' he explains. It's not just data and charts but a proper method of thinking, of visual journalism. 'Infographics are a compromise between art and information – you want to be informative but in a magazine you also have to entertain the reader. There has to be an aesthetic appeal.' Franchi is often invited to lecture about his work, and he has a beautifully crafted set of infographic slides he uses to add resonance to his words – a perfect example of his beliefs put into action.

When asked about a possible interest in interactive data visualizations, his response reveals a lot about his work: 'Infographics are already partly interactive in print. They are non-linear, the reader can follow things around the page and zoom in and out. If you move all these aspects to the iPad, it could be even better.'

IL
Detailed analysis of Iran's nuclear ambitions is contrasted with cultural facts across the top of this spread.

OPPOSITE Even a fashion shoot set in a branch of IKEA is accompanied by infographics illustrating the international reach of the furniture store.

IL

Designed as a magazine within a magazine, 'Rane' ('Frogs') is a provocative cultural section that takes its visual inspiration from early twentieth-century Italian Futurist publications. The full title of the section ('Qui non si canta al modo delle rane') translates as 'This is not the manner of singing frogs', a quotation from medieval Italian poet Cecco d'Ascoli that was used by 1913 Futurist publication *Lacerba*. The frog theme is carried through the section in the form of repeating icons.

AMLETO S'È PERSO NELLA RETE

Issue 34, October 2011

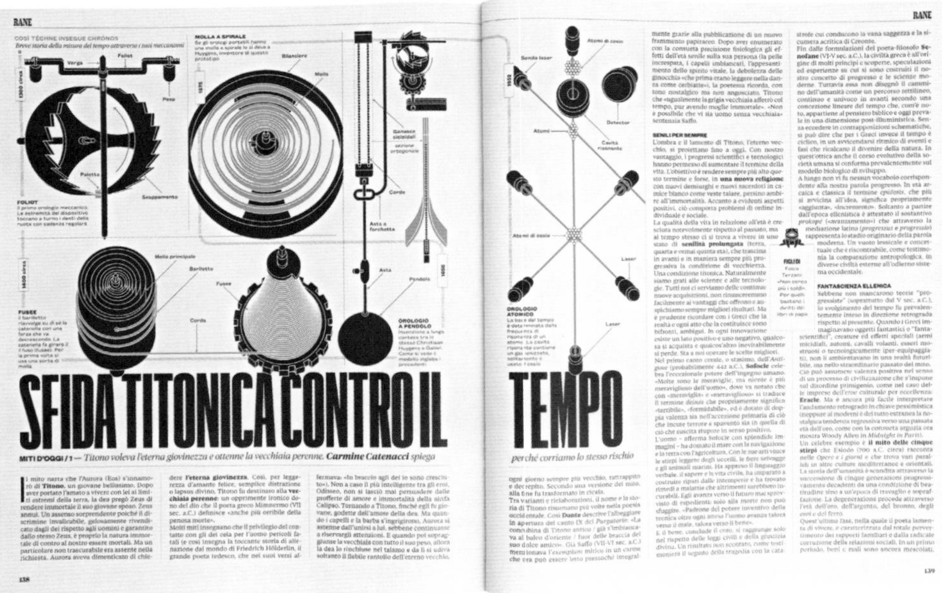
RANE

SFIDA TITONICA CONTRO IL TEMPO

MITI D'OGGI / 1 — Titono voleva l'eterna giovinezza e ottenne la vecchiaia perenne. Carmine Catenacci spiega perché corriamo lo stesso rischio

Issue 38, October 2012

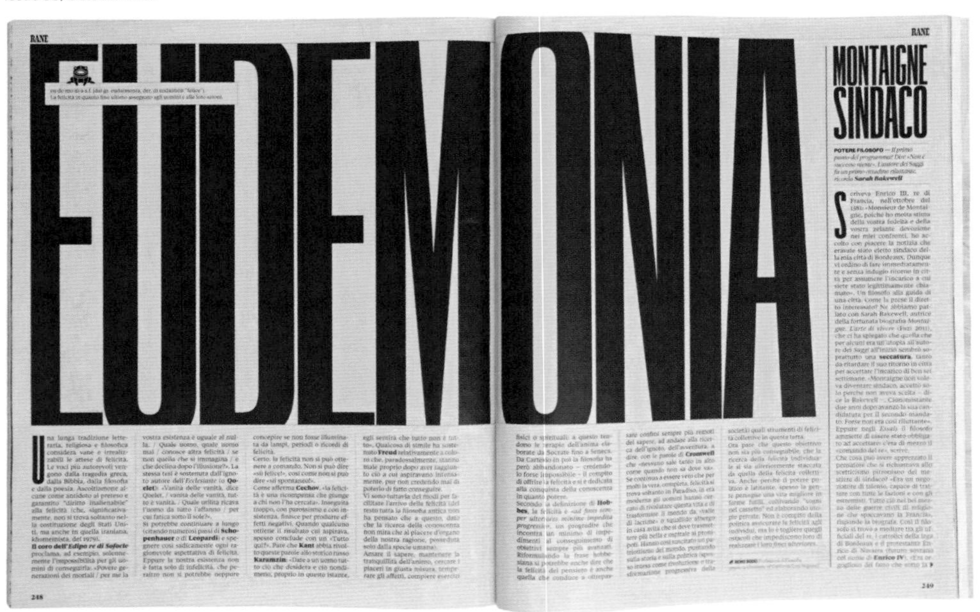
RANE

EUDEMONIA

MONTAIGNE SINDACO

Issue 34, October 2011

LA POLEMICA

PRECARI

Ma chi ha imposto ai giovani scrittori una certa immagine dei giovani stessi? ***Latronico*** **p. 220**

AMLETO SENZA TESTO

Le mappe dei rapporti di forza tra i personaggi shakespeariani dello ***Stanford Lab*** **p. 226**

CHI HA SFASCIATO LA NOSTRA STORIA

Ha cominciato la cultura storiografica fascista a deformare il Risorgimento a uso e consumo del regime. Ha continuato l'opera, nel dopoguerra, l'intellighenzia comunista. ***Parlato*** **p. 230**

LE DUE SAFFO

Le nuove interpretazioni politicamente corrette uccidono la poetessa di Lesbo. ***Catenacci*** **p. 242**

CONTRO SLOW FOOD

Caro Petrini, sicuro che il piacere di mangiare sia un diritto umano? ***Borghini*** **p. 246**

X NYC = Y BEY

Farinelli *ritorna sulle nuove, strane simmetrie geografiche del dopo 11 settembre* **p. 239**

Musica • Helmut Lachemann *Grido* (quartetto d'archi), 2001; *...got lost...* (musica per soprano e pianoforte), 2006; *Berliner Kirschblüten* (arrangiamento su variazioni di una canzone popolare giapponese)

RANE

Anno	I	· Qui non si canta al modo delle ·	Numero	1

ARMANO • BIGLIARDI • BODEI • BONINO • BORGHINI • CANTÙ • CATENACCI • COPPOCK • DA EMPOLI • DI NAPOLI • FARINELLI • FILONI • LATRONICO • MASIERO • MORUZZI • PARADISI • PARLATO • PETRIOLI • PIETRONI • SAVOIA • SGOBBA • TASSANI • ZOLO

GIUSEPPE DI NAPOLI

Noi abitanti dell'iconosfera siamo continuamente assediati da immagini di ogni tipo, televisive, fotografiche, digitali, da illustrazioni e da manifesti che inondano i nostri occhi con caleidoscopiche riproduzioni. Questo fatto condiziona ovviamente il nostro modo di percepire gli oggetti: ci induce a vedere degli stessi oggetti soltanto ciò che viene riprodotto in immagine. Una delle cause di questo fenomeno è riconducibile al fatto che tanto le immagini quanto le forme che percepiamo guardando un oggetto sono entrambe generate dallo stesso tipo di proiezione ottica centrale, che ha origine da un punto nello spazio, quello in cui si trovano momentaneamente il nostro occhio o l'obiettivo fotografico. È evidente che qualsiasi oggetto può essere visto in momenti diversi da più punti di vista, in svariati orientamenti spaziali presentando di volta in volta profili molto differenti tra loro. Le cose, quindi, non hanno un solo contorno, ma, tanti quanti sono i punti di vista dai quali possono essere osservate. Il nostro occhio, però, focalizza la sua attenzione soltanto su quelli che possiedono le informazioni visive necessarie al riconoscimento della forma dell'oggetto osservato. Questo perché la maggior parte dei punti di vista accidentali presenta una quantità ridotta di informazioni visive, proiettata, cioè, profili deformati. Sfruttando la possibilità di configurare svariate figure con le ombre proiettate su di una parete da un oggetto, il famoso teatrino delle ombre cinesi fatto con le mani cattura l'immaginazione dei guardanti da secoli. Ma i criteri che adotta l'occhio per selezionare in ogni oggetto la forma ottica di maggiore informazione visiva sono soltanto di natura percettiva, ottica e geometrica o anche estetica, culturale e simbolica? Spesso, sono proprio i profili più ambigui e ambivalenti ad essere preferiti dai pittori. Basti osservare con quanti inconsueti orientamenti sono state dipinte le mani nelle diverse epoche. Talvolta "il miglior contorno", in termini pittorici, quello più "espressivo", non risponde affatto al criterio di massima informazione visiva. Sotto determinati scorci prospettici anche la forma di un comune oggetto (una caraffa, una sedia o un albero) può apparire con i profili di figure curiose da indurre a vedervi qualcosa di più e/o di diverso dall'oggetto che delimita. Le immagini anamorfiche dimostrano come la stessa forma dipinta sulla superficie di un muro o di una tela, se osservata da punti di vista differenti può visualizzare immagini molto differenti ed enigmatiche. Esempi in tal senso sono molto frequenti nei dipinti di Hans Holbein e di Jean François Niceron. Il fine dell'arte non è riducibile alla riproduzione delle cose visibili in modo naturalistico: la storia della pittura è ricca di esempi in cui la forma ottica di un oggetto è stata deformata al fine di esprimere tutt'altro significato da quello del mero riconoscimento visivo. A conclusione di queste considerazioni poniamo un problema percettivo e cognitivo di particolare interesse, a patto di non ridurlo a mera curiosità, perché eleva il tema al piano della metafisica della visione: dal momento che ogni cosa può essere osservata da infiniti punti di vista, e, considerato che, come è a tutti noto, Dio è onnivedente (vede cioè tutto e di ogni singola cosa tutto ciò che è visibile e invisibile), che tipo di forma vede il suo occhio mentre guarda una brocca contemporaneamente da tutti i suoi punti di vista?

NELL'OCCHIO DI CHI GUARDA

Come funzionano le forme? Perché vediamo in un modo piuttosto che in un altro? **Giuseppe di Napoli**, docente emerito all'accademia di Brera, spiega che l'occhio umano è veramente divino.

219

173

'Rane' opening page, issue 34, October 2011. Section title *Christian Schwartz*.

Der Wedding
Germany, Issue 4, 2012 (210 × 270mm, 8½ × 10¾ inches)
Editor and art director *Axel Völcker*
SEE MORE DER WEDDING p207

Volume
The Netherlands, Volume 13, 2007 (200 × 266mm, 8 × 10½ inches)
Editor-in-chief *Arjen Oosterman*; Design *Irma Boom and Sonja Haller*

White Zinfandel
USA, Issue 2, TV Dinners, Fall/Winter 2012 (230 × 330mm, 9 × 13 inches)
Editor and creative director *Jiminie Ha*

OPPOSITE
Froh!
Germany, Issue 8, May 2012, 'Games' (220 × 285mm, 8¾ × 11¼ inches)
Editor-in-chief *Dr. Sebastian Pranz*; Art director *Klaus Neuberg*
SEE MORE FROH! p179

Playground
UK, Issue 8, 2011 (165 × 240mm, 6½ × 9½ inches)
Editor *Carianne Whitworth*; Design *Joseph Hales*

Infographic approaches can be applied in all sorts of contexts and use many different production techniques. Conceptual architecture magazine *Volume* photographed a live installation of images as a background to a graph; *Froh!* maps the content of an issue, linking common elements; *Playground* records the process by which it came to exist using a flowchart.

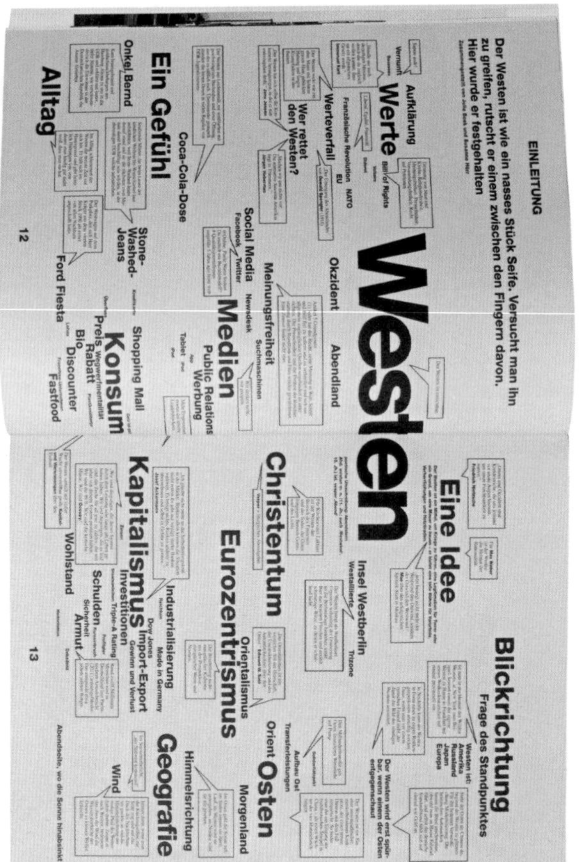

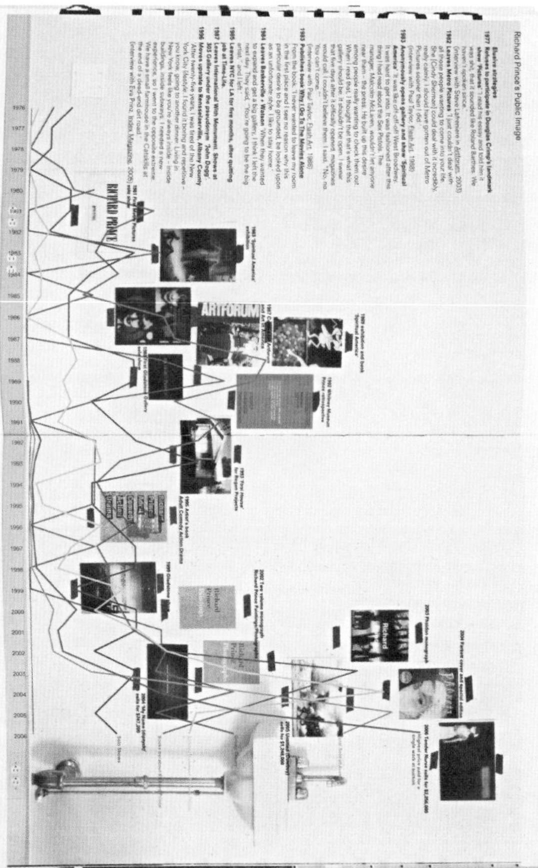

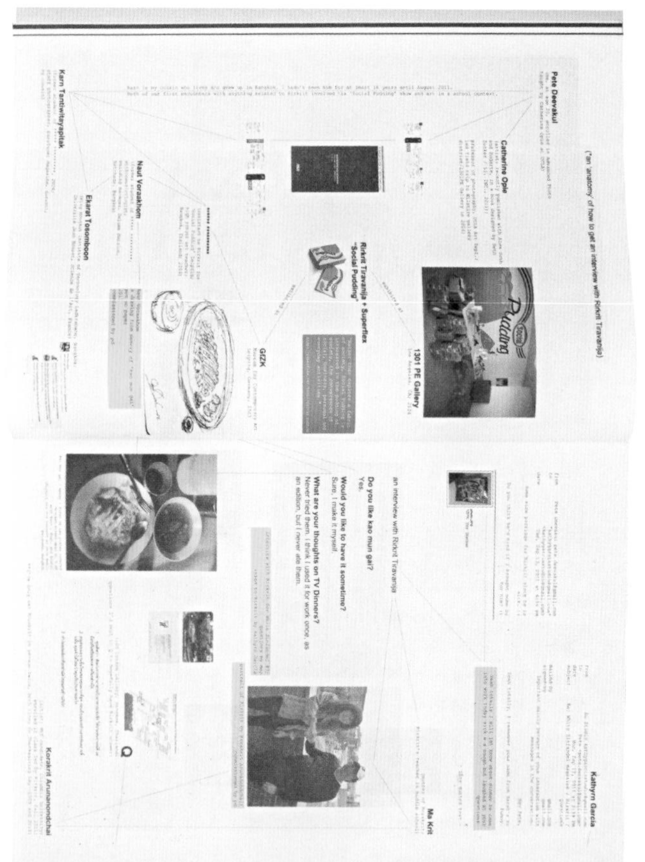

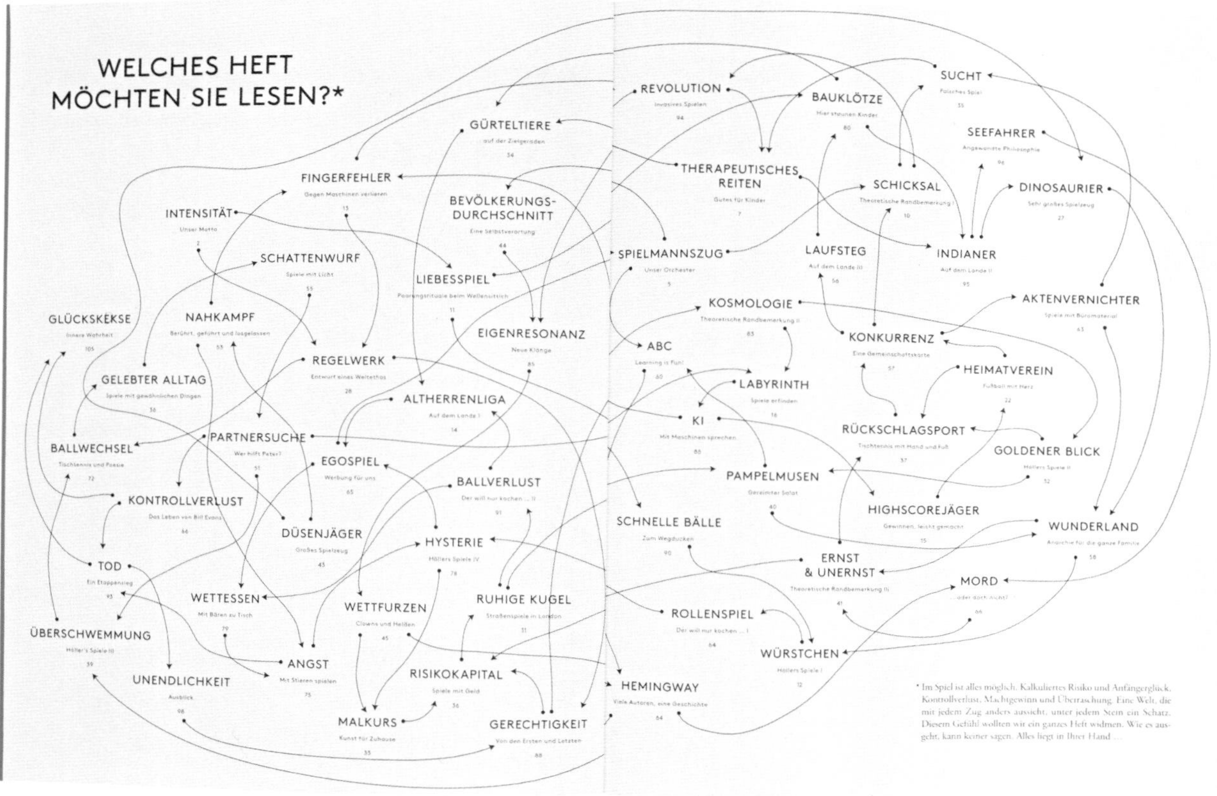
WELCHES HEFT MÖCHTEN SIE LESEN?*
REVOLUTION
BAUKLÖTZE
SUCHT
GÜRTELTIERE
SEEFAHRER
FINGERFEHLER
THERAPEUTISCHES REITEN
SCHICKSAL
DINOSAURIER
INTENSITÄT
BEVÖLKERUNGS-DURCHSCHNITT
SPIELMANNSZUG
LAUFSTEG
INDIANER
SCHATTENWURF
LIEBESSPIEL
KOSMOLOGIE
AKTENVERNICHTER
GLÜCKSKEKSE
NAHKAMPF
EIGENRESONANZ
ABC
KONKURRENZ
REGELWERK
HEIMATVEREIN
GELEBTER ALLTAG
LABYRINTH
ALTHERRENLIGA
KI
RÜCKSCHLAGSPORT
BALLWECHSEL
PARTNERSUCHE
GOLDENER BLICK
EGOSPIEL
PAMPELMUSEN
BALLVERLUST
KONTROLLVERLUST
HIGHSCOREJÄGER
SCHNELLE BÄLLE
DÜSENJÄGER
WUNDERLAND
HYSTERIE
TOD
ERNST & UNERNST
MORD
WETTESSEN
WETTFURZEN
RUHIGE KUGEL
ROLLENSPIEL
ÜBERSCHWEMMUNG
WÜRSTCHEN
ANGST
UNENDLICHKEIT
RISIKOKAPITAL
HEMINGWAY
MALKURS
GERECHTIGKEIT
* Im Spiel ist alles möglich. Kalkuliertes Risiko und Anfängerglück, Kontrollverlust, Machtgewinn und Überraschung. Eine Welt, die mit jedem Zug anders aussieht, unter jedem Stein ein Schatz. Diesem Gefühl wollten wir ein ganzes Heft widmen. Wie es ausgeht, kann keiner sagen. Alles liegt in Ihrer Hand …

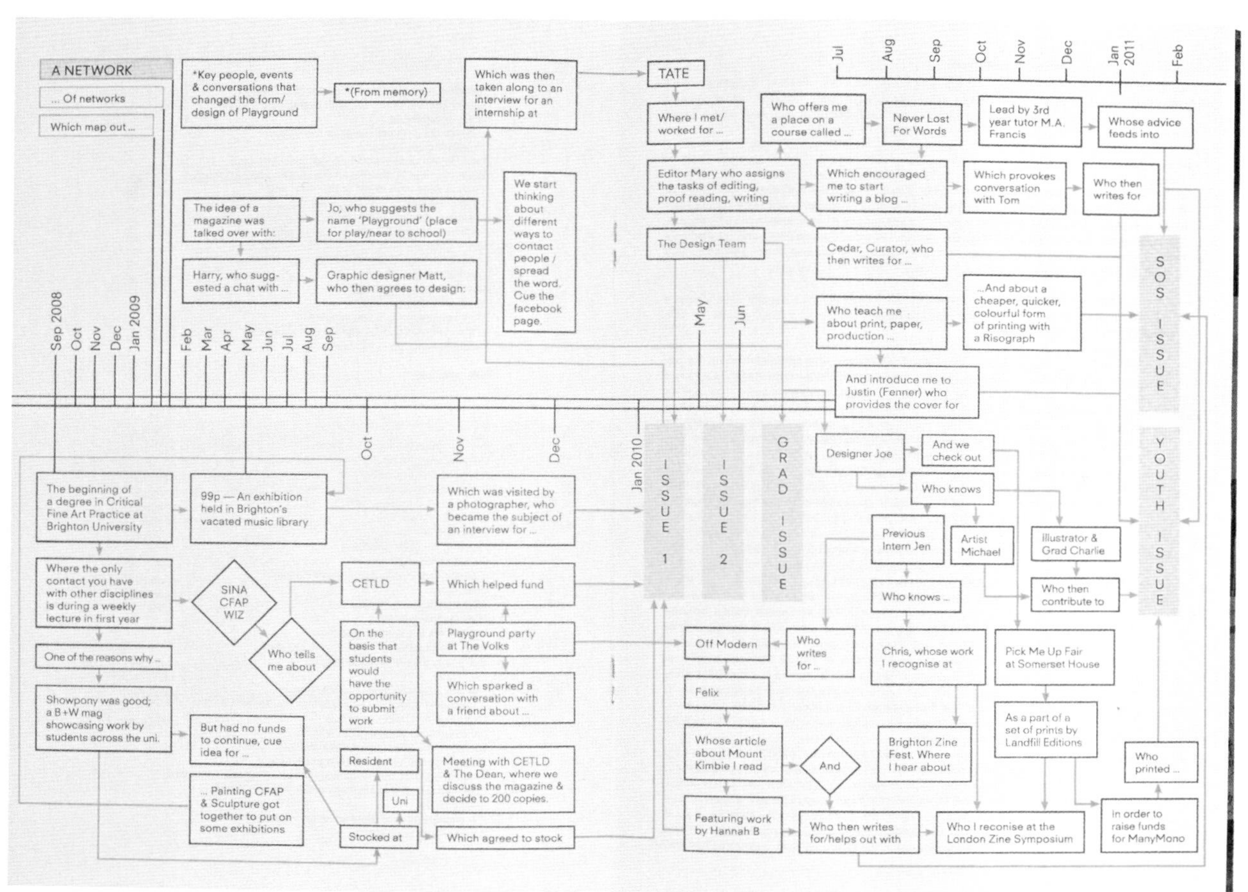
A NETWORK
... Of networks
Which map out ...
*Key people, events & conversations that changed the form/design of Playground
*(From memory)
Which was then taken along to an interview for an internship at
TATE
Jul Aug Sep Oct Nov Dec Jan 2011 Feb
Where I met/worked for ...
Who offers me a place on a course called ...
Never Lost For Words
Lead by 3rd year tutor M.A. Francis
Whose advice feeds into
Editor Mary who assigns the tasks of editing, proof reading, writing
Which encouraged me to start writing a blog ...
Which provokes conversation with Tom
Who then writes for
The idea of a magazine was talked over with:
Jo, who suggests the name 'Playground' (place for play/near to school)
We start thinking about different ways to contact people / spread the word. Cue the facebook page.
The Design Team
Cedar, Curator, who then writes for ...
Harry, who suggested a chat with ...
Graphic designer Matt, who then agrees to design:
...And about a cheaper, quicker, colourful form of printing with a Risograph
Who teach me about print, paper, production ...
SOS ISSUE
Sep 2008 Oct Nov Dec Jan 2009 Feb Mar Apr May Jun Jul Aug Sep
May Jun
And introduce me to Justin (Fenner) who provides the cover for
Oct Nov Dec Jan 2010
ISSUE 1
ISSUE 2
GRAD ISSUE
Designer Joe
And we check out
YOUTH ISSUE
The beginning of a degree in Critical Fine Art Practice at Brighton University
99p — An exhibition held in Brighton's vacated music library
Which was visited by a photographer, who became the subject of an interview for ...
Who knows
Previous Intern Jen
Artist Michael
Illustrator & Grad Charlie
Where the only contact you have with other disciplines is during a weekly lecture in first year
SINA CFAP WIZ
CETLD
Which helped fund
Who knows ...
Who then contribute to
One of the reasons why ...
Who tells me about
On the basis that students would have the opportunity to submit work
Playground party at The Volks
Off Modern
Who writes for ...
Chris, whose work I recognise at
Pick Me Up Fair at Somerset House
Showpony was good; a B+W mag showcasing work by students across the uni.
But had no funds to continue, cue idea for ...
Which sparked a conversation with a friend about ...
Felix
As a part of a set of prints by Landfill Editions
Resident
Meeting with CETLD & The Dean, where we discuss the magazine & decide to 200 copies.
Whose article about Mount Kimbie I read
And
Brighton Zine Fest. Where I hear about
Who printed ...
... Painting CFAP & Sculpture got together to put on some exhibitions
Uni
Stocked at
Which agreed to stock
Featuring work by Hannah B
Who then writes for/helps out with
Who I reconise at the London Zine Symposium
In order to raise funds for ManyMono

Futu

Poland, Issue 6, 'Label', September 2008 (230 × 280mm, 9¼ × 11 inches)
A series of stylized graphs comparing the intangible value of brands (each colour dealing with a different commercial sector) but also an exercise in making dry information look as dynamic as possible.
Editor *Martyna Bednarska-Cwiek*; Art director *Matt Willey*

Issue 20, February 2011. Illustration *Jeremyville*

Issue 22, March 2011. Illustration *Michael Michael Motorcycle*

Issue 22, March 2011. Illustration *Michael Michael Motorcycle*

El Fanzine
Mexico (280 × 370mm, 11 × 14½ inches)
This free culture publication has an extraordinarily exuberant, colourful graphic approach that gets the most out of the dull newsprint stock it's printed on. Editorial director *Mariano Rocha*; Art director *Daniel Coca*; Publisher *Landy Bustamante*; Editor-in-chief *Andrés Medina*

HIGHLIGHTS

Some call it "black music for white people," some see it as a celebration of yesteryear; for *Tim Small* the current resurgence of R & B is a rare convergence of the public's and the critic's desires, proving that beauty — and smoothness, and melody — does not have to be dull.

26

Illustrated Examples

Every season, new and old ideas surface in the form of combinations, materials and specific styles. A few of each came to mind this fall and we had Wayne Pate illustrate a handful of our favorite examples.

01 Hiking Boots

02 Patterned Socks

03 Double Breasted Blazers

04 Sweater Accessory

05 Cargo Pants

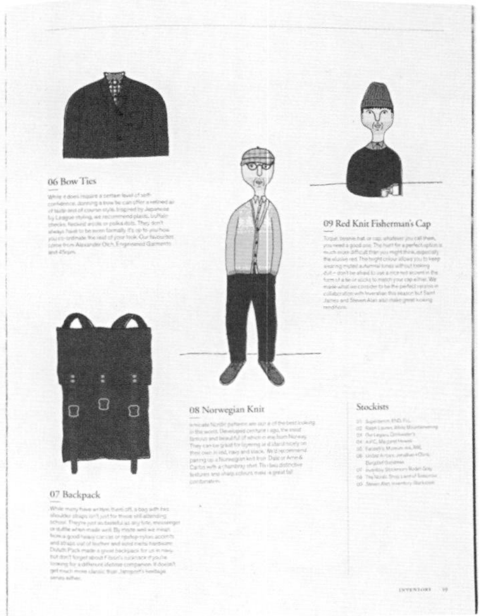
06 Bow Ties

07 Backpack

08 Norwegian Knit

09 Red Knit Fisherman's Cap

Stockists

Secret City
Carlos Bosillo

Bar, Barred
Barcelona, Spain

Fraser Nelson

Le Lunch
London, UK

Kaleidoscope
Italy, Issue 14, Spring 2012 (220 × 288mm, 8¾ × 11½ inches)
Illustration commissioned from Milan-based Chinese street portraitist *Lin Chin*.
Editor-in-chief *Alessio Ascari*; Art direction and graphic design *OK-RM*

Inventory
Canada, Number 1, Fall/Winter 2009 (215 × 287mm, 8½ × 11¼ inches)
The problem of displaying generic examples rather than specific branded items is solved by commissioning illustrator *Wayne Pate*.
Editor-in-chief and creative director *Ryan Willms*; Art director *Chris Allen*

Port
UK, Issue 4, Winter 2011 (230 × 290mm, 9 × 11½ inches)
The regular 'Secret City' section of the magazine is always illustrated by *Dan Williams*
Editor *Dan Crowe*; Creative Directors *Kuchar Swara* and *Matt Willey*
MORE PORT p197

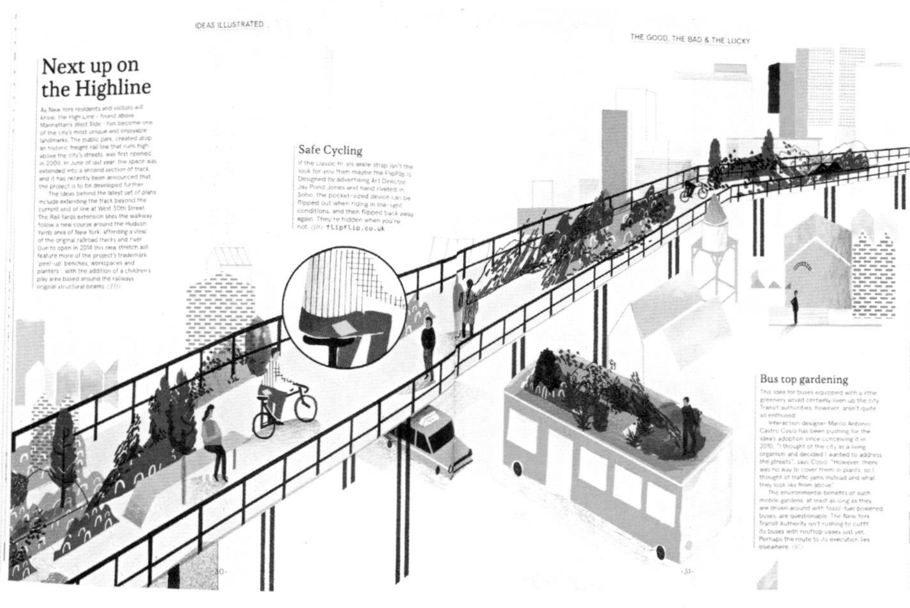

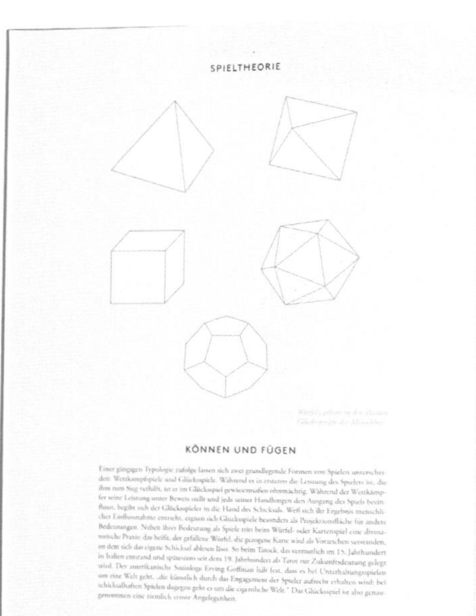

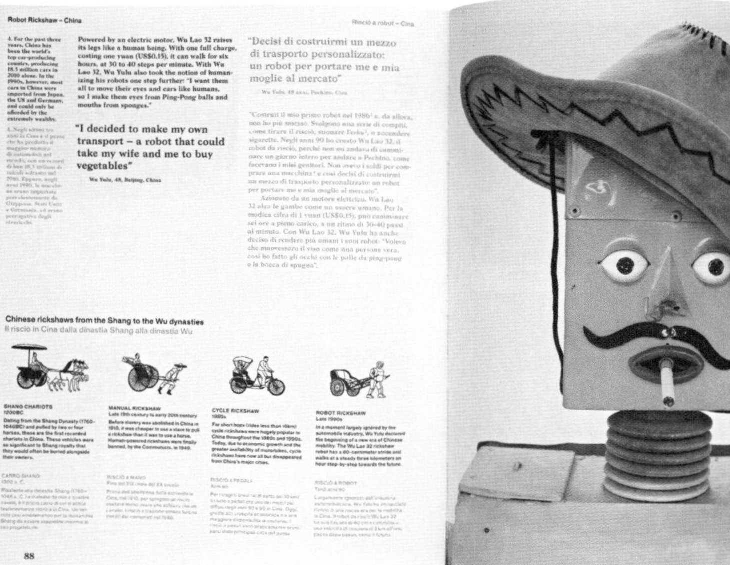

Ideas Illustrated
UK, Issue 5, 2012, 'The Luck Issue' (210 × 270mm, 8¼ × 10¾ inches)
Illustration can sometimes give a better general impression of a place than photography, an example being this drawing of Manhattan's Highline park by Luke Fenech.
Editor *Nick Defty*; Art director *Alex Hunting*

Froh!
Germany, Issue 8, May 2012 'Games' (220 × 285mm, 8¾ × 11¼ inches)
This themed magazine relies on mutliple illustration styles throughout, such as these found images of dice and visual explanations of budgerigars' gender differences.
Editor-in-chief *Dr. Sebastian Pranz*; Art director *Klaus Neuberg*

Colors
Italy, Issue 81, 'Transport', Summer 2011 (228 × 289mm, 9 × 11½ inches)
Illustration also has an important role as small drop-in explanations, such as those in this visual history of Chinese rickshaws.
Editor *Jonah Goodman*; Creative director *Patrick Waterhouse*

THE MONOCLE 100
FAVOURITE THINGS

25–29
Kamakura
A PLACE TO GROW OLD

ILLUSTRATIONS/
Satoshi Hashimoto

246 — ISSUE 49

ISSUE 49 — 247

Issue 49, December/January 2012. Illustration *Satoshi Hashimoto*

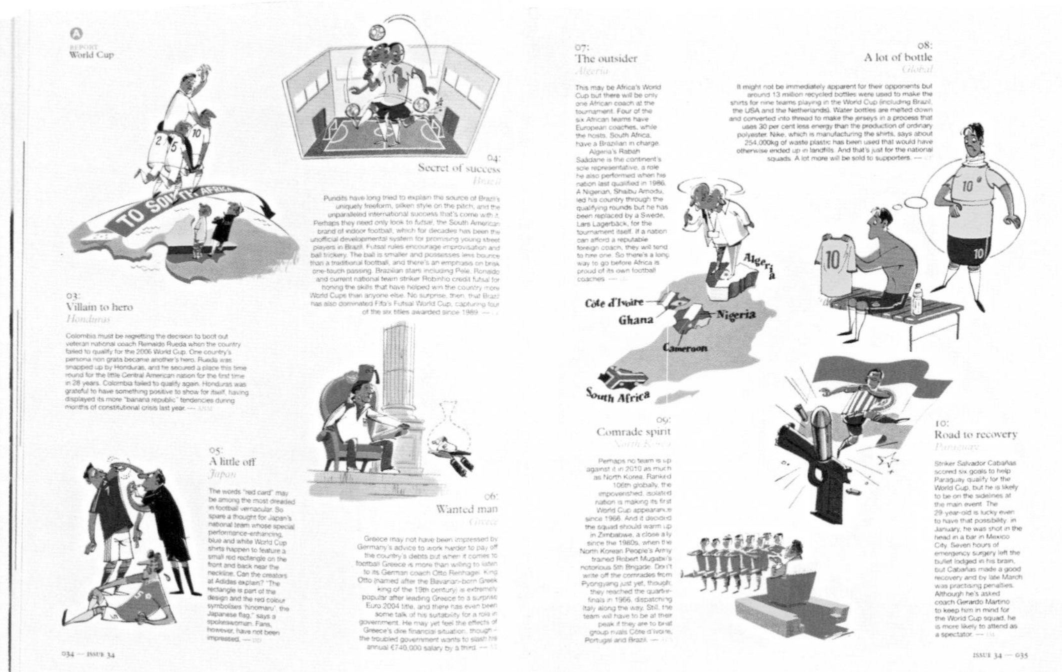

REPORT
World Cup

03:
Villain to hero
Honduras

04:
Secret of success
Brazil

05:
A little off
Japan

06:
Wanted man
Greece

07:
The outsider
Algeria

08:
A lot of bottle
Global

09:
Comrade spirit
North Korea

10:
Road to recovery
Paraguay

034 — ISSUE 34

ISSUE 34 — 035

Issue 34, June 2010. Illustration *Satoshi Hashimoto*

Monocle

UK (200 × 265mm, 8 × 10½ inches)
Illustration is a key part of the visual identity of this global business and culture magazine, bringing colour and wit to pages that otherwise feature quiet monochrome typography and unsaturated photography.
Editor-in-chief and chairman *Tyler Brûlé*; Creative director *Richard Spencer Powell*
SEE MORE MONOCLE p196

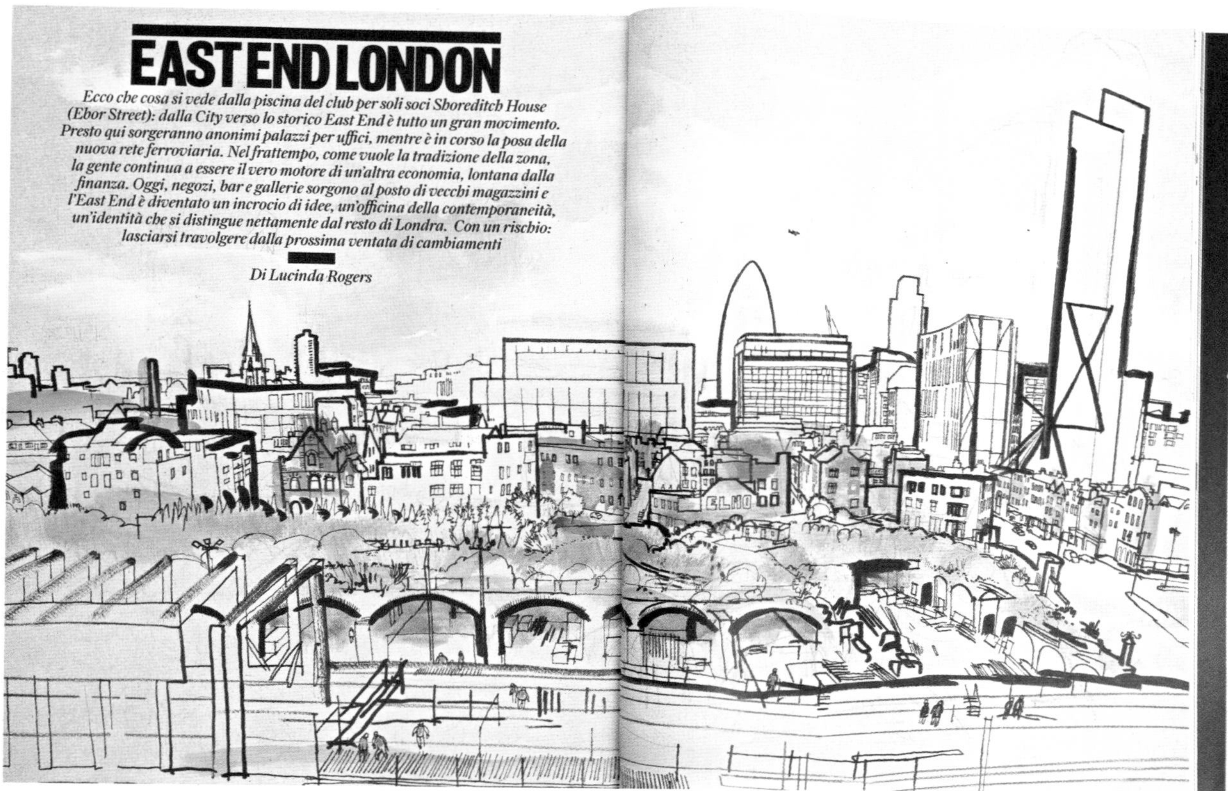

EAST END LONDON

Ecco che cosa si vede dalla piscina del club per soli soci Shoreditch House (Ebor Street): dalla City verso lo storico East End è tutto un gran movimento. Presto qui sorgeranno anonimi palazzi per uffici, mentre è in corso la posa della nuova rete ferroviaria. Nel frattempo, come vuole la tradizione della zona, la gente continua a essere il vero motore di un'altra economia, lontana dalla finanza. Oggi, negozi, bar e gallerie sorgono al posto di vecchi magazzini e l'East End è diventato un incrocio di idee, un'officina della contemporaneità, un'identità che si distingue nettamente dal resto di Londra. Con un rischio: lasciarsi travolgere dalla prossima ventata di cambiamenti

Di Lucinda Rogers

Issue 122, November 2008. Illustration *Lucinda Rogers*

Issue 126, April 2009. Illustration *Michael Kirkham*

Case da Abitare

Italy. (227 × 287mm, 9 × 11½ inches)

This interiors magazine uses full-page illustration to change the pace of pages usually full of photography. The style of artwork varies considerably, as these examples demonstrate.

Editor *Francesca Taroni*; Art director *Kuchar Swara*

The New Yorker

USA (200 x 272mm, 8 x 10¾ inches)

Since its 1925 inception *The New Yorker* has run illustrated front covers by leading artists and designers, relating to the seasons, current news stories or general cultural observations. Subscribers receive these unadorned covers; newsstand copies have an additional flap on the left side of the cover carrying content details.

FROM LEFT:

Imagining a future where ebooks and author souvenirs have replaced printed books; to mark the date US tax returns are due, tax forms are folded to make origami military hardware, a reference to the increasing US defence budget; each year, the magazine celebrates its anniversary with a front cover featuring its 'mascot' character, Eustace Tilley. In 2012 he appeared blurred and with a download icon, marking the then recent launch of the magazine's iPad app; contemporary Hallowe'en, with parents' faces lit by their smartphones as their children go trick-or-treating.

Editor *David Remnick*; Art editor *Françoise Mouly*

December 5, 2011, 'Black Friday'. Artist *Daniel Clowes*

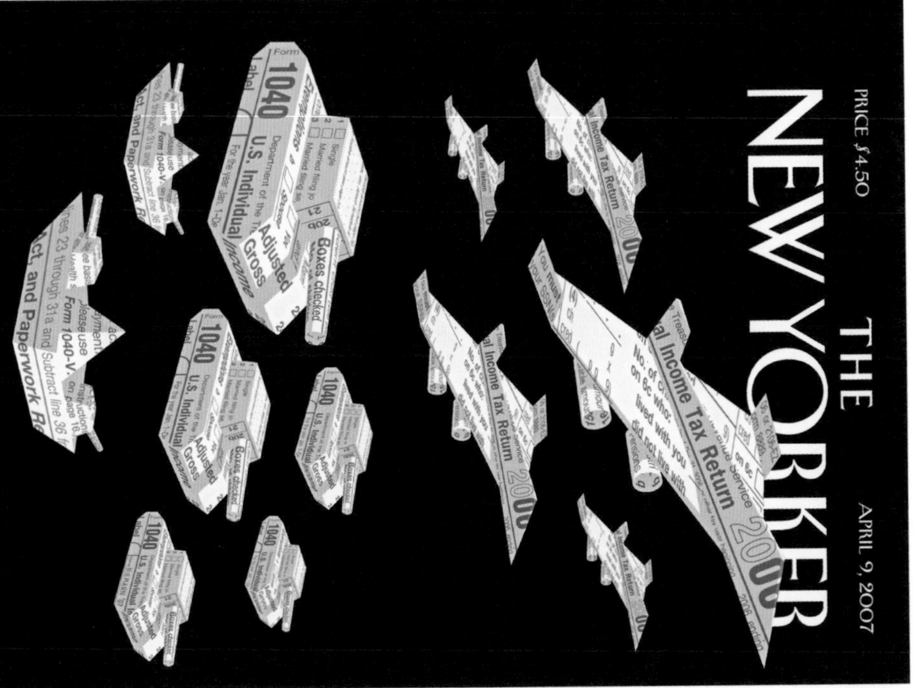

April 9, 2007, 'T-Day'. Artist *Christoph Niemann*

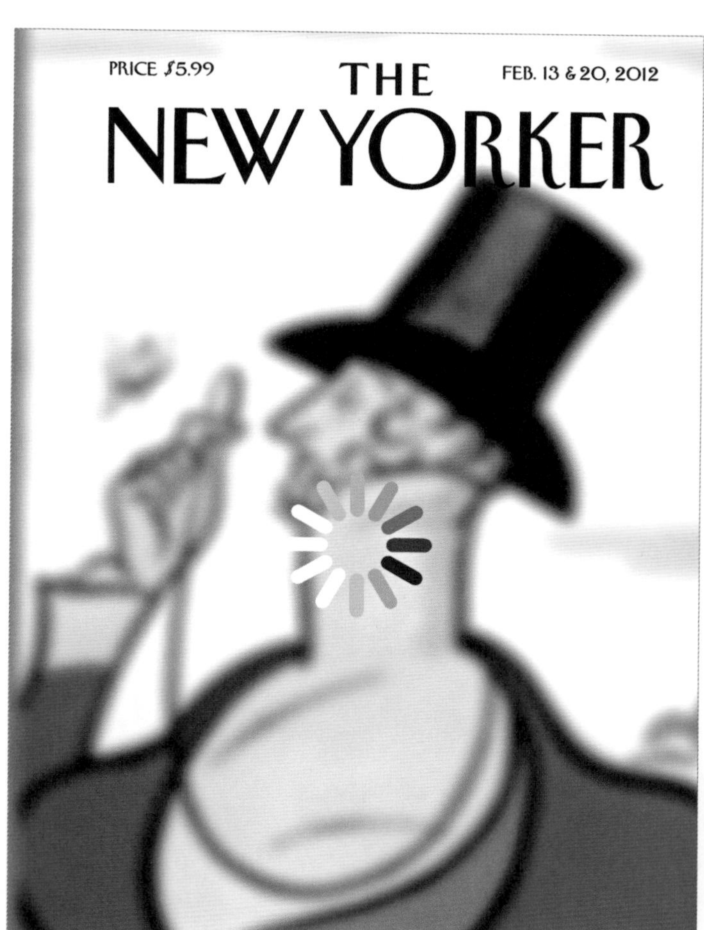

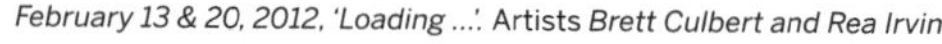
February 13 & 20, 2012, 'Loading ....' Artists *Brett Culbert and Rea Irvin*

November 2, 2009, 'Unmasked'. Artist *Chris Ware*

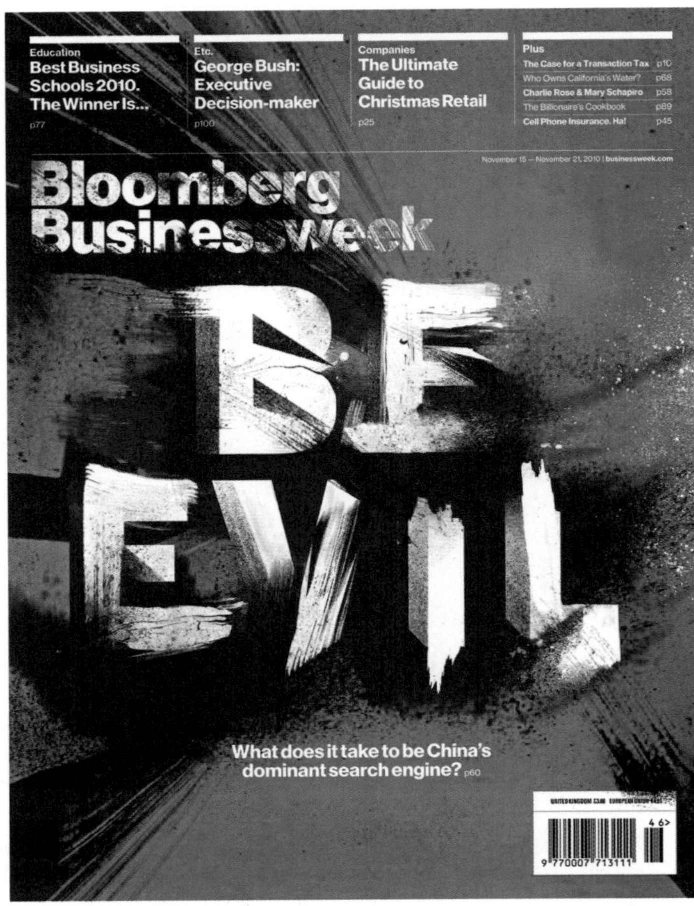

November 15, 2010. Typography *Hellovon*

August 15, 2011. Photograph *Corriette Schoenaerts*

June 18, 2012

July 2, 2012

April 13, 2012

July 2, 2012. Illustration *Jennifer Daniel*

August 6, 2012. Illustration *David Parkins*

April 18, 2011

November 1, 2010. Illustration *Nick White*

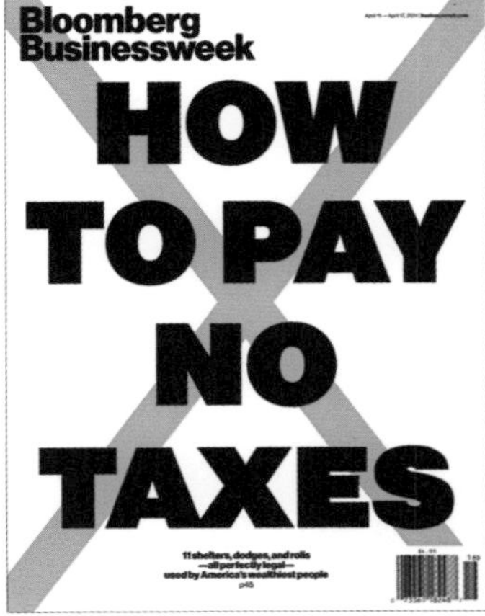

April 11, 2011

August 19, 2011. Illustration *David Foldvari*

May 28, 2012

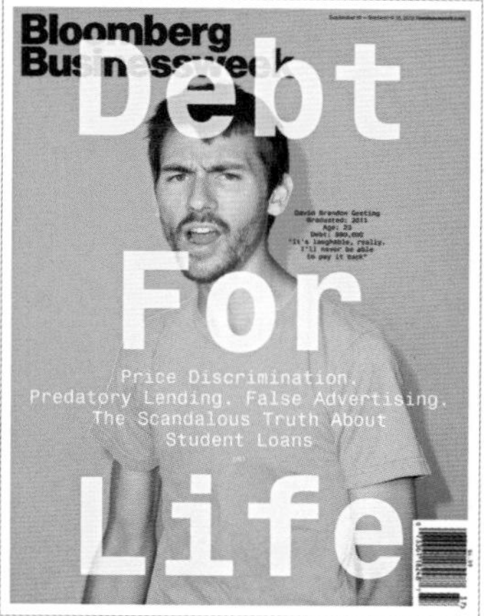

September 10, 2012. Photograph *Charlie Engman*

July 9, 2012

October 31, 2011. Illustration *Justin Metz*

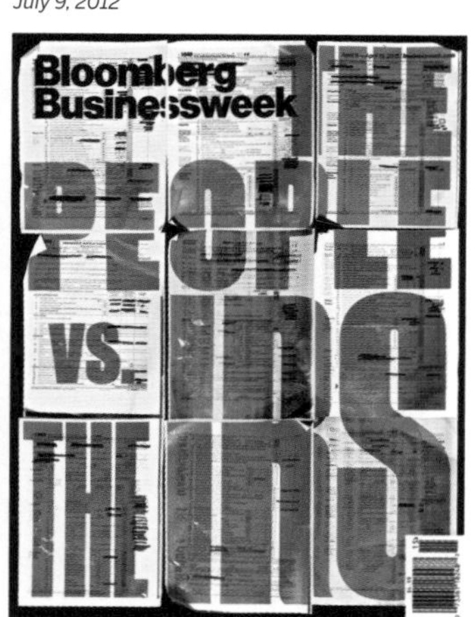

April 9, 2012

Bloomberg Businessweek
USA (200 × 266mm, 8 × 10½ inches)
Since its 2010 redesign this weekly has made a feature of its covers, employing strong typography, illustration, infographics and photography to ensure they have become a weekly publishing news event in their own right.
Editor *Josh Tyrangiel;* Creative director *Richard Turley*

December 20, 2010 – January 2, 2011 | **businessweek.com**

Bloomberg Businessweek
Year in Review

2010

Barack Obama
The New Normal
Normal, IL
Deepwater Horizon
"I want my life back"
Mark Hurd
Foreclosure
"End the Fed!"
Volcano
Toyota
WikiLeaks
8-inch Hailstones

365 days, 61 Charts, 289 Pictures, 7 Essays. The Business Year in Perspective

Sarah Palin
Gold
Euro
Bacon
Unemployment
Lady Gaga
Unobtanium

$4.99
DISPLAY UNTIL JAN. 19, 2011
52>
0 75470 18255 6

December 20, 2010. Design Richard Turley, Jennifer Daniel and Kenton Powell

June 27, 2011

Bloomberg Businessweek
USA (200 × 266mm, 8 × 10½ inches)
The weekly business magazine reinvented for today's businessmen, using design and illustration techniques more usually found in fashion and culture magazines.
Editor *Josh Tyrangiel*; Creative director *Richard Turley*

'Richard and I sit directly across from each other; we don't have meetings. He'll kick me under the table and I'll zip around to see his screen. Most of our conversations about the front covers happen in a series of 30-second back-and-forths.'

JOSH TYRANGIEL
EDITOR
BLOOMBERG BUSINESSWEEK

June 13, 2011, The Popularity Issue.

Bloomberg Businessweek
The magazine has developed a reputation for infographics thanks to infographics designer Jennifer Daniel. The 2011 Popularity Issue (TOP, THIS PAGE AND OPPOSITE) was a typically inventive issue, the pages flowing together into one continuous diagrammatic investigation of the year's most popular products, people and trends. Both on highly developed pages like these and on simpler, weekly pages (OPPOSITE, BOTTOM), the design works on two levels. The reader can flick through and enjoy the surface level, or dig deeper for a longer read.

Bloomberg Businessweek (USA)

EDITOR JOSH TYRANGIEL
AND DESIGN DIRECTOR RICHARD TURLEY

First published in 1929, *Businessweek* survived the Great Depression of the 1930s to establish itself as the voice of US business, providing rare nationwide coverage of finance, marketing and labour news, along with related political issues. But by the late 2000s it was a magazine in decline, suffering like most from the drop in advertising revenue caused by the latest recession. It went through several redesigns before finally being sold to multinational media business Bloomberg in 2009. The subsequent turnaround in its fortunes is a remarkable example of how design can help reinvent a magazine.

Bloomberg renamed the magazine *Bloomberg Businessweek* and brought in a new creative team. Editor Josh Tyrangiel was hired from *Time* magazine, where he had been responsible for hiring Luke Hayman for its 2007 redesign. As part of the interview process Tyrangiel prepared a 5,000-word outline of what he would do with the magazine. 'The old *Businessweek* was unfathomable to me. I literally didn't know where I was in the magazine, the navigation was so poor and the art direction confused. I laid out a whole plan, central to which was finding a great creative partner.'

Tyrangiel called in several design directors to offer their thoughts and quickly settled on young British art director Richard Turley, then designing the 'G2' section of *The Guardian* newspaper. What had initially been a one-off redesign project became a formal job offer to run the magazine. 'Richard came in and it was just clear that his sensibility and my sensibility worked together. What's unusual is that I think we have more respect for the other person's discipline than for our own.' They also share a conviction that the best idea counts, regardless of whose it is.

Such mutual regard for each other's role has always been a vital part of successful editor–designer relationships, but Tyrangiel and Turley take it to a deeper level than most. The larger staffs found at US publishers have often led to hierarchical office arrangements that separate people from one another. Senior figures tend to expect their own office-space, and even junior staff members have individual booths of their own. But not at Bloomberg. Learning from his experience running the Time.com website, on arrival at Bloomberg Tyrangiel set up an open-plan office arrangement that mixed departments and staff across the floor.

Our interview took place in one of a few separated breakout spaces at Bloomberg HQ, from where Tyrangiel was able to point out his team: 'What you see out there is everyone sitting right next to each other. The news section is run by those two women there ... Cindy is our design director ... Eleanor's the executive editor ... they sit next to each other and are constantly conceiving stories.' This mixing of disciplines sounds an obvious idea but remains rare in an industry where staff tend to be arranged by discipline. It is a very modern sensibility, and extends to editor and design director – no corner offices with views across Manhattan for them. 'Richard and I sit directly across from each other; we don't have meetings. He'll kick me under the table and I'll zip around to see his screen. Most of our conversations about the front covers happen in a series of 30-second back-and-forths.'

Those front covers have been the most high-profile part of the new *Bloomberg Businessweek* to date. Together they form a working sourcebook of editorial ideas, making impressive use of everything available to the magazine designer. Photography, illustration and typography are all called into use

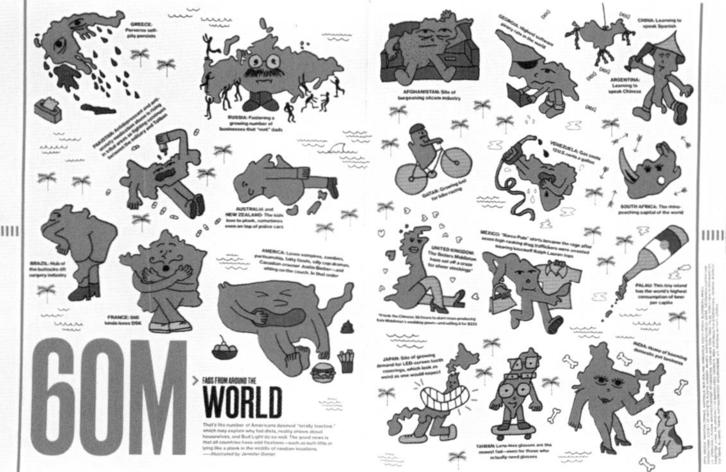

at different times, and sometimes combined. This is nothing new in itself, of course, but it's the style and wit with which work is commissioned that makes the covers stand out. It has brought a new excitement to the US weekly news magazine market, which still tends towards a more craft-orientated approach to illustration. At the time of my visit to the Bloomberg offices, one of the other news weeklies had a beautifully rendered piece of artwork as a cover, which I'm sure was a perfect response to the brief but one I struggled to make immediate sense of. By contrast, *Bloomberg Businessweek*'s covers share a directness of vision, an unapologetic willingness to get to grips with a story and shout about it. Turley: 'The illustrated Coke cover (see page 184) was one of those moments where you do something you don't see much of over here. It was, basically, a 'G2' cover.' And having done it, the parameters shift again for the next cover: 'Sometimes there's not enough time to think about another idea so you end up being more radical with the covers just because there's no time to do anything else.'

If Tyrangiel brings an absolute belief in the importance of making the most of print – 'You have to explore every avenue of storytelling and the visual is 50 per cent of that' – then Turley brings a talent for responding to story ideas at a spontaneous, instinctive level. In his previous role at *The Guardian*'s daily 'G2' section, his ability to quickly conceptualize and execute a cover, often with same-day turnaround, proved a highlight of the early days of the newspaper's 2005 redesign and prepared him well for life at Bloomberg. It also makes a virtue of characteristics for which he was criticized at school – 'being intuitive and not always thinking things through'. It is this immediacy that provides the linking character between the very different covers. As the examples shown here demonstrate, there is no single stylistic direction to the designs – instead a pervasive mood of excitement and thrill in the process shines through and provides the thread week to week. There's a sense of brinksmanship here, spontaneity adding an excitement to the process of creation, that comes across in the cover designs and helps the magazine position itself as a vital news weekly.

Look at the cover designs and you'll see references to magazines far beyond the business realm. Turley's admiration for the editorial work of Scott King (*Sleazenation*, UK), David Carson (*RayGun*, USA) and Neville Brody (*The Face*, UK) is evident. '*RayGun* was just an incredible moment. You couldn't have had Scott Dadich (*Wired*) without Carson and his expressive, poetic way of manipulating editorial design.'

With the covers setting the tone for the project, the inside pages flesh out the pair's desire to surprise their readers. Again, you can see influences from pop culture and beyond. They are making a magazine for the business world – 'white men in suits' was a phrase

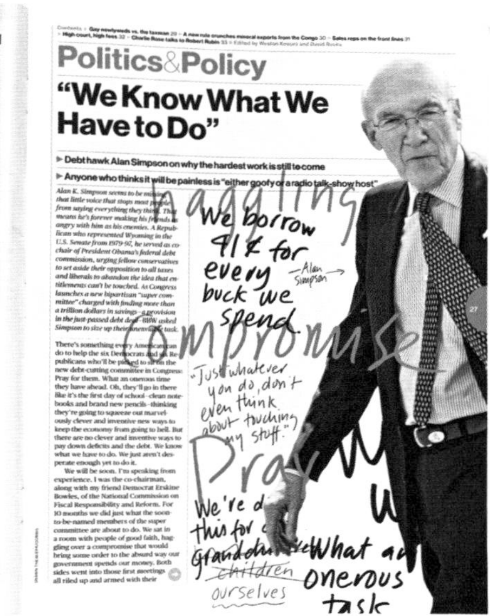
Politics&Policy

“We Know What We Have to Do”

Debt hawk Alan Simpson on why the hardest work is still to come

Anyone who thinks it will be painless is “either goofy or a radio talk-show host”

August 8, 2011

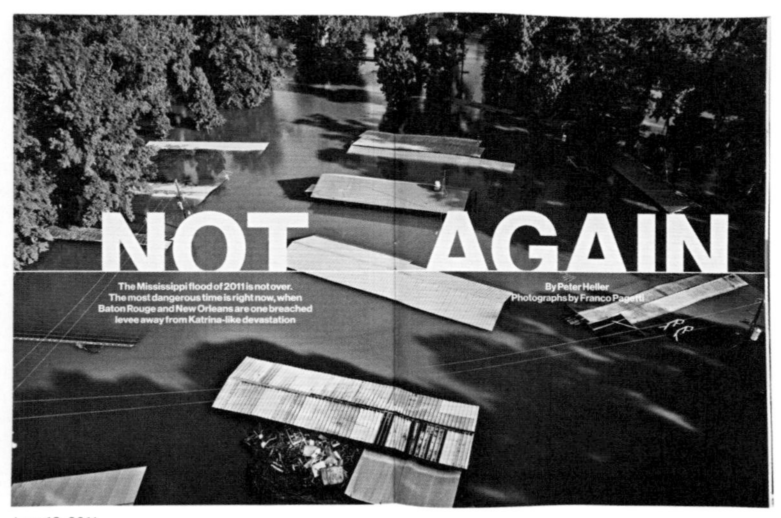

NOT AGAIN
The Mississippi flood of 2011 is not over. The most dangerous time is right now, when Baton Rouge and New Orleans are one breached levee away from Katrina-like devastation
By Peter Heller
Photographs by Franco Pagetti

June 13, 2011

Empire
At
The
End
Of
The
Earth

A journey to the Siberian stronghold of Gazprom, the company that keeps the Kremlin in business
By Brett Forrest. Photographs by Alexander Gronsky

February 13, 2012

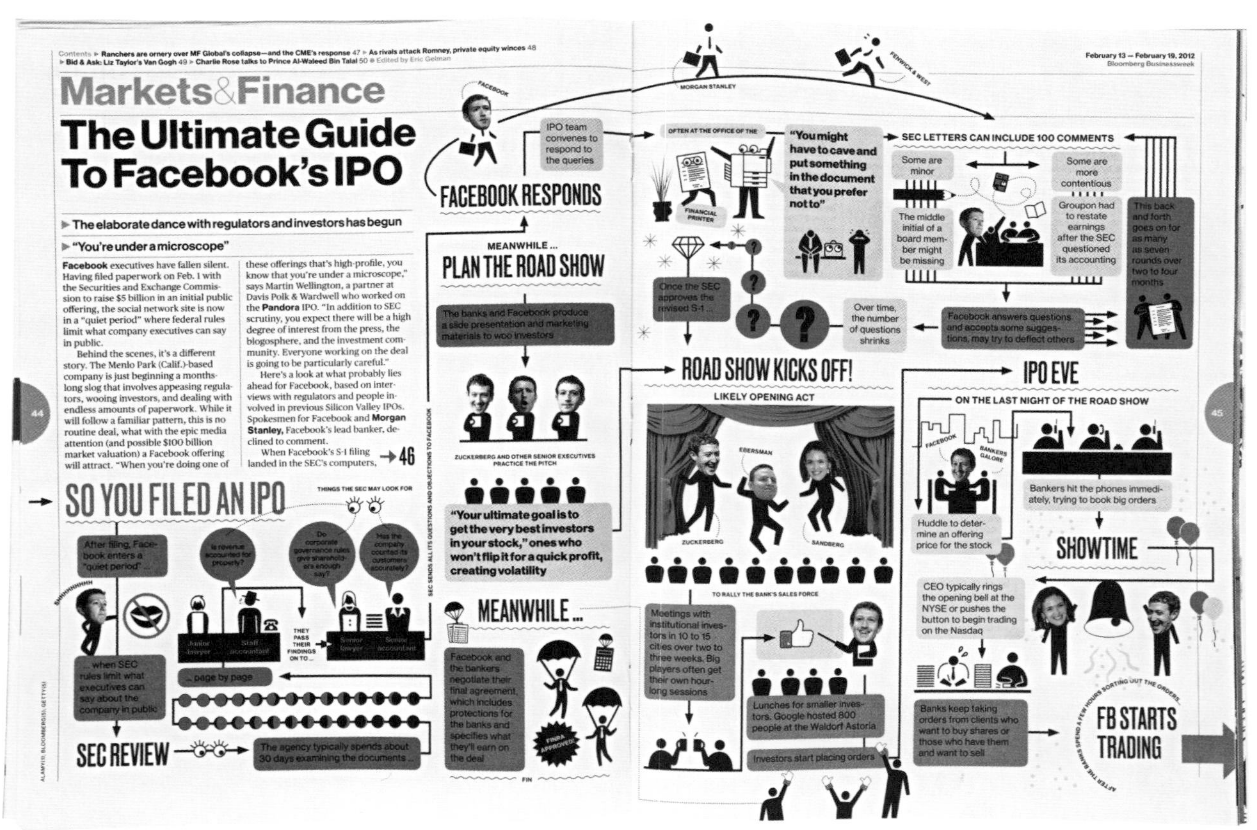

Contents ▶ Ranchers are ornery over MF Global's collapse—and the CME's response 47 ▶ As rivals attack Romney, private equity winces 48 ▶ Bid & Ask: Liz Taylor's Van Gogh 49 ▶ Charlie Rose talks to Prince Al-Waleed Bin Talal 50 ● Edited by Eric Gelman

February 13 — February 19, 2012
Bloomberg Businessweek

Markets&Finance

The Ultimate Guide To Facebook's IPO

▶ The elaborate dance with regulators and investors has begun

▶ "You're under a microscope"

Facebook executives have fallen silent. Having filed paperwork on Feb. 1 with the Securities and Exchange Commission to raise $5 billion in an initial public offering, the social network site is now in a "quiet period" where federal rules limit what company executives can say in public.

Behind the scenes, it's a different story. The Menlo Park (Calif.)-based company is just beginning a months-long slog that involves appeasing regulators, wooing investors, and dealing with endless amounts of paperwork. While it will follow a familiar pattern, this is no routine deal, what with the epic media attention (and possible $100 billion market valuation) a Facebook offering will attract. "When you're doing one of these offerings that's high-profile, you know that you're under a microscope," says Martin Wellington, a partner at Davis Polk & Wardwell who worked on the **Pandora** IPO. "In addition to SEC scrutiny, you expect there will be a high degree of interest from the press, the blogosphere, and the investment community. Everyone working on the deal is going to be particularly careful."

Here's a look at what probably lies ahead for Facebook, based on interviews with regulators and people involved in previous Silicon Valley IPOs. Spokesmen for Facebook and **Morgan Stanley,** Facebook's lead banker, declined to comment.

When Facebook's S-1 filing landed in the SEC's computers, → 46

February 13, 2012

Bloomberg Businessweek
Various feature openers show the visual influence of non-business magazines (TOP, THIS PAGE AND OPPOSITE). A story such as this one about Facebook's share offer (BOTTOM) might start out as a purely written piece before developing into an infographic.

ptember 24, 2012. Photograph *Ka Xiaxi*; Illustration *Pinar & Viola*

What would happen if you took the collective wisdom of Steve Jobs, Eric Schmidt, Steven Spielberg, and Anna Wintour and poured it into one campaign manager's head? Barack Obama will find out in November. By Joshua Green

Jim Messina Has a President to Sell

June 18, 2012

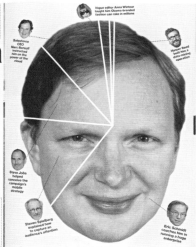

mentioned several times – but there's a shared appreciation that those white men in suits are no longer interested to see themselves in print. Tyrangiel points out that business is a more fascinating world than it is often given credit for, as 'there's no more conflict, drama or tension in any other subject than business. Yet most magazines devoted to it are bloodless, they're condescending even to expert readers.' The challenge they've set themselves is to keep readers interested by surprising them – not a new idea in itself but the extent to which they set out to do so *is* new.

This desire for the new doesn't stem from a love of novelty but comes from a strategy that ties together creative excellence and value. Tyrangiel regularly mentions the price of the magazine, pointing out the need to make readers feel they have got their money's-worth from every single page, let alone every issue. 'We've been through some very difficult times in journalism and publishing, and we all bear the scars. We'd better defend our future by making every page good,' he says. 'We publish over 40,000 words a week, and I'm probably the only person who's going to read every word. Even our most devoted readers are going to skip pages here and there. But when they're moving past those pages there should be something that catches their attention,' explains Tyrangiel.

The result is a page design that operates on two distinct levels. The front section of the magazine is the clearest example of this. There's a strong structural base featuring a tight three-column grid and very clear navigational elements. At this level there are few surprises: it is easy to read, immediately recognizable and guides the reader well.

Over that, a second layer of surprises is added paragraph by paragraph, column by column, page by page. These are the mini graphics, drop-in photos, diagrams and visual jokes that litter the pages, breaking up the content visually and editorially. 'Our pages got more and more intense as people got more confident about designing them. You can now flick through them, have a really rich experience and feel like you've had your five bucks'-worth' – value again, this time from Turley – 'without having actually read anything. And when you are interested in a story you'll find it a pleasant reading experience.'

Art director and editor both see the many design and editorial elements available to them as tools in their quest for reader attention. Stories are discussed in terms of the best way to present them, with the question 'How can we do it better?' forever being asked. 'Some stories are very hard to bring to life visually – private equity, for instance – so we may go heavier on text than on art. By and large I like to get that 50:50 point where everything is enriching everything,' says Tyrangiel.

The final part of this armoury is the infographics, something the magazine now has a name for but which was at first a peripheral feature in the redesign. Turley had doubts about this currently fashionable form of visual explanation ('sometimes there's this assumption that there's great data available, but when you go looking for it the story quickly disintegrates'), but he was excited when Tyrangiel proposed doing an entire issue using only charts and diagrams. That issue, the '2010 Review', confirmed their reputation for the form and led to infographics design specialist Jennifer Daniel being hired.

Both admit their intense approach to magazine creation is an exhausting one, and there is a sense that the inevitable result of their continual self-questioning will be to replace themselves. But the combination of sales growth and award-winning creativity proves their belief that quality works.

Bloomberg Businessweek
Steve Jobs
1955—2011

Remembering that you are going to die is the best way I know to avoid the trap of thinking you have something to lose.
You are already naked.
There is no reason not to follow your heart.

Simple can be harder than complex. You have to work hard to get your thinking clean to make it simple.
But it's worth it in the end.

The only way to be satisfied is to do what you believe is great work.

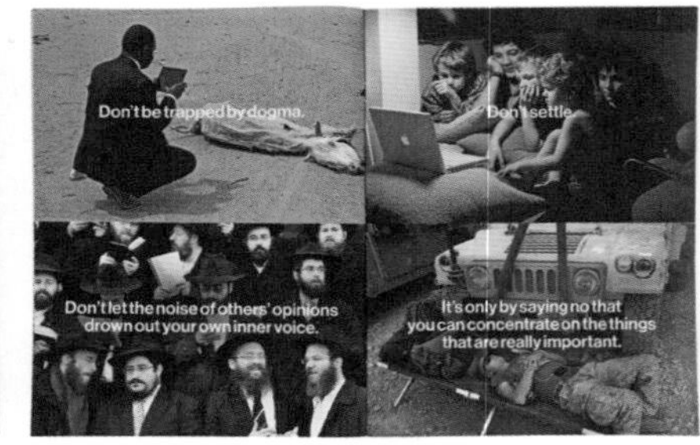
Don't be trapped by dogma.
Don't settle.
Don't let the noise of others' opinions drown out your own inner voice.
It's only by saying no that you can concentrate on the things that are really important.

A lot of times, people don't know what they want until you show it to them.

Things don't have to change the world to be important.

Creativity is about connecting things,
When you ask a creative person how they did something,
they may feel a little guilty because they didn't really do it,
they just saw something.

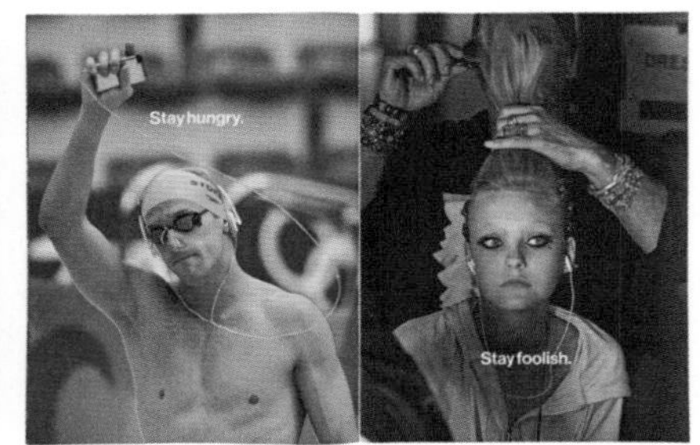
Stay hungry.
Stay foolish.

And one more thing...

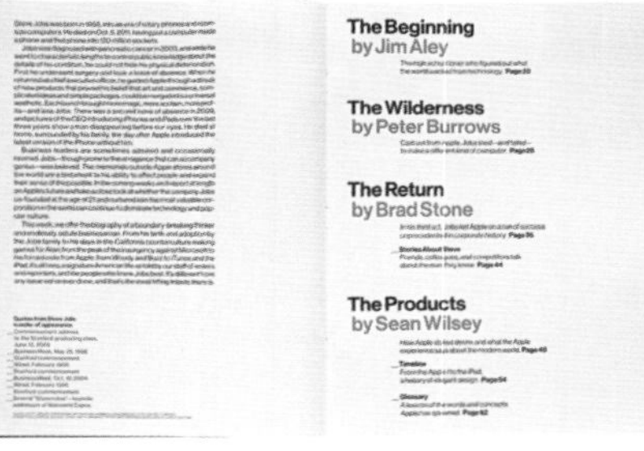
The Beginning by Jim Aley
The Wilderness by Peter Burrows
The Return by Brad Stone
The Products by Sean Wilsey

1955—1985 The Beginning By Jim Aley

No Bozos. Ever.
By John Sculley

DESIGN × CONTENT

1985—1997 The Wilderness By Peter Burrows

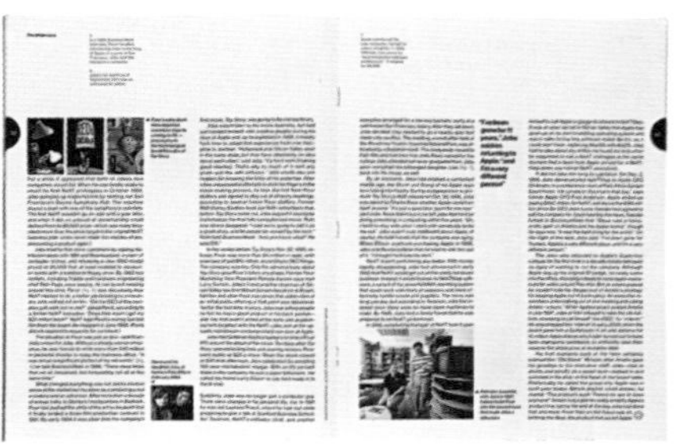

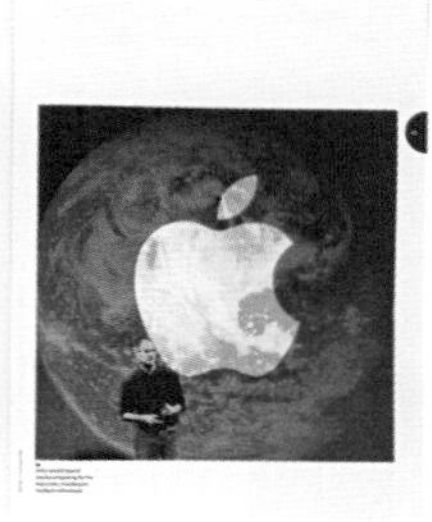

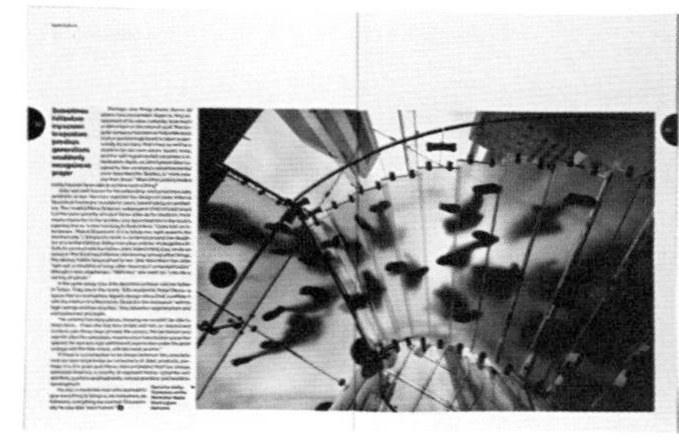

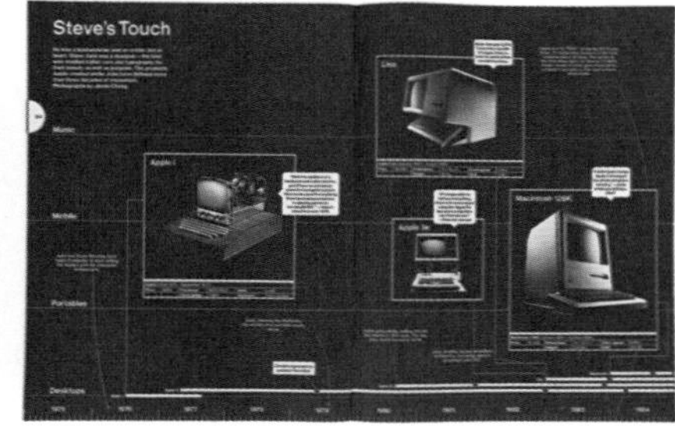

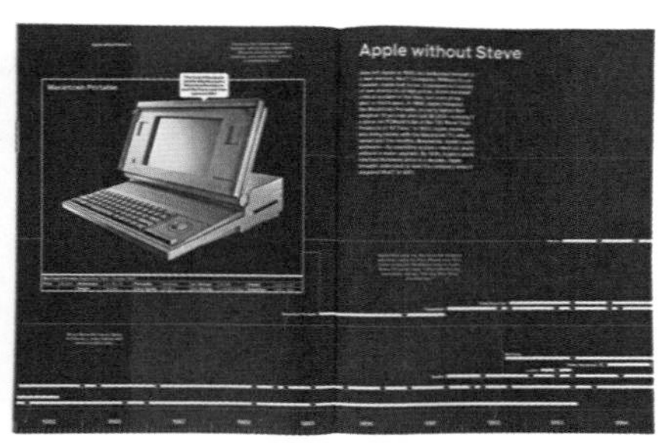

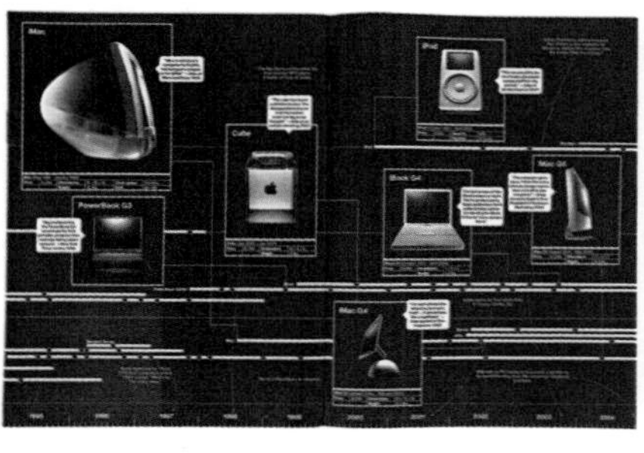

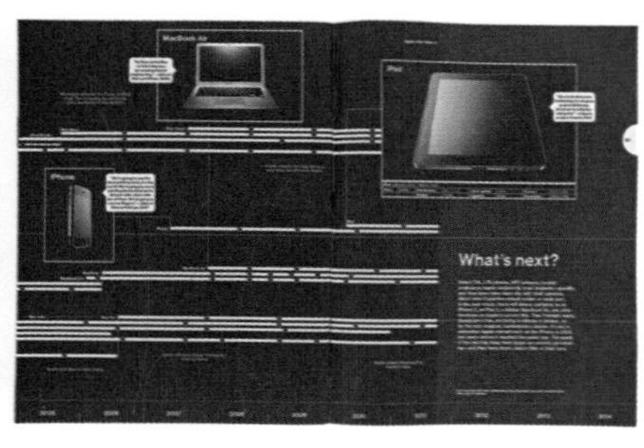

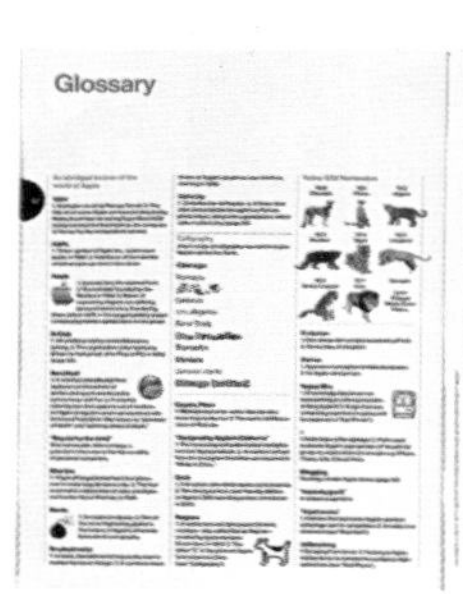

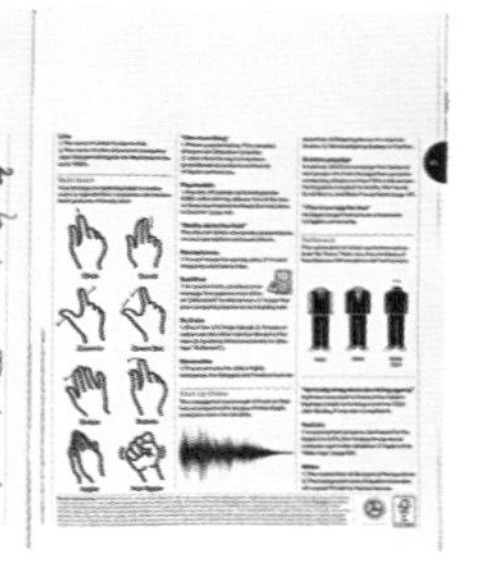

Bloomberg Businessweek
October 10, 2011
As the regular weekly edition was due to go to press on October 5, the news broke that Steve Jobs had died. The issue was completely restarted and a special tribute to Jobs created literally overnight. This is the entire issue.

The Thing About Mexican Cement: Tercer Un Quinto

Headline design *Ramiro Espinoza/Tomate*

Headline design *David Jonathon Ross*

Headline design *The Church of London*

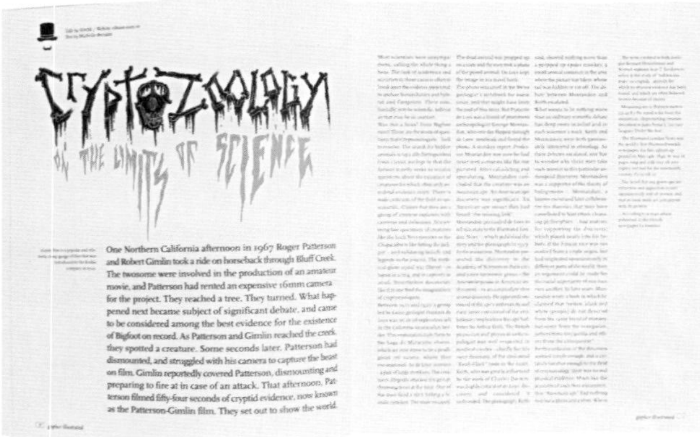

Headline design *Hase*

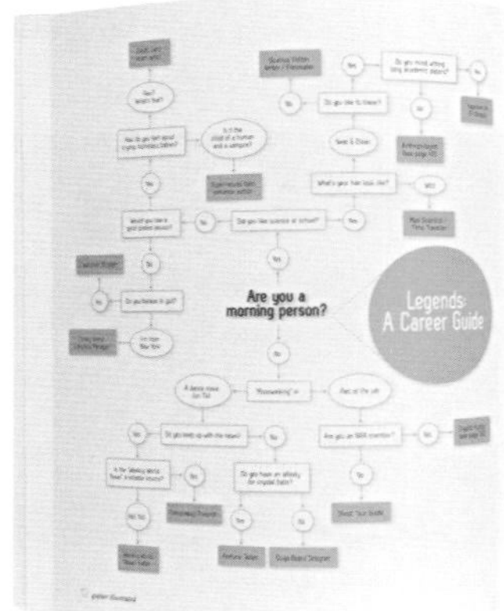

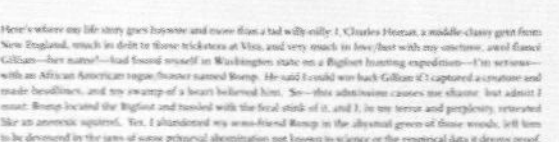

Headline design *Áron Jancsó*

Headline design *Mike Cina*

LEGEND HAS IT

Headline design *Billy Ben*

Headline design *Negro*

Surprise Ending
KNIFING IN CENTRAL PARK
Homo killer on the prowl
WORK OUT

ESSAY
Dressed to Kill:
Lifting the shirt on Gere, Pacino and cinematic masculinity circa 1980
Text Stuart Henderson
Electronic Music Score
MALE REAR NUDITY

Little Joe

UK, Issue 1, 2010 (140 × 210mm, 5½ × 8½ inches)

An appreciation of pre-digital cinema aligned with the editor's discovery of his own sexuality. *Little Joe* uses a different typeface for each headline, sitting them in the centre of each page.

Editor and designer *Sam Ashby*

OPPOSITE **Gopher Illustrated**

USA, Volume 1, 2010 & Volume 2, 2011 (205 × 255mm, 8¼ × 10 inches)

An international culture and literature magazine that commissions different people to design each headline. Completely counter to most design advice, but surprisingly effective.

Editors *Michelle Benaim Steiner and Lope Gutiérrez-Ruiz*;

Art director *Lope Gutiérrez-Ruiz*; Senior designer *Alexander Wright*

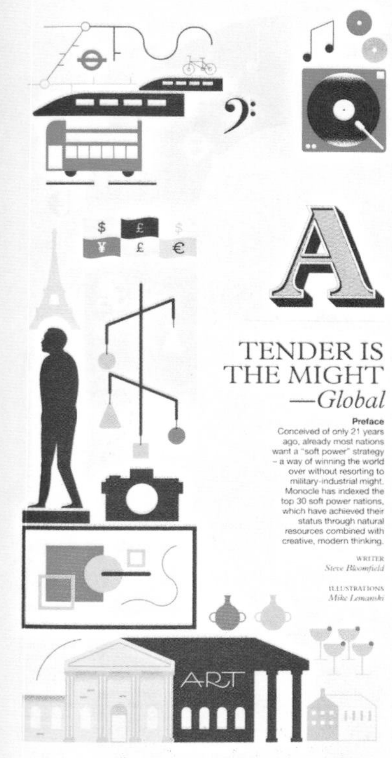

AFFAIRS
Soft Power Survey

A

TENDER IS THE MIGHT —*Global*

Preface
Conceived of only 21 years ago, already most nations want a "soft power" strategy – a way of winning the world over without resorting to military-industrial might. Monocle has indexed the top 30 soft power nations, which have achieved their status through natural resources combined with creative, modern thinking.

WRITER
Steve Bloomfield

ILLUSTRATIONS
Mike Lemanski

Everyone wants it, some have it, few know how to use it. There is barely a foreign ministry on the planet that doesn't have a soft power unit, a soft power strategy or, at the very least, a memo from a minister returning from an overseas conference urgently asking his advisors what this soft power business is all about.

The phrase "soft power" has been around for two decades, devised by the American foreign policy expert, Joseph Nye (who talks about the future of soft power on page 44). But until MONOCLE and the Institute for Government compiled the first ever Soft Power Survey 12 months ago, it remained a relatively nebulous concept whose definition depended on which foreign minister you were talking to.

Our first survey prompted some anguished responses from foreign ministries and cultural institutions. Ministerial advisers got in touch to point out soft power nuggets we had apparently overlooked, various heads of public diplomacy made personal pleas to be ranked higher next time around, while the head of one august cultural institution was rather put out by our failure to name-check his organisation.

Our joint winners last year, the UK and France, have both suffered soft power setbacks over the last 12 months. As last year's survey was heading off to the printers the UK's new coalition government announced it was taking an axe to one of the country's greatest soft power icons, the BBC World Service. The government's insistence on following a path of austerity – regardless of the economic merits or otherwise – has created

ISSUE 49 — 041

Issue 49, December 2011/January 2012

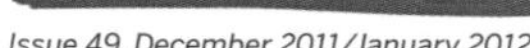

Issue 49, December 2011/January 2012

Issue 14, June 2008

Issue 49, December 2011/January 2012

Issue 50, February 2012

DESIGN × CONTENT

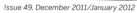

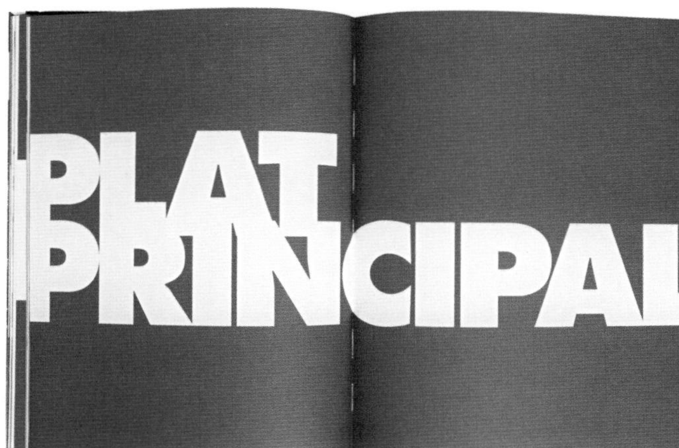

Swallow LEFT
USA, Issue 1A Nordic Issue, 2008 (235 × 310mm, 9¼ × 12¼ inches)
This food magazine uses meal courses as bold section headings.
Editor and creative director *James Casey*

Port RIGHT
UK, Issue 5, Spring 2012 (230 × 290mm, 9 × 11½ inches)
The magazine is split into several numbered sections, in this issue presented using bold, coloured numerals.
Editor *Dan Crowe*; Creative Directors *Kuchar Swara and Matt Willey*
MORE PORT p229

Monocle OPPOSITE
UK (200 × 265mm, 8 × 10½ inches)
Each issue is split into five sections – Affairs, Business, Culture, Design and Edits – which are signified by the 'engraved' A, B, C, D and E characters (ad pages blacked out).
Editor-in-chief *Tyler Brûlé*; Creative director *Richard Spencer Powell*
MORE MONOCLE p229

TWO
ENTERTAINING FOR TWO

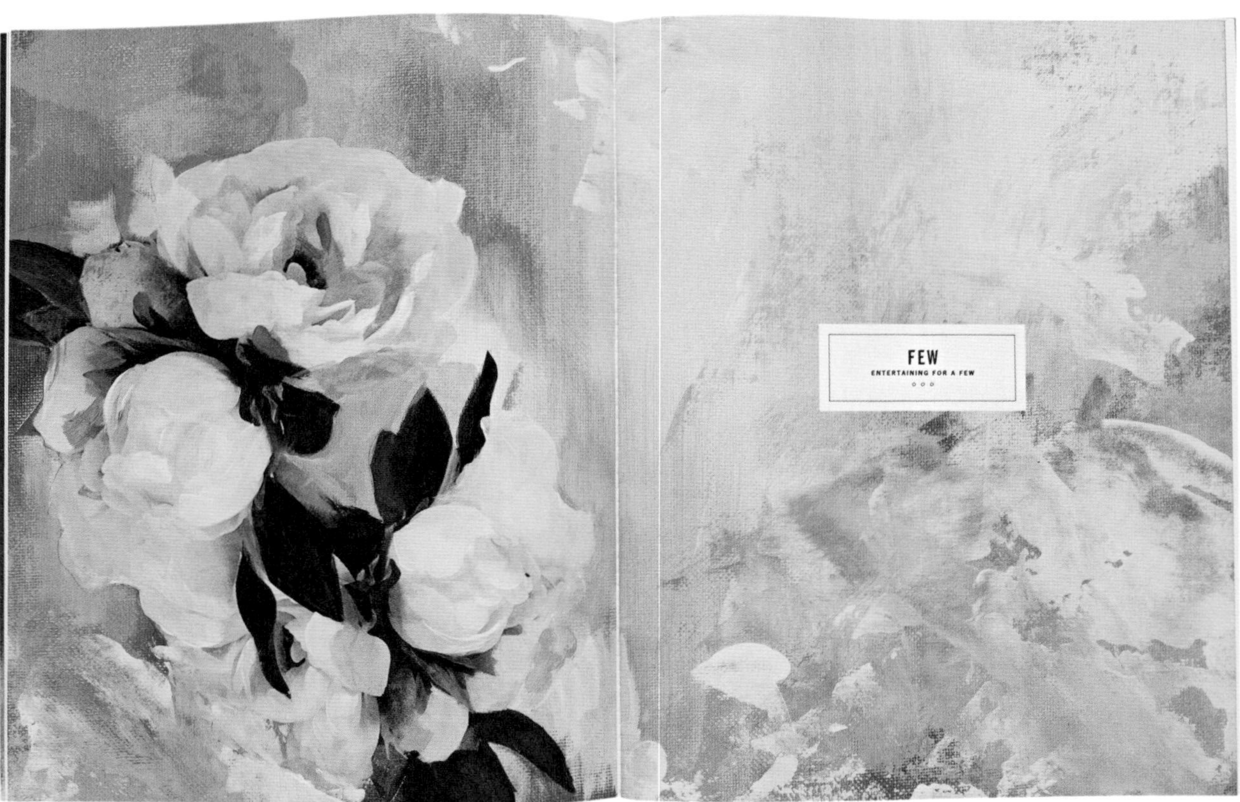
FEW
ENTERTAINING FOR A FEW

Underscore
Singapore, Number 4, The Flight Issue, Autumn/Winter 2012
(190 × 260mm, 7½ × 10¼ inches)
Each issue of this themed global culture magazine is divided into five chapters with pictorial opening spreads relating to the theme. The chapter numbers pick up from the previous publication, emphasizing the continuation from issue to issue. This fourth edition carries chapters 16–20.
Editor-in-chief *Justin Long*; Creative director *Jerry Goh*

OPPOSITE **Kinfolk**
USA, Volume 2, 2011 (214 × 275mm, 8½ × 11 inches)
This 'guide for small gatherings' is divided into three sections, each of which begins with an opening spread: One (Enteraining for one), Two (entertaining for two) and Few (Entertaining for a few).
Editor *Nathan Williams*; Designer *Amanda Jane Jones*

Self Service

France, Issue 14, Spring/Summer 2001 (235 × 310mm, 9¼ × 12¼ inches)
A pictorial story based on the simple premise of collecting 100 everyday inspirational things. Carefully curated but fitted together on the page with little editorial direction, it's akin to a highly designed scrapbook.
Editor-in-chief and creative director *Ezra Petronio*; Art direction *Work in Progress*

OPPOSITE

33 Thoughts

UK, Summer 2006 (170 × 230mm, 6¾ × 9 inches)
A customer magazine published for accountants BDO Stoy Hayward, each issue contained 33 brief articles ranging from a single-sentence quotation to several hundred words of text. These 'thoughts' were presented in a highly expressive illustrated notebook format.
Editor *Jane Lewis*; Art direction *James Grubb*

onehundredthings
An ode to the surprising everyday points where inspiration begins. No hype, no spin, just those rare personal instants that put our thoughts in a whole new light. Move out of context and look around for yourself. You'll be surprised at what you might find.

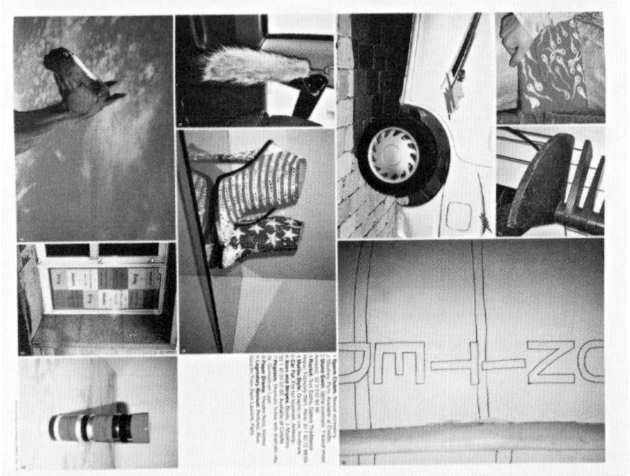
UNITED

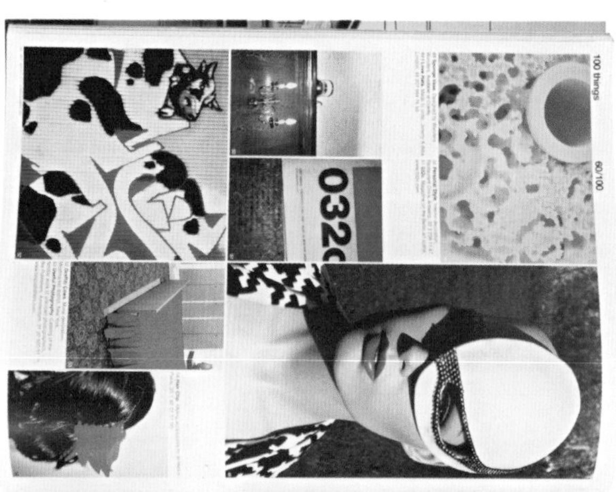
100 things
60/100
032c

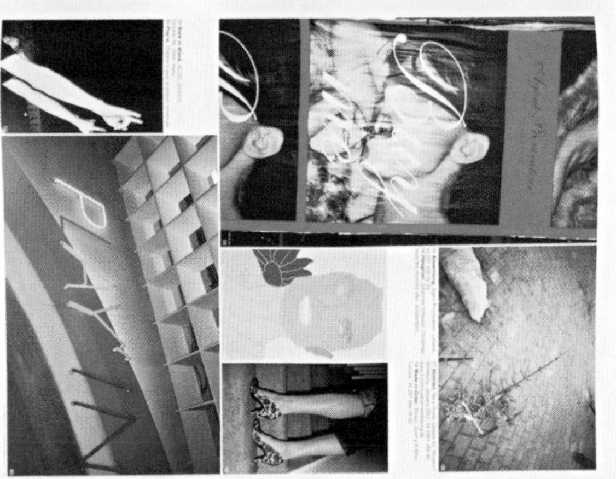
PLAY IN

100 things
42/100
HiT

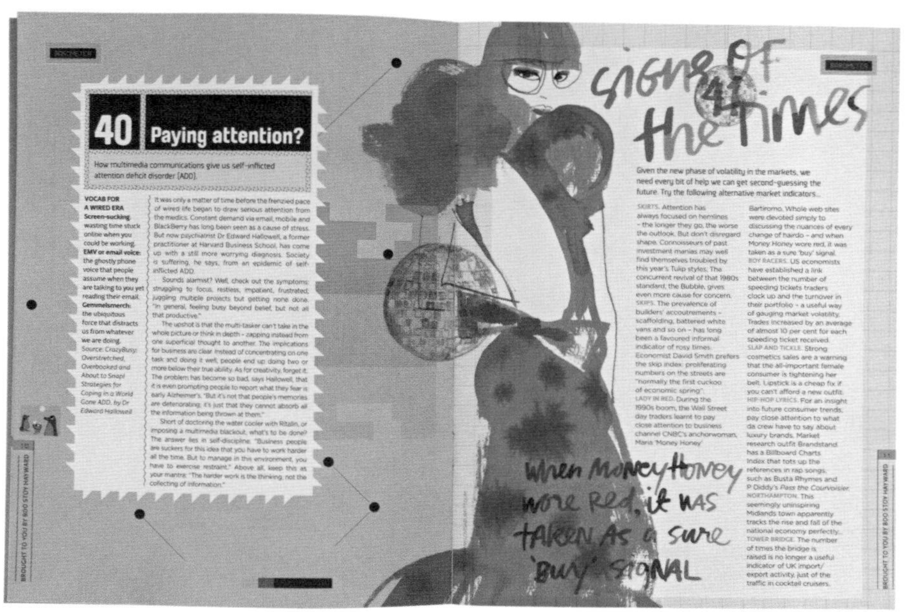

40 Paying attention?

How multimedia communications give us self-inflicted attention deficit disorder (ADD).

Signs of the times

Given the new phase of volatility in the markets, we need every bit of help we can get second-guessing the future. Try the following alternative market indicators...

When Money Honey wore red, it was taken as a sure 'buy' signal

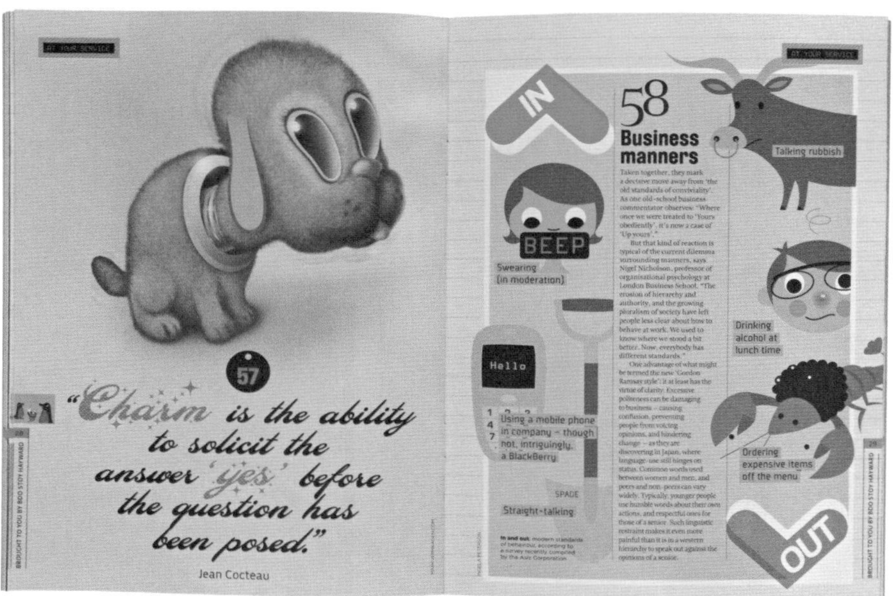

57

"Charm is the ability to solicit the answer 'yes' before the question has been posed."

Jean Cocteau

58 Business manners

53 Be Free

There is always a fine line between a successful giveaway and a financial and public relations disaster.

54 Be Frugal

Business folklore is stuffed with tales of tight-wad billionaires, but the truly frugal company is a rare beast indeed.

Under The Influence

France, Issue 08, Autumn/Winter 2010/11 (240 × 335mm, 9½ × 13¼ inches)

The centre section of this large-format fashion title carries the written content, which is printed in green and uses a simple, strong graphic language to provide a unifying identity.

Creative director *Mark O'Sullivan*; Editor-in-chief *Susan Connie Marsh*; Design director *Xavier Encinas*

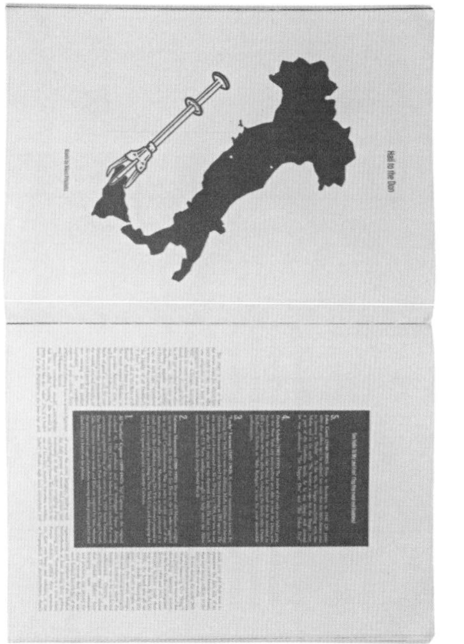

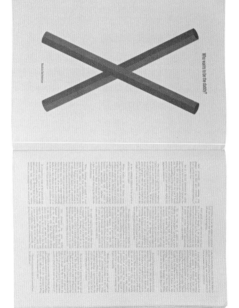

Little White Lies

UK, Issue 43, Sept/Oct 2012 (200 × 245mm, 8 × 9¾ inches)

Each issue of this movie magazine focuses on a single new movie. For its 'On the Road' issue, it paid homage to author Jack Kerouac's method of writing the original novel on a single long scroll of paper. All the features relating to the film were designed on a single continuous scroll of paper, writers typing the text and illustrators adding images. The scroll was then split into pages with elements from the previous part of the scroll still present.

Editor *Matt Bochenski*; Creative director *Paul Willoughby*

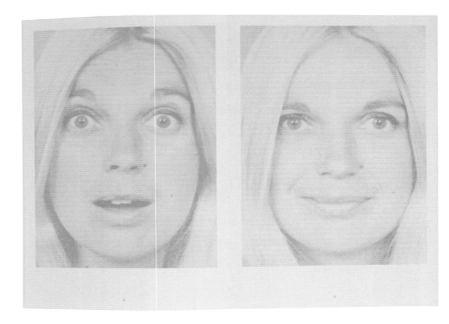

Fillip

Canada, Issue 16, Spring 2012 (170 × 245mm, 8 × 9¾ inches)
A carefully constructed, simple design is brought to life and given increased continuity by the use of gentle colour gradient fades across text columns and images.
Editor *Kristina Lee Podesva*; Design *The Future*

OPPOSITE

Bad Day

Canada (148 × 229mm, 6 × 9 inches)
This culture magazine uses a different-coloured paper stock and single ink colour for each issue. A single full-colour photo-story in the centre emphasizes the monochrome nature of the rest of the publication.
Editor-in-chief *Eva Michon*; Creative director *Colin Bergh*; Publisher *Jackie Linton*

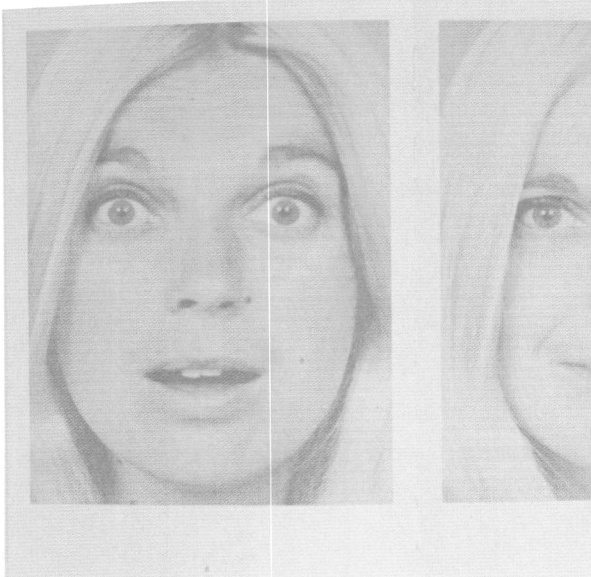

Over the past two decades, Mike Mills' quiet, consistent contribution to popular culture is difficult to quantify. Looking over his resumé of music videos and design work, it's hard not to exclaim, "He did that, too?" The art for Air's *Moon Safari*, as well as their music videos; the *Washing Machine* cover for Sonic Youth; that Supreme logo with the accent over the 'e'; and all the X-Girl graphics.

54

Issue 11, 2011

Issue 13, 2012

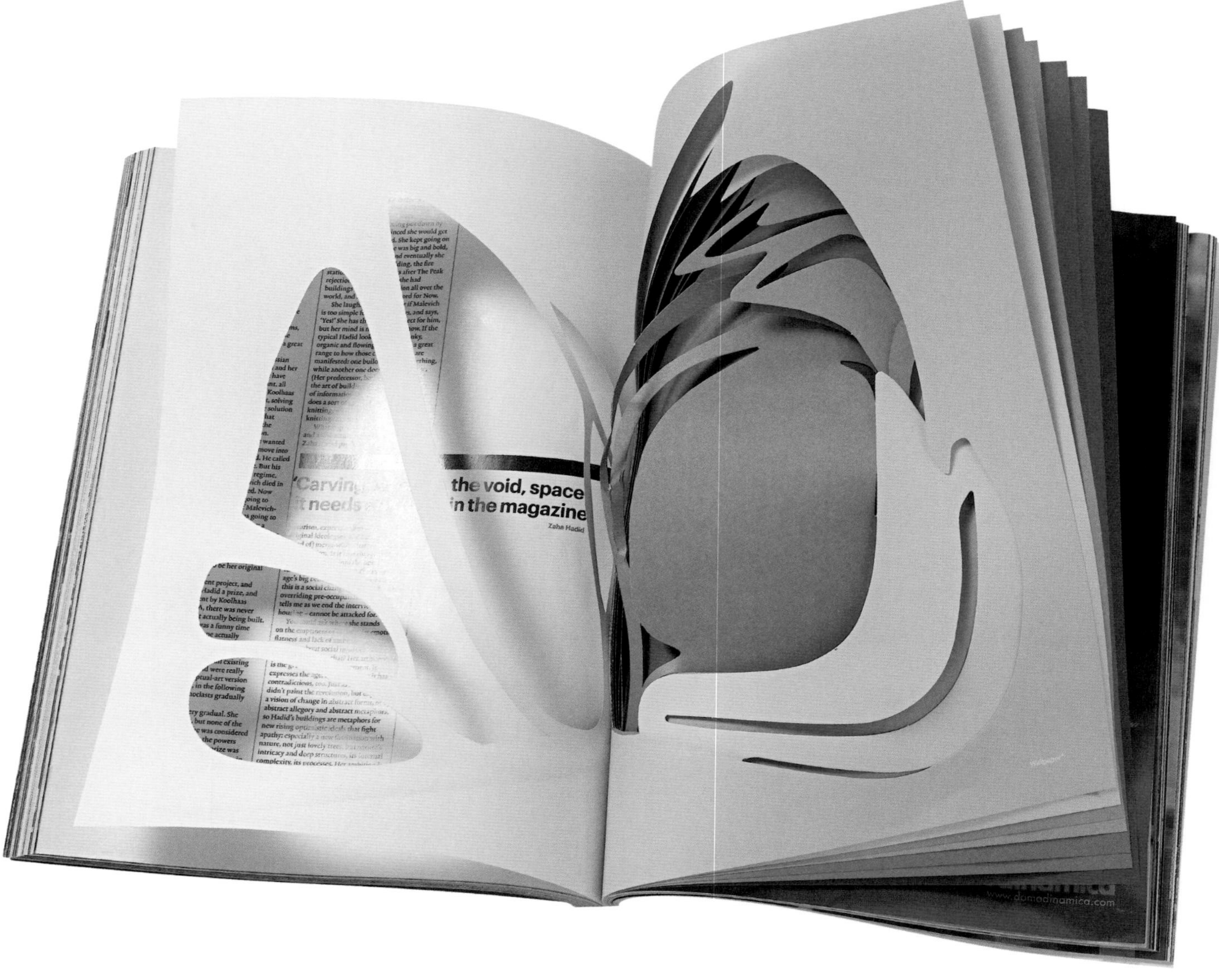

Wallpaper
UK, Issue 115, October 2008 (220 × 300mm, 8¾ × 12 inches)
For a special issue guest-edited by architect Zaha Hadid, a section of the magazine used laser-cut card to reproduce her designs for a room at the Venice Biennale. The pages could be folded to make a 3-D model of the room.
Editor-in-chief *Tony Chambers*; Art director *Meirion Pritchard*

Der Wedding
Germany, Issue 2, 2012 (210 × 270mm, 8½ × 10¾ inches)
A page of tracing paper is used to physically separate each half of an image of a single building divided into two homes.
Editor and art director *Axel Völcker*; Photograph *Mirko Zander*

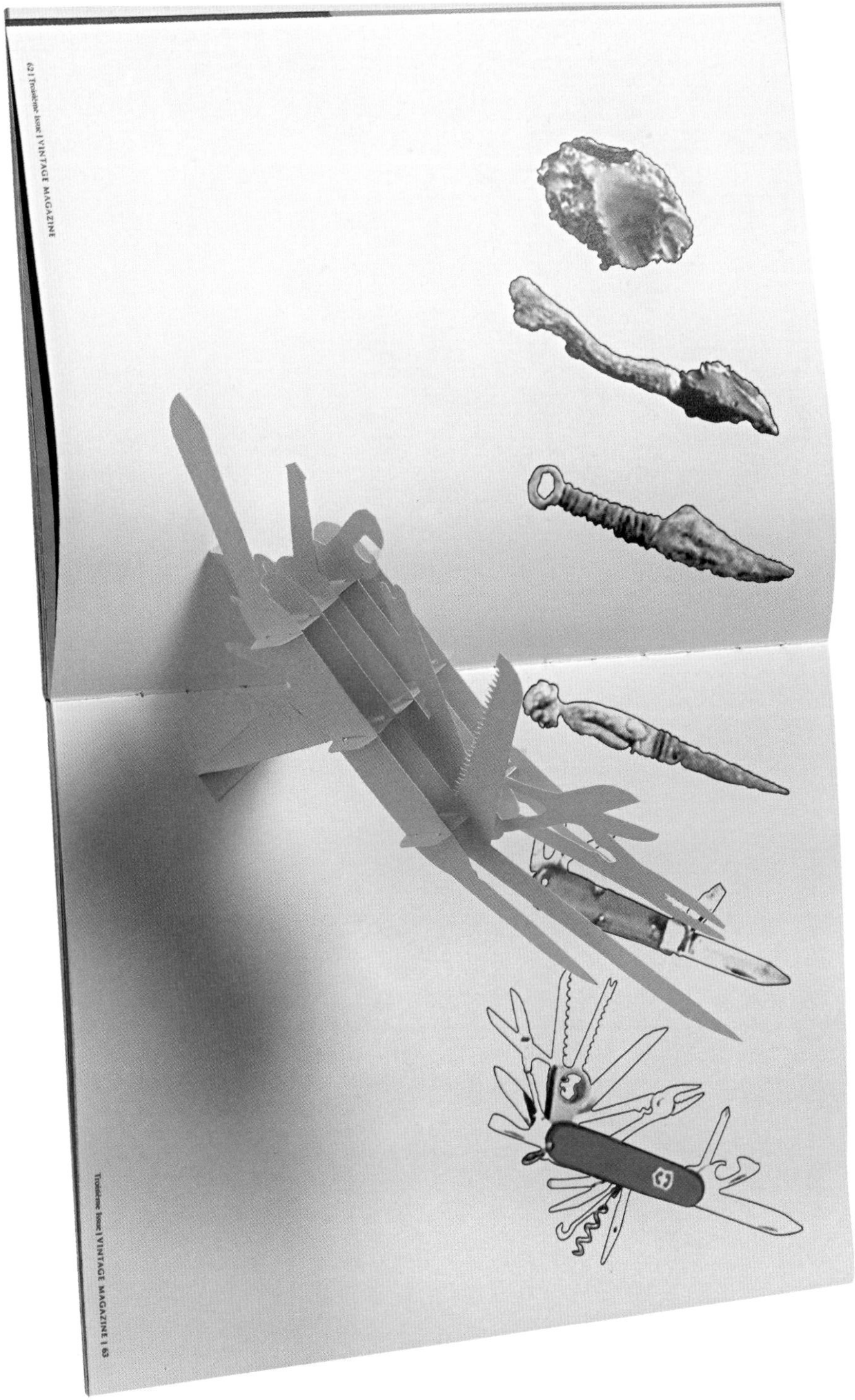

Vintage Magazine
USA, Issue 3, 2009 (225 × 296mm, 9 × 11¾ inches)
Vintage Magazine always has plenty of surprises: tipped-in items, die cuts, etc. This is perhaps one of the most spectacular: a life-size pop-up paper sculpture reproduction of a Swiss Army knife by Shawn Sheehy.
Editor-in-chief *Ivy Baer Sherman*; Art director *Regis Scott*

OPPOSITE **Amelia's Magazine**
UK, Issue 2, Autumn/Winter 2004 (200 × 245mm, 8 × 9¾ inches)
The intricate cover design by Rob Ryan is laser-cut into card and a die-cut hole contains a Swarovski-crystal charm bracelet.
Publisher, editor and art director *Amelia Gregory*

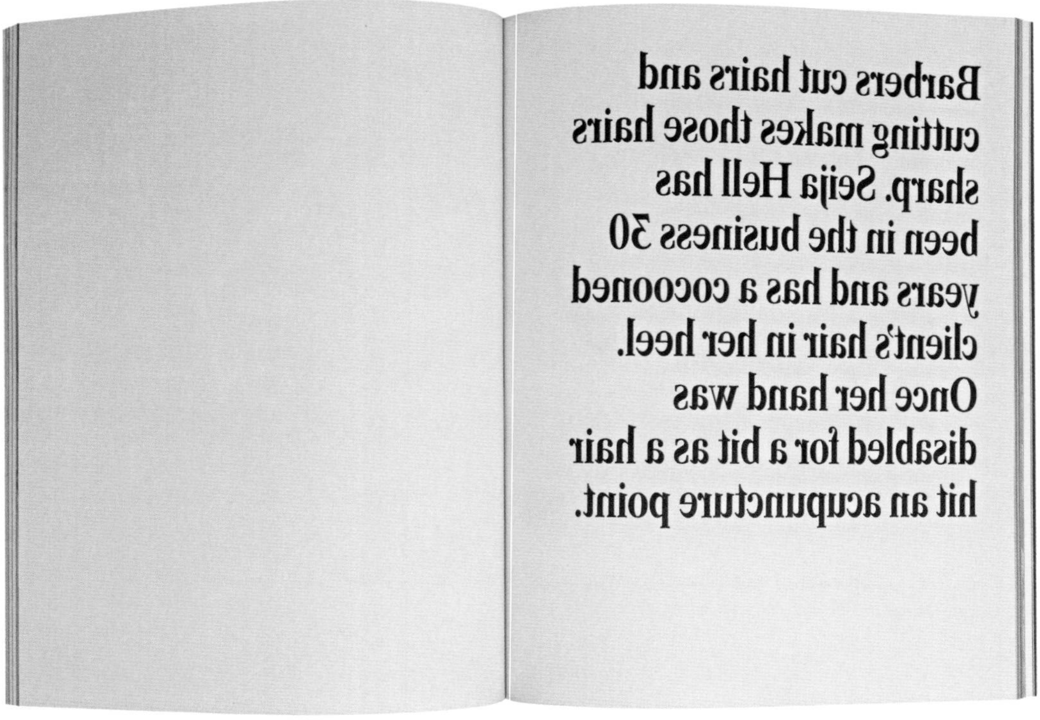

Kasino Creative Annual
Finland, Issue 1, About Hair, 2010 (162 × 210mm, 6½ × 8¼ inches)
Text is printed backwards on paper thin enough for the words to be read through the reverse side, the effect subtly highlighted by blue underscoring on the reverse.
Creative director *Pekka Toivonen*; Editor *Jonathon Mander*; Director of photography *Jussi Puikkonen*

OPPOSITE **GQ**
USA, June 2010 (203 × 275mm, 8 × 11 inches)
A trompe l'oeil effect allows the headline to this feature to be read through a 'rip' in the page.
Editor-in-chief *Jim Nelson*; Design director *Fred Woodward*; Photographs *Inez van Lamsweerde and Vinoodh Matadin*

AMONG THE GLORIOUS WINGED CREATURES THAT WALK DOWN THE RUNWAY FOR VICTORIA'S SECRET, NONE IS MORE LOVELY THAN THE AUSSIE MIRANDA KERR. OR MORE DANGEROUS. JUST ASK THE POOR SAP WHO ALMOST GOT FIRED FOR LOOKING AT ONLINE PICTURES OF HER AT WORK. NOW, HERE AT GQ, WE LIKE SEXY, BUT WE ALSO LIKE EMPLOYMENT. SO THIS MONTH WE OFFER NOT ONLY FRESH PHOTOS OF MIRANDA BUT ALSO HELPFUL ADVICE ON HOW TO ENJOY THEM WITHOUT GETTING S#!TCANNED BY STEPHEN SHERRILL
PHOTOGRAPHS BY
INEZ VAN LAMSWEERDE
& VINOODH MATADIN
DIRTY
ANGEL
GQ | 175

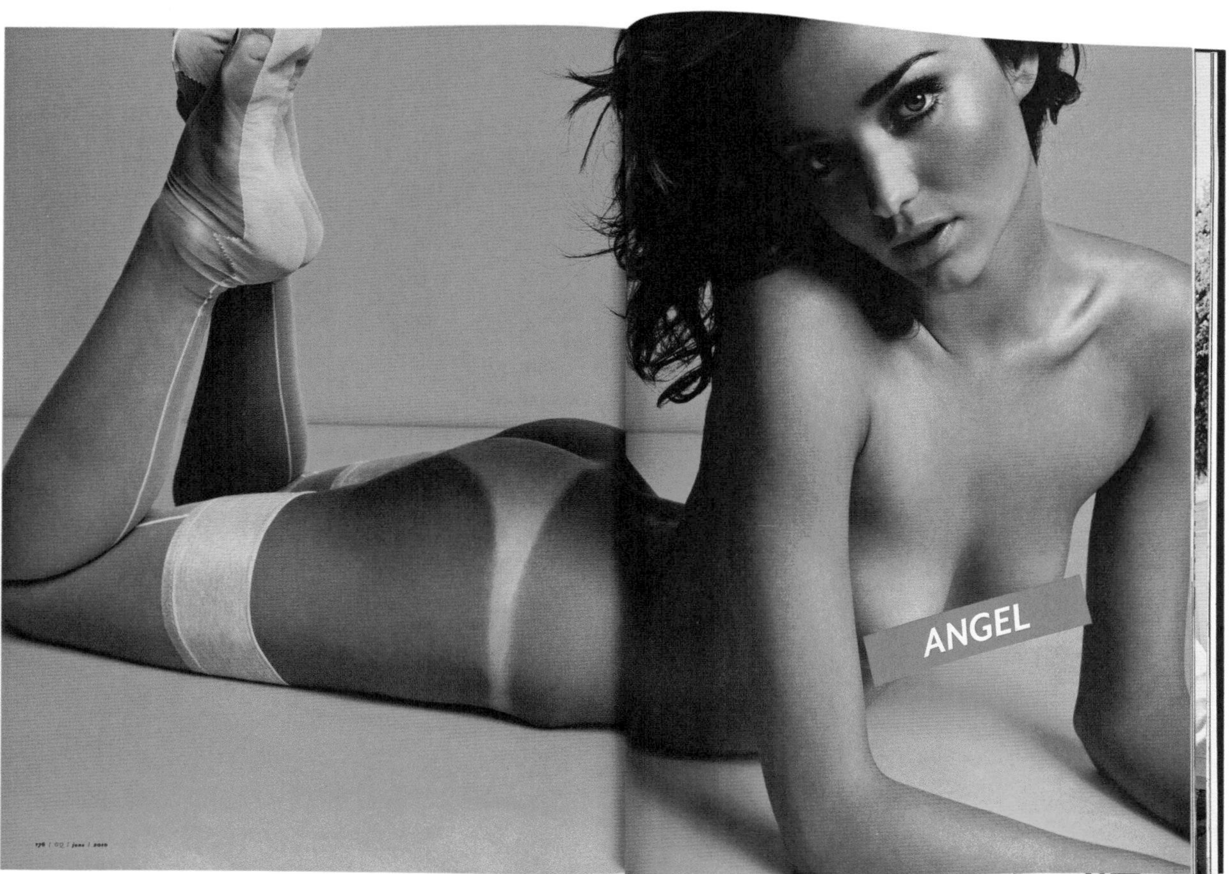

ANGEL

GQ © Condé Nast

This is a Magazine

Italy, June 2006 (230 × 290mm, 9¼× 11½ inches)

The first of three printed compendiums from experimental online magazine thisisamagazine.com, this hardback book used print and finishing effects to allude to some of the animation and colour effects created online using Flash.
Editors and art directors *Andy Simionato and Karen Ann Donnachie*

THIS PAGE The pages are split into three horizontal flaps that can be mixed up, with content on both sides of the paper creating new combinations. The blank pages actually contain die-cuts.

OPPOSITE A series of artworks by Sergei Sviatchecnko use die-cuts to exaggerate his layering and cutting style.

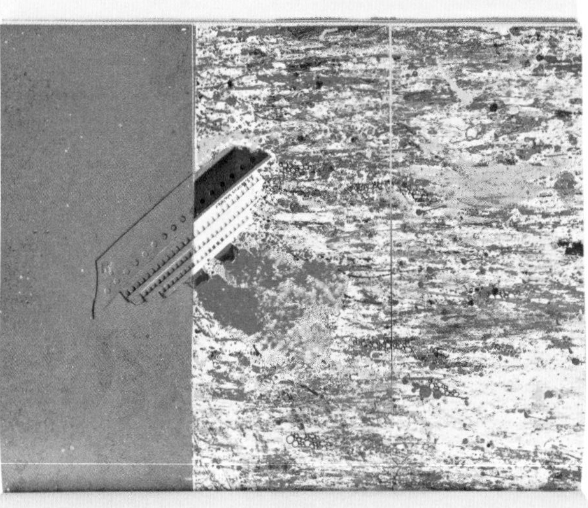

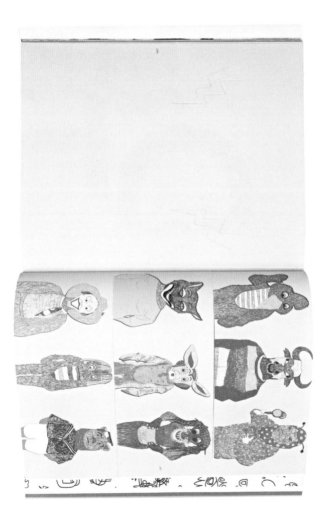

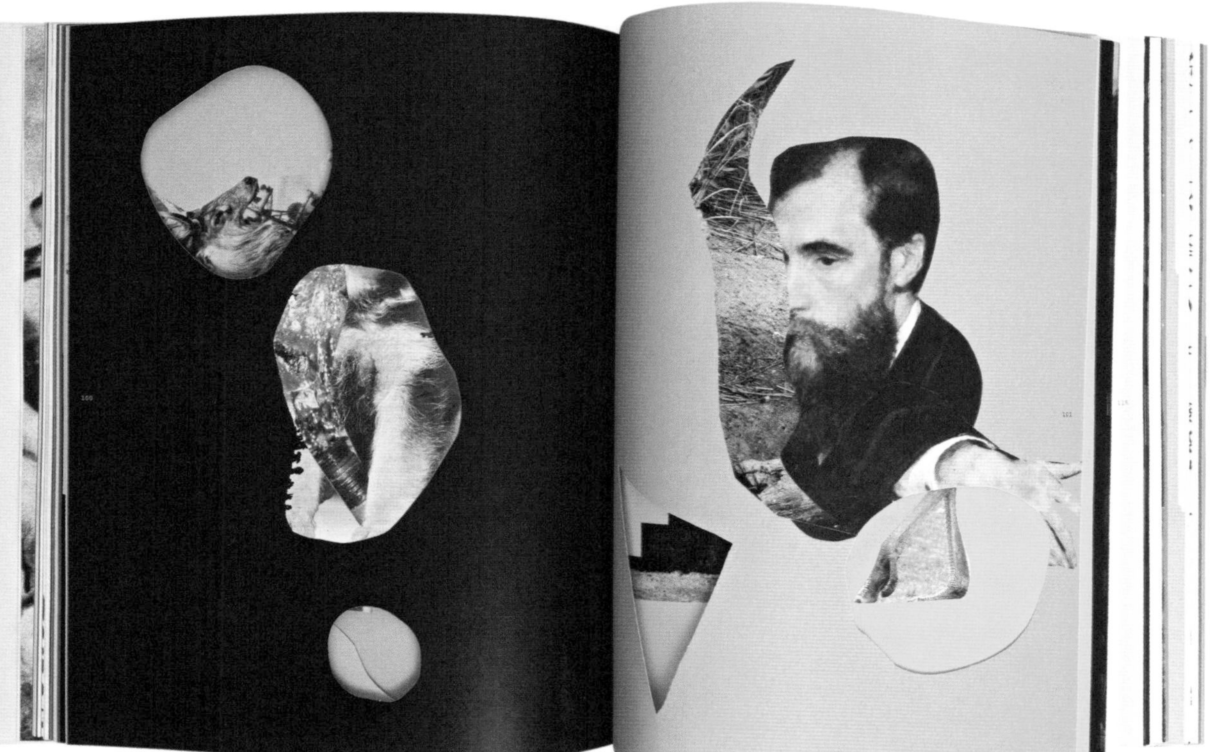

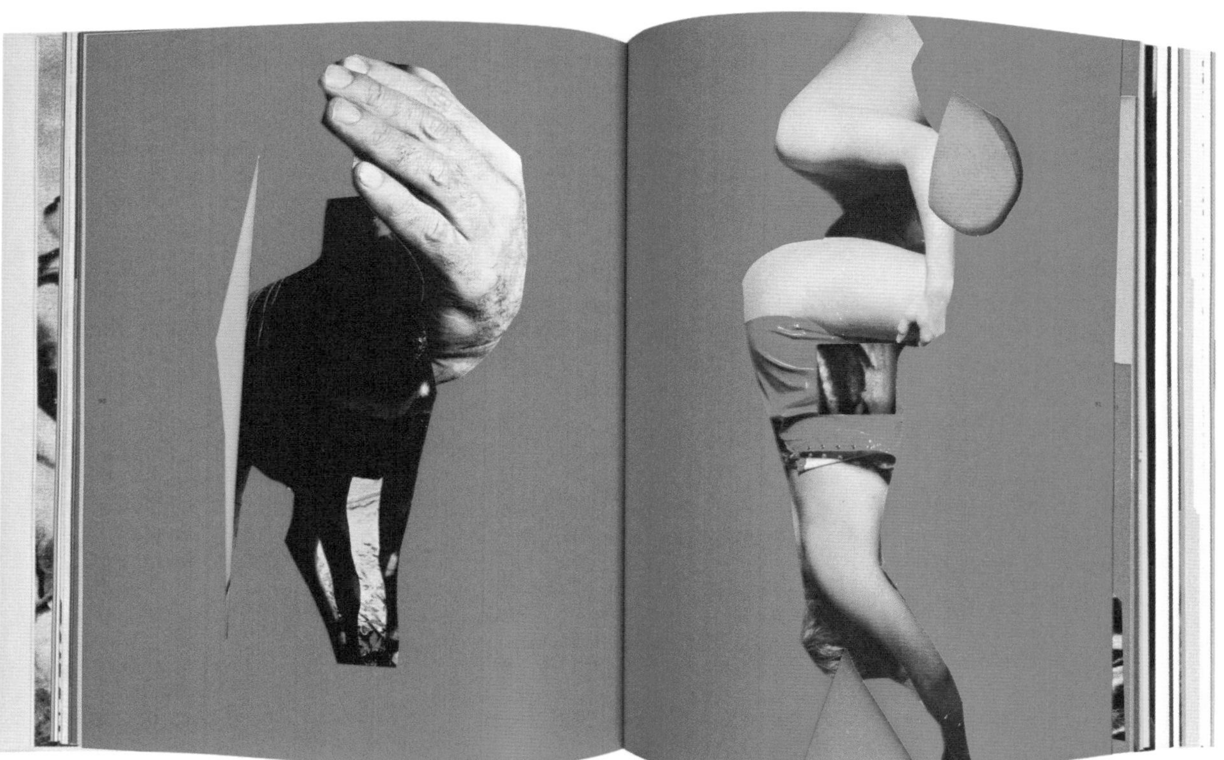

PRINT × DIGITAL

New technology has always had a formidable effect on magazine-making. As noted in my introduction, the medium developed in parallel with broader industrialization and has benefited from regular advances in technology: the introduction of colour presses, hot metal and then photo-typesetting methods, improved proofing systems and more reliable paper stock. But such advances were not automatically accepted without question.

In researching this book I re-read earlier books about magazine design and noted how new technology regularly surfaces as a concern. In the 1969 book *Magazine Design*, Ruari McLean describes the options provided by the new photo-typesetting technology as 'useful if wisely used: but they are also temptations which put the designer to the risk of infatuation with distortion for its own sake'. By 1991 William Owen was writing in *Modern Magazine Design* about 'the influence of television on readers' expectations and habits', before echoing McLean when describing the 'obtrusive idiosyncrasies that we see in much computer-based design today ... which stem from its limitations and from the over-exuberance typical of anyone who has been given a new toy'.

More recently, the general shift in the industry from the once-prevalent layout software QuarkXPress to the new Adobe InDesign (following the latter's launch in 1999) has introduced several more new toys for the designer. Drop shadows on headlines have never been so easy to add, nor so commonly applied.

However, technology has undoubtedly improved magazines. The smooth integration of layout, photographic manipulation and illustration software, allied with the increased processing power of the desktop computer, has meant the editor and designer now have a degree of control unthinkable even ten years ago. The technology empowers them as visual journalists; what both McLean and Owen were expressing was the hope that, given the scope of available options that each technological development provided, the creative decisions taken would be the right ones. I hope this book demonstrates that today many visual journalists are indeed making carefully considered use of technology.

It would be absurd to argue that the arrival of the Internet is merely another step in this technological timeline. Since the early 1990s era of dial-up modems and monochrome web browsers, the Internet has sped through its own timeline of advances, culminating in today's always-connected mobile broadband access. This is far from simply a new challenge; for some, the Internet presents the ultimate challenge for the printed magazine. Yet, in the context of the previous changes in technology, the Internet can be seen in a different light. New media always arrive to fanfares about replacing old media, and we've been hearing about the web replacing magazines for over a decade now. But the relationship between magazines and websites is far more complex than that. Whatever their long-term relationship, in the short-term magazines have benefited creatively from the arrival of the Internet and other digital forms.

Many independent magazine makers discovered their voices writing blogs; others, such as *Karen* (UK) bypass the web but apply a highly personal sensibility, inspired by blogging. Increasing numbers of bloggers have found a use for printed publications alongside their website. *It's Nice That* (UK) launched a biannual print edition to balance the disposability of their daily posts with a more precise editorial voice. Blog and magazine live side by side, supporting each other through their distinct roles; founder Alex Bec notes that having a physical representation of their output meant advertisers and clients took *It's Nice That* more seriously. Another blogger, Michael Bojkowski of LineFeed, identified common themes in his posts and created the printed *LineRead* (UK) as a vehicle to investigate those themes in more depth. Slanted, HypeBeast and my own magCulture have all experimented with printed variations of their posts.

Some of the most interesting crossovers occur when the two media are entwined. *Things Our Friends Have Written on the Internet* (UK) was a one-off newspaper project that combined print and digital sensibilities. Content was sourced by its editors from a selection of their favourite blogs and websites and reproduced without the permission of the originators. Instead, the blogging convention of providing URL links was used. The result was a printed newsfeed – a collection of unrelated content, a curated snapshot of the web.

Print-on-demand services such as HP's MagCloud (as used by *LineRead*) mean individual copies of a magazine are printed to order. While expensive for the individual buyer, they mean the publisher avoids the heavy investment involved in printing copies in advance of sales, and also in distributing them afterwards.

All publishers rely on modern computer technology not only to write and design their magazines, but also to research, promote and sell them. For the smaller, independent publisher, free services such as Gmail, Skype and Facetime provide vital communication with both contributors and readers, while Facebook, Twitter and blogs such as Coverjunkie and magCulture, help promote them. The Internet has also revolutionized distribution, vastly increasing the reach of independent magazines. Platforms such as Big Cartel and Shopify allow the creation of custom online stores, using PayPal to give direct, international access to online sales. As a result, smaller, specialist magazines can now seek international markets without incurring the cost of third-party distribution services, or increasing their print run to supply stores across the world.

The Internet has also laid down a creative challenge to publishers: how do you make the most of print? This has seen a renewed interest in alternative paper stocks as mainstream publishers turn away from what was once the default gloss finish. International franchise *Grazia*'s (UK) gravure printing on matt stock marked a sea change in attitudes, as did food title *Jamie*'s (UK) use of uncoated. Unheard of in a genre traditionally reliant on glossy stock to highlight food photography, the decision was possible thanks to digital print profiling that meant pre-press could prepare images to deal with the extra absorption of uncoated paper, ensuring the food still looked appetizing.

Special inks, metallic blocking and die cuts are some of the other print-only effects available in the quest to become more 'magazine-y' and distinct from digital editions. *Wallpaper** (UK) magazine has been very successful at using these techniques on its front covers; its August 2010 DIY cover went further and used a web interface to provide a set of elements for each reader to design their own personal front cover – a spectacular print–digital collaboration that resulted in 22,000 different digitally printed front covers.

Condé Nast vice president of design and platforms, Scott Dadich, sees this development continuing as sales become split between print and tablet editions of his magazines. 'If I replace the $1 cost of printing a magazine with the 25c it costs to deliver a digital file, I can take that saving and put it back into the print product. More pages, better paper stock and improved production values. The magazine becomes more of a keepsake – print changes but it doesn't go away.'

The digital file to which Dadich is referring is an iPad app. Until the arrival of the Apple iPhone in 2007, attempts to earn income from digital publishing had been limited to online advertising, paid-for PDFs and experiments with paywalls; ad income had disappointed, PDFs felt like a stopgap measure and paywalls were successful in only a few specialist markets. The launch of the Apple App Store, and its rapid stocking with apps of all types, presented publishers with a much better opportunity to charge people for digital content.

Screen size remained an issue – although that didn't prevent *The Guardian* (UK) newspaper launching an iPhone app that, even today, remains a great example of efficient, customizable

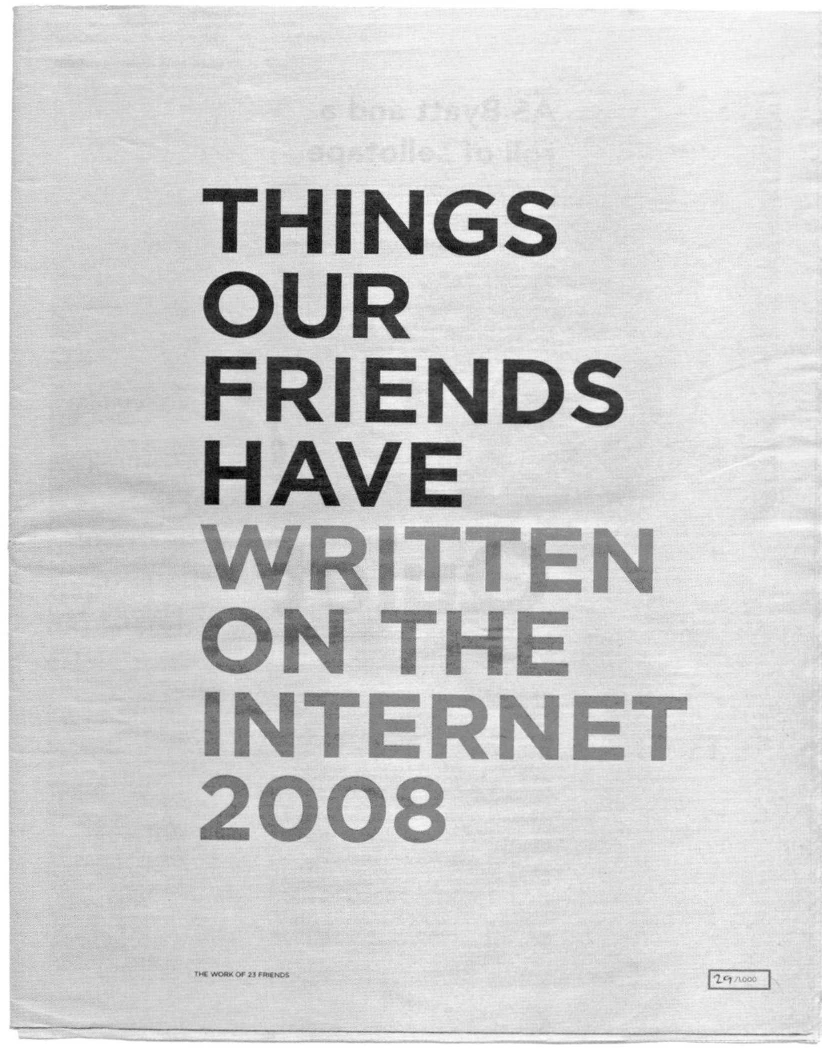

Things Our Friends Have Written on the Internet
UK, 2008 (290 × 380mm, 11 × 15 inches)
The content for this newsprint publication was reproduced from websites enjoyed by the publishers, who added blog-style credits for their sources.
Editor *Russell Davies*; Designers *Ben Terrett* and *Alex Parrott*

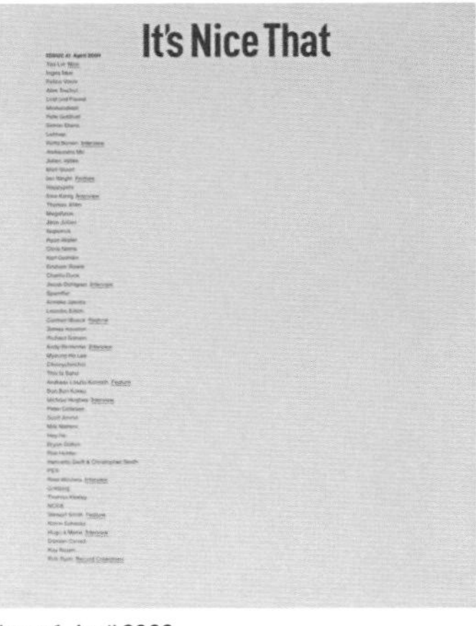

Issue 1, April 2009

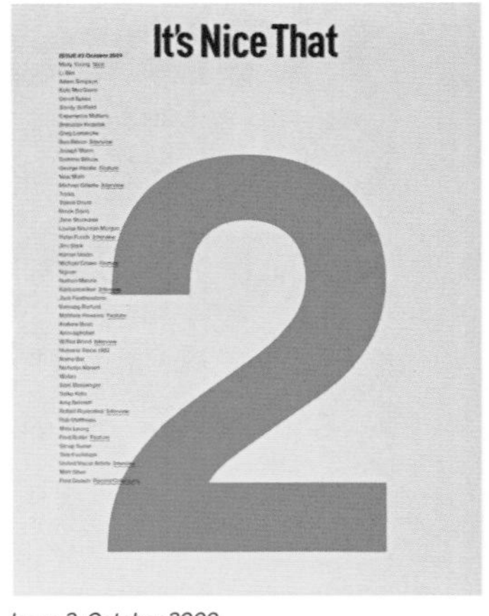

Issue 2, October 2009

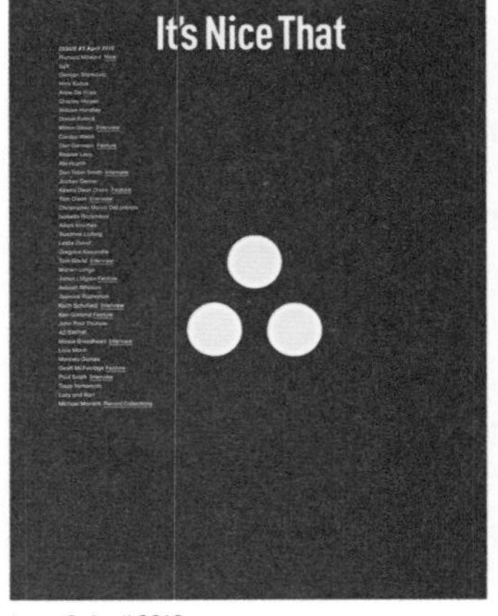

Issue 3, April 2010

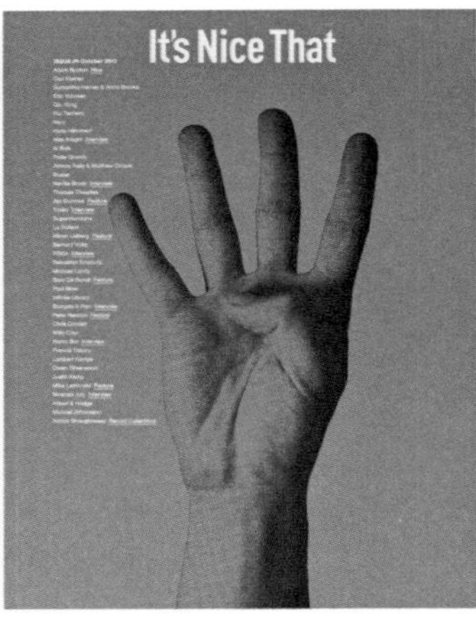

Issue 4, October 2010

It's Nice That
UK, Issues 1–4 (210 × 275mm, 8¼ × 11 inches)
The first eight editions of the magazine show its development from blog spin-off to a more magazine-like cover format.
Editors *Will Hudson and Alex Bec*; Design *It's Nice That and Joseph Burrin*
UK, Issues 5–6 (210 × 275mm, 8¼ × 11 inches)
Editor *Alex Moshakis*; Design *It's Nice That and Joseph Burrin*
UK, Issues 7–8 (228 × 300mm, 9 × 12 inches)
Editor *Alex Moshakis*; Art director *Ray O'Meara*

news delivery – but Apple had firmly established a market for apps.

The arrival of the iPad in 2010 played to publishers' hopes. Apps were seen as the digital equivalent of printed magazines: they could be sold singly or as part of an ongoing subscription. Was this the device that would finally let publishers transfer their long-standing business model into the digital realm?

App production using Apple's X-code was a challenge quickly resolved, as Adobe and various third-party suppliers devised plug-ins for InDesign that allowed editorial staff to create apps based on print layouts without having to know code. *Wired* (USA) was an early adopter, and the app creation tools they helped devise with Adobe soon became available to all as their Digital Publishing Suite (DPS, see interview on page 226). Woodwing (later bought out by Adobe) were there early on too, and others including Mag+ and QuarkXPress followed with their own digital-content platforms.

It's still too early to tell if tablets (the iPad has been joined by multiple competitors) will live up to publishers' expectations. Fundamentalists from either side of the print–digital divide will tell you that app magazines are doomed to fail, yet much resource continues to be devoted to them. There is a growing feeling among publishers that they can work; while some hold back, the majority are getting on and experimenting. Dadich is bullish about his company's apps and can point to *The New Yorker*'s app (USA) as a success story. After one year, 16 per cent of the magazine's sales are app-only, and Condé Nast claims a good number of new rather than ex-print readers among them. Businesses that pre-date the tablets (Exact Editions, Issuu) also report increased sales of their simpler, PDF-based digital magazines since the launch of Apple's Newsstand.

Setting aside these unresolved complications of business models and production, what should a magazine app look like? The two interviews in this section of the book feature very different views.

The *Wired* app continues to work a busy, clamorous visual direction (a contemporary iteration of the need to use all the new toys at once?). It was the perfect app with which to show off your new iPad – all bells and whistles, with specially shot video and animation effects throughout. It was the first outing for Adobe's Digital Publishing Suite (DPS) navigation design, an efficient but overbearing structure that is uncustomizable. The resulting apps always feel as though there are two layers of interaction – the rigid navigation, and the content itself.

It's worth revisiting here the aims of magazine design first mentioned in the introduction to the previous section, Design × Content: to help the reader (navigation) and to provide a visual character that reflects the content and establishes the project's identity. In print, the balance between these sometimes contrary aims is a defining quality of the end result. The tablet promises an easier empathy between navigation and character, yet tools such as DPS apply the same rigid navigation devices each time. The noisier visuals of *Wired* can cope with its nature, while a gentler app, such as that of *The New Yorker*, has a jarring relationship with the same navigation system.

An often overlooked issue is the difference between print and tablet screen in terms of how the same design devices and elements will appear. The backlit screen will make even a simply adequate photograph look stunning; but it also lacks the inherent subtlety of print that clarifies visual hierarchies on the page. Detailed items in print – thin rules, small text, discreet navigational elements and paler colours – are recessive when compared to bolder headlines, larger graphics and

Issue 5, April 2011

Issue 6, July 2011

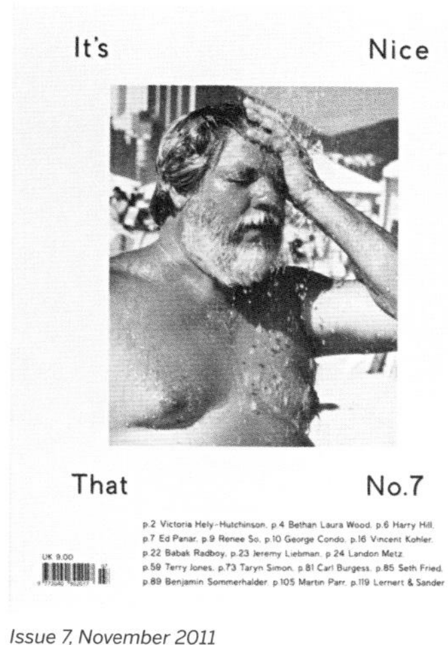

Issue 7, November 2011

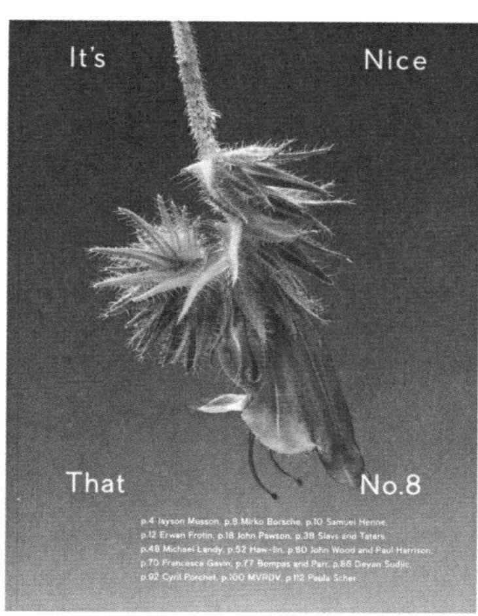

Issue 8, March 2012

brighter colours. Transfer that same hierarchy to the iPad and all have the same shiny, backlit presence; the hierarchy is obscured.

I have more sympathy with Tim Moore's desire to get out of the user's way and let them interact directly with his content in *Letter to Jane* (USA). Publishing from scratch without a printed edition allows him to move away completely from the print flatplan and 'pages'. The result is a calm, reflective experience, with navigation that appears as it is needed. The app includes slideshow and video content, and the reader is gently encouraged to enjoy and finish these elements rather than jump to the next button or effect.

For the series of apps I designed for *Port* magazine (UK) I tried both methods; the first used Adobe DPS and I collaborated with Moore on the later two. I was trying to reflect the aesthetic of the print magazine rather than create a replica of it, and found working from scratch with Tim a far more satisfying way to do so.

However, both processes share the use of hard-set 'pages' linked together with code. The apps are effectively streams of screengrabs through which the user navigates. This leads to huge app files even before video is added to the mix. The natural next step is to start creating apps with HTML5 – websites, basically – and some publishers will tell you that, before long, printed magazines will also be designed using HTML5 in order to streamline the joint production process.

Whatever the production method used, a key factor in an app's success or failure will be its ability to link and share content with other parts of the digital world through social networking – something the *Flipboard* app has focused on since its launch. *Flipboard* applies a design algorithm to the user's social network streams and other selected content providers to create a seamless experience of updated text and images. It is surprisingly effective, and its page-flip effect remains a rare print reference in digital format that is both satisfying and effective.

The Little Printer is a piece of hardware that also allows users to channel content from their social networks and other sources into one output. In this case, London design studio Berg has developed a system to link digital feeds via Wi-Fi to a small printer in the user's house that prints the content onto rolls of receipt paper.

If that seems fanciful, consider this: are iPads and the other tablets really the future of publishing? The reality is that they are currently just one part of a growing trend towards multiple channels. Everyone is experimenting, nobody is standing still; the apparent success of *The New Yorker* iPad app has already led to the development of an iPhone version. It's a surprisingly satisfying experience: as a subscriber, I can now read the magazine in any of three formats – the two digital ones having the added benefit of audio and sometimes also video. Did I mention they have a website too? Meanwhile, *Monocle* has ignored tablets altogether and instead launched a digital radio station (on which the flagship show is a review of printed magazines), opened a chain of shops selling *Monocle*-branded products and is planning a similar move into cafés.

Perhaps the lesson from all this experimentation is a rather simple one: today's magazine makers must work in multiple channels and get the most out of each of them. It is more important than ever that we get under the skin of the stories we are telling and select the best way(s) to share them with our audience(s). Radio? Video? Tablet? Events? Print? All have their place as part of the modern magazine. From a business point of view, this is a hugely challenging time. But creatively, the cross-pollination between these different channels is driving a new golden age of magazine making.

TERRY JONES AT VOGUE

Ever wondered what UK Vogue looked like when Terry Jones was art director, before he left to launch i-D? Here's the cover and some spreads from an issue dated 1 September 1975 that will have a familiar feel to anyone who enjoys i-D.

MAGAZINE OF THE WEEK #5: CARL*S CARS

Carl*s Cars is a long-time favourite of mine but the recent publication of issue 17 gives me the chance to post a few images and thoughts about the magazine. Published from Oslo, Norway by Karl Eirik Haug (parking lot boy/editor-in-chief and, presumably, the Carl of the title) and Stephanie Dumont (hood girl/creative director), Carl*s Cars is about cars but pulls a master-stroke by selling itself as 'a magazine about people'. This is not a minor point; most car mags are resolutely focused on vehicles, their engineering and statistics. This magazine is about the relationship between the driver and their car.

THAT END OF PRINT THING

THREE DAYS IN NEW YORK

COLOPHON2007 UPDATE

TYPOGRAPHIC ISSUE 65

Typographic is published twice a year by the International Society of Typographic Designers. Each issue is designed by a different designer, with previous designers including Designer's Republic, Nick Bell and Cartledge Levine. Issue 65, The Advertising Issue, was published last June but I've only just caught up with it. Designed by advertising typographer Paul Belford and typographer David Jury, I'm not that excited by the general page design but what is clever is the way it has been conceived to appear as if it has been printed on the back of multi-sheet advertising hoardings.

NEW YORKER COVER

Every New Yorker cover features illustration but not all are as simple yet expressive as this week's design by Christoph Niemann.

MONOCLE

First impressions: there's a lot of it, 244pp plus Manga insert; from the black cover and on it looks, and is, very serious; it must be the only mainstream magazine out there without a single celebrity in it; it is full, and I mean FULL of words; it is single-pace throughout, with almost no change of visual tone; the cover is, I assume, deliberately crap; lovely uncoated but hi-white paper stock; the content is truly international; it is absolutely not Wallpaper* mk2, appearing to be a victory of content over style rather than that magazines' opposite position; two unassuming fonts, Miler and Helvetica; arguably it's a book, not a magazine (the standfirsts are titled 'preface'); it is the antithesis of the quick-fix read-it-on-a-tube-journey magazine – it's something for your upcoming long haul trip; the little M monogram is too like Habitat's 'home is where the heart is' logo; it is far less pretentious than many will have expected; and finally, how are they going to achieve this volume of content ten times a year?

COLOPHON SHALL BE OURS

ARE YOU A COOLMAN?

BEHIND THE TIMES

TOO MANY ADS?

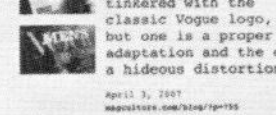

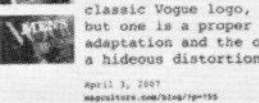

VOGUE FOR MEN

Two very different ways to do Vogue for men. On top is the European magazine Vogue Homme International, made in Paris by French Vogue editor-in-chief Carine Roitfeld (more on this in another post to come), while below is the recently launched US Men's Vogue, edited by US Vogue editor-in-chief Anna Wintour. Both magazines have tinkered with the classic Vogue logo, but one is a proper adaptation and the other a hideous distortion.

KASINO A4

Sometimes a new, independent magazine turns up out of the blue and genuinely surprises me. The latest example is Kasino A4, brought back from Helsinki by my colleague Ian.

no manifesto

A disconnect has occurred. Previously established ways of doing things are falling away. In areas such as politics, design, economics, entertainment fracture is everywhere. Nothing replaces anything anymore, everything proliferates. There is simply 'more' – more formats, more networks, more access points, more things to do make and do. The dust may never settle so muck in and let's get dirty.

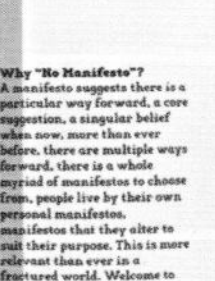

Disconnected identities: Google obliterate their own logo

magCulture/paper
UK, Issue 1, 2010 (290 × 380mm, 11 × 15 inches)
Editor and designer *Jeremy Leslie*

LineRead
UK, Issue 3, 2010, 'Disconnect the Fracture' (210 × 275mm, 8¼ × 10¾)
Editor and designer *Michael Bojkowski*

Cover Junkie Magazine
The Netherlands, Issue 1, 2012 (250 × 325mm, 9¾ × 12¾ inches)
Editor and designer *Jaap Biemanns*

Three bloggers who moved to print for different reasons: *magCulture/paper* celebrated five years of posts on the magCulture blog by drawing attention to the large archive of material sitting behind the latest posts; *LineRead* developed themes that had begun to emerge on the LineFeed blog; *Cover Junkie Magazine* took content from the blog and curated it carefully, adding art directors' favourites and grouping themes.

Club Donny
The Netherlands, Issue 6, 2010/11 (297 × 325mm, 8 × 11¾ inches)
The content for this magazine about our relationship with nature in urban environments sources content via its website. Submissions are published unedited in an unbound format that draws attention to the random nature of the material published.
Publishers *Samira Ben Laloua, Frank Bruggeman and Ernst van der Hoeven*

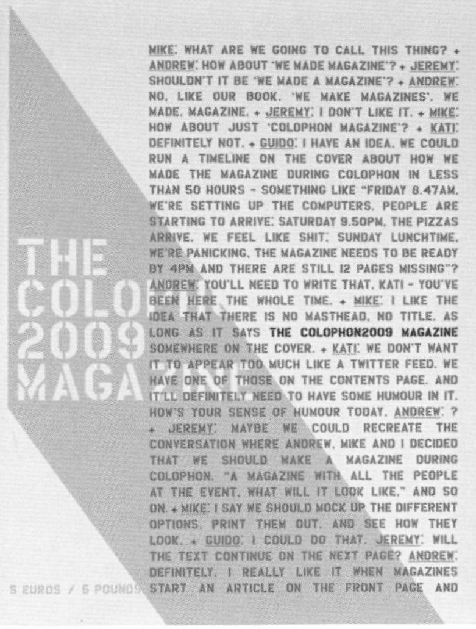

THE COLOPHON2009 MAGAZINE

MIKE: WHAT ARE WE GOING TO CALL THIS THING? + ANDREW: HOW ABOUT "WE MADE MAGAZINE"? + JEREMY: SHOULDN'T IT BE "WE MADE A MAGAZINE"? + ANDREW: NO, LIKE OUR BOOK. 'WE MAKE MAGAZINES'. WE MADE. MAGAZINE. + JEREMY: I DON'T LIKE IT. + MIKE: HOW ABOUT JUST 'COLOPHON MAGAZINE'? + KATI: DEFINITELY NOT. + GUIDO: I HAVE AN IDEA. WE COULD RUN A TIMELINE ON THE COVER ABOUT HOW WE MADE THE MAGAZINE DURING COLOPHON IN LESS THAN 50 HOURS – SOMETHING LIKE "FRIDAY 8.47AM, WE'RE SETTING UP THE COMPUTERS, PEOPLE ARE STARTING TO ARRIVE; SATURDAY 9.50PM, THE PIZZAS ARRIVE. WE FEEL LIKE SHIT; SUNDAY LUNCHTIME, WE'RE PANICKING, THE MAGAZINE NEEDS TO BE READY BY 4PM AND THERE ARE STILL 12 PAGES MISSING"? ANDREW: YOU'LL NEED TO WRITE THAT, KATI – YOU'VE BEEN HERE THE WHOLE TIME. + MIKE: I LIKE THE IDEA THAT THERE IS NO MASTHEAD, NO TITLE, AS LONG AS IT SAYS **THE COLOPHON2009 MAGAZINE** SOMEWHERE ON THE COVER. + KATI: WE DON'T WANT IT TO APPEAR TOO MUCH LIKE A TWITTER FEED. WE HAVE ONE OF THOSE ON THE CONTENTS PAGE. AND IT'LL DEFINITELY NEED TO HAVE SOME HUMOUR IN IT. HOW'S YOUR SENSE OF HUMOUR TODAY, ANDREW: ? + JEREMY: MAYBE WE COULD RECREATE THE CONVERSATION WHERE ANDREW, MIKE AND I DECIDED THAT WE SHOULD MAKE A MAGAZINE DURING COLOPHON. "A MAGAZINE WITH ALL THE PEOPLE AT THE EVENT, WHAT WILL IT LOOK LIKE," AND SO ON. + MIKE: I SAY WE SHOULD MOCK UP THE DIFFERENT OPTIONS, PRINT THEM OUT, AND SEE HOW THEY LOOK. + GUIDO: I COULD DO THAT. JEREMY: WILL THE TEXT CONTINUE ON THE NEXT PAGE? ANDREW: DEFINITELY. I REALLY LIKE IT WHEN MAGAZINES START AN ARTICLE ON THE FRONT PAGE AND

5 EUROS / 5 POUNDS

Colophon Magazine
Luxembourg, 2009 (235 × 310mm, 9¼ × 12¼ inches)
Created in 48 hours to record the Colophon magazine conference.
Editor *Kati Krause*; Art director *Guido Krüger*

OPPOSITE **London2012 Olympics magazine**
UK, 2012 (210 × 295mm, 8¼ × 11¼ inches)
Published daily throughout the Olympics, these 68-page magazines previewed events and presented highlights from the previous day.
Editor *David Edwards*; Art director *Chris Barker*

Endurance publishing

The pressure that builds up during the making of a magazine can be both thrilling and exhausting. The desire to make the end result as good as possible eventually comes into direct conflict with the hard fact of the deadline. Interviewees can delay their contribution, writers can grab an extra few days, editors can sit on copy, photographers and illustrators can be late. But whoever initiates a delay, it's the design studio that has to make up the lost time. Being responsible for design and pre-press preparation of pages brings the advantage of complete control but also adds responsibility for the final schedule.

The computer technology available to even the smallest magazine today has made this possible, and has also all but removed the divide between print and digital in production terms. As we design pages for print onscreen, we are reading blogs, receiving tweets and updating our Facebook pages. As noted on page 216, Adobe has made print and iPad app production a part of the same software.

As the lines between print and digital production have become blurred, it was surely inevitable that a hackathon approach would be applied to magazine production (hackathon being a time-limited, intense innovation workshop favoured by coders and engineers). The print version of this has become known as endurance publishing, and involves setting a 48- or even 24-hour deadline to create an entire magazine. Speed and spontaneity are usually more important here than perfection, exaggerating the usual compromise between quality and timing.

My first involvement with such a project was at the Colophon2009 conference that I co-curated with Mike Koedinger and Andrew Losowsky. We wanted a record of this three-day celebration of independent magazine publishing, so we invited all the attendees – writers, editors, designers and image-makers – to collaborate in creating a magazine. I produced a basic page template, a studio was set up to the side of the main conference hall and we proceeded to create content for a 96-page publication. Led by art director Guido Kruger and editor Kati Krause, the magazine team worked for 48 hours and hit the deadline. The finished magazine was a good reflection of the weekend's talks and events – conveying the busy, upbeat mood of the conference and featuring most of its participants.

The Colophon2009 publication was produced as a magazine, but an alternative format became popular that same year with the launch of the Newspaper Club. Conceived to open up print production to non-designers, the Newspaper Club was soon picked up by designers themselves as a means of quickly producing small-run publications. Founders Ben Terrett, Russell Davies and Tom Taylor had produced a one-off publication (*Things Our Friends Have Written on the Internet*, UK) based on their friends' blog posts at the end of 2008. To produce it they used a newspaper printer, and in the process realized that such printers had significant downtimes when their otherwise busy presses were dormant. Their response, initially greeted by printers with some scepticism but subsequently embraced, was to act as a conduit for that downtime by providing an easy upload process for anyone to order very small print runs of tabloid newspapers. Designers could upload bespoke PDFs, non-designers could use the Newspaper Club's free templates. Either way, within a few days you could receive anything from a single copy to thousands of copies of your publication. This was a natural fit for endurance publishing, adding speed to the production side.

In the USA, two ad hoc projects were launched where the magazine itself was the event. *Long Shot* pulled together a group of magazine professionals to create a themed publication to a 48-hour schedule and distributed it via print-on-demand service MagCloud. The occasional *Twenty-four Magazine* project cut the deadline of a similar project by half. While the content of each is engaging, it's fair to note that *Long Shot* benefitted from more design time.

These were experimental, investigative projects looking at how print and digital techniques can combine. *Bloomberg Businessweek* (USA) took the idea into the mainstream with their overnight Steve Jobs issue (see page 192), but a more thorough and practical test of the potential for endurance publishing was carried out during the London2012 Olympics, when UK publisher Haymarket won the contract to publish a daily programme throughout the Olympics and Paralympics. Each edition had to be printed and ready at each of the Olympics venues by 7am every morning of the 16 Olympic days and 11 Paralympic days.

It was unworkable to start from scratch each day; months of planning went into preparing as much as possible in advance. Editor David Edwards and art director Chris Barker had a pretty tight plan in place long before the opening ceremony. 'I suggested we should have a section where every one of the day's events was listed in chronological order so the reader would realise that, as well as being at a particular event in a particular venue, they were also a part of this giant festival of sport,' recalls Barker. 'Senior editor Johnny Aldred latched onto this, and suggested that was what the whole publication should be, with features, interviews and other content all hanging off the timeline.' For editor-in-chief Simon Kanter, this simple idea persuaded him and client LOCOG that 'we could create a magazine-style product that still had the functionality of a programme'. The timeline dictated the running order and meant that every sport got a look in. 'We had something on every event happening that day, wherever you were as a reader,' says Barker. 'This was our USP, the one thing we could do that the newspapers couldn't.'

The design team – alongside Barker were three designers, two picture editors and he had advice and direction from Haymarket's group art director Martin Tullett and design director Paul Harpin – settled on a flexible 36-column grid that allowed a modular approach to the content. They knew the event schedule but the final team selections couldn't be confirmed until weeks before the actual games. 'We had a mammoth task to create the flatplans for each day. Starting in about February, myself and David would sit with lists of each day's events and piece them together like a jigsaw along the timeline we had created, using the official schedules,' says Barker. 'We would move through a day at a time, saying things like "stick a 'how it works' in there!", "interview with GB star!" and "live update panel". This process took weeks and was probably the most fun I've ever had in my career.'

Subsequent months were spent by journalists and designers preparing words and infographics to fill in each day's timeline. The cover stars were in constant flux due to injuries and form: 'People that seemed like a dead cert in January looked like a laughable choice come July.' Barker reckons that to cover all options the journalists prepared 50 per cent more content than was required, while on the design side they had a tight structure backed up by a toolkit of elements that could be used in the case of an emergency. 'The pre-press department did thousands of cut-outs for us so we could hit the ground running during gamestime,' says Barker. Up-to-date material was added on the fly. 'I felt that if enough of a percentage of it looked like high-quality magazine content then the whole piece would hang together,' says Barker.

The resulting magazines successfully fulfilled two roles for visitors: they were great event guides, but also acted as perfect souvenirs. Despite the prior preparation they retained a vivid spontaneity and remain one of the few really successful executions of the controversial London2012 identity. The angular typeface works well as an editorial character font and the front cover designs in particular brought a very human feel to the visual presentation of the games.

The 27 magazines – over 1,800 pages – were designed and produced from Haymarket's west London office, while client liaison and on-site reporting took place the other side of the city at the Olympic Park. Googledocs played a key behind-the-scenes part in the project, allowing status checks on all aspects of production to be made via the web from anywhere at anytime. A lot of effort went into making the process look as simple and easy as possible.

By contrast, production of one-off publication *The Good Times* (UK) was designed to be as open and accessible as possible. London agency The Church of London produced this tabloid newspaper (printed via the Newspaper Club) to explore their ideas of collaborative content creation. Published to cheer up a February Monday deemed 'the year's most depressing day', it was created in five days and the entire process carried out publicly. Appeals for content were issued via Twitter, and the collating and editing of content shared in real time on open Googledoc spreadsheets. In a process they describe as 'mutualisation', anyone was able to access the files and offer improvements and additional ideas, or simply watch the green 'in progress' flags turn red one by one as text was edited and laid out. In a complete subversion of the usually discreet edit–design process, the entire creation and production of *The Good Times* could be accessed step by step, becoming an event in its own right. The printed newspaper was later distributed free around London and was also available online as a PDF.

THE OFFICIAL OLYMPIC GAMES DAILY PROGRAMME
London 2012
Day 1
28.07.2012
£5
Every sport inside
Cav
Cavendish leads out Team GB's medal mission
PLUS All the best pictures from the build-up to the Games

THE OFFICIAL OLYMPIC GAMES DAILY PROGRAMME
London 2012
Day 2
29.07.2012
£5
Becky
Can Adlington be the golden girl again?
Every sport inside
PLUS All the best pictures from yesterday at the Games

THE OFFICIAL OLYMPIC GAMES DAILY PROGRAMME
London 2012
Day 3
30.07.2012
£5
Tom
Daley and Waterfield go diving for gold
Every sport inside
PLUS The greatest pictures from yesterday at the Games

THE OFFICIAL OLYMPIC GAMES DAILY PROGRAMME
London 2012
Day 4
31.07.2012
£5
Zara
Phillips and Team GB jump to it
Every sport inside
PLUS The greatest pictures from yesterday at the Games

THE OFFICIAL OLYMPIC GAMES DAILY PROGRAMME
London 2012
Day 5
01.08.2012
£5
Every sport inside
Bradley cycles for gold in the Time Trial
Wiggo

THE OFFICIAL OLYMPIC GAMES DAILY PROGRAMME
London 2012
Day 6
02.08.2012
£5
Victoria
Pendleton leads British team into Velodrome action
Exclusive to venues

THE OFFICIAL OLYMPIC GAMES DAILY PROGRAMME
London 2012
Day 7
03.08.2012
£5
Jess
Ennis spearheads Great Britain's Athletics attack
Exclusive to venues

THE OFFICIAL OLYMPIC GAMES DAILY PROGRAMME
London 2012
Day 8
04.08.2012
£5
Exclusive to venues
Get set...
Bolt

THE OFFICIAL OLYMPIC GAMES DAILY PROGRAMME
London 2012
Day 9
05.08.2012
£5
Exclusive to venues
History time
100m

THE OFFICIAL OLYMPIC GAMES DAILY PROGRAMME
London 2012
Day 10
06.08.2012
£5
Beth
Tweddle's final fling at Olympic gold medal
Exclusive to venues

THE OFFICIAL OLYMPIC GAMES DAILY PROGRAMME
London 2012
Day 11
07.08.2012
£5
Hoy
Sir Chris is on track for a record sixth gold medal
Exclusive to venues

THE OFFICIAL OLYMPIC GAMES DAILY PROGRAMME
London 2012
Day 12
08.08.2012
£5
Exclusive to venues
Shanaze
BMX star Reade ready for Olympic redemption

THE OFFICIAL OLYMPIC GAMES DAILY PROGRAMME
London 2012
Day 13
09.08.2012
£5
Keri-Anne
Marathon woman swimming for gold
Exclusive to venues

THE OFFICIAL OLYMPIC GAMES DAILY PROGRAMME
London 2012
Day 14
10.08.2012
£5
Stevenson takes on the world in Taekwondo
Exclusive to venues
Sarah

THE OFFICIAL OLYMPIC GAMES DAILY PROGRAMME
London 2012
Day 15
11.08.2012
£5
Farah's 5000
Exclusive to venues

THE OFFICIAL OLYMPIC GAMES DAILY PROGRAMME
London 2012
Day 16
12.08.2012
£5
The greatest!

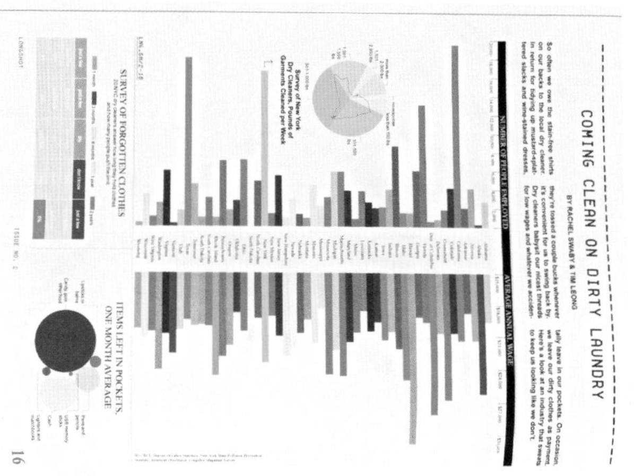

COMING CLEAN ON DIRTY LAUNDRY

BY RACHEL SWABY & TIM LEONG

So often we owe the stain-free shirts on our backs to the local dry cleaner. In return for tidying up mustard-splattered slacks and wine-stained dresses, they're tossed a couple bucks whenever it's convenient for us to swing back by. Dry cleaners babysit our nicest threads for low wages and whatever we accidentally leave in our pockets. On occasion, we leave our dirty clothes as payment. Here's a look at an industry that sweats to keep us looking like we don't.

NUMBER OF PEOPLE EMPLOYED — AVERAGE ANNUAL WAGE

Survey of New York Dry Cleaners, Pounds of Garments Cleaned per Week

SURVEY OF FORGOTTEN CLOTHES

ITEMS LEFT IN POCKETS, ONE MONTH AVERAGE

LONGSHOT — ISSUE NO. 2 — 16

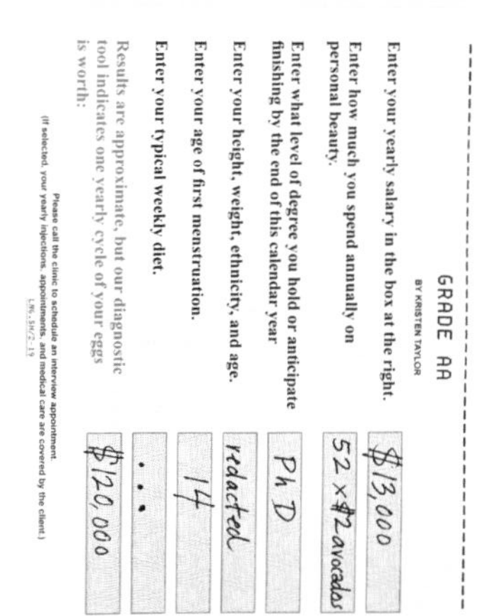

GRADE AA

BY KRISTEN TAYLOR

Enter your yearly salary in the box at the right.	$13,000
Enter how much you spend annually on personal beauty.	52 × $2 avocados
Enter what level of degree you hold or anticipate finishing by the end of this calendar year	PhD
Enter your height, weight, ethnicity, and age.	redacted
Enter your age of first menstruation.	14
Enter your typical weekly diet.	. . .
Results are approximate, but our diagnostic tool indicates one yearly cycle of your eggs is worth:	$120,000

Please call the clinic to schedule an interview appointment.
(If selected, your yearly injections, appointments, and medical care are covered by the client.)

THE PRICE OF LIFE

BY TIMOTHY LESLE

JUL 29–31 2011 — 17

Eyjafjallajökul
eyjafjallajokull
jyaeajfllojaukll
ajyjaellfjoakllu
jjaylleajfoklual
jayjealeaoflkula
leafjjjelofkullala
jjjeaaayflllouk
teksayflukuajjal
takeiteasyiceland

Longshot
USA, Issue 2, 'Debt', July 2011 (210 × 275mm, 8¼ × 10¾)
Set up by a group of US magazine makers, *Longshot* has a simple premise. Once a year, the team announces a date, a theme, then for 24 hours accepts content submissions from volunteers on that theme. 24 hours later they upload the completed magazine to MagCloud from which copies can be ordered.
Editors *Mathew Honan, Alexis Madrigal and Sarah Rich*; Art directors *Eveything Type Company*

Stranded
USA, 2010 (210 × 275mm, 8¼ × 10¾)
When he found himself stranded in Ireland due to flight cancellations after the Icelandic volcano eruption in spring 2010, writer Andrew Losowsky used the Internet and social media to call together contributions from others in the same predicament. The resulting print-on-demand publication is a record both of people's stories and the process of making the magazine.
Editor *Andrew Losowsky*; Art director *Matt McArthur*

London2012 Olympics magazine OPPOSITE
UK, 2012 (210 × 295mm, 8¼ × 11¼ inches)
The covers of these daily magazines caught the mood of the UK as it celebrated daily events using (mostly) TeamGB stars and their nicknames.
Editor *David Edwards*; Art director *Chris Barker*

MILK
THINK QUARTERLY

OPPOSITE **Think Quarterly**

UK, Summer 2011, The People Issue, (205 × 250mm, 8 × 10 inches)

Each edition of this high-spec, low-print-run magazine published by Google is personalized for the person it is posted to. The nature of the personalization changes according to the theme. For the People Issue, a huge monochrome artwork was drawn by a team of illustrators over three days (BACKGROUND); this was then divided into 2,000 individual sections and each section digitally printed and applied to a single edition of the magazine as its cover (the red square (BOTTOM RIGHT), highlights the part of the artwork used on the featured cover). Editor *Matt Bochenski*; Creative director *Rob Longworth*; Illustrators *Ryan Chapman, Jasper Dunk, Dale Edwin Murray, Daniel Frost, Matthew Hams, Yasmeen Ismail, Jean Jullien, Chetan Kumar, Paul Layzell, Maggie Li, Dominic Owen, Hattie Stewart, Toby Triumph, Robbie Wilkinson, Paul Willoughby and Dan Woodger*

Wallpaper*

UK, August 2010 (220 × 300mm, 8¾ × 11 inches)

Using a set of elements available for manipulation on the magazine website, readers were able to create their own personalized front cover design for this edition of *Wallpaper**. Over 22,000 readers did so and their designs were digitally printed and added to their individual copies of the magazine. Editor-in-chief *Tony Chambers*; Creative director *Meirion Pritchard*; Technical development *Kin*

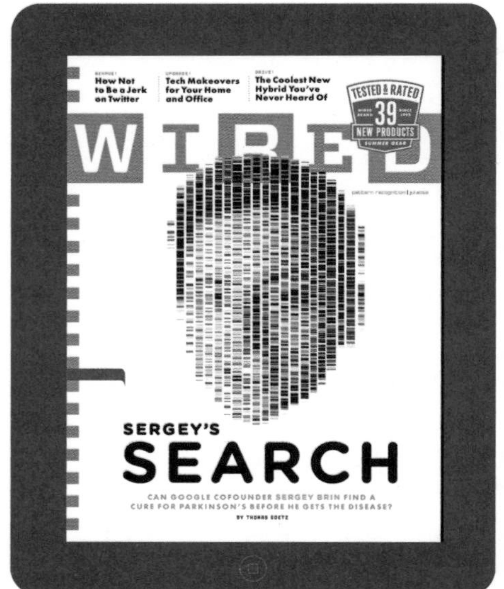

Wired
USA, July 2010 (iPad app created using Adobe DPS)
At the time of writing, this is the earliest of the *Wired* iPad apps still available. These screengrabs show the journey from 'front cover' (TOP LEFT), via two possible navigation routes, to the cover story (OPPOSITE, BOTTOM). The digital and print editions carry the same content. See the print version of this design, p.117. Editor-in-chief *Chris Anderson*; Creative director *Scott Dadich*

Wired (USA)

CREATIVE DIRECTOR SCOTT DADICH
(NOW VICE-PRESIDENT EDITORIAL PLATFORMS AND DESIGN, CONDÉ NAST)

During the second half of 2009, speculation grew that Apple was about to launch a new device based on their hugely successful iPhone. This, as yet un-named, tablet was quickly seized upon by magazine publishers as the potential answer to providing digital content in a paid-for format. In the absence of any real news or facts it became known as the 'Jesus Tablet', the industry's saviour. The iPhone and its related App Store had established the starting business model – now the publishers just had to figure out a way to create the content and get it onto the device that was launched in April 2010 as the iPad.

Despite no advance direction from Apple in terms of the size or specification of the iPad, in early December 2009 two tablet-content demos went viral online. First came *Sports Illustrated* (US), with plenty of video and interactivity overlaid on print-like page designs. Despite little basis in reality – there was no detail of how the material was created – the visuals helped establish some of the key issues facing the new medium, and made it clear that a magazine app was a genuine prospect.

A couple of weeks later Swedish publisher Bonnier released the result of their collaboration with London design studio Berg. This more sophisticated video outlined issues to do with navigation and the challenge of designing for a dual-orientation (i.e. both horizontal and vertical) environment. It also presented a convincing prototype of how the tablet itself might look and feel, as well as the relationship between device and content. From this demo, Bonnier later developed its own bespoke app creation tool, Mag+, a plug-in for Adobe InDesign.

Both demos lacked key elements – *Sports Illustrated* was all magazine content and little invention, while Bonnier's *Mag+* was all concept and no magazine content – but together they contributed enormously to the discussion about what a tablet magazine might be.

Meanwhile, a stronger combination of technological innovation and editorial content had been under development for several months in San Francisco, where the creative team at *Wired* (US) had been collaborating with software giant Adobe.

Wired's creative director Scott Dadich had already established *Wired* as the magazine of the moment in terms of design (see page 116). In April 2009 he had his annual review meeting over lunch with editor-in-chief Chris Anderson. An enthusiastic supporter of Google's idea that 20 per cent of your work time should be applied to innovative, personal projects, Anderson asked Dadich what he might do given that time. Sitting eating in South Park, Dadich quickly sketched on a napkin his first thoughts of how tablet publishing might work. 'Chris's response was: put someone else on the print magazine, take a designer and go build a prototype,' explains Dadich. He and designer Margaret Swart went off for a month to refashion existing *Wired* layouts and work on an interface. They followed several different navigation routes, but pretty quickly settled on the up/down-sideways interface still used in Adobe's Digital Publishing

Suite (DPS) software today. 'We ended up producing a four-minute video that simulated all the actions.'

Over the summer of 2009 that video was shown to both Apple and Adobe. Adobe's Director of Experience Design, Jeremy Clark, had similar ideas to Dadich, and by August 2009 they were working together on developing a *Wired* tablet app. The Adobe offices are about three blocks away from those of *Wired*, so from that point the two teams were in daily contact. Dadich describes the set-up: 'Eight of us worked together – me, Margaret and Wyatt Mitchell from *Wired* and Jeremy, Bruce Bell, Justin van Slembrouck, Bob Walton and Amy Haynes from Adobe. We made everything – the navigation model, the icons, the look and feel.' The project got the green light from the Condé Nast board in December 2009, just as those other demo videos went viral.

At this point the problems of working with digital technology kicked in – not so much in terms of the technology itself, but the politics surrounding it. The app project had been developed using Adobe's Air technology (an application that allows a single piece of code to work across different operating systems), and when Apple confirmed on 27 January 2010 that the iPad was coming, the Wired-Adobe team felt well ahead of the game. They would create everything using Flash, and use Air to transcode (translate) it into the iOS-friendly form for Apple devices. But that reliance on Air was to prove a critical problem in March, when Apple announced a ban on transcoding from Flash. Overnight, the team lost their core technology.

'We had an emergency meeting and Adobe said that, despite being only six weeks away from launch, they'd rebuild the app to suit Apple,' explains Dadich. 'Adobe's InDesign team had just completed InDesign 5 and had some free time, so they took up the build of the app using HTML5. Next thing you knew, we had ourselves an app.' That first *Wired* app launched in mid-May 2010, about a month after the US launch of the iPad.

While many developers regarded Flash as a slightly shaky platform, a view Apple endorsed as they banned its use in iOS, there are plenty of people convinced it was merely Adobe-bashing on Apple's part. As well as leading to a rebuild of that first *Wired* app, it also meant Adobe's app-creation tool based on the *Wired* project, DPS, had to start again from scratch. Such jostling for control is a common feature of the technology world – something magazine publishers have struggled to come to terms with. As they move into this new digital realm they leave behind over a century spent in the relative comfort of print, and face multiple challenges.

In addition to the creative challenges of making their editorial content work on tablets – multiple devices, each with different screen sizes and resolutions – they must come to terms with ceding distribution control to the various app stores (it can take days for Apple to clear a new app for sale in its App Store), as well as seeing their shiny new apps alongside not just magazine competitors but games, movies, music and books. Strategy involves not just print and digital, but print, web, tablet, mobile and social networks, combined in different ways for individual projects.

Has Dadich nailed what a magazine app should be? 'I see two directions. First there's the common platform, Adobe DPS or another system. This is a digital magazine, it's up/down, right/left, it has these controls and this is how we make it. You don't need a PHD to do it, you can be a designer working hands-on in InDesign.' He cites the magazines he is now responsible for to illustrate how different types of project can use the same platform: 'Creative teams at *Allure* and *Vanity Fair* and everything in between can ideate and produce their own content that's interesting, engaging and beautiful.' The other direction is more bespoke, such as *The New Yorker*'s 'Goings On' app, where 'it's just about listings and theatre tickets and accessibility'.

'Looking forward, you get into the two-/three-/five-year plan and it becomes more about the granules of content rather than this lumped-together thing called a digital magazine. It's about making a really compelling video story and tagging it so it knows it'll go into the digital edition – it needs to go to my iPhone, to my living-room television, and all I had to do was tag it the right way.'

Where does all this leave print? 'That remains a fundamental part of it all. InDesign sits at the centre of the ecosystem, and we'll see the day soon when HTML5 comes out of InDesign and that code is going to go on to tablets, phones and websites.' He doesn't expect to be designing in print alone again – instead he talks of making the technology transparent, 'going back to the idea of making a great magazine story and it just happens it has a print and digital component. All we have to think about is making it beautiful.' As I leave our interview he tells me, 'As a designer, I can't imagine a better time to be in the business.'

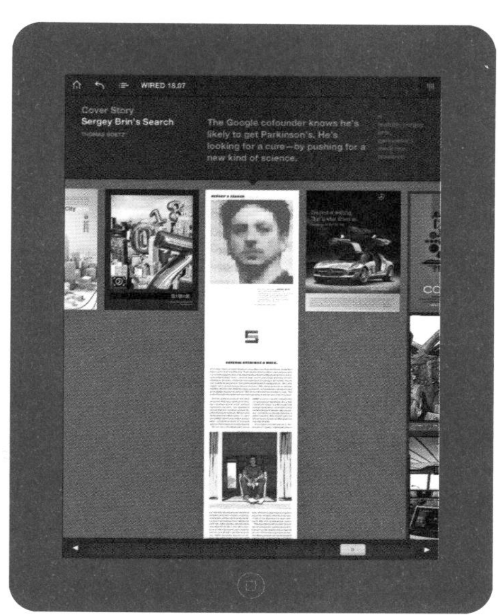

SERGEY'S SEARCH by Thomas Goetz

Google cofounder **SERGEY BRIN** has a 50 percent chance of developing Parkinson's. It's coded in his DNA. So he's pushing for a new kind of science—heavy on the data—to find a cure before the disease finds him.

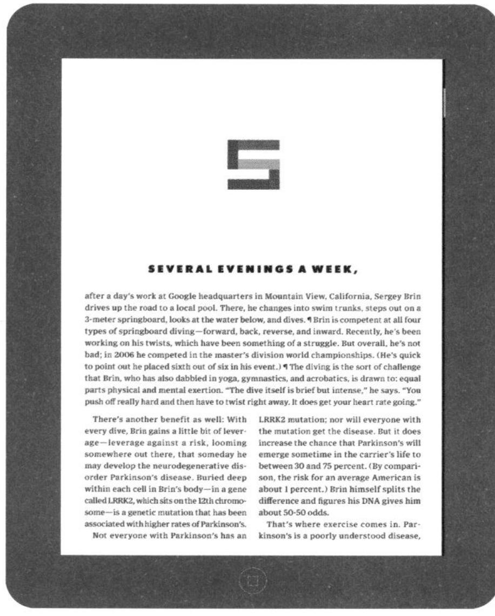
5

SEVERAL EVENINGS A WEEK,

after a day's work at Google headquarters in Mountain View, California, Sergey Brin drives up the road to a local pool. There, he changes into swim trunks, steps out on a 3-meter springboard, looks at the water below, and dives. ¶ Brin is competent at all four types of springboard diving—forward, back, reverse, and inward. Recently, he's been working on his twists, which have been something of a struggle. But overall, he's not bad; in 2006 he competed in the master's division world championships. (He's quick to point out he placed sixth out of six in his event.) ¶ The diving is the sort of challenge that Brin, who has also dabbled in yoga, gymnastics, and acrobatics, is drawn to: equal parts physical and mental exertion. "The dive itself is brief but intense," he says. "You push off really hard and then have to twist right away. It does get your heart rate going."

There's another benefit as well: With every dive, Brin gains a little bit of leverage—leverage against a risk, looming somewhere out there, that someday he may develop the neurodegenerative disorder Parkinson's disease. Buried deep within each cell in Brin's body—in a gene called LRRK2, which sits on the 12th chromosome—is a genetic mutation that has been associated with higher rates of Parkinson's.

Not everyone with Parkinson's has an LRRK2 mutation; nor will everyone with the mutation get the disease. But it does increase the chance that Parkinson's will emerge sometime in the carrier's life to between 30 and 75 percent. (By comparison, the risk for an average American is about 1 percent.) Brin himself splits the difference and figures his DNA gives him about 50-50 odds.

That's where exercise comes in. Parkinson's is a poorly understood disease,

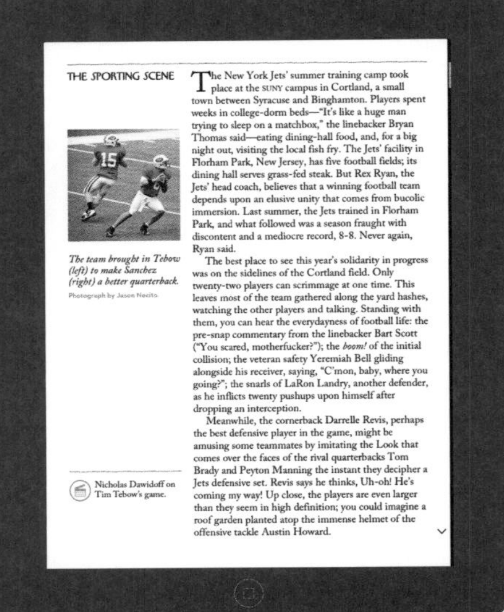

THE SPORTING SCENE

The New York Jets' summer training camp took place at the SUNY campus in Cortland, a small town between Syracuse and Binghamton. Players spent weeks in college-dorm beds—"It's like a huge man trying to sleep on a matchbox," the linebacker Bryan Thomas said—eating dining-hall food, and, for a big night out, visiting the local fish fry. The Jets' facility in Florham Park, New Jersey, has five football fields; its dining hall serves grass-fed steak. But Rex Ryan, the Jets' head coach, believes that a winning football team depends upon an elusive unity that comes from bucolic immersion. Last summer, the Jets trained in Florham Park, and what followed was a season fraught with discontent and a mediocre record, 8-8. Never again, Ryan said.

The best place to see this year's solidarity in progress was on the sidelines of the Cortland field. Only twenty-two players can scrimmage at one time. This leaves most of the team gathered along the yard hashes, watching the other players and talking. Standing with them, you can hear the everydayness of football life: the pre-snap commentary from the linebacker Bart Scott ("You scared, motherfucker?"); the *boom!* of the initial collision; the veteran safety Yeremiah Bell gliding alongside his receiver, saying, "C'mon, baby, where you going?"; the snarls of LaRon Landry, another defender, as he inflicts twenty pushups upon himself after dropping an interception.

Meanwhile, the cornerback Darrelle Revis, perhaps the best defensive player in the game, might be amusing some teammates by imitating the Look that comes over the faces of the rival quarterbacks Tom Brady and Peyton Manning the instant they decipher a Jets defensive set. Revis says he thinks, Uh-oh! He's coming my way! Up close, the players are even larger than they seem in high definition; you could imagine a roof garden planted atop the immense helmet of the offensive tackle Austin Howard.

The team brought in Tebow (left) to make Sanchez (right) a better quarterback.

Photograph by Jason Nocito

Nicholas Dawidoff on Tim Tebow's game.

The New Yorker TOP

USA, September 17, 2012 (iPad app created using Adobe DPS)

The print magazine's cover flap device is mimicked in its digital app, while its longform journalism and design adapts easily to the new medium.

Editor-in-chief *David Remnick*; Creative director *Wyatt Mitchell*; Illustration *Chris Ware*

MORE NEW YORKER p237

Flipboard BOTTOM

USA, launched March 2010 (bespoke iPad app)

This app takes the user's social media feeds and presents them together within an algorithm-controlled page design. The page-flip effect that led to the app's name is a rare successful example of adapting a print 'effect' to a digital environment.

Designer *Marcos Weskamp and team*

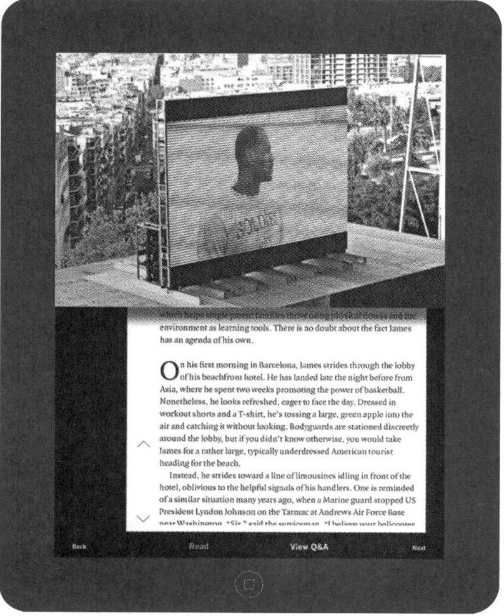

Port
UK. Issue 4, Winter 2011 (iPad app)
Following an earlier app created using Adobe DPS, this edition was developed in Xcode and uses its own navigation system, based on the principle that only buttons relevant to the moment should be present at any time at the bottom of the screen). Several master gestures – such as three taps to return to the contents list – were universally available. The content was taken from the same print edition of the magazine but heavily reformatted for the iPad.
Editor *Dan Crowe*; App design *Jeremy Leslie*; Coding *Tim Moore*

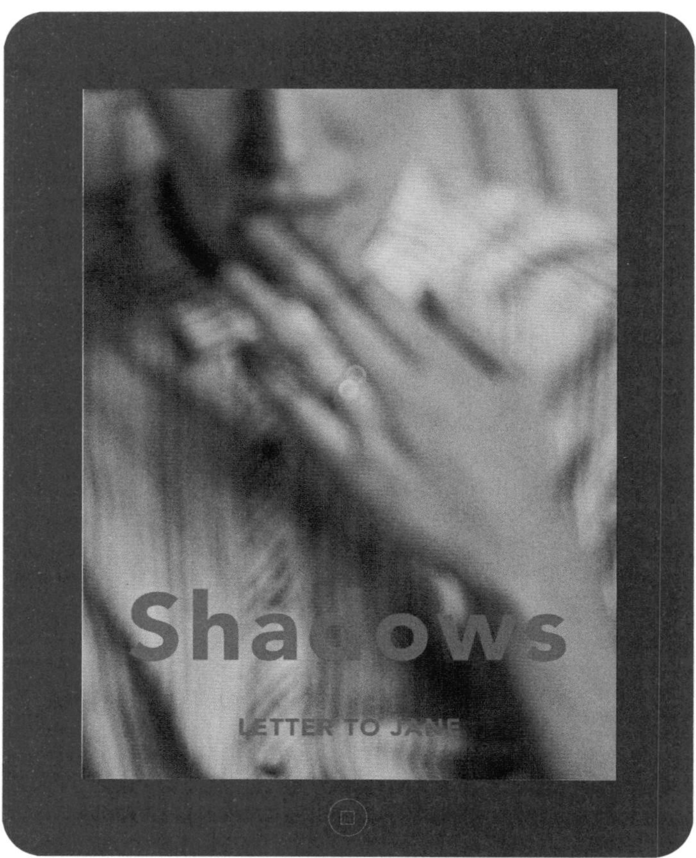

Letter to Jane (USA)

EDITOR, DESIGNER AND CODER TIM MOORE

While most people trying to conceive an iPad magazine approach the project from within the magazine world and with an awareness of the subsequent commercial and creative imperatives, Oregon-based photography graduate Tim Moore had a very different reason to try out the new medium. 'I realized before I graduated that my education in photography and film studies was basically useless. I had no money and no idea about what to do so I just did the only thing I knew how to do, and that was create content.'

He saw there were many people – musicians, artists, designers, film-makers – doing their own thing and making a living from it, and interviewed them in the hope that he could learn from them. Meanwhile, he was trying to compile a portfolio of his own photography work to show potential employers, and had the idea that he could combine the interviews and images to make a magazine to pass around. *Letter to Jane* was born.

The first issue was made on his six-year-old MacBook and distributed free as an 180-page PDF on Christmas Day 2009. Moore received a slightly confounding response: 'Instead of getting job offers, I got a ton of offers from people who wanted to be in the magazine. I figured I'd got something here, so I got to work on the second issue.'

In between these first two issues, the iPad was announced. He fell in love with the tablet straight away: 'It was such a better way to read than a desktop screen. I knew I'd never have the budget for print and didn't really know how to do print anyways, so I started to learn how to make an iPad magazine.' This was prior to any other iPad magazine project being published, but the relevant toolkits had been available for iPhone apps for some time, and Moore used tutorials on YouTube and other sample projects to teach himself coding. His first app was released a month after the iPad launch, featuring a small selection of imagery and a simple navigation that pointed the way for future issues. 'I felt I'd found something. I'd been trying out all these formats that never really felt like a fit, but looking at my work on an iPad really felt natural.'

The name of the project points to Moore's inspiration. '*Letter to Jane* is the title of a short experimental film by Jean-Luc Godard and Jean-Pierre Gorin. It's a Marxist diatribe about the photo of "Hanoi Jane" and I'm doing something completely different, but what I like about it is that it's a simple film made with one photo and a tape recorder. The point of the film was to say to the audience: I didn't use any special equipment or expensive setup and I still made something interesting.'

Letter to Jane arrived in the app store as one of the first magazine apps, alongside far larger projects that used third-party suppliers to create their apps. *Time* used Woodwing, *Popular Science* used Mag+ and *Wired* soon appeared using the beginnings of Adobe DPS. 'I'd look at the suppliers' websites and I knew I would never have enough money to even get a callback,' explains Moore, 'so the only option I had was to code, but honestly that was the most appealing option.' He had his MacBook, Apple's Xcode was a free download and a developer's licence of only $99 a year made for a very low barrier to entry – 'cheaper than any other creative endeavour I can think of'. He expected

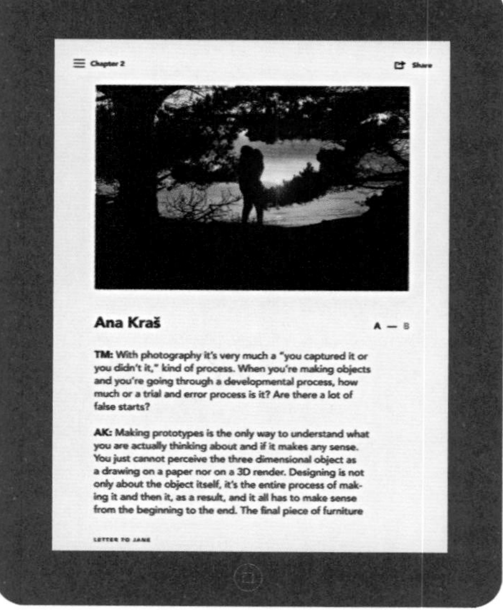

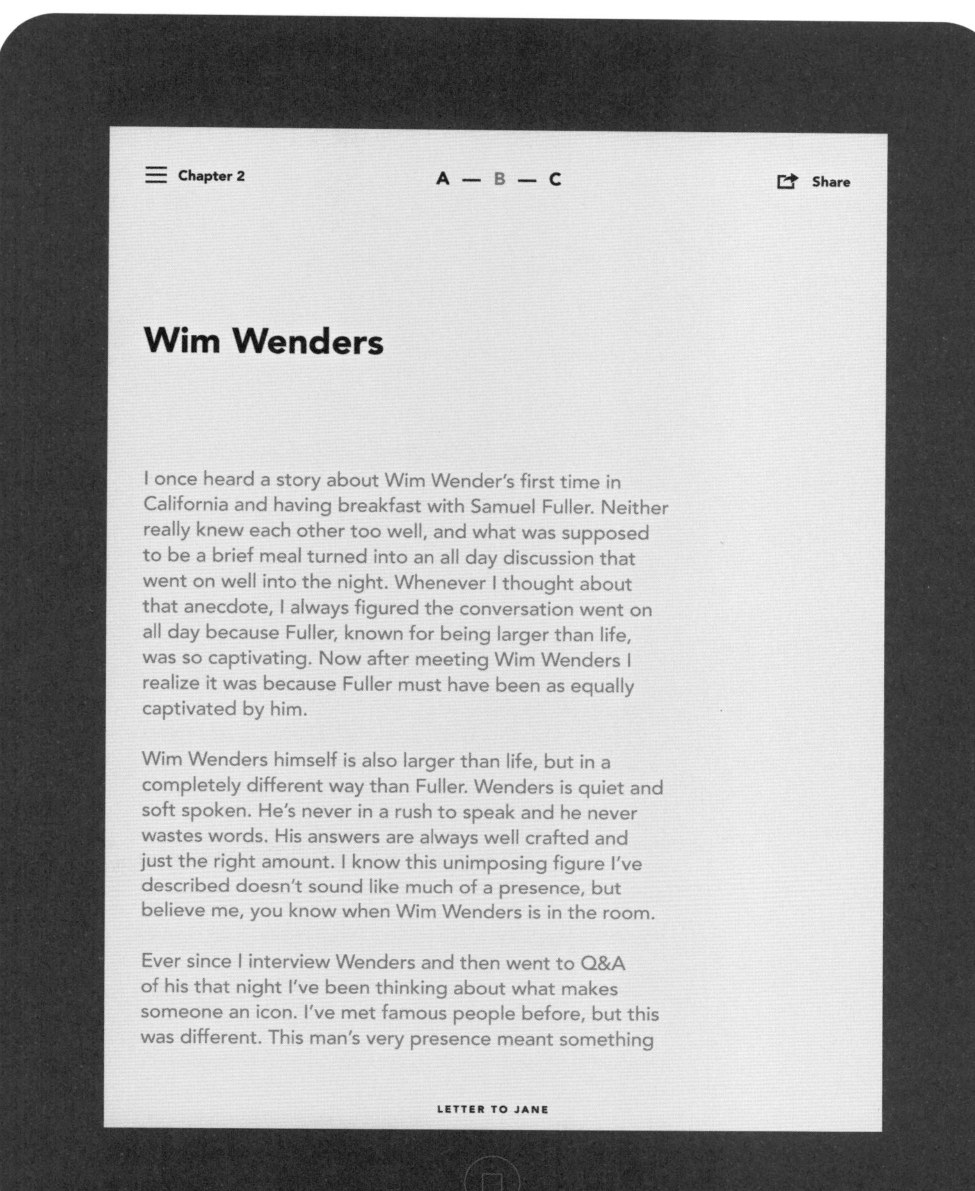

Chapter 2
A — B — C
Share
Wim Wenders
I once heard a story about Wim Wender's first time in California and having breakfast with Samuel Fuller. Neither really knew each other too well, and what was supposed to be a brief meal turned into an all day discussion that went on well into the night. Whenever I thought about that anecdote, I always figured the conversation went on all day because Fuller, known for being larger than life, was so captivating. Now after meeting Wim Wenders I realize it was because Fuller must have been as equally captivated by him.
Wim Wenders himself is also larger than life, but in a completely different way than Fuller. Wenders is quiet and soft spoken. He's never in a rush to speak and he never wastes words. His answers are always well crafted and just the right amount. I know this unimposing figure I've described doesn't sound like much of a presence, but believe me, you know when Wim Wenders is in the room.
Ever since I interview Wenders and then went to Q&A of his that night I've been thinking about what makes someone an icon. I've met famous people before, but this was different. This man's very presence meant something
LETTER TO JANE

Letter to Jane
USA, Issue 4, Winter 2012 (bespoke iPad app)
The fourth edition of this self-published app continues its investigation of how editorial apps can avoid using the legacy concept of 'pages' and instead provide more fluent ways to experience editorial text and images.
Editor, designer and developer *Tim Moore*

Adobe to supersede his project with DPS, but when it arrived, 'the costs were over the top, the software looked horrible and I hated (and still do) their vertical columns approach.'

Moore sees *Letter to Jane* as an alternative, aligning it with independent print magazines: 'With the Apple Newsstand and all the major publishers now on the iPad, I feel like there's a great opportunity for something different. The majors have carved their narrow path, leaving a bunch of interesting trails for the rest of us to explore. With print I look at the newsstand and see the big magazines lining the shelves and they have a certain aesthetic. Then there is the shelf with the indie publications. You can just tell they're different, you don't even have to touch them, their presence alone defines something right off the bat. Adobe is the digital glossy, and now I have the chance to create the digital indie.'

Letter to Jane benefits from not starting life as a piece of print, and from not feeling it necessary to add every single effect available. Most apps are added on to the end of the production process and use Adobe DPS or similar tools to add interactive effects to existing text and images laid out in InDesign. Too often these effects overwhelm rather than improve the content – the app structure and navigation becomes the content. Moore wants his magazine app not to feel like an app, and starts with raw content. Issue by issue he's tried to simplify the onscreen navigation and let that content shine through. 'The better I get at designing for iOS, the more I can figure out how to get out of the way of the user.' Without formal design training he has an instinctive understanding of how magazine design works, and talks of 'taking care of the reader'.

The result is a refreshingly simple experience. It can seem quiet – *Letter to Jane* is not an app to show off your whizzy new iPad with – but in the longer term is far more engaging than most magazine apps. It shares the immersive quality of print magazines. Additional information and navigation appears as you read. Moore: 'I want the text to feel like it responds to the reader and that the magazine can adjust to the reader's needs. That kind of interaction is more subtle and takes more thought, but it creates a better overall experience.'

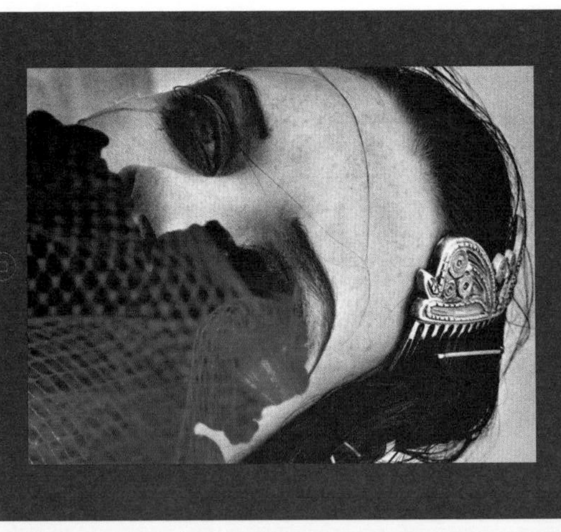

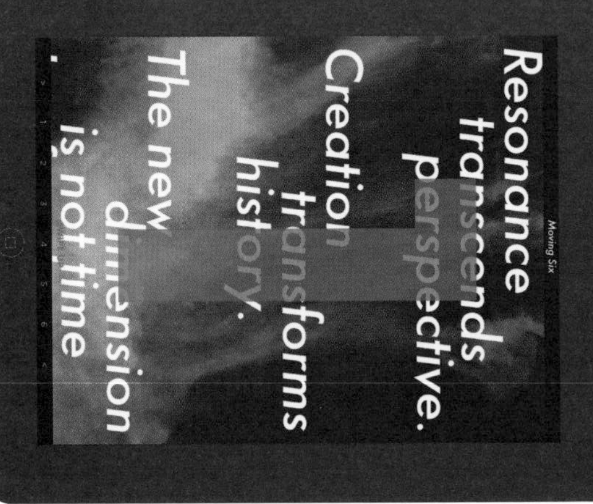

Moving Six

Japan, October 2012 (bespoke iPad app)
Archive material from Commes des Garcons' print publication *Six* (1988–91) is repurposed for the iPad. Purely visual content allows the designers to play with gesture and tilt control to create an exciting, if chaotic, experience. It includes the hugely satisfying counter-intuitive gesture of holding a finger on the screen to *stop* images changing.
Digital art direction *Remi Paringaux and Benjamin Cooper*

OPPOSITE, LEFT

Opening Ceremony

USA, Issue 1, Sports, September 2012 (bespoke iPad app)
This app stems from a print publication published by the fashion store of the same name. It doesn't repeat the printed content, but instead presents seven specially created, slick, digital experiences that have a game-like approach to interaction – users can layer images and write or draw across images. An effective addition to the printed magazine.
Editor-in-chief *Rory Satran*; Creative director *Emmett Shine*

OPPOSITE, RIGHT

Katachi

USA, Fall 2012 (iPad app built using their bespoke OrigamiEngine tools)
Katachi is a showcase for the publishers' own app creation software. Many of the effects are visually stunning – it's clear why they call the software Origami – but are overused and confusing as an overall editorial experience.
Editor-in-chief and Creative director *Ken Olling*

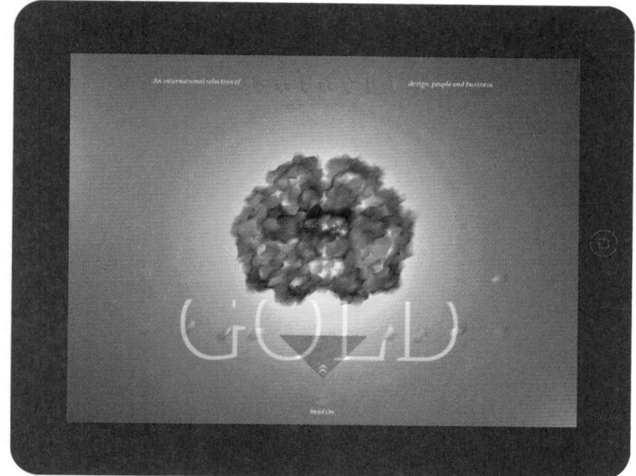

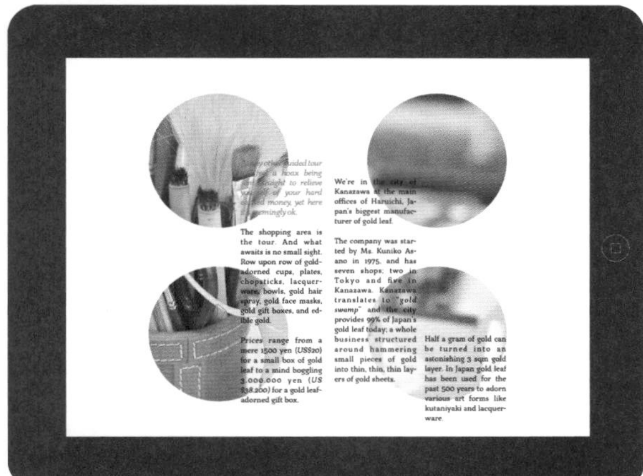

Editions29

USA, The Museum, Issue 1, October 2012 (bespoke iPad app)

This series of apps covers areas of design and creativity: architecture, cars, music and, in this example, museum design. The emphasis is on strong photography and calm, gentle pans and moves. Static pictures are repeated on the same screen, closer up and moving; other images take up the whole screen and a swipe reveals the rest of the picture. Captions, text and audio are all easily accessible but can also be ignored in favour of the visual.
Edioria/design direction *Ninan Kurien*

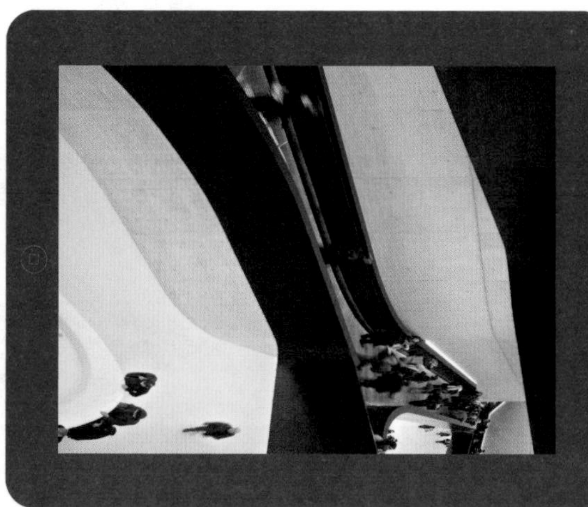

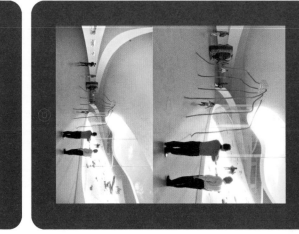

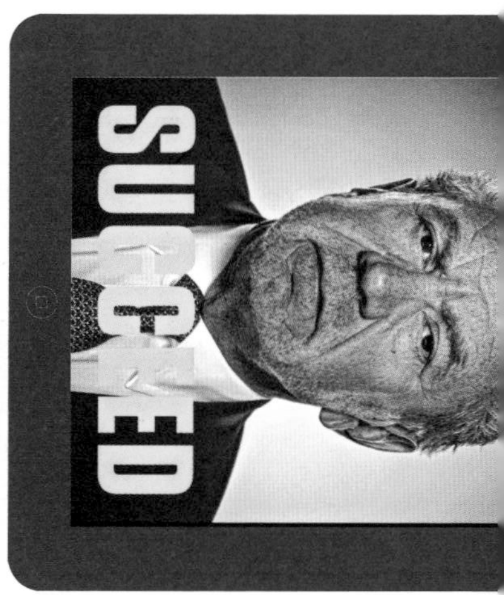

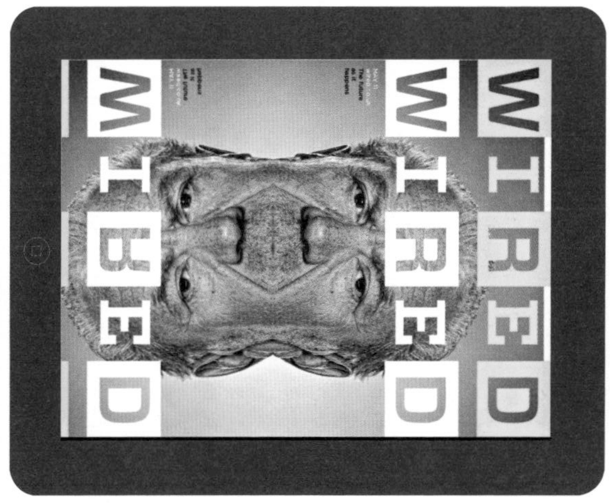

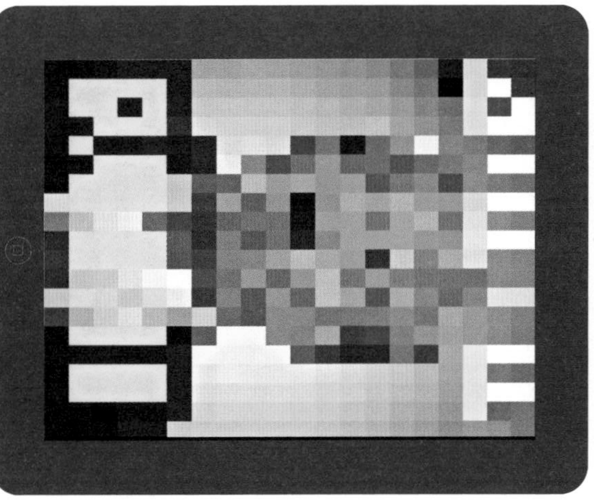

LEFT **Wired**
UK, May 2011 (iPad app created using Adobe DPS)
The print-edition front cover was animated to emphasize the 'Failed' theme. See page 122 for the print version of this design.
Editor *David Rowan*; Art director *Andrew Diprose*

ABOVE **Monocle24 app**
UK, 2011 (iPhone)
Apps aren't neccesarily complete renditions of printed editions. *Monocle* founder Tyler Brûlé has consistently spoken against magazine apps, preferring to focus on launching the Monocle24 digital radio station. A logical extension of Monocle24 is, however, this iPhone app that allows the user to download audio content from the radio station. A good example of how apps are best tailored to your content.
App development *Paul Regan*

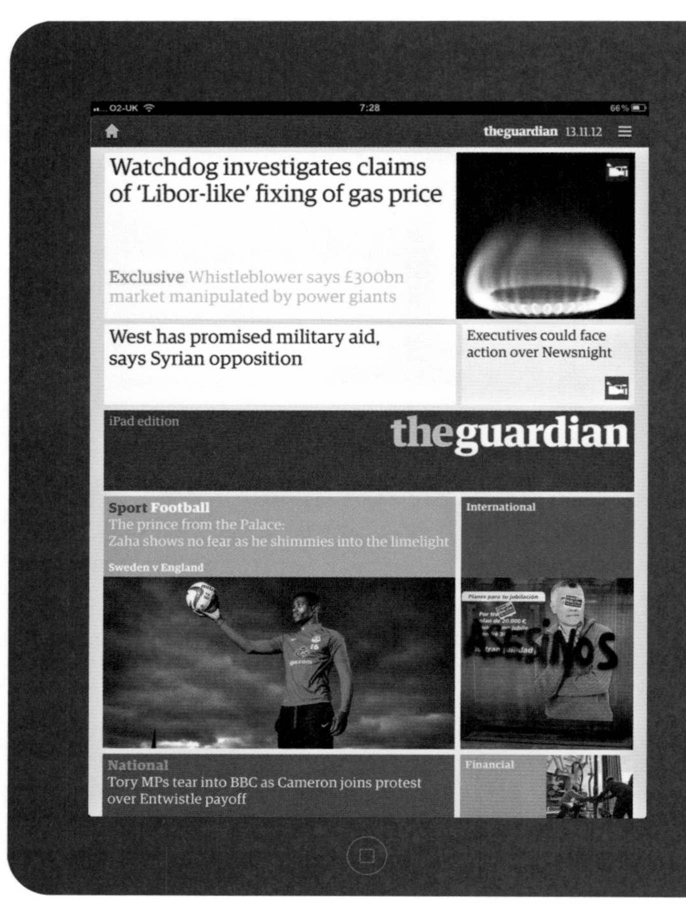

O2-UK
7:28
66 %
theguardian 13.11.12
Watchdog investigates claims of 'Libor-like' fixing of gas price
Exclusive Whistleblower says £300bn market manipulated by power giants
West has promised military aid, says Syrian opposition
Executives could face action over Newsnight
iPad edition
theguardian
Sport Football
The prince from the Palace: Zaha shows no fear as he shimmies into the limelight
Sweden v England
International
ASESINOS
National
Tory MPs tear into BBC as Cameron joins protest over Entwistle payoff
Financial

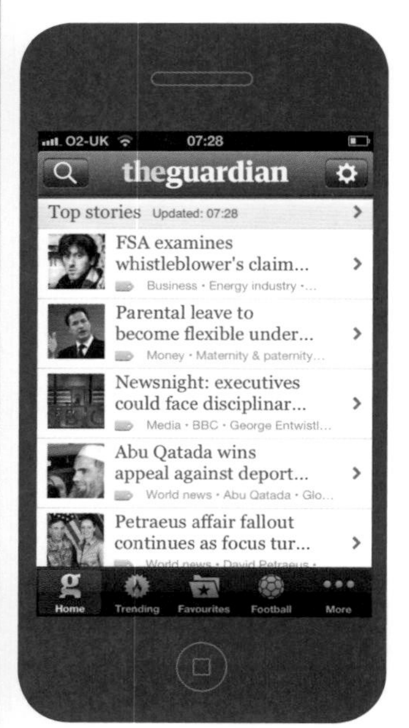

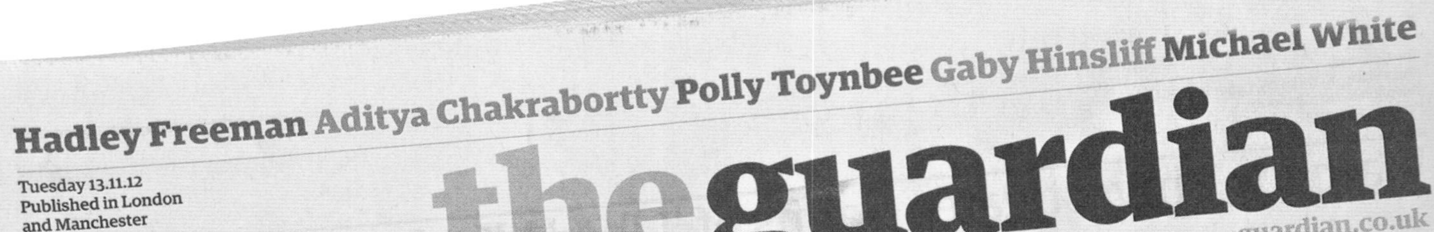
Hadley Freeman Aditya Chakrabortty Polly Toynbee Gaby Hinsliff Michael White

Tuesday 13.11.12
Published in London and Manchester
£1.20

theguardian
guardian.co.uk

9 770261 307521 46

Paul Weller and Bruce Foxton
How we made A Town Called Malice

Mike Brearley
What the Paralympians have taught us

Meet England's newest recruit
Wilfried Zaha exclusive interview

Watchdog investigates claims of 'Libor-like' fixing of gas price

Exclusive Whistleblower says £300bn market manipulated by power giants

Terry Macalister

The City watchdog, the Financial Services Authority, is investigating claims by ... that Britain's £300bn ...

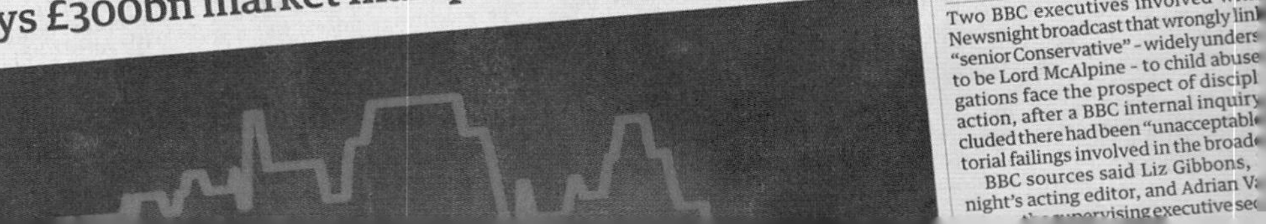

Executives could face action over Newsnight

Dan Sabbagh and John Plunkett

Two BBC executives involved with ... Newsnight broadcast that wrongly link... "senior Conservative" – widely unders... to be Lord McAlpine – to child abuse ... gations face the prospect of discipl... action, after a BBC internal inquiry ... cluded there had been "unacceptabl... torial failings involved in the broad...

BBC sources said Liz Gibbons, ... night's acting editor, and Adrian V... supervising executive se...

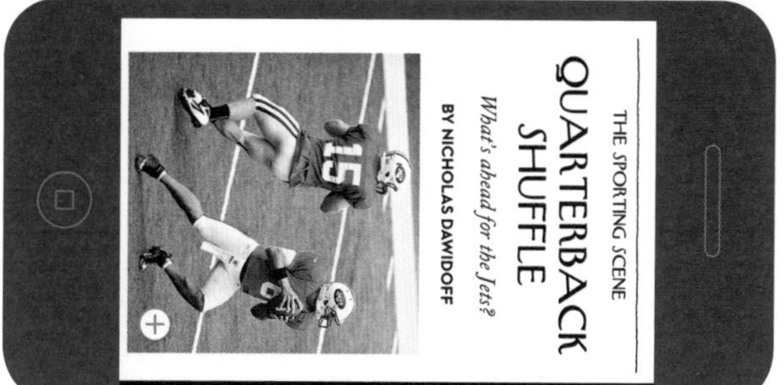

The New York Jets' summer training camp took place at the SUNY campus in Cortland, a small town between Syracuse and Binghamton. Players spent weeks in college-dorm beds—"It's like a huge man trying to sleep on a matchbox," the linebacker Bryan Thomas said—eating dining-hall food, and, for a big night out, visiting the local fish fry. The Jets' facility in Florham Park, New Jersey, has five football fields; its dining hall serves grass-fed steak. But Rex Ryan, the Jets' head coach, believes that a winning football team depends upon an elusive unity that comes from

2 of 68

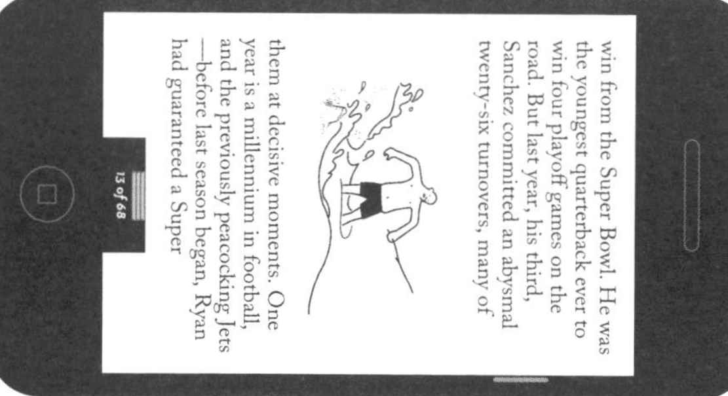

win from the Super Bowl. He was the youngest quarterback ever to win four playoff games on the road. But last year, his third, Sanchez committed an abysmal twenty-six turnovers, many of
them at decisive moments. One year is a millennium in football, and the previously peacocking Jets —before last season began, Ryan had guaranteed a Super
13 of 68

TOP **The New Yorker**

USA, September 17, 2012 (iPhone app created using Adobe DPS)

The New Yorker was one of the first magazines to publish entire issues for the smartphone alongside its iPad edition. Its long-form content is well suited to the small high-resolution screen.

Editor-in-chief *David Remnick*; Creative director *Wyatt Mitchell*; Illustration *Chris Ware*

BOTTOM **British Journal of Photography**

UK, Issue 1, 2012, Roger Ballen (iPhone app created using Mag+)

Alongside a major investement in its print edition, the BJP has launched a premium, paid-for iPad app and is also publishing free iPhone apps such as this one to provide additional content between issues.

Editor-in-chief *Simon Bainbridge*; Art editor *Mick Moore*

OPPOSITE **The Guardian**

UK, Tuesday, November 13, 2012 (Newspaper, bespoke iPad and iPhone apps)

The newspaper runs its entire news operation from a single database, meaning the print, website and app editions share the same content. The iPad app repurposes the entire print edition each day, the iPhone app is more regularly updated and allows the user to select favourite areas of content.

Creative director iPad *Mark Porter*; Senior designer iPad and iPhone *Andy Brockie*

INDEX

Thank you

To all the art directors, designers, editors and publishers whose cooperation made this book possible, particularly those who gave their time to be interviewed: Jop van Bennekom, Marissa Bourke, Scott Dadich, Chris Dixon, Sarah Forbes Keough, Francesco Franchi, Luke Hayman, Penny Martin, Mike Meiré, Ralph McGinnis, Tim Moore, Adam Moss, Richard Turley, Josh Tyrangiel and Marco Velardi.

David Bate for patiently helping throughout with design, photography and production, Andrew Losowsky for giving the main texts an invaluable read and Jo Lightfoot, Susie May and Kim Sinclair at Laurence King Publishing for their help and support.

Emily Anderson, Greg Beckel, Michael Biedowicz, Andrew Blauvelt, Tony Brook, Patrick Burgoyne, Alex Capes, Milena Carstens, Andrew Diprose, Sarah Douglas, Hayley Dunlop, Simon Esterson, Steven Gregor, John Jervis, Terry Jones, Mina Kaneko, Ellen Lupton, Jörg Koch, Mike Koedinger, Danny Miller, Randy Minor, Bob Newman, Rosie Poole, Dan Robson, Mark Sinclair, Steve Smith, Sarah Temple, Khoi Vinh, Hannerie Visser, Steve Watson, Anna Weston.

Everyone who has supported the magCulture blog by submitting, reading, advertising and commenting.

And last but never least, Lesley, Cameron and Ewan.

Links to all featured magazines can be found at themodernmagazine.com

Read more at magCulture.com

Page numbers in *italics* refer to illustrations